THE WAY TO FAITH

THE WAY TO FAITH

An Examination of Newman's
Grammar of Assent
as a Response to the Search for
Certainty in Faith

DAVID A. PAILIN

WIPF & STOCK · Eugene, Oregon

Wipf and Stock Publishers
199 W 8th Ave, Suite 3
Eugene, OR 97401

The Way to Faith
An Examination of Newman's Grammar of Assent as a
Response to the Search for Certainty of Faith
By Pailin, David A.
Copyright©1969 Methodist Publishing - Epworth Press
ISBN 13: 978-1-4982-8047-1
Publication date 1/27/2016
Previously published by Epworth Press, 1969

Every effort has been made to trace the current copyright
owner of this publication but without success. If you have any
information or interest in the copyright, please contact the publishers.

Contents

I. THE PROBLEM OF FAITH   1
  1. Introduction   1
  2. The Crisis for Faith in the Nineteenth Century   4
    a. New Philosophical Positions   6
    b. Advances in Science   21
    c. Developments in Literary and Historical Criticism   31
    d. The Challenge to Authoritarian Structures   50

II. THE BACKGROUND TO THE *GRAMMAR OF ASSENT*   60
  1. Newman's Awareness of the Contemporary Crisis for Faith   60
  2. Newman's Quest for a Firm Faith   67
  3. Newman's Intellectual Background   87
  4. The Nature of Assent   92

III. THE CONDITION OF ASSENT   97
  1. Introduction   97
  2. Apprehension as the Condition of Assent   98
    a. The Nature of Apprehension   98
    b. Apprehension as Necessary for Assent   100
    c. The Implications of Apprehension being a Condition of Assent   102
    d. Criticism of Newman's View of the Nature of Apprehension and of its Relation to Assent   105
    e. Conclusion   108
  3. The Two Types of Apprehension and their Influence on Assent   109
    a. The Distinction between 'Real' and 'Notional' Apprehension   109
    b. The Application of the Distinction to the Matter of Religion   114
    c. The Difference between Real and Notional Apprehension in the Matter of Assent   117
    d. Criticism of Newman's View of Real and Notional Apprehension and Assent   120
    e. Conclusion   123

IV. THE ANTECEDENT OF ASSENT — 125

   1. Introduction — 125
   2. Reasoning and Assent — 126
      a. The Function of Reasoning as an Antecedent of Assent — 126
      b. Newman's Criticism of Locke — 132
      c. Religious Belief and Conclusive Arguments — 135
   3. Inference and Assent — 136
      a. The Nature of Inference — 136
      b. The Value of Inference as an Antecedent of Assent — 141
   4. Illation and Assent — 144
      a. The Nature of Illation — 144
      b. The Value of Illation as an Antecedent of Assent — 153
      c. Conclusion — 159

V. THE ACT OF ASSENT — 161

   1. Assent and Conscience — 161
   2. The Decision to Assent — 169
   3. Certainty and Certitude — 177

VI. CONCLUSION — 186

APPENDICES — 198

   I. Newman's Classification of the Types of Assent — 198
   II. Newman's List of His Unpublished Attempts to Write on Faith and Reason — 202
   III. Sixteen Extracts from Newman's Unpublished Private Manuscripts concerned with his Thought about the Logic of Faith — 205

NOTES — 224

INDEX — 271

Preface

I would like to express my gratitude to all who have assisted in the preparation of this book. First of all, I wish to thank Dr. John Heywood Thomas for his patient guidance and help during the several years I was engaged on this work. Without his encouragement this book would never have been finished and without his careful criticisms it would have been very much poorer. I am also greatly indebted to the Fathers of The Oratory at Edgbaston for their kind permission to examine Newman's private papers and to publish some extracts from them. In particular I thank Father C. Stephen Dessain for all his advice. His great knowledge of the Newman Manuscripts made my examination of them much more fruitful and exciting than would have been otherwise possible. I am also grateful to the Rev. Dr Percy Scott and the staff of Hartley Victoria College for their permission to start this study during my training for the Methodist ministry and to Romiley Methodist Church for never complaining when, as their minister for five happy years, I spent a considerable part of my time trying to finish this study. Several members of that Church suffered more directly when they volunteered to help with the initial typing. I am grateful for their aid. Different parts of the manuscript have been read by Professor E. G. Rupp, Professor H. Cunliffe-Jones, the Rev. Owen E. Evans and the Rev. Henry D. Rack. For their advice and suggestions I am also grateful. Finally I want to thank my wife and my parents whose support in very many ways has made this work on Newman possible.

This list of thanks may suggest that the author of this book has merely combined the ideas and aid generously given by many other people. I must also be allowed to claim responsibility for all the errors in this book!

Manchester
Christmas Eve 1966　　　　　　　　　　　　　　　DAVID A. PAILIN

TO GWYNETH

Part 1: The Problem of Faith

1. INTRODUCTION

A seventeenth-century theological rebel, John Robinson, the pastor to the Pilgrim Fathers, wrote:

> To live by *Reason* is to live the life of a man; To live by *Sense* is to live the life of a beast: But to *live by Faith is to live the life of the Son of God,* and to be (in its effects) *partakers of the Divine nature;* and that not onely in the reasonable, but in the sensitive faculties also. . . . *Reason is that wherein man goes before all other earthly creatures; and comes after God* onely, and the Angels in Heaven. . . . Now, who would not strive to excel other men in that, wherein men excel all other Creatures? How much more, in that, to which few men attain: true *faith*, and the life thereof.[1]

If we agree with John Robinson's assertion we have to answer the question, 'What is this "true faith, and the life thereof" and how do we attain it?' All our actions are the expression of some faith or other.[2] We seek 'true *faith*', that is, a faith which corresponds to what is ultimately significant,[3] in place of the false and inadequate substitutes which so largely dominate life. This 'true faith' is not limited to theories which have only intellectual significance. It is an assent which determines our practice as well as our thoughts.

Since faith is fundamental to life, we like to think that our particular faith is in some way or other sure and certain. Articles of faith generally determine our behaviour so far as we consider that they are 'certain'; we seek to build our life on a rock of certainty rather than on the shifting sands of opinion. 'I kept my heart', wrote Augustine, 'from assenting to anything, . . . For I wished to be as assured of the things I saw not, as I was that seven and three are ten.' He came to see, however, that in the end he must believe 'things not demonstrated, (whether it was that they could in themselves be demonstrated but not to certain persons, or could not at all be)'.[4] The problem for Newman, and for us, is how matters of faith can have the 'certainty' necessary for them to determine life while they are still objects of faith and not of knowledge. It may be suggested that faith is a courageous stand in the face of acknowledged uncertainty. Such courage is, however, an expression of faith and depends for its strength upon the belief that its stand is the right one to make. The 'rightness' of this belief is, in turn, viewed as 'certain' by those who hold it.

The respective territories of faith and knowledge have been variously assessed as people have felt more or less confidence in the faculty of reason. Even so, the greatest claims for our rational powers have to admit that in the end we depend upon faith—even if it is faith which is so generally held that we hardly recognize it as faith.[5] Within Christian theology there have been widely differing views about what can be held to be 'known' and what can be accepted only as a matter of 'faith'. Aquinas, for instance, held that our reason could establish some theological truths. He wrote that 'the existence of God, in so far as it is not self-evident to us, can be demonstrated from those of His effects which are known to us'.[6] Later he expounded what is meant by this as he dealt with the question 'Whether God can be known in this life by Natural Reason?' Here he stated that:

> Our natural knowledge begins from sense. Hence our natural knowledge can go as far as it can be led by sensible things. But our mind cannot be led by sense so far as to see the essence of God, because the sensible effects of God do not equal the power of God as their cause. . . . But because they are His effects and depend on their cause, we can be led from them so far as to know of God *whether He exists,* and to know of Him what must necessarily belong to Him, as the first cause of all things, exceeding all things caused by Him.[7]

Aquinas's confidence in the power of human reason was limited on two counts: first, by the recognition that 'the truth about God such as reason could discover, would only be known by a few, and that after a long time, and with the admixture of many errors'. Therefore, since 'Man's whole salvation . . . depends upon the knowledge of this truth, . . . it was necessary that they should be taught divine truths by divine revelation'.[8] Secondly, the theological truths which could be known by reason were very restricted. They needed to be supplemented by revealed truths which would be accepted by faith: 'it was necessary for the salvation of man that certain truths which exceed human reason should be made known to him by divine revelation'.[9] Thus while Aquinas held that there was some knowledge of God available to reason, this natural knowledge was not sufficient for salvation: man needed revelation also.

William Paley, a classical exponent of Christian natural theology, agreed that revelation was necessary to overcome the limitations of reasoning. In his *Natural Theology* he stated that 'it is one of the advantages of the revelations which we acknowledge, that . . . they introduce the Deity to human apprehension, under an idea more personal, more determinate, more within its compass, than the theology of nature can do.'[10] He showed, however, considerable confidence in the ability of our reason to determine theological truths. Even though he recognized the need of revelation, he tried to prove the veracity of the Christian revelation by rational arguments, seeking to meet Hume's objections to miracles by further reasoning.[11] He classed 'religion' with 'every other subject of human reasoning' and asserted that 'the truth of Christianity depends upon its leading facts, and upon them alone. Now, of these we have evidence which ought to satisfy us.'[12] In his most famous work, *Natural Theology*, Paley maintained that both the existence and some of the attributes of God could be convincingly demonstrated by reference to the natural order.

> Upon the whole, after all the schemes and struggles of a reluctant philosophy, the necessary resort is to a Deity. The marks of *design* are too strong to be gotten over. *Design* must have had a designer. The designer must have been a person. That person is GOD. . . . The *attributes* of such a being, suppose his reality to be proved, must be adequate to the magnitude, extent, and multiplicity of his operations. . . .'[13]

The evidence of 'contrivance' (or design) in nature 'proves the *personality* of Deity'[14] and indicates 'an *intelligent* author'.[15] Furthermore, 'of the "Unity of the Deity" the proof is the uniformity of plan observable in the universe', while the 'appearances of nature' also provide 'proof of the *Divine goodness*'.[16] While the need for revelation and faith is recognized by Paley, the power of reason is stressed to the point where they have little significance. According to Paley, we can know the basic truths of religion through our reason.

Paley, confident in the power of reason to teach us the existence and basic attributes of God, died in 1805. Immanuel Kant had died the previous year, having destroyed the possibility of such confidence for future theologians. In his *Critiques* and other works Kant sought to demonstrate the limits of human knowledge. He held that it was 'absolutely necessary . . . to consider all that has been done (sc. in philosophy) as undone' and was bold enough to assert that the 'possibility' of 'any future metaphysic' would depend upon its 'satisfying the demands' of his critical work.[17] So far as religion was concerned, he said that he had 'found it necessary to deny *knowledge*, in order to make room for *faith*'.[18] He did not deny *a priori* the validity of religion but wanted to make it clear that 'the acceptance of the fundamental principles of a religion is faith *par excellence* (*fides sacra*).'[19] We can perceive the significance of this claim from the distinctions which he draws in his *Critique of Pure Reason* between 'opining, knowing and believing', the three ways of 'holding . . . a thing to be true'.

> *Opining* is such holding of a judgment as is consciously insufficient, not only objectively, but also subjectively. If our holding of the judgment be only subjectively sufficient, and is at the same time taken as being objectively insufficient, we have what is termed *believing*. Lastly, when the holding of a thing to be true is sufficient both subjectively and objectively, it is *knowledge*. The subjective sufficiency is termed *conviction* (for myself), the objective sufficiency is termed *certainty* (for everyone).[20]

While Kant showed in relation to the traditional proofs for the existence of God that human reason was unable to handle the concept of God without running into self-contradictions, he had not ruled out the possibility that reason might have a function in leading to belief. The question left to future theologians was: 'How does one come to the conviction (or certitude) of religious belief?' Its solution was made most urgent by the crisis of faith in the nineteenth century. This crisis stemmed from several contemporary developments whose combined effect was to raise fundamental doubts about faith in its traditional form.

2. THE CRISIS FOR FAITH IN THE NINETEENTH CENTURY

Paley's first major work, *Moral and Political Philosophy*, was published in 1785. In the chapter 'Of Reverencing the Deity', he attacked the 'infidelity' which 'is served up in every shape that is likely to allure, surprise, or beguile the imagination'. By it 'the Christian testimony is depreciated and traduced' and the believer finds himself 'unsettled and perplexed'. Paley believed that this widespread 'infidelity' could be met by the message of Jesus Christ, a message that was authenticated by 'prophecy and miracles' and offered to 'the wisest of mankind . . . an answer to their doubts, and rest of their inquiries'. He closed the chapter by asserting that 'he alone discovers, who *proves*; and no man can prove this point but the teacher who testifies by miracles that his doctrine comes from God.'[21] Dr. W. S. Wayland's preface to the 1837 edition of Paley's works tells us that the *Moral and Political Philosophy* was introduced as 'a standard examining-book in the University of Cambridge' in 1786–7 and 'still keeps its ground'.[22] Even so, the confident faith expressed in this part of the work became increasingly rare as its foundations were undermined by the intellectual revolution. The nineteenth century was not a great age of faith, following a century of rationalism and doubt. Paley's work largely reflected the intellectual situation in the eighteenth century. Although many did not share his particular faith, there was widespread confidence in man's ability to find the truth about life. In the nineteenth century this confidence was replaced by serious doubt.

The first quarter of the nineteenth century was a time of furious activity in the Church in Britain. In the 1780s 'a handful of men and women shocked by the decay of English religion and the corruption of English morals' had begun a movement for national reform. In *Fathers of the Victorians*, Ford K. Brown has described how this movement 'grew rapidly into huge proportions' until 'in thirty years it had covered England with reforming institutions' and 'left a lasting impression on all English-speaking countries'.[23] Superficially it seemed that the Church, with its traditional faith, was solidly established throughout the land. G. M. Young describes the 'typical average man' of Victorian England in terms of a printer whose family went 'to church or chapel' on a Sunday morning and in the evening practised 'hymns on the harmonium'. Of course there were many who did not behave this way—the intellectual doubters and the 'swarming, drinking, fighting multitude' of 'the class below'—but the reputation of the majority has justifiably survived as God-fearing, church-going respectability. This reputation obscures the fundamental unbelief that was spreading through the land. As G. M. Young comments, his printer probably 'would rather slip off to a quiet game of bowls . . . than be marched off to church' and it is far from certain that 'what he heard on Sunday he lived up to on weekdays'.[24] The conference of the Evangelical Alliance in 1851 was told that while 'believers are multiplied, . . . the tone of piety is often lowered by the worldliness of our bustling age'.[25] The speaker held that 'the isolation of thought to which our insular position has often led, and the quiet acceptance of inherited opinion, are melting away before the spirit of the age, and have left the minds of too many utterly confused and unsettled, mistrustful of their old creed, and ready to be carried about by every wind of doctrine.'[26] Another speaker asserted that 'infidelity' formed 'one of the most prominent features of our social history' although he comforted his audience with the assurance that this infidelity 'can in our day scarcely do more than revive old objections, and advance old theories'.[27] His comfort was illusory: the growing infidelity involved new and radical reappraisals of fundamental beliefs. Elliott-Binns is correct when he rejects 'the widespread assumption' that the Victorian age was 'an age of confidence and certitude', and holds that it 'was not an age of faith, though it undoubtedly witnessed an increased vigour in practical religion'.[28]

While the Reformation produced in both Protestant and Roman Catholic a fresh understanding of the Christian faith, it was more a renewal and re-emphasis of old ideas than a break with established principles. In spite of their bitter disputes, Protestant and Roman Catholic accepted the same fundamental principles of ancient and medieval Christianity. The sixteenth century saw a 'reformation' of old truths, not a revolution. The real revolution in Christian thought occurred during the nineteenth century, following upon the intellectual developments of the previous two centuries. It was then that the old foundations were radically questioned and the need for new bases for faith became widely recognized. What had previously been assumed as self-evident truths became suspect. There had been rebels and doubters in the previous century but their influence had been restricted. The general decay in religious life had blunted the challenge of their ideas. Ironically it was the Evangelical Revival, because it quickened religious life, that gave these and other criticisms popular significance. The more important belief became, the more important it became to refute the challenges to faith. What were the new factors that made the nineteenth-century criticisms of the Christian faith so fundamentally disturbing and created such widespread uncertainty about what previously had been accepted? Basically there were four: new philosophical positions, advances in science, developments in literary and historical criticism, and the growth of 'democratic' ideas.

a. New Philosophical Positions

Medieval philosophers attempted to create a synthesis in which all the elements of thought were related in a consistent system. They achieved a large measure of success but in the work of Duns Scotus and William of Occam we see it beginning to break down. After the Renaissance philosophers tried to reconcile the new ideas to the traditional conceptions so that some kind of synthesis could be preserved. Such a reconciliation became increasingly difficult as the medieval 'religious' world-view began to be replaced by a 'scientific' one until even its possibility was doubted.[29] In the middle of the eighteenth century Hume published his investigations and at the end of the century Kant let loose his *Critiques*, having been 'roused' by Hume from 'his dogmatic slumber and compelled to seek a solid barrier against scepticism'.[30] In a letter to Herder, Hamann comments that Kant 'certainly deserves the title of a Prussian Hume', and we may apply to Hume also Heine's description of Kant as 'the arch-destroyer in the realm of thought' with 'his destructive, world-annihilating thoughts'.[31] The critical inquiries of these two philosophers shook the foundations of the philosophical tradition which had prevailed fundamentally unchanged since Plato and Aristotle and had been 'baptized' by Christianity as the vehicle for its self-understanding. The collapse of the old philosophy threatened the structure of faith which had been expressed in terms of it. What was the nature of this collapse and the threat that it posed? Here we can give only a brief suggestion of the answer in its metaphysical and ethical aspects.

Hume and Kant both seek to determine the limits of man's knowledge by analysing the way in which man comes to know things. In the Introduction to *A Treatise of Human Nature* Hume says that:

> all the sciences have a relation . . . to human nature. . . . Even *Mathematics, Natural Philosophy,* and *Natural Religion,* are in some measure dependent on the science of MAN; since they lie under the cogniscance of men, and are judged of by their powers and faculties.[32]

Hume proceeds to offer a 'science of man' which is based on a thoroughgoing empiricism of 'experience and observation'. He rejects as 'presumptuous and chimerical' any attempt to go 'beyond experience'.[33] The sole foundation of our knowledge is the data of experience. The result is a sceptical empiricism which can be regarded as the father of logical positivism. Thus the notion of 'substance' is restricted to a collection of experienced attributes while the notion of 'cause' is reduced from necessary connexion to regular succession. When Hume applied his highly critical mind to religion, he showed the unsatisfactory quality both of the ontological, cosmological, and teleological arguments for the existence of God[34] and of the use of miracles to prove 'the truth of the *Christian* religion'.[35] Man has neither the evidence nor the mental capacity to give a 'reasonable' defence of the Christian faith. Hume further suggested that the origin of religious belief can be explained phenomenologically as primitive man's imaginative identification of the unknown forces which largely governed his life as existing personal beings.[36] If, therefore, 'a wise man . . . proportions his belief to the evidence',[37] he will find it difficult on the basis of Hume's position to have much confidence either in the theistic arguments of natural theology or in the dogmas of revealed theology. For a time the force of Hume's work was not fully appreciated[38] but eventually his criticisms could not be ignored. They began to effect people's confidence in faith and it was realized that attempts must be made to counter them. Any reappraisal of the foundations of religious faith soon had to take into account also Kant's critical philosophy.

Kant had no doubts about the significance of his critical philosophy. He claimed that it was 'absolutely necessary' to make all future metaphysical thought accord with his position and 'to consider all that has been done (sc. before Kant) as undone'.[39] The essence of his 'Copernican revolution' was to 'suppose that objects must conform to our knowledge' whereas 'hitherto it has been assumed that all our knowledge must conform to objects'.[40] While Hume had held that our knowledge is wholly derived from the data of experience, Kant argued that all knowledge is the result of interaction between the knowing self and the object to be known. Our knowledge of something depends both upon the way we are able to experience it and upon the way our mind interprets that experience by its in-built structures of understanding. Our knowledge, therefore, is limited to 'phenomena'—that is, to things, as they appear to us. We cannot know what things are like 'in themselves'; the realm of 'noumena' is completely closed to our understanding. Attempts to reason about 'noumena' result in confusion and contradiction.

The most famous part of the application of Kant's thought to religion is his refutation of the ontological, cosmological, and teleological arguments for the existence of God. They showed, for Kant, that 'reason . . . stretches its wings in vain in thus attempting to soar above the world of sense by the mere power of speculation.'[41] Even though the refutations are open to criticism, they were generally regarded as conclusive in the nineteenth century. Kant was widely regarded as having decisively ended traditional natural theology. He himself considered that this part of his work showed that 'speculative reason' can neither prove nor disprove the 'objective reality' of God.[42] On the other hand, he held that the concept of God as an *ens realissimum* is an important regulative principle in thought.[43] Although this 'transcendental ideal' has an important function in our thinking, 'we are left entirely without knowledge as to the existence of a being of such outstanding pre-eminence'.[44] When we turn to morality, the object of our *practical* reason, we find that Kant holds that our 'consciousness of our duty' to seek the *'summum bonum'* implies 'the supposition' of the existence 'of a supreme intelligence'. A proper appreciation of morality thus requires that we 'postulate . . . the reality of a *highest original good*, that is to say, of the existence of God'.[45] Kant is careful to point out that the 'moral necessity' of postulating the existence of God is a 'subjective' not an 'objective' necessity. Our need to introduce the notion of 'God', if we are fully to explain our moral consciousness, is no proof that God exists objectively. For the practical reason God is a 'principle of explanation' or 'a hypothesis'.[46]

Kant's distinction between 'noumena' and 'phenomena' raises in a critical way the problem of whether we can talk about God even if we suppose that He does exist. Whereas our knowledge of objects is in terms of time and space, since these are the forms of intuition, in God's case 'the conditions of time and space' do not apply.[47] In the *Critique of Practical Reason* Kant states that 'the condition of time is nothing' to God. God's actions are restricted to the realm of noumena: He can be held to be 'the cause of the existence of . . . noumena' but 'it is a contradiction . . . to say that God is a creator of appearances'.[48] Since our knowledge is of phenomena, we seem to be left with the position that God knows one world and we know a different one. While Kant regards 'noumena' as in some way causally related to phenomena, we cannot specify the relation between the two worlds since, strictly speaking, the notion of 'cause' itself is one of our categories of understanding and so refers only to the world of phenomena, not to the world of noumena.[49] Kant thus concludes that any knowledge we have of God is 'only for practical purposes'. He is confident that we cannot specify 'one single attribute' of God which could extend our 'theoretical knowledge' once we have abstracted 'from it everything anthropomorphic'.[50] We can only talk about God in terms of 'a *symbolical* anthropomorphism' which indicates His relation to the world. As for what God is really like, 'we . . . acknowledge that the Supreme Being is quite inscrutable and even incogitable *in any determinate way* as to what He is *per se*'.[51]

Kant's own view of his achievement is contained in a famous sentence in his Preface to the Second Edition of the *Critique of Pure Reason*: 'I have therefore found it necessary to deny *knowledge*, in order to make room for *faith*.'[52] He considered that it was possible to talk about God so long as the statements were recognized to belong to the logic of faith. Although he gave a few indications of a possible answer,[53] Kant left the problem of determining the precise nature of faith-statements to his successors. For some the combined effect of the work of Hume and Kant was effectively to rule out the possibility of talking about God in a way that could be metaphysically justified. Others took up the challenge and offered their interpretations of the logic and meaning of faith-statements. There were two ways of doing this. Either one could produce a natural theology which was not open to the criticisms of Hume and Kant or one could give a radical place to faith in religious statements. Both responses prolonged and increased the shaking of faith's foundations. The nineteenth-century believer could not rest in untroubled certainty and at the same time be seriously aware of the movements of contemporary thought. The basis of faith was challenged. Faith would survive only by meeting the challenge.

There were many attempts in the nineteenth century to produce an acceptable natural theology upon whose foundations a firm faith could be established. In some cases the intention was to provide an acceptable foundation for faith as traditionally understood. Other attempts involved a conscious reinterpretation of the content of the faith as part of the apologetic task. Consequently three different questions had to be answered: what are we talking about when we make statements of faith? how can we talk about these things? how can we justify such faith-statements? Here we cannot pretend to give more than a cursory survey of the answers that were offered to these questions. We want merely to suggest the kind of thinking that was involved as an indication of the depth of the crisis for faith in the nineteenth century.

The most important attempt to defend a recognizably orthodox understanding of the Christian faith was made by Schleiermacher.[54] His natural theology started from man's experience of himself rather than from his reason. In *On Religion: Speeches to Its Cultured Despisers*, published in 1799, he holds that we will find the ground of religion not by understanding doctrinal systems but when our 'whole soul is dissolved in the immediate feeling of the Infinite and Eternal'. Doctrines are reflective attempts to express and interpret such experience and they are 'only to be understood by it and along with it'.[55] The experience is:

> the immediate consciousness of the universal existence of all finite things, in and through the Infinite, and of all temporal things in and through the Eternal. Religion is to seek this and find it in all that lives and moves, in all growth and change, in all doing and suffering. It is to have life and to know life in immediate feeling, only as such an existence in the Infinite and Eternal. . . . Yet religion is not knowledge. . . . In itself it is an affection, a revelation of the Infinite in the finite, God being seen in it and it in God.[56]

Schleiermacher developed his position systematically in *The Christian Faith*. He starts from the 'consciousness' or 'feeling of absolute dependence' which 'accompanies our whole existence'. This 'feeling' makes known to us a real and not merely an imagined situation. Hence when we speak of 'God', we signify 'simply that which is the co-determinant in this feeling and to which we trace our being in such a state'. Thus our 'feeling of absolute dependence' is the same as being 'conscious of being in relation with God'. We know God only through such 'feeling' —we cannot speak of God in terms of an 'outwardly given . . . perceptible object'.[57] Schleiermacher builds up a system of doctrine which derives the articles of faith from this basic position and restricts their meaning to what can be so derived. In this way he produced a statement of faith which could hope to meet the challenge of the critical philosophy. The reference of theological statements was located not in the fields of 'knowing' and of 'doing' but primarily in that of 'feeling or of immediate self-consciousness'.[58] It was thus possible to talk about God so long as we restricted our statements to what we grasped of God as the correlate of our primary 'feeling' and did not claim to know what God was like in Himself. Theological statements were justifiable so long as they could be reasonably derived from this special kind of experience.

Schleiermacher's attempt to restate natural theology in response to the critical philosophy received only limited support. Many people would not accept his view that theological statements are primarily statements about a fundamental 'feeling' and secondarily statements of what that 'feeling' indicates about our existential situation. Although Schleiermacher's presuppositions seemed to rule out such a possibility, believers and non-believers regarded some religious statements as some kind of objective descriptions of God and of His activity. They found little comfort in Schleiermacher's solution to the philosophical aspects of the crisis for faith.

They would have found probably less comfort in the alternative response which Kierkegaard offered. We say 'would have' because, in fact, Kierkegaard's work was not widely known in the nineteenth century. Kierkegaard treated the place of faith with radical seriousness. He presented to his readers various fundamental attitudes to life and pointed out the differences between them. In *Either/Or* he distinguished between the aesthetic and the ethical stances, in *Fear and Trembling* between the ethical and the religious. For the latter he used the story of Abraham and Isaac since 'the ethical expression for what Abraham did is, that he would murder Isaac; the religious expression is, that he would sacrifice Isaac.'[59] Having pointed to the differences, Kierkegaard deliberately thrust the responsibility of choosing a position on to the reader.[60] At the same time he left his reader in no doubt about the necessity for unreserved commitment to what he determines to be the truth—'there is only one relation to revealed truth: believing it.' The authenticity of faith is proved by the individual's willingness to 'suffer' for it.[61]

Kierkegaard's view of the life of faith led him to deny even the possibility of a philosophy which comprehends all truth objectively. He persistently criticized the Hegelians for claiming finality for their system. The attack was pressed home in the *Concluding Unscientific Postscript* where he argued that while 'a logical system is possible, ... an existential system is impossible.' Since a 'logical system' must not incorporate anything 'that has any relation to existence', it can neither 'boast of an absolute beginning, since such a beginning, like pure being, is a pure chimera', nor be significant for actual life. On the other hand, 'an existential system cannot be formulated', because 'reality itself ... cannot be a system for any existing spirit.'[62] The fundamental error of 'speculative philosophy' is to forget that 'the knower is an existing individual'. This error is avoided when we recognize that 'subjectivity is truth, subjectivity is reality.'[63] In terms of religion this meant that Kierkegaard was not disturbed by the impossibility of demonstrating the existence of God.[64] For him the important question was faith, 'the mode of the subject's acceptance' of Christianity, because 'it is only in subjectivity that its truth exists, if it exists at all; objectively, Christianity has absolutely no existence.'[65] The essence of religion, then, is faith in which 'an objective uncertainty' is 'held fast in an appropriation-process of the most passionate inwardness'.[66] The 'absurd' or 'paradoxical' content of faith is stressed to emphasize this rational 'uncertainty'. In particular the absurd element in Christian faith is seen in two claims—the claim that God is deeply concerned about the fate of individual human beings,[67] and the claim that 'the eternal truth has come into being in time, that God has come into being ... precisely like any other individual human being.' The object of faith, however, is 'not a doctrine' but a personal relationship centred on 'God's reality in existence as a particular individual'.[68] For faith to be real, this relationship must exist at first hand in the present.[69] The believer is not a disinterested spectator but a totally committed participant in a contest which offers him life or death.

In this way Kierkegaard provided an answer to the crisis of faith brought about by the critical philosophy. He did not challenge its destruction of natural theology. Instead he tried to show that a true understanding of the Christian position was not disturbed by these views simply because it was based on *faith* and not on untenable claims to knowledge. Kierkegaard's stress on the 'absurd' element in the content of faith and on the necessity for a commitment which could not be rationally justified made many of his readers wonder if his apology for Christianity were not in the end a condemnation of it. If faith demanded unreserved assent to what was recognized to be objectively most uncertain, could they as rational persons give such assent? Did not their consciousness of their 'rationality' rule out faith? Many who wanted to 'believe' felt unable to seek faith on Kierkegaard's terms. The necessity for rational justification was a presupposition which most people in the nineteenth century could not bring themselves to challenge. The type of solution offered by Kierkegaard was as little satisfactory, though for different reasons, as that of Schleiermacher. The crisis for faith continued.

We have room to notice only two of the attempts by British theologians to meet the crisis. The work of Coleridge and Mansel must serve to indicate how theology was being forced to reconsider its position in Britain. John Stuart Mill described Coleridge as one of 'the two great seminal minds of England in their age',[70] while Maurice suggested that Coleridge's works reflect 'the struggles of the age'.[71] Coleridge states that his studies of the empiricists failed to provide 'an abiding place for my reason' but that he found in Kant and his followers ideas which 'invigorated and disciplined my understanding'. While his views resembled those of Schelling, he claimed that they were fundamentally his own. Any resemblances were to be accounted for in their common discipleship of Kant.[72]

Coleridge vigorously attacked the highly popular 'rational' theology such as was to be found in the works of Paley. Although he recognized Paley's merits, he felt 'bound in conscience to throw the whole force of my intellect in the way of this triumphal Car, on which the tutelary Genius of modern Idolatry is borne'.[73] Paley was fundamentally in error because he placed religion primarily in the realm of the intellect and tried to prove conclusively 'the verities of religion', thus denying the vital element of moral choice in such matters.[74] Such 'rational religion' was neither rational nor religion.[75] Reason must be restricted to 'objects of sense' since it falls into error when it is applied to 'spiritual realities . . . beyond the sphere of possible experience'.[76] The existence of God, the foundation of religion, 'is absolutely and necessarily insusceptible of a scientific demonstration'. It is 'necessarily' undemonstrable because the acceptance of doctrines of religion is a matter of 'belief' and, therefore, of the 'will'.[77] According to the *Biographia Literaria*, we are led to faith by the indications of our understanding and the demands of our conscience, but in the end faith is a moral commitment, not a 'cold . . . worthless, because compulsory, assent' of the intellect alone.[78] Coleridge thus located the foundations of faith in the moral nature of man. Faith is not derived from 'abstract or speculative Reason' but from 'the *Practical* Reason of Man, comprehending the Will, the Conscience, the Moral Being . . . that Reason . . . which is . . . the Source of living and actual Truths'.[79] Theological doctrines are tested not by 'speculative' reason but against 'the dictates of Conscience, and

... the interests of Morality'.[80] Coleridge further argues that his sense of moral responsibility requires him as an 'absolute duty to believe ... that there is a God ... in whom supreme reason and a most holy will are one with an infinite power'.[81] This emphasis on the place of conscience and will does not lead in Coleridge to an irrational fideism. Although the divinely given 'faculty of Reason' is limited in its abilities, it is neither 'totally useless' nor 'wholly impotent' but may prevent faith from becoming ridiculous.[82] Whately overstates his case when he condemns Coleridge's position because 'it makes each man's own feelings the sole test of what he is to believe.'[83] He fails to recognize both the rational and cognitive elements in these 'feelings' and the external evidence supporting them.

Fundamentally Coleridge opposes the 'religion' of Paley and 'rational' theology because it sees faith primarily in terms of the intellect. For Coleridge religion is a matter of practice. The 'knowledge' of God given by faith comes from the dictates of conscience which govern the whole life of the individual. In the *Theological Notes* he asserts that 'religion has no speculative dogmas; that all is practical, all appealing to the will' and that 'Christ is not described primarily and characteristically as a teacher but as a doer.'[84] Consequently his answer to those who have doubts and problems about the doctrines of faith is to assert that 'Christianity is not a Theory, or a Speculation, but a *Life*. Not a *Philosophy* of Life, but a Life and a living Process. . . . TRY IT.'[85] The 'proof' of faith is not found in abstract reasoning but in the experience of those who live by it. He thus diagnoses the need of the age as an 'enthusiasm' in which the individual is absorbed 'in the object contemplated from the vividness or intensity of his conceptions and convictions'.[86]

In Coleridge, therefore, we find an attempt to meet the crisis for faith by concentrating on the subjective and practical elements of religion. As Maurice pointed out, the importance of Coleridge was that he took seriously the principles of the critical philosophy and applied them to theology.[87] He recognized that attempts like that of Paley to found religion on reason were doomed to failure because of the inherent logic of the attempt. Religion must, as Kant and Hume had seen, be based on faith.[88] In his references to the moral will and conscience Coleridge suggested what might be the structure of faith. His writings on this point are tantalizingly fragmentary but they reflect an awareness in British theology of the philosophical aspects of the crisis for faith and an attempt to meet them. His concept of faith, however, was too subjective and irrational for most people. Coleridge pointed to the problem rather than offered a widely acceptable solution.

In the work of Mansel we find another attempt to apply the critical philosophy to theological doctrines. The result was regarded by some as a virtual surrender to agnosticism while others hailed it as a valuable piece of apologetic. Mansel was a disciple of the Scottish philosopher Sir William Hamilton who held that we could grasp 'only the limited, and the conditionally limited' since 'the infinite and the absolute . . . are . . . equally inconceivable to us'.[89] In his essay on *Metaphysics* Mansel suggests that 'the existence of the finite is inexplicable . . . unless we admit the existence of the infinite' and so 'we cannot escape from the conviction that the infinite does in some manner exist.' At the same time he insists that 'we can form no positive conception' of the nature of this 'infinite' for 'the conception of the infinite itself appears to involve contradictions'. These contradictions are due to 'the impotence of thought' when it tries to overcome the 'limitations in our power of comprehension'. Since our 'consciousness' is 'relative' and 'limited', it 'cannot comprehend the infinite'. All we can do is to accept on authority what we can never discover through our reason. Attempts to reconcile by reason apparent incompatibilities in theological assertions are doomed to fail because we can never hope to understand the true content of any attribute of God.[90] Thus Mansel ends his essay on *Metaphysics* by suggesting that 'Metaphysical speculation' will have been useful if it only teaches us 'of the laws and limits of Reason; and, by consequence, of the just claims of Faith'.[91]

In his famous Bampton Lectures, *The Limits of Religious Thought*, Mansel developed his views, using as a motto Berkeley's statement that 'the objections made to faith are by no means an effect of knowledge, but proceed rather from an ignorance of what knowledge is.'[92] By defining 'the provinces of Reason and Faith, the limits of our knowledge and of our ignorance', Mansel attempted to determine the proper place of revelation.[93] He argued that 'the fundamental conceptions of Rational Theology' are 'self-destructive' since mutual, internal contradictions are involved in attributing to 'one and the same Being' the 'three conceptions' of 'the Cause, the Absolute, and the Infinite'.[94] These contradictions do not belong to the nature of the Infinite and Absolute but reveal the limitations of our mode of understanding.[95] From this Mansel concluded that 'human reason' is impotent as 'an *a priori* judge' of theological truths. Reason can neither prove nor disprove any belief.[96] Because of its evident limitations, we must not confine our faith to the bounds of reason but must 'believe in that which we are unable to comprehend'.[97] An analysis of our religious consciousness, as attempted by Schleiermacher, offers no more hope of a coherent knowledge of God. It may compel men to believe that there is a God but it cannot exhibit His nature.[98] To try to know what God is like in Himself is to attempt the impossible: we must be content to know only 'how He wills that we should think of Him' in the 'types and shadows' by which He reveals Himself.[99] Mansel defends this limited view of theological knowledge on the grounds that 'the highest principles of thought and action, to which we can attain, are *regulative,* not speculative.' This means that 'they do not tell us what things are in themselves, but how we must conduct ourselves in relation to them.'[100] We must not pretend to know what God is like in Himself but be content to believe that the revelation He has given us of Himself is 'true' (as far as we are capable of seeing the 'truth' in such matters) and 'is best adapted to our wants and training'.[101] The function of reason in religion is to provide various internal and external 'evidences' to support the claim to revelation. Mansel thus concludes that 'there can be no such thing as a positive science of Speculative Theology' for we are unable to 'apprehend' the 'Nature and Attributes of God in His Infinite Being'.[102] Philosophy denies the possibility of rational theology in order to establish the place of faith and revelation.

Mansel's views received a mixed and often vigorous reception. Maurice was stung into impassioned attack since he believed that Mansel rejected the essence of Christianity when he denied the possibility of a direct knowledge of God.[103] J. B. Mozley wrote more temperately to R. W. Church that he thought the lectures 'put forward the absolute unintelligibility of the Divine nature . . . too nakedly'.[104] Newman on the whole approved of the lectures.[105] Within the camp of faith some defenders considered that Mansel was building up the fortifications while others felt that he was undermining them by conceding too much to the critical philosophy. Among the enemies outside the camp, Mansel's work found some approval.[106] The ideas of Hamilton and Mansel provided a foundation for Herbert Spencer's naturalistic and agnostic position.[107] On the other hand Mill described Mansel's work as 'a detestable to me absolutely loathsome book', since it put forward a view of God and religion which was 'profoundly immoral'.[108] Mansel's defence of faith thus helped to deepen the crisis. Some, like Newman, valued the work but for many it only made the possibility of faith more doubtful still.

At the same time that these disturbing attempts were being made to find an apologetic for a recognizably orthodox Christian faith, other philosophers were extending the crisis for faith by suggesting that the true content of its doctrines had been misapprehended. Their expositions of the 'real meaning' of the Christian faith made the believer, already struggling to defend his faith, even more bewildered. Again we can do no more than briefly indicate the kind of views that were offered for consideration.

In an early theological essay, Hegel defined 'the aim and essence of all true religion' as 'human morality'. Its doctrines and practices were to be interpreted in accordance with this view of its nature.[109] This Kantian restriction of religion to morality was eventually modified by an understanding of theological doctrines as pictorial expressions of metaphysical truths. In *The Phenomenology of Mind* Hegel describes religious language as 'presentative pictorial thought' using 'figurative ideas' to describe the 'Absolute Being' at 'the level of imaginative thought'.[110] In a later work, *The Philosophy of Mind*, in which he also recognized an essential connexion between morality and religion,[111] Hegel asserts that 'the content of religion and philosophy is the same.' The fundamental difference between them is that whereas philosophy grasps the Absolute Spirit under 'the forms of speculative thought', religion uses 'the terms and conditions of finitude in general' to express 'the truth *for all men*'.[112] Religion thus sacrifices precision and consistency to the demands of comprehensibility. This position is developed in Hegel's *Lectures on the Philosophy of Religion* which were published posthumously. The 'true' religion expresses 'the absolute truth' that God is the 'universal Spirit which particularizes itself' in the processes of life.[113] God is 'no longer a Being above and beyond this world' but is known outwardly in the events of history and inwardly in the consciousness of 'the finite spirit'.[114] Properly understood, the doctrines of the Incarnation and the Trinity express pictorially important truths about the Absolute Spirit of the Hegelian system.

For some this position offered a philosophically respectable way of entertaining religious beliefs. At first sight the doctrines of religion might seem to be untenable. The apparent difficulties disappeared once the doctrines were translated from their pictorial form into the language of Hegel's metaphysic. By such translation, it was claimed, their proper content was revealed. There was considerable dispute about the correct resolution of such 'demythologization' but many real Victorians are represented by Mrs. Humphrey Ward's Gray, who held that 'all religions somehow contain, amid all the dross, the pure, august, uninviting philosophic truth of religion.'[115] Many others, then as now, could not accept such 'demythologization'. They felt that the Hegelian programme secured for the Christian faith a doubtful metaphysical acceptability by sacrificing some of its fundamental truths. The attempt to change the form had resulted in a loss of essential content. There might be some similarities but there were also vital differences between Hegel's

'Absolute Mind' and the Christian 'God'. The differences prevented any unobjectionable identification of the two.

Even less acceptable was the radical translation of Christian doctrine offered by Feuerbach. He argued that religious doctrines are properly to be understood as descriptions of human perfections.

> Such as are a man's thoughts and dispositions, such is his God; so much worth as a man has, so much and no more has his God. Consciousness of God is self-consciousness, knowledge of God is self-knowledge. By his God thou knowest the man, and by the man his God; the two are identical.[116]

To say that 'God is love' is equivalent to saying that 'Love is God', for 'that which in religion is the predicate we must make the subject, and that which in religion is a subject we must make a predicate.' To attribute anything to God is to assert a goal for human life. God is 'the mirror of man' which reflects his ideals and his needs.[117] Feuerbach thus attempted to make religious statements acceptable by resolving 'the religious essence into the human essence'.[118] *The Essence of Christianity* was translated into English by George Eliot and appeared in 1854. In contrast to her translation of Strauss's *Life of Jesus* the work received little attention and was a financial failure.[119] It does, however, indicate the radical reappraisal of Christian beliefs which could be found in certain intellectual and literary quarters. This reappraisal stretched from the simple theism of F. W. Newman's *Phases of Faith* through Leigh Hunt's *Religion of the Heart* to the atheistic propaganda of Bell's *The Task of Today* and the 'Religion of Humanity' of the British disciples of Comte. It lay behind Adam Bede's remark that 'doctrines was like finding names for your feelings.'[120] These attempts to make Christian beliefs acceptable by reinterpretation seemed to many believers to deepen the crisis for faith rather than to alleviate it. In certain cases the elements of faith could still be perceived, even if faintly, in the new forms. In other cases the 'demythologized' forms of the old beliefs seemed rather to express a non-theistic position.

The crisis for faith was further extended by various philosophical and ethical systems which offered 'ways of life' that were not dependent upon theistic beliefs. These challenged the final bastion of much popular apologetic for faith—the claim that a good life was not possible apart from some theistic faith. An effective alternative was offered in the practice of autonomous ethics. Victorian non-believers such as John Stuart Mill, T. H. Huxley, and Leslie Stephen displayed a moral integrity which was at least the equal of that shown by any believer.

Fundamental religious uncertainty was often accompanied by confidence and certainty in ethical matters.[121] George Eliot was typical of many in that she 'affirmed the sovereignty of impersonal and unrecompensing Law' although she had lost her faith in God.[122] The high morality practised by many unbelievers had a theoretical side in attempts to find a philosophically acceptable foundation for an autonomous ethic. The divorce of faith and practice was apparent here also, for the maintenance of high moral standards did not depend upon the discovery of satisfactory theoretical backing. Mill pointed out that the sanctions of religion did not necessarily produce any improvement in moral behaviour. While religion may initially have brought men to acknowledge 'moral truths', these 'moral truths' are 'strong enough in their own evidence' not to need the support of religion. Indeed, religious authorization is detrimental to true morality for it directs morality to promises of punishment and reward instead of cultivating the 'unselfish feelings' which value morality for its own sake. Morality is annihilated if it is subordinated to the will of God.[123] In his *Utilitarianism* Mill outlined an ethic based on 'the greatest happiness principle' which he had learnt from Bentham. The ultimate sanction for this ethic is no transcendent Power but 'the conscientious feelings of mankind'.[124] It was an ethic and a sanction which evoked considerable response—although both Mill and Sidgwick, as well as many of their followers, displayed in practice a recognition of a categorical imperative which went beyond their professed principles.[125]

A very different ethical system was propounded by Herbert Spencer. Here evolutionary ideas were applied to ethics. Spencer's thought had been dominated by evolutionary models for several years before Darwin's *Origin of Species* appeared, and his views were only partly modified by those researches. The application of a theory of evolution to metaphysical and ethical issues by Spencer raised questions which Darwin was unwilling to investigate.[126] Spencer allowed that religious beliefs are probably 'not absolutely baseless' but they are not significant because they concern matters which are essentially incomprehensible.[127] The evolutionary process is explicable in terms of the physical laws of matter and motion without reference to an intelligent will. The development of morals is part of this cosmic process. In the history of races and nations we see 'the process of moral adaptation, which is a continual approach to equilibrium between the emotions and the kinds of conduct required by surrounding conditions'.[128] According to Spencer, the evolutionary order moves ethically from egoism through ascending stages of altruism towards an ideal state in which individual and general interests will be at one. Man's moral responsibility is to live in accordance with the dictates of this 'evolutionary hedonism'.[129] His happiness is found in his harmony with the cosmic order. In Leslie Stephen's *Science of Ethics* the conclusion is reached that 'Happiness is the reward offered not for virtue alone, but for conformity to what I have called the law of nature, of which it is the great commandment, "Be strong".'[130] Since it was fashionable to be 'scientific', the pseudo-scientific nature of such ideas gave them great popular appeal. In spite of considerable philosophical and ethical criticisms, they offered an understanding of life which was an attractive alternative to the uncertain position of religion. They were apparently based on 'scientific knowledge' while religion was notoriously based on questionable 'faith'. It was some time before the unscientific nature of the 'science'[131] and the errors in some of the 'knowledge' were widely perceived. Meanwhile many were attracted to evolutionary ethics as a viable way of life. Others preferred to stand with T. H. Huxley in judgement on the apparent development of the cosmic process. The ways of nature were not to be copied by man but countered by obedience to the standards of absolute goodness.[132] While the authority for such standards might be unclear, their appeal was regarded by many as intrinsically compelling. Nevertheless, whether man was to follow or to counter the evolutionary process, was a question which could be, and often was, determined without reference to God. There were alternatives to theism for reaching decisions about the meaning and values of life.

Autonomous ethics did not only offer an alternative to religious belief. They further contributed to the crisis for faith by providing the basis for attacks on those beliefs. Within the fold of faith the clash between Christian doctrines and Christian ethics at certain points was not unnoticed. Attempts were made to reconcile the conflicting elements. The problem could be avoided by asserting the inscrutable wisdom of God—but this was to attempt to meet the problem for faith by a demand for deeper faith. Others tried to correct the ethically objectionable elements by reference to other doctrines. Maurice challenged the notion of everlasting punishment, while McLeod Campbell presented an alternative to the substitutionary theory of the Atonement. In each case the morally objectionable element was countered by reference to the love and justice of God. All this was done by rearrangements within the realm of faith. The non-believer was not restricted to such schemes and refused to join in the mental gymnastics employed by some theologians to get round these problems. A conflict between belief and ethics was a condemnation of the belief. Mill wrote that religion was worth considering only when it had 'freed itself from the pernicious consequences which result from its identification with any bad moral doctrine'.[133] Among the ideas that could be classed as 'bad moral doctrine' were those of predestination, everlasting torment, substitutionary punishment and retributive justice. They could be found at the heart of most contemporary expressions of the Christian faith. They helped to render that faith unacceptable to minds already characterized by ethical certainty and religious uncertainty.

The extreme point of the ethical rejection of Christianity was reached by Nietzsche who proclaimed that the Christian ideal was the negation of true manhood.[134] Nietzsche's influence in Britain was small.[135] Believer and non-believer on the whole shared the same ethical values. The non-believer might find that this common ethic led him to criticize religious belief and offered him a substitute for it. On the other hand, when that common ethic was assailed, he recognized that the values he stood for were in practice those pursued also by the Christian. The believer thus found, often to his bewilderment, that his values were defended by those who denied his fundamental faith. This aggravated the crisis for faith.

b. Advances in Science

Not only developments in philosophy and ethics disturbed the security of faith in the nineteenth century. Scientific advances posed a threat which was equally menacing. Addressing The Religious Science Congress at the end of the century, Auguste Sabatier described the present relation between religion and modern culture as one of 'conflict'. Religion views 'the discoveries of modern science' as 'nothing but menace and danger' while science regards religion 'as the great obstacle to the bringing in of a better state of things'. For many the inescapable choice confronting 'modern culture' is either 'the destruction of religion or the domestication of science, the triumph of irreligious culture or the triumph of superstition'.[136] When 'science' was popularly regarded as the way of proof and progress, the believer, harrassed by philosophical problems, could not be happy about the security of his faith. The crisis for faith deepened. What led to this situation?

The revolution which underlies modern science occurred in the sixteenth and seventeenth centuries. During the period from Copernicus to Newton it was established that questions about the natural order were to be answered by observation and experiment. Previously they had been answered by reference to the authorities of classical philosophy. The struggle to free thought about the natural world from domination by Aristotle reached a dramatic climax in the case of Galileo. As A.N. Whitehead puts it, Galileo and his opponents were 'at hopeless cross purposes' because 'Galileo keeps harping on how things happen, whereas his adversaries had a complete theory as to why things happen'.[137] Although Galileo was forced to recant, ultimately the victory went to those who defended their views by reference to the facts and not to *a priori* theories. By the nineteenth century, the victory was absolute. When Mill wrote that 'the rules of experimental inquiry are the contrivances' for discovering the 'Laws of Nature', he expressed an undisputed assumption.[138] With this revolution in the way to knowledge came a tremendous increase in the sum of knowledge. The faith by which men lived had to be related to an increasingly complex knowledge of the world in which they lived.

Where faith was not tied to classical philosophy,[139] there was no reason to suspect that the scientific revolution would lead to any serious conflict with religion. Whitehead suggests that the revolution was stimulated in part by the concept of God as a being 'with the personal energy of Jehovah and . . . the rationality of a Greek philosopher'. This concept had become part of 'the instinctive tone of thought' through 'the unquestioned faith of centuries'.[140] It provided a faith in the rationality of creation which underlay all scientific investigation. Many of the foundation fathers of modern science did not experience any tension between their work and their religious convictions. Isaac Newton was a devout Christian who expounded the Apocalypse as well as the law of gravitation. Boyle wrote extensively about religion. The new discoveries could be interpreted as revelations of the nature of God. Kepler saw the glory of God in the regularity of the universe.[141] Ray entitled one of his books *The Wisdom of God Manifested in the Work of the Creation*. Derham and Paley founded their religious apologetics upon the discoveries of science.[142] In spite of Hume's philosophical criticisms, the President of the Royal Society, the Archbishop of Canterbury, and the Bishop of London showed no embarrassment when they asked eight people to fulfil the will of the Earl of Bridgewater by writing 'On the Power, Wisdom, and Goodness of God, as manifested in the Creation'.[143] The Earl wrote his will in 1825 and died four years later. The Bridgewater Treatises marked the end of an era. Although Paley was read at Cambridge throughout the nineteenth century, the period is characterized by growing tension between the discoveries of scientists and the faith of believers. Instead of being its ally, science increasingly appeared as the enemy of faith. The challenge it offered did not only depend upon the logical implications of the new discoveries. To a large extent science threatened faith through the psychological effects of its findings. No scientific discovery logically disproved the existence of God. The cumulative effect of different discoveries was to destroy belief in God by suggesting that any event could be explained by natural causes alone. There might be a God but His remoteness from actual events made Him insignificant. Again, science could not logically refute a teleological understanding of the world. Psychologically science rendered it unacceptable by advancing only mechanistic explanations. The conflict between objectivity and subjectivity in morality was decided in favour of the latter, not by scientific demonstrations but by the indirect psychological effects of scientific explanations.[144] It is now time to examine some of the particular points of conflict between science and faith in the nineteenth century which contributed to the crisis for faith.

The very size of the universe made it difficult to believe in a God who was its Creator with the intimacy and personal relationship that hitherto had characterized faith. Traditional belief appeared incredible when it claimed that the Creator was interested in people individually and had revealed Himself in a particular historical figure. As we have already remarked, Kierkegaard described the 'offence' of Christianity as its assertion that 'this particular individual . . . exists *before* God 'and 'is invited to live on the most intimate terms with God'. The 'absurdity' of Christianity is its assertion that 'God has come into being . . . precisely like any other individual human being.'[145] The 'offence' and 'absurdity' that Kierkegaard recognized philosophically was felt by others through the revelations of astronomy. The remote God of eighteenth-century Deism seemed more commensurate with the vastness of the universe. Tennyson expressed the mood of many contemporaries when he wrote:

> I falter where I firmly trod,
>   And falling with my weight of cares
>   Upon the great world's altar-stairs
> That slope thro' darkness up to God,
>
> I stretch lame hands of faith, and grope,
>   And gather dust and chaff, . . .[146]

The more astronomy revealed about the universe, the harder it was to have faith. A man might believe *that* a Creator existed but to believe *in* such a Creator required a faith which was increasingly difficult. God seemed to be too big to be believed in!

Not only the size of the universe but also the age of the world threatened faith. Both Protestant and Roman Catholic, assuming the inerrancy of the Bible, based their beliefs on its records. In 1823 Coleridge, without embarrassment, explained climatic changes in Siberia by reference to 'the Noachian deluge, as related and described by the great Hebrew historian and legislator'.[147] Maurice repeated in 1853 the view that human history began with Adam in 4004 B.C.[148] The Bible provided the truths of faith. Any attack on the Bible's veracity would seem to be an attack on the fundamentals of faith. The developing science of geology made such an attack. It challenged the Mosaic account of the world's beginnings. In consequence the nineteenth century was the scene of a running battle between the geologists and the Bibliolaters. As early as 1814 Thomas Love Peacock ridiculed 'the very Scientific narrative of that most enlightened astronomer and profound cosmogonist Moses'.[149] In the following decades Buckland, a clergyman, Lyell, a layman, and others argued persuasively from geological evidence that the age of the world must be regarded not in terms of a few thousand years but in millions.[150] On the same grounds the story of the Flood must be severely modified. The presence of fossils deep in the earth could not be explained by a universal flood only a few thousand years ago.[151] Some believers responded simply by asserting the Biblical record in the face of its critics.[152] Others tried to get round the problems by devious compromises. Gosse suggested that God had put misleading fossils into the rocks as a test of faith! Buckland declared that the 'days' of creation in Genesis 1 were vast epochs, not periods of twenty-four hours.[153] In 1839 John Pye Smith, the Divinity Tutor at Homerton College, published *The Relation between the Holy Scriptures and some parts of Geological Science*. He suggested that the conflict between geology and the Bible should be solved by recognizing that the inspiration of the Bible is restricted solely 'to religious subjects' and expressed in terms 'suited to the men of primeval times'. On the basis of these principles he asserted both that 'the Scripture does use language . . . concerning . . . God . . . which we dare not say is *literally true*', and that 'the alleged discrepance between the Holy Scriptures and the discoveries of scientific investigation, is not in reality, but in semblance only.'[154] We find the same principles used by C. W. Goodwin in his paper *On the Mosaic Cosmogony* in *Essays and Reviews*. Goodwin suggested that theologians should 'accept frankly . . . that those things for the discovery of which man has faculties specially provided are not fit objects of a divine revelation'. Geology and theology are not to be reconciled by tampering with 'the plain meaning of the Hebrew record', nor by claiming that science fills in details omitted by the 'Mosaic writer'. We must recognize that the Bible contains 'erroneous views of nature' since it is written 'from a different point of view from that which we now unavoidably take'. Difficulties arise because we will not accept the Bible as 'a book of religious instruction' which need not be and is not 'scientifically exact'. Our problems will disappear if we abandon the *a priori* view of 'how God ought to have instructed man' and recognize instead how He has in fact chosen to instruct him.[155] Here the scientific appeal to the facts is applied to the question of Biblical authority. In this way Goodwin attempted to fulfil the aim of *Essays and Reviews* 'to illustrate the advantage derivable to the cause of religious and moral truth . . . from a free handling . . . of subjects peculiarly liable to suffer . . . from traditional methods of treatment'.[156] The principles adopted by Pye Smith and Goodwin were acceptable only to a few believers. Those principles made possible a reconciliation which seemed to others to be the destruction of faith. Such theories might satisfy the subtle minds of scholars but they seemed evasive to the ordinary believer. In the popular view the alternatives were either the refutation of the geologists or the abandonment of faith based on the Bible.[157] There was no middle way. If one part of the Bible could be shown to be in error, how could faith be based on any of it? If the principles of Pye Smith and Goodwin were adopted, would anything be left for faith? On the other hand, the geologists seemed to have established their case. On Tuesday, 11 April, 1848, the Theological Examiners at Cambridge asked the candidates: '1. Give the date of the deluge'. The expected answer was '2348 B.C. and 1656 after the creation of the world'.[158] The faith which allowed such questions and answers was menaced. For some it was already impossible.

The challenge of the geologists was followed by the greater challenge of the theory of evolution. Darwin's work administered a blow to faith from which it is still recovering and his portrait enjoys a place of honour as frontispiece to the second volume of Robertson's *History of Freethought in the Nineteenth Century*. This volume opens by remarking that 'the concept of Evolution' was probably the most powerful 'of all the ideas which undid the hold of traditionary creed on the general intelligence of the modern world'.[159] The theory of evolution did not originate with Darwin. It can be observed in the writings of the Germans, Oken, von Baer and Schwann, and the Frenchmen, Saint-Hilaire and Lamarck, during the first half of the century. In Britain the theory received wide publicity when *The Vestiges of the Natural History of Creation* appeared in 1844.[160] The book was anonymous, slipshod, severely criticized and extremely popular, going to many editions. Its authorship was attributed to various people—including Prince Albert! In fact it was written by Robert Chambers.[161] Darwin's contribution was to provide a mass of evidence by which the concept of evolution was developed and defended. *His Origin of Species* appeared in 1859. Four years later Huxley published his lectures entitled *Man's Place in Nature* which exhibited man's position in the evolutionary process.

Darwin finally made his own views of this issue explicit in *The Descent of Man* which came out in 1871.

Darwin himself was an agnostic who did not find any necessary contradiction between his work and a theistic belief. Could not evolution be regarded as the method of creation? Some believers supported Darwin. Hort felt that he had made his case. Asa Gray, R. W. Church, and Charles Kingsley accepted the theory without losing their faith. The majority of believers reacted with horror and repulsion.[162] They saw that if Darwin was right, they could no longer hold the traditional beliefs about creation. The theory of evolution replaced the Genesis account with the suggestion that existing creatures, including man, had come from more primitive forms as a result of a struggle for survival. The characteristics of the different species could be explained as the consequence of impersonal laws working through chance variations. The Argument from Design was undermined because there was no need to postulate a conscious purpose behind the forms of creation. The theory did not rule out the possibility of a Creator, but evolution seemed a strangely wasteful way for God to proceed. The place given to man in the evolutionary process contradicted traditional beliefs about the creation and fall of man which were at the centre of faith. If these beliefs were rejected, then the accepted doctrine of the Atonement would be in jeopardy. Man's place as the latest and highest product of evolution suggested that further progress might be possible in the future. Such views challenged any assertion of the finality of Christ and the Christian Gospel. The theory of evolution supported ideas of natural development and progress which attracted adherents increasingly throughout the century. As we have already mentioned, attempts were made to apply the theory to metaphysics and ethics. When Goodwin claimed that 'the plan of Providence for the education of man is a progressive one,' he expressed a view that had great contemporary appeal.[163] For him it was a way of defending the Biblical revelation in the face of scientific discoveries. For others it might suggest that the next evolutionary progress would come through the abandonment of the old faith. A faith whose certainty lay in past events and whose doctrines did not accord with the Darwinian position could not feel confident after 1859. The evolution of science increased the threat to faith.

The discoveries of science further threatened faith as they made men aware of what the world was really like. Believers could not content themselves with a cosy view of God's benevolence and the goodness of His creation when the facts showed that the world was harsh and unfeeling. Tennyson expressed one aspect of the problem when he wrote of the impersonal mechanism of nature:

"The stars", she whispers, "blindly run."[164]

The mechanistic understanding of events expounded by science appalled many believers. It suggested that everything happened solely because of the working out of impersonal laws. There was no loving mind, no benevolent purpose guiding events, only irresistible structures of blind force. Tennyson asked:

> And shall I take a thing so blind,
>   Embrace her as my natural good;
>   Or crush her, like a vice of blood,
> Upon the threshold of the mind?[165]

but even this choice might not be open to him. Mill wrote that 'everything which occurs in the universe is determined by the laws of causation and collocations of the original causes.' He explicitly declared that this applied to personal decisions as well as to natural events for, 'given the motives which are present to an individual's mind, and given likewise the character and disposition of the individual, the manner in which he will act may be unerringly inferred'.[166] Personal responsibility and faith seemed unreal if this was how men must understand their world.[167]

Furthermore, the real nature of things as revealed by science conflicted with traditional beliefs. Tennyson recognized this also:

> Are God and Nature then at strife,
>   That Nature lends such evil dreams?
>   So careful of the type she seems,
> So careless of the single life; . . .
>
> 'So careful of the type?' but no.
>   From scarped cliff and quarried stone
>   She cries 'A thousand types are gone:
> I care for nothing, all shall go.
>
> 'Thou makest thine appeal to me:
>   I bring to life, I bring to death:
>   The spirit does but mean the breath:
> I know no more. . . .'
>
> [Man] trusted God was love indeed
>   And love Creation's final law—
>   Tho' Nature, red in tooth and claw
> With ravine, shriek'd against his creed— . . .[168]

This poem was published in 1850, nine years before *The Origin of Species*. The doctrine and examples of survival of the fittest reinforced the clash between faith and reality as seen by science. In 1860 Huxley still felt confidence in 'the absolute justice of the system of things' but by the time of his death in 1895 he recognized 'the immorality of the cosmos'.[169] The believer found it hard to accept and yet equally hard to deny the immorality of reality. His belief in the love and goodness of God was radically challenged by the cruelty and waste of a creation which was governed by the law of the jungle. It seemed necessary to surrender belief in either the omnipotence or the omniscience or the benevolence of God. For Mill the state of nature indicated that God must be limited in one or more of these attributes.[170] Hume had vividly expounded this problem in the previous century. It was not impossible to envisage a better world than the reality opened up by science.[171] It was not easy for the believer to put his faith in a God whose creation seemed smeared with imperfections.

The more a mechanistic view of nature was accepted, the harder it became to find a place for miracles.[172] R. W. Church might speak of 'the immeasurable difference that miracle or no miracle makes in our idea of religion',[173] but for many the advances of science rendered belief in miracle suspect. Some managed to accommodate miracles to science by reinterpreting their significance. Others felt obliged to abandon any reliance upon such reports. Miracles could no longer be adduced among the useful 'evidences' for faith. Schleiermacher suggested that while miracles might be expected 'from Him who is the supreme divine revelation', the claim that a miracle has occurred is the result of faith rather than evidence for faith. Any reference to miracles can only be 'relative' since our knowledge of 'physical Nature' is so limited.[174] The compromise that miracles presupposed faith was not acceptable to those whose views were dominated by the norms of scientific knowledge. Mill followed Hume's lead in attacking belief in miracles. In his *Logic* he argued that either the evidence for an event claimed to be miraculous must necessarily be inadequate or the acknowledged laws of nature must be amended to comprehend it. Thus 'we must disbelieve the alleged fact, or believe that we were mistaken in admitting the supposed law'. Either way there was no miracle left to be adduced in support of faith. Mill recognized that his position rested upon the principle that 'whatever is contradictory to a complete induction is incredible'.[175] This assumption was assailed by those who wished to preserve miracles for faith. Maurice protested that miracles were signs that the causal nexus of natural law is not the whole story;[176] Trench argued that miracles are not 'contrary' to the nature we know, but 'beyond and above' it, for 'the miracles of earth . . . are the laws of heaven'.[177] Mozley criticized scientists for confining themselves to 'the material and mechanical laws of nature' and then proceeding to assert 'the inviolability' of these laws.[178] Newman accused Hume's followers of being irrational because they equated 'the uniformity of nature which they witnessed hour by hour' with 'a necessary, inviolable law'.[179] In strict logic Mozley and Newman were correct. In practice men trusted what they regularly experienced rather than reports of events which ran counter to their experience. The position was summed up by Baden Powell in *Essays and Reviews* when he wrote that:

> the enlarged critical and inductive study of the natural world, cannot but tend powerfully to evince the inconceivableness of imagined interruptions of natural order, or supposed suspensions of the laws of matter.[180]

He concluded that an alleged miracle can be regarded either as an instance of a natural law still unknown or as a matter of faith and not of reason.[181] Science was beginning to dominate the way men thought. Miracles, which *ex hypothesi* were contrary to the laws of nature, were out of keeping with such thought. A faith which involved belief in miracles or used miracles as evidence for its truth was in difficulties in a world which was becoming scientifically orientated.

This position was generalized in the notion of 'scientific truth' which gradually, and often unconsciously, became the accepted norm for thought. The scientist appealed to experiment and observation in confirmation of his theories. His claim to truth was limited to what the evidence demonstrated. The religious thinker, in contrast, asserted dogmatically theories which were notoriously difficult to verify. The scientific approach was intrinsically preferred by the self-consciously 'reasonable' Victorian. To describe something as 'scientific' was to give it immediate appeal. Spencer expressed this popular attitude in his confessedly 'scientific' approach to life, even though his use of evidence was often peculiar. Huxley's 'agnosticism' is the model of what this attitude could mean in practice. He acknowledged that all our actions and reasonings depend upon a 'great act of faith'. This 'act of faith', however, is not the believer's trust in God and theology but the scientific faith that 'the experience of the past' is 'a safe guide in our dealings with the present and the future'. His 'agnostic faith' is based on:

> the fundamental axiom of modern science. . . . In matters of the intellect, follow your reason as far as it will take you, without regard to any other consideration. And . . . do not pretend that

conclusions are certain which are not demonstrated or demonstrable.

The agnostic restricts himself, as the scientist does, to what can be supported by 'logically satisfactory evidence'. In all matters, even religious ones, '"ascertainment and verification" . . . must be conducted according to the strict rules of scientific investigation, or be self-convicted of worthlessness'.[182] Here the truth-values of the scientist reign supreme. Tennyson had hinted at the position in 1850 when he wrote:

> We have but faith: we cannot know;
> For knowledge is of things we see.[183]

During the nineteenth century scientific ways of thought increasingly controlled men's minds. Pragmatism and Logical Positivism were two major consequences of the development. Freud described religion as 'an illusion' and concluded 'our science is no illusion. But an illusion it would be to suppose that what science cannot give us we can get elsewhere.'[184] By 1927 this view was commonplace. Since the logic of faith was different from the logic of science, faith was threatened where the logic of science came to be accepted as the norm for truth. The articles of belief were discounted and the crisis for faith deepened.

As the century closed few people doubted that faith must accommodate itself to the scientists' discoveries. Theology, finding itself 'shouldered and jostled by the sturdy growths of modern thought' might bemoan 'the hostility' which it encountered.[185] It would gain sympathy only when it restricted its claims to sovereignty in the realms of thought. Even if it could claim to be *princeps*, it was *princeps inter pares*. No longer could theologians assume that men would accept or were even interested in their pronouncements. They had to show why men should entertain their claims to state truths. Men listened when the scientist went beyond his brief and dogmatized about religion.[186] They were not interested when the theologian objected to this trespass.[187] They protested when the theologian succumbed to the same temptation. The theologian had to learn humility in order to get a hearing. At the same time he had to show that his faith had relevance and significance.

Whitehead suggested that 'the greatest invention of the nineteenth century was the invention of the method of invention'.[188] Technological developments went along with advances in science. Man increasingly found himself in control. The autonomy he enjoyed led him to question the need for religious faith. God was a hypothesis he seemed to need less and less. 'By an irresistible effort' nineteenth-century man sought 'the final conquest and realization of his autonomy. . . . In this very effort and expansion of his inner being' he came, as Sabatier said, 'into collision with religion, as it has been established and maintained by the tradition of the past'.[189] What was left after the collision? For many religion was destroyed, man was in control, and life had lost its meaning.[190] In a causally determined universe, there was no place for God—but was man only a puppet controlled by internal springs? The advances in science during the nineteenth century, both in their rational implications and in their psychological effects, extended and deepened the crisis for faith.

c. Developments in Literary and Historical Criticism

During the nineteenth century the techniques of literary and historical criticism were applied to the Bible and the doctrines of the Church. Sometimes the results were valuable for faith because they deepened men's understanding of its foundations.[191] More often they appeared hostile to faith because they undermined traditional positions. Both the Old and New Testaments were analysed and theories propounded about their constituent materials. The authority of the Bible declined as scholars discovered errors in transmission, historical mistakes, duplications, contradictions and adaptations of its material for theological purposes. The nature of its inspiration was questioned. While the critics' conclusions were widely disputed, the propriety of their approach was increasingly recognized. No longer could faith unhesitatingly assume that the Bible was a divine oracle, virtually written by the finger of God and true in every word. The security of faith was further challenged as scholars noticed the changes that had occurred in Christian doctrines over the centuries. The Church might claim to believe the faith of the Apostles but historical research revealed how much the formulations of that faith had developed. Would the Apostles recognize the faith of the Church in the nineteenth century as their own? Here we can only indicate a fraction of the work that appeared during the century. The picture is often confused by a long time-lag between the publication of critical theories and the public's awareness of them. During most of the century, for example, knowledge of Continental Biblical studies was restricted to a small company in this country.[192] By the end of the century, however, the basic theories were widely known, even if they were not accepted. Traditional beliefs were challenged: the crisis for faith deepened.

Leadership in Biblical criticism, together with the most radical theories, came from the Continent. In 1863, R. W. Mackay wrote that German scholarship had already 'conclusively settled' questions which were still being 'or perhaps only beginning to be discussed in England'.

He located 'the progressive spirit of true Protestantism and of sound learning' in Tübingen, not in the English universities with their more cautious ways.[193] There was never any significant English support for the extreme views that could be found on the Continent—as, for instance, in the Dutch school at the end of the century which regarded all the canonical Pauline epistles as pseudepigrapha. Nevertheless, even the more cautious English scholars had to recognize that there were problems associated with the traditional acceptance of the Bible. As we have already noticed, scientific work in geology and evolution raised questions about the credibility of Genesis. Goodwin argued in *Essays and Reviews* that theology must frankly admit the presence of 'erroneous views of nature' in the Bible.[194] Literary and historical criticisms widened the breach which science made.

Traditionally believers had accepted what the Bible said as *ipso facto* true. Some continued to hold this position fundamentally to the end of the century in spite of increasing criticism and ridicule. In his Bampton Lectures in 1866, Liddon allowed that there were superficially 'heterogeneous' elements within the Bible but maintained that they were all products of 'the continuous action of a Single Mind'. Since the Bible was an organically united work, expressing one Revelation from cover to cover, it was permissible to expound the meaning of one passage by reference to any other passage. Consequently Liddon found no difficulty in accepting that the use of the plural 'Elohim' in Genesis indicated Trinitarian views of God.[195] The rejection of any part of the Bible seemed to him liable to lead to the rejection of the whole. Mozley believed that if the critics were allowed to dispose of whatever parts of the Bible offended their reason, the result would be a chaotic subjectivism. The 'whole Scripture' must be regarded 'as Divine Revelation', received on 'authority', not chosen by 'taste and predilection'.[196] As the Regius Professor of Hebrew at Oxford, Pusey preserved a traditional and uncritical view of the Bible until his death in 1882. Such a traditional acceptance of the Bible, however, did not imply any necessary agreement about what the Bible taught. There seemed no limit to the views that could be drawn out of the Bible by the skilful exegete.[197] Severe doctrinal conflicts, which disturbed the humble believer, were not absent from the ranks of the Bible's defenders.[198]

A far greater challenge to faith was posed by the growing company of rebels against the traditional acceptance of the Bible. In a letter in 1837 Whately mentions the numbers of uneducated unbelievers who deny 'the authenticity of our sacred books'.[199] The International Conference of the Evangelical Alliance, held during the Great Exhibition in 1851, was told that:

critical objections, grounded on the internal features of the text of Scripture, or contradictions in the narrative, are daily assuming a wider place in the polemics of infidelity. The works of the most sceptical of German rationalists, some of them translated and published in cheap editions for the use of the lower classes, are ransacked for arguments to overthrow the genuineness, authenticity, and veracity of the books of Scripture.

But although such 'infidel literature is decidedly on the increase', the Conference was encouraged by its faith that 'the Word of God in our hands is constructed with Divine foresight to meet the peculiar demands of every age,' and the view that 'attachment to the Word, as the test and standard of Divine truth, leavens very extensively the mass of British society'.[200] The grounds for this encouragement eroded during the second half of the century.

The subjection of the Bible to the canons of 'sound reason' was not new. Locke had published a treatise entitled *The Reasonableness of Christianity as delivered in the Scriptures* in 1695 and twice 'vindicated' his views. Toland had argued in 1696 that there was nothing 'mysterious' about the Christianity revealed in the Bible for it was 'reasonable and intelligible'.[201] The following century witnessed several deistic 'interpretations' of 'Scriptural' Christianity. They were the expression of philosophical points of view and did not greatly disturb the faithful. A great change came with the application of literary and historical techniques in the nineteenth century. Coleridge confessed to difficulties with the Bible. He criticized the 'text sparring' by which an arbitrarily selected verse of Scripture was made to support some abstruse doctrinal point. Even if the Bible were 'infallibly rational', such a method of exegesis was absurd.[202] But was the Bible 'infallibly rational'? Coleridge's doubts on this point are seen in his *Confessions of an Inquiring Spirit* which was published posthumously in 1840. What in the Bible 'found' him in the 'depths of his being', he was prepared to recognize as inspired by the Holy Spirit. But the presence of 'apparent discrepancies' in the text, as well as philosophical objections, made him unwilling to regard the whole Bible as 'dictated by an Infallible Intelligence' to writers who, 'each and all, were divinely informed as well as inspired'. The conclusion he reached was that while 'the Bible contains the religion revealed by God', this proposition did not imply 'the absolute infallibility even of the inspired writers in matters altogether incidental and foreign to the objects and purposes of their inspiration'. The existence of 'errors' in the sacred text was no real obstacle to faith.[203] Coleridge's discriminating intellect could appreciate the distinction between the essential and inessential in the Biblical material. Others were not so wise. The recognition of any error in the Bible threatened the foundations of their faith.

Two years before Coleridge's *Confessions* appeared, Hennell's *An Inquiry concerning the Origin of Christianity* was published. Its conclusions were not in any way influenced by doctrinal considerations about the inspiration of the Bible. Hennell tried to date the Gospels and to determine their historical value by literary criticism, taking into account the intentions of their authors. He decided that the Synoptic Gospels (and possibly John's Gospel also) were not written by eye-witnesses but by believers one or two generations after the death of Jesus. These authors employed source-material that had been affected by the faith and imagination of the Church. They, in turn, adapted the material to their own standpoints. Miraculous and supernatural elements in the narratives were legendary fictions. Robertson describes the work as 'the first systematic analysis, in English . . . of the gospels as historical documents'.[204] For Hennell the Gospels were significant, not as historical reports, but as expressions of the faith of the early Christians. For most of his readers[205] his denials were more significant than his affirmations. They cut through the supports of the Christian faith. This was George Eliot's experience—reading Hennell drove away her Evangelical inclinations and, in many ways, her Christian convictions.[206]

Hennell pursued his researches in ignorance of Strauss's *Leben Jesu* which had been published in 1835. A certain Dr. Brabant recognized the similarity of the ideas in the two works and sent Strauss a copy of the *Inquiry*. Strauss had it translated and published in German, contributing a prefatory note of high praise. Meanwhile Brabant's daughter had started to translate the *Leben Jesu* into English, but when she married Hennell the task was taken over by George Eliot. The publication of the translation in 1846 was a further blow to the structure of faith. For Strauss it was a presupposition that miracles do not happen. He treated the central stories of the Gospel according to this principle. The virgin birth, miracles, resurrection and ascension of Jesus were not 'historical facts' but myths enshrining 'eternal truths'. In the Gospels we find stories expressing the philosophic truths of Hegelian idealism. It was the philosophic truth of these myths and not the historical reality of the stories that mattered.[207] Thus Strauss offered a view of the Bible which was in harmony with certain contemporary thought. It was a view which horrified many believers. His treatment of the Gospel narratives removed the historical foundation upon which their faith was built. If Strauss's treatment of the Bible were accepted, Christianity would be translated into a metaphysic.

Through George Eliot's translation Strauss's views became widely known in Britain. His criticisms of the Bible were developed by other members of the Tübingen school and gradually their views were also disseminated.[208] They reinforced the threat to faith posed by Strauss's work. Baur made a critical study of the New Testament, seeking to discover the standpoint of the different authors. His 'Tendenzkritik' led him to see in the first century a fierce and prolonged struggle between Paul and Judaizers. Matthew belongs to the Jewish and Luke to the Pauline side of the struggle. Mark, James, Ephesians, Colossians, Philippians and Hebrews are ascribed mediating rôles. Only Galatians, Romans and I and II Corinthians, together with the Apocalypse, were written before the Fall of Jerusalem. The Pastoral Epistles reflect the struggle with gnosticism in the second century, while John is connected with the Montanist movement towards the end of that century. Baur's emphasis on conflict reflects his own philosophic background: he read the New Testament through the eyes of Hegelian dialectics. He considered that his work demonstrated:

> that all that which constitutes the historical Christ, what is said of him and what we know of him, belongs to the world of conception, and indeed of Christian conception, and consequently has nothing to do with a man belonging to the real world.[209]

A later member of the Tübingen school, Keim, found certain historical value in Matthew, which he dated *c.* A.D. 68; Luke was written by a moderate Paulinist, using Matthew as one of its sources; Mark used both the other Synoptics and did not appear until A.D. 100 or later; John was later still and had little historical worth. From his studies Keim produced a picture of Jesus which did not comfort the orthodox although it was less radical than those of Strauss and Baur. It was not only the conclusions of the Tübingen school that unsettled faith. The presuppositions behind this approach challenged long-established views about the Bible. A new understanding of the basis of Christian doctrine would have to be found if the Bible was properly subject to the same canons of criticism as other books. The cry of 'sola Scriptura' faded as the Scriptures were dissected by the scalpel of literary and historical criticism. The dissection might or might not reveal malignancies: the real trouble was that it was difficult to dissect without killing the body!

In February 1860 *Essays and Reviews* was published, creating a controversy that raged for several years.[210] The volume was regarded as an assault upon the Bible from within the Church. The defenders of the old faith felt with horror that they were being betrayed by those they counted as fellow-believers while they tried to resist the attacks of

Germans and infidels. We have already noticed the essays by Baden Powell and Goodwin in connexion with the conflict between science and Biblical faith. Two other essays explicitly dealt with the Bible, one by Rowland Williams and the other by Benjamin Jowett, while Henry Wilson's essay contained many sharp attacks upon the Scriptures in passing. These essays caused consternation. Rowland Williams dealt with 'Bunsen's Biblical Researches' in a deliberately provocative manner.[211] Bunsen's studies showed the untenability of the Biblical chronology and cast grave doubt on many of the Pentateuchal records. It appeared that the Pentateuch was composed of disparate materials expressing different points of view, that Isaiah and Zechariah were composite works, that Daniel was to be dated in the time of the Maccabean revolt. Even if the Suffering Servant of Isaiah 52 and 53 is not to be identified as Jeremiah, the Christian interpretation of this and many other prophecies is challenged. The Christ of Paul and the Gospels is treated as 'the moral Saviour of mankind', offering men the key to a 'healthful mind' and a 'durable society'. Abraham, Moses, Elijah and Jeremiah reflect a faith of freedom and reason. They refused 'deference to a supposed external authority as would quench these principles themselves'—an authority claimed in 1860 by 'the despairing school who forbid us truth in God or in conscience, unless we kill our souls with literalism'.[212] Williams asserted that there could ultimately be no conflict between the truths of history and the faith which God had taught men in Christ.[213] Bunsen was a champion of 'light and right'.[214] Jowett's essay, 'On the Interpretation of Scripture', was less provocative, more famous and far more influential. He pointed out that while all Christians regarded the Bible as authoritative, they interpreted it according to their different standpoints and reached an 'extreme variety' of conclusions. The only solution to this chaotic situation was to recognize that:

> in what may be termed the externals of interpretation, that is to say, the meaning of words, the connexion of sentences, the settlement of the text, the evidence of facts, the same rules apply to the Old and New Testaments as to other books.[215]

Even though in 'many respects' the Bible 'is unlike any other book', dogmatic principles must not be allowed to determine its interpretation.[216] In a period when 'the intellectual forms under which Christianity has been described' were in transition, 'a change in some of the prevailing modes of interpretation' was necessary as well as expedient.[217] Thus Jowett asserted that 'it is better to close the book than to read it under conditions of thought which are imposed from without', for such conditions 'are inconsistent with the freedom of the truth and the moral character of the Gospel'.²¹⁸ Wilson's essay caused great offence both by its criticisms of traditional theology and by its attacks upon traditional views of the Bible. He suggested that the Biblical authors may, on occasion, have recorded 'their own inadequate conceptions' rather than 'the mind of God'. Their work contained exaggerations, if not plain errors.²¹⁹ The ascription of the title 'Word of God', and the claim to infallible inspiration for the Bible, is neither 'Scriptural' nor required by the Articles of Religion. The Biblical critic may pursue his researches and publish his conclusions without fear of transgressing bounds laid down by the Church.²²⁰ The ecclesiastical authorities rose to the bait. Williams and Wilson were condemned in the Court of Arches and Convocation condemned *Essays and Reviews*. The Judicial Committee of the Privy Council acquitted Williams and Wilson on appeal, but 11,000 clergy and 137,000 laymen declared their support for the Church in maintaining 'without reserve or qualification, the Inspiration and Divine Authority of the whole Canonical Scriptures, as not only containing but being the Word of God'.²²¹ The defenders of the Bible were still a mighty army. Their opponents, however, were taking the offensive and steadily gaining strength and support.

The next crisis was occasioned by a bishop reading the Old Testament carefully. When Colenso of Natal published *The Pentateuch and the Book of Joshua Critically Examined* in 1862, the ranks of the opponents of traditional Biblicism achieved episcopal support. Critical analyses of the Old Testament were not new. Hobbes and Spinoza had questioned the Mosaic authorship of the Pentateuch in the seventeenth century. The nineteenth century opened with a Scottish Roman Catholic priest, Geddes, getting into trouble for asserting that the Pentateuch was a composite work and for denying that the God of the Pentateuch was worshipful.²²² In 1829 Milman's *History of the Jews* appeared—a work which professed to submit the books of the Old Testament 'to calm but searching criticism as to their age, their authenticity, their authorship; above all, their historical sense and historical interpretation'. Milman allowed the Biblical authors to be specially gifted 'for the communication of . . . moral and religious truth' but held that in all other respects 'they were men of their age and country, who . . . thought the thoughts of their nation and their time.' He preserved an open mind on the historicity of miracles but rejected the recorded population figures as 'untenable'.²²³ The result was a history which used the Old Testament according to the canons of historical research. Abraham, removed from his religious functions, became 'a nomad Sheik'; David was 'in his exile . . . a freebooter' and as an 'Eastern King . . . had his harem'.[224] The orthodox were not pleased by the history and raised a passionate outcry against it.[225] They were not used to such treatment of Scripture. The storm eventually blew itself out and Milman suffered no official ecclesiastical censure. Colenso was not so fortunate. The Church had grown less tolerant, more ready to condemn, since 1829. The attacks of the enemies of faith had made the Church more conscious of the need to close its ranks against those who challenged its established faith. *Essays and Reviews* had referred to certain Old Testament studies. The furore aroused by the volume turned onto Colenso. The bishop was a mathematician who could accept miracle stories but not the many arithmetical inconsistencies which he discovered in the Pentateuch. The frank way he pointed out exaggerations and legends in the sacred text irritated his fellow clergy. Colenso was condemned by the ecclesiastical authorities both in England and in South Africa but his position was safeguarded by the Courts of Law.[226] In spite of his censure, the following half-century saw a great increase in the number, depth, and extremism of Old Testament studies. The tide ran strongly against the defenders of the old view of Scripture.

In Holland, Kuenen regarded the patriarchs as personifications rather than historical personages. Moses and the Exodus were historical but most of the material about this period, in the books from Exodus to Joshua, was untenable by critical standards. While Hebrew prophecy is unique, it is to be understood in terms of 'the Israelitish spirit' without supernatural intervention. Messianic interpretations of prophecies come from Christian devotion rather than from historical reality. Kuenen's greatest work, *The Religion of Israel to the Fall of the Jewish State*, was published in 1868–70 and an English translation appeared five years later. Similar views were expressed in Germany about this time by Wellhausen. He regarded the patriarchal materials as stories, reflecting national and tribal history, which were told in the time of the kings. Moses was responsible neither for monotheism nor for the Pentateuchal legislation. The Law as a whole belongs to post-exilic Judaism and so follows the prophetic period.[227] The prophets do not prefigure the Christian Christ and the title 'Son of Man' was turned into a Messianic designation by mistake in the early Church. Wellhausen's theories aroused great interest and even greater controversy. His *Prolegomena to the History of Israel* appeared in 1885 in an English translation by Robertson Smith who averred that 'almost every young scholar of mark' was on its side.[228] How little Scottish believers were prepared to accommodate their faith to such views was seen in the treatment Robertson Smith had received when he had published similar views on his own account. In an article on the Bible in the 1875 edition of the

Encyclopaedia Britannica, he had advanced views which could not be reconciled with the traditional faith in an inerrant Bible. He had challenged the accepted views on the origin of the Pentateuch, the authorship of the Psalms, the predictive character of prophecy and the composition of the Gospels. He was acquitted on a charge of heresy in 1880 but removed from his chair in Aberdeen in the following year. It was the last important victory for the traditionalists. Popular interest in the conflict disseminated the new ideas and gained for them increasing acceptance.[229] Robertson Smith himself received appointments at Cambridge from where he exercised considerable influence in the following years. He had indicated in his writings and lectures in 1870 that he found no difficulties in reconciling his Christian faith to the new critical insights.[230] Others were finding the same truth for themselves, only it was not the old traditional faith solidly based on an inerrantly inspired Bible that they held. The decline of the old faith was epitomized in 1882 by the appointment of S. R. Driver as Regius Professor of Hebrew at Oxford on the death of Pusey. As Pusey had stood for the old faith, so the cautious Driver became the symbol of those who challenged its Biblical positions. His *Introduction to the Literature of the Old Testament* was the English classic of the critical approach. In the Preface, Driver warned his readers that the 'traditional view' cannot stand 'without denying the ordinary principles by which history is judged and evidence estimated'. As in the sciences, so in Biblical studies, 'the conclusions which satisfy the common unbiassed and unsophisticated reason of mankind prevail in the end.' The work of the critics does 'not destroy the inspiration of the Old Testament' but determines how that inspiration has in fact operated.[231] This seemed close to blasphemy for those who clung to the old faith as an unalterable rock. *The Times* gave the work a sympathetic review. It accepted that:

> The old order changeth, yielding place to new,
> And God fulfils Himself in many ways.[232]

What was not at all clear was what the new order would be like. The crisis for faith was still present. In spite of the confident claims of the critics that their work did not necessarily destroy the Christian faith, it was still the case that their work destroyed the old faith and no one was certain where they could find the secure foundation of a new faith.

During the latter half of the nineteenth century the assault on the Bible was carried by a motley company. Matthew Arnold, for whom God was 'the Eternal not ourselves that makes for righteousness',[233] regarded the Bible, with all its 'legend and miracle', as providing 'the springs of emotion' which nerve a life of high morality.[234] To do its proper work, the Bible must not be treated as 'a talisman to be taken and used literally'. It must be interpreted by 'discriminating experience' and the canons of 'true culture'.[235] The power of its stories lies in their literary effect and not in their historicity.[236] This suggested one way in which the Bible might be given meaning and value but it was far from the traditional faith. Theologians helped to dethrone the Bible as they re-examined the doctrine of its inspiration. Maurice denied the inerrancy of Scripture because such a doctrine presumed to determine *a priori* God's way of revelation and contradicted the living activity of the Holy Spirit.[237] T. D. Bernard's Bampton Lectures in 1864 treated the Bible as the record of a progressive revelation which was still to be completed. The liberal view of inspiration, that it was the personal influence of God's Spirit and not a mechanical dictation, was classically proclaimed in W. Sanday's Bampton Lectures in 1893.[238] While the theologians revised their views of its inspiration, the lower critics altered the text of the Bible. Westcott and Hort's revision of the Greek text of the New Testament, their introduction to this work and the publication of the Revised Version could not help disturbing the faith of those who uncritically and often unconsciously accepted that God had dictated the Authorised Version.[239] Even some who stood for the Catholic tradition in the Church of England, far from radical in theology and in temperament, helped to undermine the traditional faith in the Bible. A collection of essays, *Lux Mundi*, pointed the way to an acceptance of moderate historical and Biblical criticisms by members of the High Church party. A key essay was by the editor, Gore, on *The Holy Spirit and Inspiration*. In attempting 'to put the Catholic faith into its right relation to modern problems',[240] he held on to as much of the traditional view of the Bible as he could, but he had to allow that Moses did not write Deuteronomy, that Job, Jonah, and Daniel are basically 'dramatic compositions', that the pre-Abraham narratives are 'of the nature of myth' and that Paul was restricted to contemporary modes of argument.[241] Even though *Lux Mundi* did not go as far as the liberals and radicals, it showed that fundamentally the critics had established their point. Any attempt to found faith on an inerrant Scripture was doomed from the start in the minds of all but die-hard conservatives. The crisis for faith deepened as the 'truth' about the Bible was published.

If faith could not rest securely on the Bible, could it rest on a knowledge of Jesus Christ? Could Jesus Christ be known sufficiently for faith when practically the only records about Him were in the Bible? The quest for the historical Jesus was the attempt to answer part, at least, of these questions. In the process the foundations of the Christian faith were shaken. Each claim to reveal the real Jesus seemed rather to express the investigator's own metaphysical standpoint. An unknown or unknowable Jesus was no surer a foundation for faith than a faulty Bible. Here we can indicate only a fragment of the relevant material.[242]

Hennell's *Inquiry concerning the Origin of Christianity* offered a 'true account of the life of Jesus Christ' without any supernatural content. Jesus is portrayed as an Essene revolutionary, an enthusiast exercising extraordinary power through His moral purity and sense of unity with the will of God. He is regarded as a wonder-worker because of the effect of His personality on certain types of illness. It is possible that He mistakenly considers that He has miraculous power. Eventually He asserts Himself as the Messiah but is thwarted by the Roman and Jewish authorities. He refuses to retreat or to compromise and accepts martyrdom, proclaiming that His death will bring in the Kingdom of God. After His crucifixion, His body is secretly moved from the tomb by Joseph of Arimathea and Nicodemus. His disciples are misled into believing that He has risen and so, filled with new hope, preach that He was the Messiah and will soon return with divine power and glory. This Jesus might be 'one of the most extraordinary persons in history'[243] but the portrait did not match the Christ of faith. For Hennell the Christ of faith was the imaginative production of the early Church; for the believer Hennell's Jesus was a threat to his faith. But could the believer develop from the evidence a more convincing portrait of Jesus upon which his faith could rest? Historical and literary criticism did not give him much hope.

The next blow came with Strauss's *Leben Jesu* which appeared in English eight years after Hennell's *Inquiry*.[244] It enjoyed considerable influence in spite of being clearly dominated by Hegelian philosophy. Strauss treated the Gospel narratives consistently as mythical constructions which had been attached to the story of Jesus in the early Church. They express profound religious truths which originated in the Messianic faith of the first disciples and not in historical fact. Although he claimed that 'the essence of the Christian faith is perfectly independent of his criticism',[245] few Christians could accept this. By destroying the historicity of the Gospel stories, Strauss destroyed the possibility of a faith based on a historical revelation. The stories of Jesus might be illuminating as stories but the Christian faith needed to find a considerable element of fact in them. Shortly before his death, Strauss declared that we know too little about the historical Jesus to justify any religious dependence upon Him.[246] That this was the implication of his views had been seen by many Christians for a long time. They saw the choice before them as either to locate a historical Jesus or to surrender their faith.

The security of faith was not always helped when historians did claim to locate a historical Jesus. The pictures of Jesus that were presented, for instance, by Renan and Seeley could hardly be reconciled with the Christian's faith in Him. Even when Jesus became factual and not mythical, faith could still be in jeopardy. Renan's *Vie de Jesus* was published in 1863 and quickly achieved great fame.[247] It was an attempt to get behind the 'legendary' and 'Gnostic' accretions to the real Jesus, judged according to the canons of credibility adopted by nineteenth-century reason.[248] Mystery, miracle, and the supernatural were ruled out *a priori*: Jesus was to be understood in precisely the same way as any other historical figure. So far the believer might not feel too unhappy. It might be difficult to relate an incarnational belief to the historical actuality but at least Jesus was being treated as a historical actuality and not as a mythical construction. The unhappiness grew as the 'historical actuality' was delineated. At first Jesus, a peasant with a profound message of life through love, presented His insights to the people. His 'maxims' and His 'delicate communism of a band of children reposing in confidence on the bosom of their Father' were suited to 'a country where life is nourished by the air and the light' and 'a simple sect constantly persuaded that its Utopia was about to be realized'.[249] The message did not appeal to all. In the face of opposition, Jesus became 'irritated', even 'harsh and capricious'.[250] In the second part of His ministry He deliberately fulfilled Messianic prophecies, performed apparent miracles and, maybe unwittingly, took part in a faked resurrection of Lazarus.[251] In these ways He tried desperately to establish the supernatural quality of His mission. He failed and was executed. His death secured for Him the position His ministry had failed to establish: 'he began upon the gibbet the Divine life which he was to live in the heart of humanity throughout infinite ages.'[252] Renan's Jesus combined high moral integrity and reforming zeal with charlatanry and deception. In spite of these violent contradictions, Renan managed to affirm of Jesus 'the title Son of God . . . since he has advanced religion as no other has done, or probably ever will be able to do'.[253] Few others could manage it. If this was the historical Jesus, He must be condemned by Victorians more confident of their morality than of their faith.[254]

The portraits of Jesus offered by Schenkel and Keim were more reverent and correspondingly less objectionable. Nevertheless, they, too, had no place for the miraculous and supernatural in history. This rejection included a physical resurrection—though Keim replaced it by a psychical event which seemed almost as extraordinary. Their Jesus was essentially human, a person worthy of emulation and even of such worship and faith as can ever be directed by man towards a fellow human being. Was this sufficient for faith? The extremely popular *Ecce Homo* brought the issue to a head in England.[255] The work avoided many historical problems and Seeley confessed that it was only a 'fragment' of a life of Jesus.[256] Jesus is presented as a teacher and legislator, called at His baptism to be the Messiah, seeking to establish a divine commonwealth among men. He is conscious of possessing 'supernatural power' but generally abstains from working miracles with 'magnanimous self-restraint'.[257] The result was a picture of Jesus which generally steered clear of all 'theological questions'.[258] Seeley promised a later volume which would discuss 'Christ as the creator of modern theology and religion'. It never appeared and it is doubtful if Seeley had the right ability ever to do it.[259] *Ecce Homo* explained Jesus' 'object in founding the Society which is called by his name' and the nature of that 'Society' without theology.[260] If Jesus' ministry could be thus interpreted, what historical foundation was there for the dogmatic claims about Jesus which were central to the Christian faith? Seeley's Jesus could be seen as the foundation of a religion without dogma, a 'Christian morality . . . by which Christ united men together, . . . cured them of their selfishness'.[261] When the historical Jesus could be so completely separated from the Christian dogmas about Him, traditional faith was further threatened. Were these dogmas essential or were they parasites which must be removed if pure Christianity was to develop? In the 'liberal' view, they were parasites which had attached themselves to Christianity from Greek metaphysical speculation. The liberal movement stretches beyond the nineteenth century. It was largely the product of those critical investigations which sought to distinguish the actual Jesus of history from the Christ of traditional faith.

At the end of the century, Fairbairn was confident that Jesus was 'better known as He was and as He lived than at any period' since the Apostolic Church. He affirmed the 'recovery of the historical Christ' and the 'harmony of belief with history' as the contemporary situation.[262] Harnack, at the turn of the century, asserted that while 'our materials are insufficient for a "biography"', they are quite sufficient to show the historical foundation of Christianity in the ministry and teaching of Jesus.[263] In Harnack's case the result was the classical statement of liberal Christianity, but his confidence that we could discover the historical Jesus was shared by many who held a more traditional faith. Others, however, questioned the possibility of ever producing a reasonably convincing picture of the historical Jesus. Wrede held that the scanty and propagandist nature of the sources for ever prevented it.

His 'thoroughgoing scepticism' judged that 'each critic retains whatever portion of the traditional saying can be fitted into his construction of the facts and his conception of historical possibility and rejects the rest'.²⁶⁴ Schweitzer, surveying the nineteenth-century quest for Jesus and remembering the eschatological elements he found in Jesus' ministry, concluded that 'the historical Jesus will be to our time a stranger and an enigma'. This conclusion was claimed to be compatible with faith since 'the abiding and eternal in Jesus' was in His Spirit and 'absolutely independent of historical knowledge'.²⁶⁵ Such a solution made a Christian faith possible for some. For others the disappearance of the historical Jesus would mean the dissolution of the *Christian* faith. If the Bible had been the foundation of the traditional faith, the historical Jesus had been its keystone. The historians and the Biblical critics had undermined that faith.²⁶⁶

The security of faith was further undermined in the nineteenth century by increasing awareness of the changes that had occurred in Christian doctrine during its history. Whether those changes were seen as developments of latent principles or as additions to the original creeds, they indicated that the Church might no longer hold pure the Apostolic faith. They opened the door to disturbing questions about what was original and fundamental and what might be only secondary and temporary in the received faith. During the Reformation both Protestants and Roman Catholics had asserted the identity of their doctrines with those of the Apostolic Church. In the following two centuries it became apparent that certain changes had occurred. Often these changes were treated as the explicit statement of ideas already implicitly contained in the Church's faith, although some scholars claimed that novel elements had been introduced since the Apostolic era.²⁶⁷ Where development was admitted, its truth had to be justified. The Roman Catholic felt obliged to show that he still held the Apostolic faith. The Protestant was sometimes far more radical and, as we have seen in our survey of work on the New Testament, was even prepared to discover true and false developments of the teaching of Jesus within the canonical Scriptures. The fact of developments and the need to justify them helped to extend the crisis for faith.

At Tübingen in 1819 the Roman Catholic theologian Drey explained developments in terms of the Church's life as a living organism. While faith remains unchanging in essence, its particular shape will necessarily change as it relates itself to contemporary cultural forms. The task of the theologian and of the Church is to distinguish true from misleading developments. They cannot prevent developments without killing the vitality of faith. Similar views were expressed a few years later by Möhler. Again, development was interpreted as the activity of the Holy Spirit, adapting the outward forms of faith to the contemporary situation. Although these views did not command great attention, they indicate an awareness of the problem raised by investigations into the history of faith. The problem of developments was brought to a head in widely different ways by Hegel and by Newman.

Hegel's philosophy was a philosophy of development. History was the arena in which the Absolute Spirit progressively realized itself through the repeating sequence of thesis, antithesis, and synthesis. In this process new things are created and old principles are developed.[268] Religion is part of the process and subject to the same fundamental laws. Accordingly the various 'finite religions' are interpreted as 'the appearance in history' of approximations to the perfect. 'The nature and succession' of these historic faiths are 'determined by the nature of the Spirit' as it seeks 'to bring itself to consciousness of itself'.[269] When Hegel turned to the Church, he described it as the place where the Spirit is present to unite the world to itself. The Church is the 'Spiritual Community' in which the Spirit (which Hegel identifies with the Holy Spirit) is 'real, actual, and present'.[270] This means that the ultimate truth is not outside and beyond the Church but is already there 'in' its members and 'exists as actually present truth'.[271] Hegel's views influenced Christian theology in two ways. On the one hand, there were those who followed his basic dialectical principle and regarded development in theology as a process in which new views supplanted existing beliefs. They looked to future developments to create radically new expressions of the Spirit's nature. The old faith was *passé* and must be broken up that the new might appear. Thus Baur regarded the ministry of Jesus as providing a basis for a dialectical process which led through antagonisms to syntheses expressing superior apprehensions of the truth. Others accepted Hegel's view of the Church and used it to defend the unity and continuity of faith. Developments of doctrine did not supersede the old faith but exposed more of its inner 'spirit'. Although there were important differences between Hegel's view of the essence of the Christian faith and the views of orthodox believers, at least it was possible for faith to accept this interpretation of his view of the historical process. Through the developments of doctrine the Spirit increasingly revealed itself. This was acceptable to all who could accept the possibility of change. The Hegelian affirmation of change could thus help to harmonize faith with its history. Such ideas were disturbing for those whose faith assumed a fixed and unchangeable revelation. The shift from fixed principles to the leading of the living Spirit in matters of doctrine demanded a courageous faith which many believers could not muster. For them the crisis for faith deepened.

Newman was too good a historian to ignore the changes that had occurred in the history of Christian doctrine. He introduced the idea of development to English theology.[272] Both his careful researches into the history of doctrine during the first centuries and his appreciation of contemporary Roman Catholic positions made him aware of the untenability of Vincent of Lerins' principle that 'revealed and Apostolic doctrine' is 'what has been held always, everywhere, and by all'.[273] Newman explained developments in doctrine as the explication of ideas latent in the received faith. These ideas are 'implicitly received' by the believer when he consciously accepts the principles in which they are contained. Through 'the activity of our reflective powers' such an 'inward idea of divine truth . . . passes into explicit form'.[274] In the *Essay on the Development of Doctrine* Newman dealt with the problem in detail and suggested seven 'notes' by which 'genuine developments' could be distinguished from 'corruptions'.[275] Whether or not Newman's theory of development and his tests for true development were accepted, the fact of development could not be denied. Newman pointed out that 'those who find fault with the explanation here offered of its [sc. Christianity's] historical phenomena will find it their duty to provide one for themselves.'[276] Newman's theory opened for him the way into the Roman Catholic Church, the infallible authority which was the only alternative to atheism.[277] Some sympathized with his work and found it a source of enlightenment. Others, both Roman Catholic and Protestant, received it with suspicion and hostility. It disturbed the faith of Roman Catholics because it suggested that there had been progress in the Church's faith.[278] It disturbed all believers because it faced them with the fact of development and forced them to find a place for it in their faith. Newman was a believer who found peace through the theory. His theory disturbed the uncritical peace of other believers and, to that extent, contributed to the crisis for faith. While Newman strove against the 'liberalism' of the day, he could not and would not close his eyes to historical facts. If the Vincentian Canon was contrary to history, then the Canon must be abandoned.[279]

Faith was troubled by the problem of development throughout the century. The competing claims of a once-for-all revelation and the facts of the history of doctrine were not easily reconciled. The way developments had sometimes been produced in the Church was a further source of perplexity. It was not easy, as R. W. Dale remarked, to regard the Councils of the Church as inspired organs of faith when their internal politics were brought to light.[280] Nevertheless, development had undoubtedly taken place—but was it genuine development or false corruption? At the end of the century there were attempts to isolate what was claimed to be the pure, original Gospel, stripped of the accretions of ecclesiastical dogmas. In this movement theologians from Paul onwards were liable to be criticized for corrupting the Gospel of Jesus by introducing alien elements. Fairbairn, in *Christ and Modern Theology*, criticized Newman's theory of development for being narrow, logical, and abstract.[281] He described the nature of development as 'biological'—as the life of 'an organism which lives within a living world, affected by all its forces, and sensitive to its every change'.[282] The test of true development in theology is its interpretation of the 'spirit and purpose' of Christ to a particular situation.[283] Since Fairbairn believed that it was possible through modern scholarship to locate the historical Jesus, he also believed that it was possible to apply this test. In terms of 'the mind of the Master', theologians could distinguish what was of Paul or of John or of anyone else from what was genuinely of Jesus. Fairbairn's own conclusions from applying the test were on the whole favourable to orthodox opinions, propounding a kenotic Christology.[284] Other scholars started from the same assumption about the knowability of Jesus, but used it to expose as corruptions doctrines which were widely regarded as essential elements of the Christian faith. Hatch's Hibbert Lectures, which were edited by Fairbairn after their author's death, dealt with 'the influence of Greek ideas and usages upon the Christian Church'. Their problem was posed by the contrast between the Sermon on the Mount, the 'promulgation of a new law of conduct', where doctrines are assumed and are ethical and 'metaphysics are wholly absent', and the Nicene Creed which states 'partly historical facts ... partly ... dogmatic inferences', uses 'metaphysical terms which ... would probably have been unintelligible to the first disciples', and has no place for ethics.[285] In his lectures Hatch traced some of the forces involved in the journey from Galilee to Nicea and raised the question whether or not Christianity should seek to purge itself of their effects. He admitted that the changes might be 'integral and essential' to Christianity and must be further developed. He also suggested that Christianity might be 'none the loser' for throwing off the effects of Greek rhetoric, logic, and metaphysics, 'but rather stand out again before the world in the uncoloured majesty of the Gospels'.[286] While Hatch tried to be fair to both positions, it seems certain that he personally preferred the latter alternative. There can be no doubt that this was Harnack's view. He described the Gospel as 'struggling again and again to the surface', refusing to be buried under alien forms.[287] While he recognized the greatness of Paul, he also saw in Paul the first stages of a development in which 'the majesty and simplicity of the Gospel' was supplanted by a concern for correct doctrine.[288]

Like the search for the historical Jesus, the search for the pure, original Gospel of Christ and of Christianity at times disturbed faith more than it strengthened it. Mozley criticized the attempt to separate Paul's teaching from the Biblical revelation on the grounds that:

> if men once begin to cut off parts of that whole Scripture which has come down to us as Divine Revelation it is difficult to see where such a process can stop. . . . No real faith can be left in the Bible generally, when such a step has been taken. It becomes then a mere matter of a man's own choice what he accepts Scripture and what he does not; and all rests upon a footing, not of authority or command, but only of a man's taste and predeliction.[289]

For many this was true not only of the Bible but also of the whole tradition of the Church's thought. They resisted attempts to tamper with the received faith but it was not easy to defend a 'faith once delivered to the saints' when research showed that it had not been delivered in its present form at one time. The threat that the notion of development posed for the old faith by the end of the century can be seen in Hastings Rashdall. He was prepared to accept doctrines which are not 'explicitly contained in the actual teaching of Christ' and the New Testament and to reject as 'unbelievable' other things which 'have been believed by Christians—and possibly by the whole Church of some particular period'. Some 'accepted doctrines' must be given up, others corrected and new views must be given consideration since 'the development of religious thought is not finished yet'.[290] Because they could lead to such attitudes, the theory and the facts of the development of doctrine played a part in undermining faith. By raising questions about the original faith of the Church, historians and theologians upset the believer's confidence that he held the true faith. Newman met the crisis by affirming the infallible authority of the Church. Those who could not share such convictions were forced to find other ways of determining the essential faith. For some the search to establish the true faith was the way to no faith at all.

It was not only in terms of the Bible and Christian doctrine that historical studies troubled faith. Both the growing appreciation of the techniques of historical research and a sense of a pattern of progress in history contributed to the crisis for faith. Modern historiography can claim to have started in the eighteenth century with people such as Hume and Gibbon, but the discipline did not establish itself in its own right, free from domination by philosophical considerations, until the nineteenth century. This was the century of Ranke and Macaulay, Green and Carlyle, a century in which historical tomes and historical novels enjoyed great popularity. One consequence of this historical movement was to give impetus to the idea of progress—an idea which was popularly understood to be implied by the scientific theory of evolution. The classical view had been that the Golden Age was in the past—theologically in a lost Garden of Eden, secularly in Greek and Roman culture. History was then regarded as the story of corruption and decay. The new historical approach suggested that the opposite was the case: the history of mankind was the story of progress and improvement, a story which was still continuing, a story whose Golden Age was still to come. An optimistic and unsophisticated idea of progress became popular which went far beyond what could be supported by sound investigations. This view harmonized with Christian thought about a 'coming' Kingdom but it did not harmonize easily with a faith whose normative events were in the past. Faith in the activity of the Holy Spirit suited this belief in progress but the assertion that ultimate truths had been revealed once and for all time in a rather dim and primitive past did not suit its temper. Traditional faith could not easily be reconciled with prevailing attitudes. 'Modern man', highly conscious of his 'modernity', wanted a 'modern' faith. To people who were more concerned to advance than to have firm foundations, a faith with a long history was more intriguing than significant. There was great interest in the past for antiquarian reasons and for showing how man had progressed, but not for finding the basis of a living faith. In such a situation the history of faith was carefully investigated although it was considered irrelevant to contemporary life simply because of its historicity. Those who had drunk the heady wine of a belief in progress demanded new skins for their faith!

The more technical levels of history proper also raised difficulties for faith. Lessing, in the eighteenth century, had indicated certain major problems in the relation of faith to history. In the first place, how could a faith, which believers held to be certain, be based on the 'accidental truths of history'?[291] Secondly, how could it be legitimate to pass from historical judgements to 'metaphysical and moral ideas' when such a step involves a μετάβασις εἰς ἄλλο γένος (i.e. a logical typejump)?[292] Directly and indirectly, Lessing exerted considerable influence on the theology of the nineteenth century.[293] The growth of historical understanding increased the appreciation of his objections to Christianity as a 'historical faith'. Whately tried to meet the first of these problems in his pamphlet *Historic Doubts respecting Napoleon Buonaparte*. He argued that if absurdities and inconsistencies in reports about Napoleon did not lead people to doubt his historical existence, why should they dismiss Biblical reports on that ground? It was a popular *tour de force* which came to be regarded as an answer to Strauss's theories.[294] Whately argued about historical credibility on the basis of the canons of history. Later in the century many agreed in principle with Baden Powell that historical claims must be judged by historical standards and not by other considerations.[295] This was where the problem seemed to lie for faith. Could the historical claims which formed part of the heart of Christianity be justified on historical grounds? Biblical criticism, as we have seen, increasingly raised doubts that they could. Kierkegaard believed that we have sufficient historical grounds for faith but the minimum that he required was very little. He declared that:

> if the contemporary generation had left nothing behind them but these words: 'We have believed that in such and such a year God appeared among us in the humble figure of a servant, that he lived and taught in our community, and finally died', it would be more than enough.[296]

Most people considered that faith required a more 'voluminous account' and it was questionable if such could be obtained. Strauss in 1872 declared that our knowledge of Jesus was far too limited to warrant any religious dependence upon Him. This view grew in popularity. It might be that 'truth' was 'embodied in a tale' but it was far from certain that the 'tale' was historically true, 'more strong than all poetic thought'.[297] And even if the theoretical and practical uncertainties of historical judgements could be overcome, the theologian was still faced with the second problem raised by Lessing—the philosophical problem of justifying the step from historical judgements to the different category of faith. We see the difficulty when Moberly writes in *Lux Mundi* that the resurrection of Jesus 'confronts us . . . not simply as a finite historical event, but as an eternal counsel and infinite act of God'.[298] How could the two categories of truth be related? The problem was another element in the crisis for faith.

Biblical and historical studies thus joined developments in science, philosophy, and ethics in undermining the Christian faith. The nineteenth century saw a sustained and powerful attack on the foundations of traditional beliefs. It is not surprising that for many people belief became uncertain, even if it did not become impossible.

d. The Challenge to Authoritarian Structures

The nineteenth century was a period of political upheaval. The

French Revolution shattered the calm security of traditional authorities. Its rejection of the secular establishment and its repudiation of the ecclesiastical shocked many people at the time. By the middle of the century what had shocked had become acceptable, what had been resisted was increasingly practised. In 1865 Lecky wrote of the 'warm approval' with which 'the public opinion of the most advanced nations in Europe' regarded the numerous political 'insurrections' of the previous few years. Some of the changes had been inspired by a desire for powerful, just, effective, or national government. Others were due simply to the desire of 'the great majority of the nation' for a change. The new factor in all this was that both politically and theologically the desire of the majority was 'generally acquiesced in as sufficient' justification for the action.[299] The consuming interest of the age was 'liberty and not theology' and those 'who would once have been conspicuous saints are now conspicuous revolutionists'.[300] In Britain the century was the great age of reform. John Wesley had predicted that in 1832 'the beast' would ascend 'from the bottomless pit'.[301] It turned out to be the year of the first Parliamentary Reform Bill. To secure its passage through Parliament, *The Times* described how people had:

> joined the Political Unions by myriads—attended meetings by 200,000 at a time—discussed public questions with more eagerness and ability than ever—and signed and presented fresh petitions to Parliament.[302]

Most of the legal disabilities of Dissenters and Roman Catholics had already been removed, for the Test and Corporation Acts were repealed in 1828 and the Roman Catholic Relief Act was passed the following year. After 1832 reforms and improvements affected local and national government and social and economic conditions. The Chartist movement showed how universal was the desire to share in political management. It failed to achieve its 'Six Points' straight away[303] but as an expression of popular feeling it gave a powerful impetus to the demand for democracy in every structure of authority.

Carlyle described the 'irresistible' and 'ominous' advance of democracy as the mark of the age. It was not only being demanded, it was also being realized. 'From the thunder of Napoleon battles, to the jabbering of Open-vestry in St. Mary Axe, all things announce Democracy.'[304] Carlyle could point to the dangers of such democracy and anathematize Mill's *Liberty*[305] but he could not stem the tide. His advocacy of government by 'an Aristocracy of the Wise' fell on deaf ears. The established structures of authority were everywhere being scrutinized. Increasingly the sanction of authority was felt to reside in 'the people' and not in traditional hierarchies. This attitude brought into question the authority both of the Church and of its faith. Ecclesiastical privilege was often as unacceptable as political privilege. The Church's claim to be a divine institution, blessed with special power and authority, did not readily attract those who denied that monarchical and aristocratic prerogatives were of divine right. They saw in the Church a champion of the forces of privilege and reaction. In revolutionary France the Church and the Monarchy had suffered together.[306] Lecky speaks of 'the priesthood' as involved in 'a policy of toryism, of reaction, or of obstruction', while 'the organs that represent dogmatic interests' are condemned for their 'permanent opposition to the progressive tendencies around them'.[307] Marx wrote of 'the English oligarchy' and 'the Church' as twin sisters seeking to coerce 'the profane mass of the nation'.[308] Fairbairn describes how the Church represented the inequalities and injustices of society. To the working class, struggling for political justice,

> the Church was a greater offence than the State; it was the apotheosis of inequalities, loved rank and wealth, privilege and prescription, forgot the poverty of its founders, who had laboured with their hands, and of all the beatitudes most believed the one the Master had neglected to utter, *Beati possidentes*. With the Anglican Church, then, they felt that as now constituted they could have no part or lot. As Established it was the creation of privilege, as Episcopal it embodied the hated aristocratic principle, as administered, it regarded the people as children or paupers, and not as reasonable and independent men. As to the Free Churches, those of the older dissent were too plutocratic, too much governed by class feeling—an interested society, whose heart was where its interests were, with the employers and the tradesmen. . . . So they reasoned, and they acted as they reasoned; stood aloof from the churches, criticized them, disliked them, doubted their reality, denied their sincerity, and became sceptical of all they believed.[309]

When power in the Church was restricted to a privileged few, when the mill-owner controlled the local chapel, the actuality of the Church was more likely to alienate the masses than to convince them of the truth of its faith. It might be formally illogical to reject the Christian faith because of corruption in the Christian Church, but in practice the two stood or fell together. Where the Church was aristocratic, whether it reflected the privilege of family or of wealth, it was liable to fall in a democratic age. In many cases it did fall. This connexion between popular rejection of political authoritarianism and 'decay of religious faith' was noticed by Carlyle. He described the growing attitude of 'the lower classes' as one of 'revolt' on two fronts: 'decreasing respect for what their temporal superiors command, decreasing faith for what their spiritual superiors teach'.[310]

Ironically, though, what democratic practices were found in the Church served to undermine further the authority of its faith. When people helped to make decisions, they often felt they had the right to criticize or to reject what others had decided. Thus, where the Church supported the 'rights' of 'liberty', 'conscience', and 'democracy', it sometimes found that these 'rights' were used by individuals both inside and outside the Church to assert their 'freedom' to renounce articles of its faith. In the name of *Liberty*, Mill had to protest against 'the monstrous offspring of the democratic Frankenstein'.[311] Similarly the Church found that 'freedom' and 'democracy' were principles which could threaten as well as defend the security of its faith. By the end of the century many believers had learnt from experience that democracy was not necessarily the best form of government for either sacred or secular societies.[312] Nevertheless the slogans of the age were 'democracy', 'freedom', 'the rights of conscience', 'liberty',—and, like most slogans, they were ill-defined and half-misunderstood by those who used them most.

These demands could not be and were not restricted to political matters. The principles that must be applied to 'the State, and the conduct of its affairs' seemed also applicable to the Church and its religion.[313] Just as R. W. Dale, as a minister of the Church, felt bound to help people achieve their political and social rights,[314] so others demanded and asserted their political and social rights within the Church. Strife and division within the different denominations were the result. Methodism might have saved Britain from a French Revolution but it could not save itself from internal strife. The history of Methodism in most of the nineteenth century is the story of war and rumour of war. The assertion of 'democratic principles' split the ecclesiastical descendants of Wesley into a number of independent sects—and then the different groups found internal harmony hard to achieve. From their birth the Congregationalist and Presbyterian Churches had practised a Church polity in which every member enjoyed rights and privileges. This did not save them from disasters. The Presbyterian Church in Scotland divided disastrously over the right of patronage. In England it was troubled by conflicts over Unitarian views. The Congregationalists asserted their independency to the point of keeping their 'Union' chronically short of funds. 'Strictness' divided the

Baptists. The control which the 'Meeting' exercised over the individual 'Friend' led to a noticeable decline in the numbers of Quakers. Even the Mormons suffered from divisions among their leadership and 'bitter schisms tore the church asunder'.[315] In the Church of England the fact and the practice of the Establishment muted but did not eradicate the divisive stirrings of democracy. A considerable body of the clergy sought the restoration of Convocation and eventually it met. While it provided a useful talking-shop in which grievances could be aired, it was practically powerless. As for the laity, their influence on Anglican affairs was through the political control of the Establishment, and especially of the channels of preferment. In the Roman Catholic Church the 'rights of the people' were generally neglected although, as might be expected in such a diverse body, there were signs of discontent with the situation. One ray of light which shone in the darkness of ecclesiastical authoritarianism came from Newman's article *On Consulting the Faithful in Matters of Doctrine*. This essay caused great offence both by reminding its readers that at times the authorities had failed to confess the true faith and by suggesting that the *consensus fidelium* should be considered in any dogmatic definition.[316] Newman was not radical in his suggestion—'in matters of faith' he regarded 'the laity' as 'but the reflection or echo of the clergy'. Nevertheless, he also felt that there was 'something in the *pastorum et fidelium conspiratio* which is not in the pastors alone'.[317]

What was the upshot of these developments? As we have already suggested, they were generally detrimental to the Church's authority and the security of its faith. When people shared in making decisions about the Church and its faith, they were liable to limit the authority of such decisions to their personal agreement with them. Talk about an unassailable *depositum* of faith did not impress people who viewed the Thirty-Nine Articles as authorized by a Parliament whose members they elected. References to a *traditio* of true faith to be found among the faithful were unconvincing to believers who did not find the *traditio* in their own experience. Claims about a divine authority of the Church meant little to those who knew they could influence its decisions. As the mystery and the mystique of the Church and its faith disappeared in the atmosphere of popular 'democracy' and 'the rights of the individual', so their power and authority also declined. The crisis for faith deepened as the individual, influenced by these considerations, felt that there was no authority outside himself to guide him to the truth. He might listen to what the Church had to say but in the end he must decide for himself what was true—for what was the Church but a set of individuals like himself, and its faith but a creed determined by their votes? Any respect that might have been attracted by the unanimity of decisions in the Church was dissipated by conflicts within and between the denominations. What Chadwick says of the Mormons, 'the people doubted while their leaders struggled', is applicable to the Church generally.[318]

The spread of education aggravated the situation. As more people mastered the rudiments of reading, so more people could discover the disagreements between the claimants to authority. As more people were educated to be responsible for their decisions, so more people found it difficult to choose between competing claims. Sunday and Day Schools might teach people to read so that they could read the Bible for themselves. Unfortunately once people could read, they could read atheistic pamphlets as well as sacred stories.[319] Fairbairn may have been right when he applied to the Church the principle that 'adaptation to environment is a necessity to all organisms' if they are to live. He claimed that 'the Church will be able to reclaim the masses' only when it has caught up with their 'social development'. Certainly, a Church which the masses regarded as 'organized . . . for the maintenance of vested interests and conventional respectabilities' would not attract them.[320] It is ironic that where the Church attempted to adapt itself to the contemporary social ethos, it simultaneously raised doubts about the certainty both of its own authority and of that of its faith. The environment of the day did not suit plants whose structure included authority and certainty.

In England the position of the Established Church was made most difficult by secular political interference in its affairs. It was not easy to allow divine authority to a body whose official leadership was created by political appointment and whose affairs were ultimately controlled by the Crown in Parliament. Members of the Church of England had cause for unease about the status of their Church when Parliament legislated about it, when Prime Ministers promoted the Ecclesiastical Commission, and when the Privy Council decided about its doctrinal disputes. Members of every denomination and of none protested about the right of the Established Church to claim financial support from them. Tithes were commuted in 1836 but the power of the Parish Church to levy rates for its repair continued to be a source of annoyance until 1868.[321] The result was that disestablishment was desired both by members of the Church of England and by dissenters. Dissenters sought it to remove their disadvantages, both real and imagined. Catholic-minded members of the Church of England sought it so that the Church could be seen to be itself, *i.e.* the Church obedient only to God, and not mistaken for a branch of the State. The theory that identified Church and State was gradually repudiated, 'assailed' and 'destroyed' by 'the political tendencies of the age'.[322] Here Church member and unbelieving politician could find common ground. Nevertheless, while independence of the State might be good for the Church viewed internally, it was a mixed blessing when the Church tried to draw the masses into its bosom. Non-believers and dissenters might be occasionally annoyed by the fact of establishment, but this fact did allow the Church to claim that it had a responsibility for them and that they had a place within it. As the Church became in practice, if not in legal fact, separate from the State, so it began to appear more like a private club. Non-members could join it if they chose, but if they chose otherwise it was pointless to talk of their obligations to each other. The 'Catholic' demand for independence for the Church of England to control its own affairs, according to its own courts and not subordinated to the will of Parliament, helped to destroy something of the 'catholicity' of that Church. It came to be regarded as a separate group within the nation. Thus, whether the Church of England sought to remain established or to become disestablished, it seemed fated to suffer! At this point the crisis for faith, at least in relation to the Church, seems unavoidable.

As for the Church's attempt to promote itself by foreign missions, this also led ironically to some doubt about its authority. The nineteenth century was the great age of missionary endeavour. National imperialism was matched by ecclesiastical. Underlying this activity was confidence in the superiority of the Christian faith. When the missionaries went to primitive tribes which practised lurid rites based on crude beliefs, this confidence was enhanced. It was disturbed when missionaries confronted developed faiths and reported their difficulties in securing converts. Questions began to be asked about the uniqueness of Christianity and its right to proselytize throughout the world. Maybe Christians could usefully learn things from other faiths? Maybe more humility, less arrogant confidence, was appropriate to missionary zeal? A growing interest in geographical knowledge and in travelogues stimulated such questioning. By the close of the century some believers allowed that other religions enjoyed 'clear echoes of the voice of God'.[323] Stephen Neill describes the situation that developed in India:

> This was a cry that was to be increasingly heard—service but no proselytism, fellowship without aggression. Missionaries were not insensitive to this propaganda, and a hitherto unknown uncertainty is to be found in their utterances. . . . Scholarship was revealing

the spiritual treasures of the ancient religions. A more liberal theology took a rather different view of the uniqueness of Christianity.[324]

Thus, while missionaries spread the Church to nearly every nation, they began to have doubts about their methods and aims. Their reports home began to raise doubts about the absolute superiority of the Christian faith. For the most part these signs of uncertainty were faint. Usually they were swallowed up in the zeal of missionary activity. They were not completely absent, however, and constitute another, even if relatively slight, factor in the crisis for faith.

We have already mentioned the production of viable 'ways of life' which did not involve theistic beliefs. Theories about life and policies for life could be constructed without reference to God. The growing secularization of practical affairs in the nineteenth century showed that religious belief could be irrelevant in practice as well as in theory. For Lecky 'the secularization of politics', which was affecting all Europe by the middle of the century, was 'the direct consequence of the declining influence of dogmatic theology'. Decisions tended to be controlled by expediency and practical consequences rather than by general principles. Even though the Victorians were as certain about their moral principles as they were uncertain about their religious ideas, their political actions were fundamentally determined by practical considerations.[325] Throughout Europe the socialist movements were generally antagonistic to all religion. 'The spectre of Communism' which haunted Europe summoned men to freedom through revolution. Among the 'chains' which 'the proletarians' were to lose was the chain of religion.[326] It would not be missed because it had long ceased to have practical influence on the conditions of life. Marx and Engels described an industrial scene almost totally devoid of religious and ethical considerations about the condition of the worker. The 'masses' were the 'slaves' of the machine, the foreman and the boss.[327] Their salvation seemed to lie not in the advocacy of high principles but in aggressively secular political action. Nearly half a century later, Fairbairn reminded the Church that:

> the harder the struggle for existence grows, the harder does it become to be religious. . . . The conditions under which work is done are increasingly unfavourable to the cultivation of the religious spirit. . . . It is not the work that kills idealism, but the sordid conditions within and without the worker.[328]

In the practical affairs of life, religion had no great significance. When it came to making decisions and to getting things done, religious belief, in spite of (or maybe because of) the Christian Socialists, seemed to be superfluous, if not a hindrance. The crisis for faith deepened as faith was in practice divorced from large and important areas of life. It seemed to many to be an optional extra and they were too busy with the 'real' concerns of life to have time for it.

Sabatier spoke in 1897 of the 'conflict' between religion and contemporary culture. The 'modern spirit' sought the realization of the autonomy of man in every department of his life. To this spirit religious institutions appear 'as the great obstacle to the bringing in of a better state of things'. The consequence is that 'modern culture becomes irreligious, because it can see no other possibility save in the extirpation of religion itself. Religion, on the other hand, often becomes anti-scientific and illiberal.' The harmonization of religion and culture was necessary if religion was to have again any 'influence upon our conscience'.[329] Sabatier described the problem. Its solution was not so easy to discover. As we have tried to suggest, the 'spirit of the day' was opposed to authoritarian structures. The Church claimed to have some kind of divine authority both for itself and for its faith. It was not easy to reconcile the two. The 'spirit of the age' helped to deepen and to extend the crisis for faith.

In this chapter we have tried to suggest why it was that the Christian faith faced a fundamental crisis during the nineteenth century. Reports of great popular interest in and support for religion cannot hide the fact that from different sides the foundations of faith were being underminded. Some believers tried to find peace simply by shutting their minds to the challenges but they could not hope to maintain the significance of their faith while they kept it totally divorced from contemporary ideas. Some believers wanted to shore up the shaky walls of faith but were uncertain how to do it without making their faith disreputable in the judgement of contemporary thought. Some believers met the crisis by abandoning the traditional understanding of faith. They proposed new and differing interpretations of its essential content—interpretations which either seemed to other believers to omit the essential elements of faith or seemed to critics to be open to the criticisms which were levelled at traditional expressions of faith. Others reacted to the crisis by abandoning their faith. They felt that they could not give their assent to beliefs which were rebutted by views they could not discount. Believers and non-believers might not be, and very often were not, conscious of all the different views that we have mentioned. Many, however, were generally aware that the resolution of the various forces of modern thought undermined the foundations of faith as traditionally understood.

The period, then, was marked by uncertainty—uncertainty about the content of faith, uncertainty about the possibility of faith, uncertainty about what might viably replace traditional faith. Man was 'demanding a soul' and found himself 'tormented by such a request'.[330] The call to have 'faith' seemed to offer little relief for, as Browning confessed,

> How very hard it is to be
> A Christian! . . .
> . . . The whole, or chief
> Of difficulties, is belief.[331]

This was the crisis for faith which Newman attempted to meet. He tried to show that it was still possible and proper to have faith and to hold it as 'certain'. It is to Newman's work on the problem of faith that we now turn our attention. It was his personal response to the general crisis for faith.

Part II: The Background to the *Grammar of Assent*

1. NEWMAN'S AWARENESS OF THE CONTEMPORARY CRISIS FOR FAITH

Josef Pieper suggests that:

> to believe is equivalent to taking a position on the truth of a statement and on the actuality of the matter stated. More precisely, belief means that we think a statement true and consider the stated matter real, objectively existent. . . . But then we must ask: On what basis can he [sc. the believer], like the knower, say without reservation or condition, 'Yes, it is so and not different'?[1]

This is precisely Newman's question. He wanted to understand how it was possible to be certain of something which was believed. Primarily his search was a personal one: he wanted to satisfy himself that he was justified in his absolute assent to the doctrines of the Church. This personal quest, however, was inextricably united with a desire to combat the current intellectual attitude which led to unbelief. Newman called this attitude 'liberalism' and found it present both inside and outside the Church. He described it in a sermon in 1873:

> The elementary proposition of this new philosophy which is now so threatening is this—that in all things we must go by reason, in nothing by faith, that things are known and are to be received so far as they can be proved. Its advocates say, all other knowledge has proof—why should religion be an exception? . . . Seeing and proving is the only ground for believing. . . . Faith is a mistake in two ways. First, because it usurps the place of reason, and secondly, because it implies an absolute assent to doctrines, and is dogmatic, which absolute assent is irrational.[2]

In response to this attitude, Newman sought to demonstrate how a person could justifiably be certain of what he believed. His attempts reached their climax in the *Grammar of Assent*.

While Newman's personal involvement in the problem of faith was linked with a desire to counter contemporary rationalism, we must not assume that Newman had any considerable direct knowledge of the material discussed in our first chapter. As we shall indicate later, Newman seems to have been basically a solitary thinker. His importance for the crisis for faith lies primarily in the fact that his own personal quest reflected the essential nature of the problem raised by contemporary ideas. Nevertheless, Newman was not so solitary that he was not aware of current thought. The range and size both of his own personal collection of books and of the library he built up at the Oratory at Edgbaston give the lie to this. The problem is how far Newman grappled with the material of nineteenth-century rationalism rather than merely became acquainted with its fundamental tenets. I confess that I cannot give any final answer to this question. There is, however, some evidence, relevant to a conclusion on this point, which can be found in the books Newman possessed, in the books he wrote, and in his private letters and manuscripts. To this evidence we now briefly turn.

Newman's own study at the Oratory has been preserved as it was when he died. A survey of the books on the shelves gives a very tentative suggestion of some of the things Newman might have read. Where volumes are still uncut, we know that Newman did not read *that* copy—but this is no evidence that he had not read another copy. Even where pages are cut it is not certain that Newman had cut and read them. The best—and conclusive—evidence is where we find marginal notes in Newman's hand. Regretably these are not as frequent as we might have wished! In his room, then, we find a copy of the Bohn edition of Kant's *Critique of Pure Reason*. The first 177 pages (out of 517) have been cut. A copy of Chalybaüs's *Historical Development of Speculative Philosophy from Kant to Hegel* contains marginal notes which show that Newman had read it. On Biblical criticism, we find uncut a three-volume edition of Strauss's *Life of Jesus*, but a companion volume, *Voices of the Church in reply to Dr. D. F. Strauss*, has the pages of the first essay cut. This essay is entitled 'Strauss, Hegel and their Opinions'. There is a first edition of *Essays and Reviews* with nearly all the pages cut and all readable. W. Wilberforce (junior) gave Newman Colenso's *The Pentateuch and Book of Joshua* in 1862 and all its pages have been cut. Ewald's *The History of Israel to the Death of Moses* has most of its first 137 pages cut (out of 650). The opened section deals with Hebrew sources, tradition, and historical writings. A copy of R. W. Mackay's *The Tübingen School and its Antecedents* has most of its pages cut and contains pencilled marginal notes in Newman's hand. Most of these notes indicate that Newman considered that various suggestions made in the text were unwarranted 'assumptions'. Also in the room is a copy of St. George Mivart's study of Darwinism, *On the Genesis of Species*, which Newman had received from the author on its publication in 1871. All the pages are cut and Newman's interest in the subject is shown by his long correspondence with Mivart. Most of the books in Newman's room, however, do not belong to the contemporary crisis for faith. It is these books—of devotion, orthodox theology, and literature—which Newman preferred to read. He was aware of contemporary 'liberal' thought but his knowledge of it probably came from conversation with others[3] and from synoptical treatments at second-hand rather from any considerable study of the major works.

Newman's published works confirm this impression. The authors referred to most frequently are Butler and Paley. While he has reservations about their views, they certainly cannot be classed among those responsible for the crisis for faith.[4] None of his references to current Continental philosophy cite original works. In the *Development of Doctrine* he mentions Kant and Strauss but the only book he quotes by title is Pusey's *German Rationalism*. His reference to Schelling in the same volume is derived from Dewar's *German Protestantism*.[5] When Newman dealt with *Rationalism in Religion* in one of the *Tracts for the Times*, his named targets were two popular expositions of the rationalist attitude by Erskine and by Abbot.[6] The *Tract* ends with a Postscript where he quotes from an article about Schleiermacher in an American periodical. He regards this periodical as 'a melancholy evidence' that the 'spurious Christianity' of German rationalism is infecting 'Protestant America'.[7] We may, as Zeno suggests, find approving allusions in Newman's writings to views which are Kantian but, in the absence of any direct reference to Kant, it would be dangerous to assume that Newman recognized that these views came from Kant.[8] Of the British philosophers involved in the crisis for faith, Newman's published works show that he knew something of Hume, Coleridge and Hamilton.[9] These references do not indicate how much of these philosophers may have been read by Newman.

Newman's references to historians show that he had both an extensive knowledge of their works and a considerable interest in their techniques. His first book, *The Arians*, was a historical study and he retained an interest in historical research all his life.[10] In his works we find references to several historians who, intentionally or not, shared in creating the crisis for faith.[11] Gibbon is mentioned on many occasions.[12] Newman seems to have regarded him as a great historian whose conclusions were led astray by wrong interpretative principles.[13] Even though he had 'a great difficulty' with Gibbon, he wished to include him in a course on English literature at Dublin.[14] In Newman's historical works we find occasional references to Neander, Niebuhr and various other authorities. He read both Milman's *History of the Jews* and his *History of Christianity*. The former he described in a letter to Pusey as 'a very dangerous work' although he defended its 'matter' against the criticisms of another correspondent. Its error lay in 'the profane spirit' of its attitude.[15] The latter work was reviewed at length by Newman in the *British Critic*. Here again he located Milman's fundamental error in his attempt to write sacred history 'as it would appear to a man of the world', divorced from the standpoint of faith.[16] Newman's interest in the technique of historiography is shown by his wish to have a professorship in the philosophy of history at Dublin. In a letter to Allies inviting him to take this chair, Newman criticized Schlegel for writing history with 'no *view*' and Gibbon for writing history in 'subservience' to a 'bad' philosophy.[17] In the *Grammar of Assent* he made a comparison of the views of 'Niebuhr, Mr. Clinton, Sir George Lewis, Mr. Grote, and Colonel Mure'. Their mutual differences were explained by the different presuppositions which controlled their use of historical evidence.

We have already mentioned a passing reference to Strauss in the *Development of Doctrine*. From his published works we cannot gain any real indication of Newman's own knowledge of the details of nineteenth-century Biblical criticism. As an undergraduate he attended Buckland's lectures on geology but there was nothing in them to disturb faith in the Bible. Newman, in fact, considered that the lectures confirmed the Biblical record.[18] In *The Idea of a University* he mentions that 'geology may deny Moses'[19] but on the whole he did not consider that scientific investigations posed any real threat to faith. Difficulties would arise only if science and faith encroached on each other's proper territory. A true understanding of each would prevent this happening.[20] Although the Bible 'does declare a few momentous facts ... of a physical nature', they are few in number and the Church has not laid down any definite interpretation of what they mean. Until the Church does define their meaning, the believer is at liberty to interpret them as compatible with scientific discoveries in whatever way their expressions allow. There is no reason to anticipate a conflict between the truths of science and those of the Biblical revelation.[21] At this point Newman differs from the majority of contemporary believers whose faith was greatly troubled by the claims of science. Newman mentions Renan in terms of an article in a periodical[22] but he deals with Seeley's *Ecce Homo* in a long critical review. His conclusion was that 'you either accept

Christianity, or you do not: if you do, do not garble and patch it; if you do not, suffer others to submit to it ungarbled.'[23] Presumably this was Newman's general view of the attempts to produce a critical life of Jesus Christ. In 1883-4, he wrote two essays about the inspiration of the Bible.[24] They do not show what Biblical criticism Newman had read but they do show that while he firmly adhered to the doctrine of the inspiration of Scripture, his adherence was combined with an acceptance of some moderately critical positions. Thus he believed that Moses wrote the Pentateuch but used 'foreign documents', that Daniel may not have written all the book attributed to him, that David may not have written all the Psalms, that there may have been two Isaiahs, and that there may be extraneous material in the received text of Mark and John.[25] On the other hand, whatever Biblical scholarship might tell us about the human aspects of the Bible's production, in its 'substantial fulness' the Scripture must be accepted '*de fide* as true' since 'it has God for its author'.[26]

Newman's letters show that he was often consulted by people who were experiencing personally a crisis of faith.[27] The first six volumes of his letters after he became a Roman Catholic contain several discussions of this problem but none of them refers by name to any of the authors considered in our first chapter. This is presumably because in the particular cases the crisis was not related to any specific rationalistic work. The only author that Newman does discuss in relation to faith and its certainty is Butler. Here he is mainly concerned to defend himself against misinterpretations of his position due to a too close identification of his views with those of Butler.[28] In a series of letters to Meynell in 1859-60, which have not yet been published, Newman discussed Mansel's Bampton Lectures, showing that he had read them carefully and with some approval.[29] In a letter to his sister Jemima, in February 1840, Newman wrote about his expectation of 'a great attack upon the Bible' and described the different positions from which the attack might come. On the one hand there was Carlyle whose:

> view is that Christianity has good *in* it, or is good *as far as it goes*, which, when applied to Scripture, is of course a picking and choosing of its contents. Then again you have Arnold's school, such as it is, (I do hope he will be frightened back) giving up the inspiration of the Old Testament, or of all Scripture (I do not say Arnold himself does). Then you have Milman clenching his History of the Jews by a History of Christianity, which they say is worse, and just in the same line. Then you have all your Political Economists, who *cannot* accept, (it is impossible) the Scripture

rules about almsgiving, renunciation of wealth, self denial &c. And then you have Geologists giving up parts of the Old Testament. All these and many more spirits seem uniting and forming into something shocking.[30]

Other later letters and manuscripts which have not yet been published in full show that Newman read Darwin's *Origin of Species* without finding in it any great threat to faith. He corresponded at length with St. George Mivart and was interested in Mivart's criticisms of Darwin's theory. Newman pointed out, though, that he personally had no 'great dislike or dread of his [sc. Darwin's] theory' and to another he wrote that, 'I see nothing in the theory of evolution inconsistent with an Almighty God and Protector'.[31] Among Newman's private papers we also find two short discussions of Mill and three notes which tell us that he had been reading about Kant in Chalybäus's *Historical Survey of Speculative Philosophy from Kant to Hegel*.[32] As more of Newman's letters and papers are published we may discover more about what he had read. It is unlikely, however, that any forthcoming evidence will significantly alter our judgement of his acquaintance with contemporary thought. Although Newman was generally aware of current views affecting faith, he had no extensive, detailed, and personal knowledge of the ideas which were creating the crisis for faith.

Newman, on the other hand, was acutely conscious of the principles which lay behind the crisis for faith and used the term 'liberalism' as a name for them. The term thus refers in his works to those views which were the essence of the crisis for faith. After an early flirtation with this 'liberalism',[33] Newman felt that a great part of his life's work must be to battle against it and its influences.[34] In the *Apologia* he dates his break with 'liberalism' as 'the end of 1827' but, as Boekraad reminds us, his first University Sermon, preached in July 1826, shows that Newman was already warning his hearers against such tendencies.[35] In *The Idea of a University* he discussed several times this 'form of infidelity of the day' which he regarded as 'in some shape unavoidable in an age of intellect and in a world like this'.[36] In the *Apologia* he defines 'liberalism' as 'the anti-dogmatic principle and its developments' which currently expresses itself in a 'deep plausible scepticism, . . . as being the development of human reason, as practically exercised by the natural man'.[37] Newman appended a long note to the *Apologia* to expound this definition. Here he states that:

> by liberalism I mean false liberty of thought, or the exercise of thought upon matters, in which, from the constitution of the human mind, thought cannot be brought to any successful issue,

and therefore is out of place.... Liberalism then is the mistake of subjecting to human judgment those revealed doctrines which are in their nature beyond and independent of it, and of claiming to determine on intrinsic grounds the truth and value of propositions which rest for their reception simply on the external authority of the Divine Word.[38]

At the end of the note Newman lists eighteen propositions which express the essence of this 'liberalism', propositions which Newman 'earnestly denounced and abjured'.[39] They show that he understood the principles that lay behind the crisis for faith and was firmly opposed to them.

At the start of this chapter we quoted from a sermon by Newman in 1873 in which he attacks this 'spirit of infidelity' which is 'the great evil of our times'.[40] For final proof of Newman's unwavering opposition to the principles of the rationalism which was undermining faith, we may refer to his speech on 12 May, 1879, when he received the 'biglietto'—the official summons to receive his Cardinal's biretta from the Pope. Newman took this opportunity to deliver another attack on 'liberalism'. He said:

Liberalism in religion is the doctrine that there is no positive truth in religion, but that one creed is as good as another, and this is the teaching that is gaining substance and force daily. It is inconsistent with any recognition of any religion as *true*. It teaches that all are to be tolerated, for all are matters of opinion. Revealed religion is not a truth, but a sentiment and a taste; not an objective fact, not miraculous; and it is the right of each individual to make it say just what strikes his fancy.

This 'liberalism', this movement away from true faith, was 'the great *apostasia*'—but Newman did not fear for the future. The power of God was on the side of true faith and in the end must conquer.[41]

Newman's struggle against 'liberalism', however, was not primarily a struggle against those forces and attitudes in contemporary thought which he recognized to be inimical to true faith. Primarily it was a struggle to answer a problem which he felt personally and deeply. He wanted to know for himself, as well as to be able to show others, how a person could be certain in matters of faith. But while Newman's life-long quest for an answer to this problem was at heart a personal matter, it was also a concrete expression of the fundamental problem in the nineteenth-century crisis for faith. Newman's personal attempts to determine the logic of faith were also an attempted answer to this crisis. We now turn to examine Newman's views of faith and of its certainty. They constitute an important Christian response to the crisis for faith, a response which has significance not only for its own age but also for ours.

2. NEWMAN'S QUEST FOR A FIRM FAITH

Newman himself tells us that the *Grammar of Assent* was the result of a long intellectual struggle. This work differed from his other works in that it was not written in response to an immediate 'call'.

> As to the 'Assent' I had felt it on my conscience for years, that it would not do to quit the world without doing it. Rightly or wrongly I had ever thought it a duty, as if it was committed to me to do it. I had tried to do it again and again and failed, and though at length I did it, I did it after all with great difficulty—but it was a great relief to me in 1870 to have done it.[42]

Many of Newman's unfinished and as yet unpublished attempts to write on this subject have been preserved at the Oratory at Edgbaston. From these, as well as from his published works, we can see how persistently he was troubled by the problems of the relationship between faith and reason. The full title of the *Grammar of Assent*, viz., *An Essay in Aid of a Grammar of Assent*, suggests that he had reservations about his success in solving these problems when finally he did produce a treatise on them. It is interesting that all his many attempts to solve the problem embody the same basic ideas. The views on the subject found in the *Oxford University Sermons* are fundamentally the same as those which are found in the *Grammar of Assent* and in the writings of the intervening years.

In 1816, after a period of youthful scepticism, Newman experienced conversion. His experience lacked the emotional element which characterized contemporary Evangelical life.[43] Its dominant feature was a change in Newman's intellectual attitude towards religion. In the *Apologia* he describes it as 'a great change of thought' in which 'I fell under the influences of a definite Creed, and received into my intellect impressions of dogma, which, through God's mercy, have never been effaced or obscured.'[44] From this time Newman regarded dogmatic certainty about fundamentals as an essential element in real religion. Here is the source of his opposition to that 'liberalism' which will not allow certainty to any religious position.[45]

This experience, and the reading which followed it,[46] meant that Newman arrived in Oxford in 1817 firmly convinced of the truth of his religious beliefs. For the first few years of his University career he seems to have preserved his dogmatic certainty although he was aware of the difficulty of faith. For instance, in October 1819 he wrote that, 'As I understand the Bible, faith is *a* (perhaps *the*) most difficult grace',[47] but when his father warned him in January 1821 against falling into delusion and pride, Newman's comment was:

> How good is God to give me the assurance of hope! If any one had prophesied to me confidently that I should change my opinions, and I was not convinced of the impossibility, what anguish should I feel![48]

The following June, however, he had a dream in which he was aware of the limitations of human reason in theological matters.[49] By August he had begun to have doubts about his beliefs. He writes in his Journal that he wishes above all 'to attain a strength of faith, of which at present I feel the want very much. Every now and then momentary clouds of doubt cross my mind.' He finds comfort in the recollection that even though he is 'thus afflicted', he still has 'what may God in his mercy continue, a "full assurance of hope" concerning my final perseverance, and have had it from the time of my conversion.'[50] During this period Newman poses the problem before him thus: 'I know I am right. How do you know it? I know I know. How? I know I know I know &c &c.'[51] In June 1822 we find him thankful that a growing temptation 'is not one of painful and perplexing doubts and fits of unbelief',[52] but an entry in his Journal dated February 1824 announces that:

> It is painful to think how unsettled my principles are. On hardly a point have I made up my mind. Hawkins, however, has been declaring his opinions on some points, as appears to me, very erroneously, and feeling I am as a poor child without sense or strength, I trust God will enlighten me, and tell me what is the truth.[53]

These quotations show that for Newman doubt was not simply a matter of intellectual concern. Doubt about the basic doctrines of his faith caused him personal unhappiness, yet he could not avoid subjecting his beliefs to the scrutiny of his reason.

Newman's intellectual development at Oxford was particularly influenced by Richard Whately. Although he claimed that it was Whately who 'opened my mind and taught me to think and to use my reason',[54] he does not tell us how Whately's influence affected his attitude towards religious belief. He only says that on matters of doctrine he was always opposed to the Noetic Whately.[55] From this time we find Newman both in published works and in unpublished materials trying to establish the reasonableness of holding faith to be certain. His first University sermon, preached on 2 July 1826, was entitled 'The Philosophical Temper, First Enjoined by the Gospel'. It opens with the statement that 'Few charges have been more frequently urged by unbelievers against Revealed Religion, than that it is hostile to the advance of philosophy and science.'[56] While admitting some truth in the charge,[57] Newman claims that Christianity produces the character which is best suited to scientific and philosophical enquiry.[58] The danger is that in the future such enquiry may increasingly 'be found to separate from the Christian Church' and become autonomous. His only answer to this threat is to urge 'that early religious training, to which . . . all persons . . . should be submitted.'[59] At this point Newman has seen the problem rather than any indication of its answer beyond a warning against 'over-confidence in our own acuteness and powers of reasoning'.[60] In his next University sermon, preached on 13 April 1830, we see the beginnings of Newman's apologetic for faith as he explores 'the connexion between Natural and Revealed Religion'.[61] Two ideas are found here which have an important rôle in his later thought. The first is the place of conscience: for Newman 'Conscience is the essential principle and sanction of Religion in the mind.'[62] Secondly, he stresses the importance of '*facts* and *actions*', in contrast to 'inductions' or 'generalized laws', as 'the media' of the 'impressiveness' and 'truth' of religion.[63] This is an early indication of the distinction between the 'real' and the 'notional' which we will find in Newman's later understanding of living faith. In this sermon he holds that revealed religion, which completes natural religion, finds its confirmation in the natural order.[64]

Newman's confidence in human reason had declined by December 1831, when he preached on 'The Usurpations of Reason'.[65] Here Newman declared:

> there is . . . no truth of religion to which a captious reason may not find objections; and in truth the evidence and matter of Revelation are not addressed to the mere unstable Reason of man, nor can hope for any certain or adequate reception with it.[66]

Reason is limited in 'its range' and must be restricted to its proper sphere. It is intruding when it seeks to be 'an independent authority' in religious issues for faith is the basis of religion.[67] The function of reason in religious apologetics is to refute objections to faith rather than to convince inquirers.[68] Faith is discerned by 'some secret faculty' which is part of 'the instinctive power of an educated conscience . . . and without any intelligible reasoning process'. In a footnote to the

1872 edition, Newman explains that by the last phrase he means that the mind uses '*implicit* . . . reasoning'.[69] If such a positive assertion was originally intended when the sermon was composed, we find here an anticipation of Newman's position in the *Grammar of Assent* which is that we come to faith through a complex act which includes unconscious reasoning (the work of the 'Illative Sense' in the *Grammar of Assent*) and the judgement of conscience. Newman's next University sermon[70] confirms the presence of such ideas in his mind. Again he is concerned about the propagation of religion in face of the power of secular reason. He suggests that reason is unable to cope with the intricacies of 'Truth' as a whole.[71] The 'real influence' of 'Truth' 'consists directly in some inherent moral power . . . not in any evidence or criterion level to the undisciplined reason of the multitude'.[72] In this sermon we also find a recognition of the limitations of language for expressing moral truth.[73] Another important theme of the *Grammar of Assent* which is found in the University sermons of this period is the distinction between the 'real' and the 'notional'. In the sermon 'Contest between Faith and Sight' Newman argues that 'the world' overcomes faith more by its effect on our imagination than by its appeal to our reason and passions.[74] A faith which consists of the acceptance of general principles is soon crushed by 'the world' while the faith which conquers 'the world' is one which 'addresses itself to our senses and imagination'.[75] This faith is not understood primarily as an intellectual assent to doctrines but as 'implicit reliance in God's command and promise, and a zeal for His honour; a surrender and devotion . . . to Him'.[76] With this basic character of obedience[77] faith is opposed to the growing 'wilfulness' of contemporary 'liberal' attitudes.

Although Newman's work on *The Arians of the Fourth Century* was not published until October 1833, he states that 'it was ready for the Press in July, 1832.'[78] This volume casts further light on Newman's understanding of faith. The connexion between faith and morals is clearly stated. While 'relaxation of morals' leads to 'coldness in faith',[79] an 'improved moral sense (or what Scripture terms '*the Spirit*')' is necessary for the discovery of 'moral and spiritual . . . truths'. These lie beyond the 'province' of reason alone[80] but have 'a claim of acceptance on the conscience'.[81] 'Uneducated men' may have an 'implicit' faith in which they have no 'precise' grasp of the objects of their faith, but faith is possible for 'cultivated' minds only if they have some apprehension of its object. The doctrines of the Church are attempts to provide normative images for such apprehension. This apprehension is not limited to a merely notional understanding, for living faith is not found in 'assent to a form of words' but in 'habits which are realities'.[82]

Newman criticizes the Arians for their rationalistic 'axiom that there could be no mystery in the Scripture doctrine respecting the nature of God'. For him the condition of faith is an apprehension which may be more or less adequate, not a comprehensive understanding which is unable to tolerate any mystery.[83]

In 1835 Newman continued his attacks on rationalism or 'liberalism' with a Tract entitled *On the Introduction of Rationalistic Principles into Revealed Religion*. Rationalism is described as 'a certain abuse of Reason', for it is:

> a use of it for purposes for which it never was intended, and is unfitted. To rationalize in matters of Revelation is to make our reason the standard and measure of the doctrines revealed. . . . And thus a rationalistic spirit is the antagonist of Faith; for Faith is, in its very nature, the acceptance of what our reason cannot reach, simply and absolutely upon testimony.[84]

The heart of Rationalism is an 'egotistic' attempt of 'the Rationalist' to be 'his own centre, . . . he does not go to God, but he implies that God must come to him'.[85] Faith, for the rationalist, is 'never more than an opinion', arising from 'independent enquiry, dispassionateness, and the like',[86] whose content must be 'clear . . . complete and definite'. Newman contrasts this with the Gospel whose truths are 'also deep and therefore necessarily mysterious'.[87] The legitimate function of reason is to lead us to faith by ascertaining 'what things are attainable by reason, and what are not', and by indicating the acceptability and meaning of statements claiming our belief.[88] 'Right reason', then, does not seek to measure 'a divine revelation by human standards' but combines with faith 'to take what is given as we find it, to use it and be content'.[89] Newman claims the support of Butler for this understanding of the relationship between faith and reason.[90]

In other writings of this time Newman continues to attack rationalism while he defends his own position by appeal to the authority of the Church in its Catholic and Apostolic tradition. He suggests that the consequence of believing that everyone has 'a duty to exercise the "sacred right of private judgment"' is 'quot homines, tot sententiae'.[91] While he agrees with Locke, Hoadley, Hampden, and Chillingworth that 'private judgment' is incompatible with 'dogmatic certainty',[92] he draws the opposite conclusion from this. Whereas they sacrifice certainty to private judgement, Newman holds that we must subordinate private judgement to the Apostolic tradition contained in the Church's teaching and thereby preserve certainty.[93] Scripture is to be understood in the light of the 'external' and 'infallible' interpretation of 'an ecclesiastical Tradition, derived in the first instance from the Apostles'.[94] Newman thus defends the Anglican Church on the grounds that 'our Apostolical communion inherits, as the promises, so the faith enjoyed by the Saints in every age, the faith which Ignatius, Cyprian, and Gregory received from the Apostles.'[95] This copies the method of defence in 'the primitive Church'.[96] The rejection of 'private judgment', however, does not release the believer from an obligation to know the reasons for his belief. If we are to maintain our faith and 'to direct the faith of others', we must learn 'to analyse and to state formally our reasons for believing what we do believe'.[97] Newman's position is developed in his *Lectures on the Prophetical Office of the Church*, the first volume of *The Via Media*, which was published in 1837. We must 'submit to what God Himself has revealed' through the Scriptures and the Apostolic tradition of the Church because our reason is too limited to make known to us all the truth necessary for salvation.[98] The 'strange preference ... of inquiry to belief' makes 'doubtful what really was certain' and leads to the 'loss of labour, division, and error'.[99] At the same time 'Romanism' is rejected since it 'considers unclouded certainty necessary for a Christian's faith'. For Newman 'religious faith' is here a stand made in the face of some doubt and uncertainty. This is 'its trial and its praise'.[100] Faith is distinguished from opinion on the basis of personal involvement, not in terms of objective discernment: 'action', not intellectual entertainment, 'is the criterion of true faith'.[101] We come to faith as we perceive 'that on the whole facts point to certain definite conclusions, and not to their contraries' and then 'adopt those conclusions unhesitatingly' by the act of 'a vigorous will'.[102] In this act of our 'private judgment'[103] we are guided by 'internal' and 'external' as well as by 'supernatural' factors.[104] Our 'Private Judgment in matters of Faith' is restricted, however, to those issues which have not been determined already by 'Church authority'.[105] In spite of what he says about the rôle of 'Private Judgment' in attaining faith, Newman severely limits its range, making it subordinate to our duty to accept what we are told by authority.[106] His fear of 'rationalism' does not allow him the confidence in our reasoning powers which is found in the *Grammar of Assent*.

We find similar views about the nature of faith in the *Lectures on Justification* published in 1838. The faith that is necessary for justification is a personal faith which inspires action.[107] Newman contrasts this with the 'mere faith'[108] of the 'Roman Schools'[109] which is an assent without any essential personal involvement.[110] In either case, faith is 'an original means of knowledge' distinct from our senses and reason and extending beyond their range.[111] It is founded 'on a supernaturally implanted instinct' which is 'developed by religious obedience'.[112] In *Tract 85*,[113] which also appeared in 1838, Newman attacks the rationalists by arguing that 'Nature' itself condemns the 'critical, cold, investigating temper' when it attaches 'happiness . . . not to *their* temper, but rather to confiding, unreasoning faith'. The argument rests on Newman's claim that 'what is right and what is happy cannot in the long run and on a large scale be disjoined.'[114] Our faith is a stance or 'choice', made in the face of uncertainty and mystery,[115] which is fundamental to our life and activity.[116]

A major and comprehensive attempt to determine the relationship between faith and reason occurs in the four Oxford University Sermons which Newman preached in 1839 and 1840.[117] These discourses foreshadow the *Grammar of Assent*. They show a greater understanding of the rôle of our reasoning powers in matters of faith than appears in most of Newman's previous work. Newman distinguishes between the use of reason to confirm the doctrines of faith and the claim that 'Faith is actually grounded on Reason in the believing mind itself.'[118] He even holds that we may not only be unconscious of the reasons for our faith but also of the faith itself and so fail to recognize it when it is expressed.[119] Reason may 'test and verify' faith without some conscious process of reason being its source and condition.[120] Such testing and verifying, in fact, can reduce the force of faith by making its structure familiar to us. This is the danger of using reason in matters of faith.[121] With this proviso that faith is not determined by our reason, Newman holds that since the act of faith can be described as an assent 'upon certain grounds' to things not immediately present to us, it shares the basic character of 'an exercise of Reason'.[122] Because of this it is open to the criticism that it is a 'faulty exercise of Reason as being conducted on insufficient grounds'.[123] Newman points out that religious faith is not the only exercise of reasoning which is open to this criticism for it applies also to many of our decisions in such subjects as politics, economics, and literature.[124] The 'varied proofs of Christianity' have value, then, as 'an encouragement . . . and a means of confirming faith', but their force depends upon 'presumptions'[125] which may or may not be granted. Whereas the assent of reason is determined by the evidence, the assent of faith is 'mainly swayed by antecedent considerations . . . prepossessions, and (in a good sense of the word) prejudices'.[126] The fact that faith is dependent upon presumptions which are assumed makes it no more illogical than any other rational decision. Unbelief shares the same logical nature as faith for it rests upon 'presumptions and prejudices as much as faith does, only presumptions of an opposite nature'.[127] Even the clearest and most systematic argument finally depends upon something assumed 'which is incapable of proof'.[128] Since 'we are given absolute certainty in nothing', our actions must of necessity arise from a faith dependent upon presumptions.[129] The problem that arises is how we can justify the 'presumptions' or 'antecedent probabilities' that lead to the Christian faith. If we cannot justify them, we will have no defence against all kinds of 'superstition and fanaticism'.[130] Newman argues that 'the safeguard of Faith' is not 'Reason' but 'a right state of heart'.[131] We believe correctly not because of our 'natural reason' but 'because we love'.[132]

Newman recognizes the limitations of syllogistic reasoning and suggests that the higher the form of knowledge, the more obscure is the means of attaining it.[133] 'Divine Truth' is attained through reasoning which is 'subtle and indirect' and requires 'special delicacy and abstruseness'.[134] Here we have a clear preview of what is called the 'Illative Sense' in the *Grammar of Assent*. In this reasoning our 'mind ranges to and fro . . . with a quickness which has become a proverb, and a subtlety and versatility which baffle investigation'.[135] This is the way in which 'all men . . . commonly reason,—not by rule but by an inward faculty'.[136] Attempts are sometimes made, however, to reduce these natural and unconscious reasoning processes to rules.[137] The 'boldest, simplest, and most comprehensive theory' is that of Aristotelian logic.[138] Newman, accordingly, distinguishes between implicit and explicit reasoning,[139] the former our natural and unconscious way of reasoning, the latter conscious and obeying rules. He points out, further, that 'clearness in argument certainly is not indispensable to reasoning well'.[140] We may reason correctly without being aware of our method. People, furthermore, vary in their ability to apply natural reasoning to different subjects and in their appreciation of its arguments.[141] Newman suggests that 'the proof of Christianity' is 'of this subtle nature' of unconscious reasoning and so 'cannot be exhibited to advantage in [sc. syllogistic] argument'.[142] The connexion between faith and morality appears at this point as well as in reference to our acceptance of 'presumptions'. Since faith is 'created in the mind, not so much by facts, as by probabilities', the argument for faith depends upon 'a correct moral judgment and view of things'.[143] Only with a right moral attitude will we be able correctly to judge the value of evidence 'which falls short of a proof in itself'.[144] Faith is 'a test of moral character'[145] because the way in which a person treats the evidence offered to him depends upon 'the character of his mind'.[146] Newman therefore holds that 'right faith is the faith of a right mind, . . . a reasoning upon holy, devout and enlightened presumptions.'[147] This attitude is not 'natural to fallen man' but comes 'only of supernatural grace'.[148] Newman quotes I Corinthians, Chapter

2, to show that 'a certain moral state', produced by the Holy Spirit's 'regenerating and renewing influences', is 'the means of gaining the Truth'.[149] When we come to analyse the *Grammar of Assent* we will find that these sermons contain in a less systematic form most of the ideas found in that later treatise. Newman described the sermons as having 'the nature of an exploring expedition into an all but unknown country'.[150] They show that by this time he had reached in embryo the conclusions which were to be expounded in the *Grammar*. The main difference between these sermons and the later treatise is that they do not deal with the necessity of apprehension before belief.

Newman's interest in the relationship between faith and reason is reflected in some of his remaining publications as an Anglican. The nature of theological argument is succinctly described in his critical review of Milman's *History of Christianity*:

> A theory does not prove itself; it makes itself probable so far as it falls in with our pre-conceived notions, as it accounts for the phenomena it treats of, as it is internally consistent, and as it excels or excludes rival theories.[151]

This was published in January 1841 and in the following month Newman provided an example of such argument in his letters to *The Times*, later republished under the title *The Tamworth Reading Room*.[152] In these letters he attacks the idea that 'in becoming wiser a man will become better'[153] as 'the veriest of pretences which sophist or mountebank ever professed to a gaping auditory'.[154] Newman argues that 'the consciousness of a duty is not all one with the performance of it.'[155] It is not 'Knowledge' but divine 'Grace' which is 'a quickening, renovating, organizing principle' in man.[156] In a passage which is quoted at length in the *Grammar of Assent*[157] Newman holds that we cannot argue people into faith for 'man is *not* a reasoning animal; he is a seeing, feeling, contemplating, acting animal.'[158] People are influenced by 'direct impressions', not by conclusions.[159] Furthermore, life is too short 'for a religion of inferences; . . . if we insist on proofs for everything, we shall never come to action: to act you must assume, and that assumption is faith.'[160] As for 'scientific pursuits', they have no 'power of impressing religion upon the mind of the multitude'.[161] While they may provide us with data, our inference of 'religious truths' from that data will depend upon our presuppositions: 'the truth is that the system of Nature is just as much connected with Religion, where minds are not religious, as a watch or a steam carriage.'[162] Newman concludes that 'whereas man is born for action, action flows not from inferences, but from impressions,—not from reasonings, but from Faith.'[163] His concern to refute the errors of this rationalism is also seen in his essay entitled 'Private Judgment' which appeared in July 1841. He suggests that 'when Private Judgment moves in the direction of innovation' we may treat it 'with suspicion', since 'change is really the characteristic of error'.[164] We are to use our 'Private Judgment' only when God commands, for 'Divine aid alone can carry anyone safely and successfully through an enquiry after religious truth.'[165] After discussing the rôle of 'Private Judgment' in conversion Newman holds that its real task is to determine 'what and where is the Church'.[166] Men 'have neither the time, the patience, nor the clearness and exactness of thought, for processes of investigation and deduction' in matters of doctrine. All that is therefore required by 'Providence' is that men should discern the true 'teacher of doctrine'—and this limited task is within their illative power.[167]

In his last two Oxford University Sermons[168] Newman is again concerned with faith and reason. He speaks of 'an instinctive Reason, which is prior to argument and proof' by which men 'choose light or darkness'.[169] In bringing us to faith, God's 'grace does not supersede' our reasoning powers but 'uses . . . and renews them'.[170] Faith itself is a 'reaching forward to truth, amid darkness or confusion' on the basis of 'slender evidence'[171] and 'antecedent notions'.[172] It 'starts from probabilities' and ends in 'the absolute acceptance of a certain message or doctrine as divine'.[173] The function of reason which Newman emphasizes is its ability to minister to faith by making explicit what is implied in its beliefs.[174] He is careful to make it clear, however, that in this activity reason must always be subordinate to faith[175] and that faith does not have to be explicit in order to be genuinely possessed.[176] This aspect of the function of reason in matters of doctrine is expounded in Newman's final publication as an Anglican, *An Essay on the Development of Christian Doctrine*. In this work Newman recognizes that we argue both in natural science and in a religion not by formal syllogisms but by 'converging evidence in favour of certain doctrines'.[177] This is the method used by our 'Illative Sense' in the *Grammar of Assent*. While formal, explicit logic may be used to organize ideas which have been discerned by 'moral perception',[178] it is inferior to 'the spontaneous process which goes on within the mind itself'.[179] Faith is 'the absolute acceptance of the divine Word with an internal assent' which, 'being an act of the intellect, opens a way for inquiry, comparison and inference . . . in subservience to itself'.[180] The reasons for believing 'are for the most part implicit' and:

> consist . . . rather of presumptions and ventures after the truth than of accurate and complete proofs; . . . probable arguments,

under the scrutiny and sanction of a prudent judgment, are sufficient for conclusions which we even embrace as most certain.¹⁸¹

Newman claims the support of 'the unanimity of Catholics, ancient as well as modern', in rejecting Locke's view that 'doctrines are only so far to be considered true as they are logically demonstrated'.¹⁸² He thus asserts the absolute character of faith while recognizing that reason can at best only show its doctrines to be probable. In the *Grammar of Assent* he seeks to refute Locke directly, not simply by appeal to authorities. We have already noted how this study of development in doctrine contributed inadvertently to the crisis for faith.¹⁸³

In the *Apologia* Newman states that since he became a Catholic 'I never have had one doubt'. At his conversion he was not 'conscious ... of any change, intellectual or moral, wrought in my mind' and since that time he claims he has experienced only 'perfect peace and contentment'.¹⁸⁴ Nevertheless, materials among his private papers as well as certain passages in his publications show that after 1845 he was still trying to clarify his thoughts on the problems of faith and reason. In a note in *The Journal, 1859–79*, dated 30 October 1870, Newman lists some of his different attempts. Many of these attempts and other papers and fragments dealing with the problem are preserved at the Oratory at Edgbaston.¹⁸⁵ From these materials we can see what Newman meant when he said that the *Grammar of Assent* was 'the upshot of a very long desire and effort'.¹⁸⁶

In June 1846 Newman published an appreciation of Keble's *Lyra Innocentium*. In it he argues that we must choose between rationalism and submitting to an infallible authority.¹⁸⁷ There is no genuine third alternative. Since the Anglican Church does not claim 'to have the power of absolutely determining the truth in religious matters', the choice is between Roman Catholicism and rationalism.¹⁸⁸ But while this may be the choice before us, our problem is how to justify the certainty ascribed to our decision. In some notes made at this time¹⁸⁹ Newman endorses Aquinas's recognition of three forms of judgement or assent; there is perception, which comes 'from sense or intuition (intellectus or visio)', knowledge, which is 'from strict reasoning into principles known (scientia)', and the 'assent of faith', which is 'from faint reasoning supported and carried through by will'. He comments that this view of faith as 'cogitatio cum assensu' is '*precisely* my main distinction in my University Sermons' as opposed to the faulty 'Protestant theories of faith' which say that '*reason comes first* and *then* comes the will and *faith*.' Newman's view is that 'presumption supported by the *will*' is 'the proof—or cogitatio and assensus going together'. The act of faith is a complex activity: 'it begins from reason which is not strong enough to prove, but sways the will—and the will rules and determines the intellect' which assents.[190] In a letter dated 13 December 1846 Newman says that people in Rome 'at first misunderstood' him when he talked of 'probable arguments' preceding faith because they thought he was asserting that 'we could not get beyond a probable conclusion in opposition to a moral certainty'. He points out in clarification that he uses ' "probable" as opposed to demonstration, not to certainty'.[191] The certainty of our faith depends upon an act of will which is influenced but not controlled by our reasoning. We find here a consideration of the place of the will in the act of faith which has been previously lacking.

At the beginning of 1848 Newman preached a series of sermons at St. Chad's Cathedral, Birmingham. These sermons indicate how Newman related his understanding of faith to ordinary believers. In the first of these sermons he states that 'Faith is the beginning of religion'.[192] He then argues that a real faith in God arises from the confirmation by miracles of our assumption that He is almighty.[193] This weak argument is popular rather than convincing, for Newman does not seek to justify the belief that God has wrought miracles. The danger with presuppositions is recognized in a later sermon when Newman points out that they may lead us to misinterpret the evidence. He illustrates this by reference to the understanding of Scripture.[194] Our duty in bringing others towards faith is not to argue with them but 'to win the mind, to melt the heart, to influence the will' with the 'cords of love'.[195] Moral purity is the way to find the truth for 'when the heart is wrong the reason goes wrong too'.[196] Above all we must bring our 'proud intellect into subjection' and 'believe' what is pronounced by authority even though we can neither 'explain' nor 'prove' it.[197] In the end faith is not within our control since it is supernaturally inspired—it is 'the fundamental grace which God gives us'.[198]

Sometime during Easter 1848 Newman tried again to understand how faith could be held to be certain. He posed the problem thus: 'Faith is conceived to be inconsistent with *doubt*. How then can it be the result of *reasoning*? for no reasoning, in moral subjects, leads to an indubitable conclusion.' How then is it that 'faith is *preceded* by reason, yet does *not depend* upon it'? Newman distinguishes here between 'objective' certainty which is 'a quality of conclusiveness' and subjective certainty (or certitude) which is 'a state of mind'. This state of mind follows our judgement that there is sufficient evidence 'for conviction' and that 'the conclusion *ought* to be believed'. Our mind takes the conclusion which it holds to be '*fide dignum* or *credibile*' and 'by an act of the will imposes belief on itself'. In the state of belief 'it drops altogether the logical considerations which led to that conclusion ... and uses that conclusion as a first principle, absolutely true'. The degree and type of evidence which makes a proposition credible varies from one individual to another. The only test that can be applied is that the 'proof of credibility' should lead the 'mind *prudently* to receive the conclusion for certain'. 'A probable argument' on its own 'can never be sufficient in prudence for certainty' but an accumulation of probabilities may lead to 'credibility in the conclusion and certainty in the mind'.[199]

In another series of notes which he probably wrote at this time, Newman expresses similar ideas but includes a recognition of the supernatural aspect of faith.[200] Faith is described as '*certus* because its assent is without doubt or fear' and '*inevidens*, because its method of proof is imperfect'. A distinction is drawn between 'human faith, or fides acquisita' and 'divine faith'. Human faith entertains conclusions as 'not more than credible', that is as 'morally (or practically) certain, though not without doubt and fear; or highly probable, or prudent to believe; or sufficient in itself, but not sufficient considering the great importance of the subject'. In other words it is the faith which we decide to adopt while recognizing that its antecedent reasonings 'do not absolutely lead to conviction'. 'Divine faith', however, 'receives' the conclusions 'as *certain*'. It is therefore 'not resolvable into its motiva' but is 'supernatural, and a divine gift'.[201] This view of faith is given dramatic expression in *Loss and Gain*, a semi-autobiographical novel which Newman published in 1848. In this 'Story of a Convert' faith is described as 'a duty' when we have 'good grounds for believing',[202] even if those grounds are not absolutely conclusive.[203] We fulfil our duty as we 'embrace' faith 'by an act of the will'. This adoption of faith is not simply of human origin for 'faith is a gift' which comes from God.[204]

Two brief unpublished notes of 1851[205] show Newman considering how he might write about the certainty of faith. There is nothing new in these sketchy outlines of his ideas. Two years later he gave some lectures on faith and certainty which are preserved for us in notes made by Father Edward Caswall.[206] Newman comments that he seems 'to have given these lectures ... with my Paper of Easter 1848 before me'.[207] In these lectures, as in the earlier paper, a distinction is drawn between 'objective' and 'subjective certainty'. Subjective certainty alone is 'certainty proper' being a 'state of mind' which 'admits of no degree'. Although Newman says that it is 'more properly called *certitude* than certainty,' he does not persist with this terminology. This state of mind is generated by 'a certain degree of moral proof' but once certainty is reached it 'does not vary' with its antecedent proofs. Newman recognizes that our certainty may in fact be erroneous but holds that the state of certainty appears the same to us whether its object is the truth or an error.

> When subjective certainty is the result of a truth it is called certainty. When subjective certainty is the result of error it is called obstinacy. The two states of mind are different in God's sight, but there is no human criterion for distinguishing them. . . .

All we can do is to 'look to the general effect in multitudes through a course of time'. According to Caswall's notes 'the Father [sc. Newman] thinks that the whole world of religion comes from conscience'. We attain faith as we recognize that while a conclusion is 'not absolutely demonstrated' yet the evidence for it makes it 'my duty to believe'. Regarding the conclusion as 'id quod prudenter credi debet' we follow our conscience and determine to believe it. The supernatural side of faith now appears as 'grace' which creates a 'fides divina' by raising our 'fides humana' 'above nature' and making 'the conclusion stronger than any human certainty'.

In 1853 Newman made three attempts to write about faith and certainty.[208] The first two are clearly related, the second being a development of the themes found in the first paper and written a fortnight after it. They deal with the nature of certainty. 'Assent' is divided into 'absolute assent', which includes 'certainty, persuasion, prejudice, unbelief', and 'conditional assent', which covers 'belief, doubt, conjecture, suspicion, scruples, etc.'.[209] Whether an assent 'shall be absolute or conditional' depends upon the will, for while antecedent reasoning indicates what form of assent should 'naturally' be given to its conclusion, the will alone finally determines what kind of assent is given. In this decision 'the will acts as a moral agent', acting rightly or wrongly according to whether or not it reflects the nature of the conclusion reached by the 'antecedent act of reason'. When an 'objective fact' is regarded as a 'subject of certainty', it is not viewed in relation to its premises but 'stands absolute, . . . as a first principle, and a starting point as if with an axiomatic force'. This is the basic distinction 'between conviction and certainty, the former is a conclusion, the latter a commencement; the former reasons, the latter perceives? feels.'[210] A further difference lies in the fact that:

> certainty . . . which . . . naturally follows upon conviction, . . . is under the control of the will. . . . The will cannot absolutely create it, for it is the natural and direct result of conviction, but the will can hinder that direct result taking place.

It can 'stifle certainty' and grant only a conditional assent. On the other hand 'the will cannot hinder an inference from premisses, when the premisses are clearly perceived, for that inference is of a necessary character.'[211]

The third unpublished paper from 1853 is entitled 'On the Certainty of Faith'. It is a much longer and more comprehensive study of the nature of assent and shows that Newman has reconsidered the ideas of the previous papers. Whereas we can demonstrate that some propositions are true, in other cases we can only prove that they are 'credible or rather *credificative*', i.e. that they are the proper object of belief. This latter proof is not 'by syllogism, but by induction, . . . not by one direct single and sufficient proof but by a complex argument consisting of accumulating and converging probabilities'. In a note in the margin Newman adds: 'Enlarge 1. on converging probabilities—question—whether they can make up a proof sufficient for *feeling*. I have no doubt of it.' In the *Grammar of Assent* we find this enlargement in the treatment of the 'Illative Sense'. While 'the logical process is always the same,' nevertheless 'the principles or premisses' of some subjects are easier to master than those of other subjects. In subjects which have 'difficult and recondite subject matter' the expert who has studied the material is more likely to come to the right conclusion than a person who is virtually unacquainted with the issues involved. In such cases it is wise to accept the decisions of the expert according to the dictum 'Cuique in arte suâ credendum'. Newman distinguishes the proof of credibility from scientific proof on the grounds that it does not invariably rest 'on generally received principles and . . . exact syllogisms' but is derived from 'the action of the individual mind, which knows what others may or may not know, and acts not necessarily by rule, but by practical expertness'.[212] The 'mental faculty' which considers the 'Evidentia Credibilitatis' is called our 'Prudentia or Judgment'.[213] He describes it as 'partly a natural endowment common to all, or a special gift to certain persons, partly the result of experience; and it varies in its worth . . . with the subject matter in which it is employed.' Each act of faith is preceded by some reasoning which shows the 'credibilitas' of its object. By our 'Prudentia', which is also called 'sagacity, common sense, . . . shrewdness, acuteness, . . . instinctive perception', we judge whether or not there is proof of credibility. Certainty involves 'a deliberate act of reflection' in which we consciously affirm our existing apprehension of a truth, whether known or believed, with reference to 'the motiva and . . . the evidentia of that apprehension'. Certainty is thus 'the judgment of a judgment, or an assent of the intellect to an assent'. Since certainty is an assent, it 'does not admit of degrees', but it has a greater or lesser effect on our actions 'according to the quality of the motiva/evidentia in the particular case'. Newman concludes this paper with a section 'On the process of supernatural faith, and the portion of it which is supernatural'. He holds that 'every step of the process . . . up to the assent to the credibilitas . . . is natural' and 'may be mastered by a mind destitute of the grace of Christ'. This process involves the judgement of the evidence and the assent of our 'prudentia' to the 'credibilitas' of the proposition concerned. This assent to 'credibilitas' may even be reflexively confirmed in an assent to its certainty. At this point, however, the mind 'does not yet believe' but only grants that the proposition is 'credible'. 'The steps which follow are rational, according to human reason, but supernatural also, or require grace' for their performance. They consist of a judgement that it is right 'to believe what is credible', a 'voluntas credendi, determining and commanding the intellect to believe', and finally 'the act of faith, in the intellect, thus commanded'. In this paper the rôle of the will is much less arbitrary and the nature of the difference between faith and certainty is perceived.[214]

In some notes headed 'Opus Magnum'[215] and dated 'In festo S. Gregorii, 1857', Newman outlines some ideas for 'a large work which is to go to defend the Church . . . as confronted with, and as against the penetrating knowledge, learning and ability of the scientific men and philosophers of the day'. From these rough notes it appears that Newman intended to defend the need to accept revelation on the grounds of the limitations of our knowledge. He writes that 'while . . . revelation must be strange, scepticism is as strange or stranger.' The existence of God may be proved 'from conscience . . . —the imperious voice' but it is a 'personal' proof, peculiar to each individual.[216] These notes soon peter out but Newman wrote several further notes about these problems on various dates between 1859 and 1865. The proof of the existence of God from conscience is developed, for instance, in a note in the Book of Sundries dated 7 November 1859.[217] Here Newman argues that while 'we may differ in moral judgment from others', we all recognize that 'feeling . . . which I call conscience'. This:

> feeling of a *law*, whatever its dictates, . . . is, not a law of the mind, but one of these phenomena which like thought or consciousness are bound up with or convey to me the idea and fact of my being *or* existence. . . . This sensation of conscience is the recognition of an obligation involving the notion of an external being obliging. I say this, not from any abstract argument from the force of the terms, (e.g. 'A Law implies a Lawgiver'), but from

the pecularity of that feeling to which I give the name of Conscience.

Thus the recognition of the existence of God is involved in my perception of 'my own existence'. Newman adds that this has been his 'own chosen proof of that fundamental doctrine for thirty years past'.[218]

In 1858 Mansel published his Bampton Lectures which we have discussed in the first chapter.[219] Mansel tried to show 'what limitations to the constructions of a philosophical Theology necessarily exist in the constitution and laws of the human mind'.[220] He argued that we must not seek for a '*speculative* knowledge' which 'aspires to behold God in His absolute nature' and results in 'nothing more than a tissue of ambitious self-contradictions'.[221] Our aim must be to accept in faith 'those *regulative* ideas of the Deity' which are revealed to us and 'which tell us, not what God is in Himself, but how He wills that we should think of Him'.[222] Newman read these lectures and wrote to Dr. Meynell about them.[223] He says that he agrees with Mansel in a number of points and wonders if Mansel has used his (i.e. Newman's) 'Protestant teaching' in forming his ideas.[224] He sent Meynell a copy of the *Oxford University Sermons* and was pleased to learn that Meynell considered he had anticipated Mansel while avoiding 'many of his errors'. Newman replied that he was not now inclined to re-issue the *Oxford University Sermons* with a new preface but 'to write . . . a new work . . . on "the popular, practical, and personal evidence of Christianity"'. The object of this book would be 'to show that a given individual, high or low, has as much right (has as real rational grounds) to be certain, as a learned theologian who knows the scientific evidence'.[225]

Two contemporaneous unpublished fragments are extant in which Newman approaches the problem.[226] The first merely indicates an intention to examine both the personal and the objective aspects of 'the motivum credibilitatis'.[227] In the second paper Newman holds that 'though the real source and cause of religious faith is beyond nature and actual reason, still reason is its antecedent, and cause *sine quâ non.*' Thus he proposes to examine the 'subjective, private, personal, and unscientific' qualities of faity and reason, following the lines suggested in the *Oxford University Sermons*. This way he hopes to show that 'even . . . children and . . . the most ignorant and dull peasant' have good grounds for their faith.[228] The following May, Meynell published an article in *The Rambler*, entitled 'The Limits of our Thought', which was inspired by Mansel's lectures. Newman wrote to say how much he had enjoyed reading it. He was especially glad to find Meynell expressing his own view that 'transcendent truths may admit of but *partial* communication to us' and so find expression in apparent 'contradictions' which are due 'to our ignorance'[229] and the 'infirmity of human thought'.[230]

The question of the understanding necessary for faith crops up in a note dated 17 September 1861.[231] Newman asserts that while 'you *can* believe what you cannot conceive', yet 'certainly I do not believe (except implicitly)—what I do not imagine.' What he means by the terms 'conceive' and 'imagine' is not very clear but this passage reveals that Newman is now beginning to consider the problems posed by apprehension as a condition of assent. The following month he was at Ventnor and wrote some outline notes headed 'Schema totius operis'[232] which deal with our ways of reasoning. In this work Book I was to discuss 'at great length' our 'faculty of semi-intuitions' and then describe 'certainty' which is 'the mind's reflexive ratification' of the conclusions of its reasoning. By 'semi-intuitions' Newman seems to be referring to our illations or informal reasoning processes. In the second book he planned to make a critique of science as 'a criterion of knowledge', showing that it depends upon 'the necessary assumption of first principles', while in Book 3 he would correlate the 'inductive' method of science and the 'deductive' method of theology.

Newman's private papers show that during the latter half of 1863 he had returned to the problem of faith and apprehension. On 7 July,[233] he noted that we cannot assent to 'mere imaginations' but only to those 'mental images' which 'are consistent in their parts' and so form 'the subject matter of judgments'. In an unfinished paper written a few months later[234] Newman deals with the problem of the meaning of statements about God. He holds that 'all our language about Almighty God . . . is analogical and figurative.' We can talk about God only 'in terms of our experience', and yet 'we are aware, while we do so, that they are inadequate'. All we can do is to 'set right one error of expression by another', and try 'to point . . . in the right direction'. During December 1863 Newman was toying with ideas which, he tells us, became the basis for his distinction between 'imaginative and notional apprehension'.[235] His immediate concern was the origin of our conceptions. Directly relevant to the emphasis he was to place in the *Grammar of Assent* on 'real' apprehension and assent is his assertion that 'the knowledge, which is most intimately our own, and directly personal to us, *lies* in our experience'. Our direct experience is extended by conceptions created by 'the association of ideas'.[236] The reality of 'past facts' is preserved by our 'memory' of them but once our conceptions are 'viewed separately from the memory of our experience' they become 'abstract and general'. These notions, as Newman was later to call them, 'are the formal life, intellectual and moral, into which our experience has developed'.[237] The self-consistency of a conception is no guarantee of its truth nor is inconceivability a necessary mark of its falsity.[238] On the other hand, the fact that an idea is strange or inconceivable is 'a strong antecedent argument' against its truth. The 'real force' of this argument 'is upon the imagination, not upon the reason'.[239] Newman here recognizes that we are much more influenced by 'images' than by 'abstract notions'. This recognition was to be very important in the *Grammar*.

The *Apologia pro Vita Sua*, which appeared in 1864, provides us with some autobiographical insights into Newman's search for certainty and his life-long opposition to 'liberalism'.[240] It reveals how Newman was constitutionally dissatisfied with faith as a stand in the face of uncertainty: he could be content only with certainty. In his Anglo-Catholic days he had a 'firm confidence'[241] in his position and describes it primarily in terms of confidence 'in the truth of a certain definite religious teaching'.[242] He writes that:

> from the age of fifteen, dogma has been the fundamental principle of my religion. I know no other religion, I cannot enter into the idea of any other sort of religion, religion as mere sentiment is to me a dream and a mockery.[243] . . . What I held in 1816, I held in 1833, and I hold in 1864. Please God, I shall hold it to the end.[244]

The limitations of reasoning in religious matters are recognized. Newman says that when people presented arguments to him he 'felt altogether the force of the maxim of St. Ambrose "Non in dialecticâ complacuit Deo salvum facere populum suum"' for he 'had a great dislike of paper logic. . . . It is the concrete being that reasons; . . . the whole man moves; paper logic is but the record of it.'[245] In the end, however, he came to the conclusion by a 'concatenation of arguments . . . that there was no medium . . . between Atheism and Catholicity'.[246] Since his understanding of his own existence, especially in terms of his conscience, compelled him to believe in the existence of God, he was 'led on into the Church of Rome'.[247] In this process he was not convinced by 'rigid demonstration' but 'by accumulated probabilities' from which God 'carries us on, if our will does but co-operate with His, to a certitude which rises higher than the logical force of our conclusions'.[248] The final '*submission* to the Catholic Church' came when this process had brought Newman to the point where he could do it 'without doubt and apprehension'.[249] Here we have an autobiographical example of the way to faith propounded in the *Grammar*. As we have already noted, Newman says that after he 'became a

Catholic', he had 'no variations to record, . . . no anxiety of heart whatever'.[250] He found in the authority of the Church the basis for a firm faith.[251]

In four fragments that have survived from 1865 we find Newman trying to clarify his understanding of 'certitude'. In one of these papers he compares 'the moral sense' and 'certitude', holding that they are 'natural' faculties which it would be 'most unnatural' of us 'never to exercise', even though we may err in using them. Certitude is not unavoidably entailed by reasoning but is 'a free act' made at the 'call of duty' on the basis of 'our best judgment'. The reasoning involved in this judgement is not 'logical demonstration' but 'practical and personal tact and skill, . . . a habit of mind which acts *pro re natâ*' and which is 'guided by practice and experience'.[252] In another fragment Newman questions whether we have any 'right . . . to indulge the feeling of certainty' in view of the fact that we cannot always distinguish between true and false feelings of certainty 'in concrete matters'. He wonders whether our beliefs 'in all concrete matters' should include 'a reserve of doubt'. This would mean that 'nothing has a claim to be believed and acted upon as absolutely true, but simply as probable, and as safe to hold and to follow'. Such is the nature of what Catholics call 'practical certainty'.[253] This was written on 26 June. By 20 July, however, Newman had given up this conditional view. He describes certitude now as 'an assent, deliberate, unconditional, and conscious, to a proposition as true' in which 'we do not at all admit the contrary idea' but regard it as 'an absurdity'. This state of mind is not controlled by 'the reasons which are its antecedents'. It 'stands by itself, as long as I choose, created and dependent on myself as an individual and free agent'.[254] These views are repeated in a fragment dated 25 September 1865, when certitude, 'viewed as a habit', is seen to admit of degrees although in itself it is 'an unconditional assent to a proposition as true'. Newman notes that certitude thus has 'a complex character, being of the form, not of "a is b" but of "that a is b is true"'.[255]

Eventually, however, Newman decided that he was approaching the problem of faith from the wrong angle. He describes the incident in *The Journal, 1859–79*:

> At last, when I was up at Glion over the Lake of Geneva, it struck me 'You are wrong in beginning with certitude—certitude is only a kind of assent—you should begin with contrasting assent and inference.' On that hint I spoke finding it a key to my own ideas.[256]

This occurred in August 1866. Newman did not finish the *Grammar of*

Assent until January 1870. From the interim we have a little unpublished material which indicates the views to be expressed in the *Grammar*.[257] Newman states in one note that 'devotion and social interchange of thought, . . . a good life and prayer for grace, and availing ourselves of the judgment of the wise' are necessary for attaining religious truth.[258] In another fragment[259] he deals with the differences between notions and 'concrete matter' as they affect inference and assent. Finally, before he published the *Grammar of Assent*, Newman submitted his material to Meynell, who was Professor of Philosophy at the Seminary at Oscott, so that he could correct anything 'which offends against doctrinal propriety or common sense'.[260]   Not altogether willingly Meynell went through the proofs and suggested some minor corrections. On 15 March 1870, the *Grammar of Assent* was published. It expressed the conclusions of Newman's life-long attempt to understand the certainty which belongs to faith. It was 'a great relief' to him when it was finished. Although Newman states that it was not written in response to a specific 'call',[261] it can be seen as his response to the 'call' of his age in the challenge of a 'liberalism' which was creating a crisis for faith.

3. NEWMAN'S INTELLECTUAL BACKGROUND

Before we turn to the *Grammar of Assent* itself we must try to determine the sources of Newman's thought and the degree to which he may have been influenced by them. In doing this, we are indebted to the unfinished and unpublished thesis of C. B. Keogh, *Introduction to the Philosophy of Cardinal Newman*, in which a great deal of the relevant material is collected.[262] One of the problems in seeking to establish the sources of Newman's thought is the fact that often he does not acknowledge any. This is probably because he himself did not remember or recognize where his ideas had come from. Newman's thought was primarily his own and while he might use ideas which he had learnt from others, he was not consciously seeking either to develop or to correct them. We might claim, therefore, that a certain idea used by Newman has come to him from someone else but we cannot be sure that Newman would admit this. In any case, the important thing for him would not be the origin but the value of an idea.

The fundamental influence on Newman's thought were the Fathers of the Church. He tells us that after his conversion in 1816 he read Milner's five-volume *History of the Church of Christ* and became 'enamoured' of its long quotations from the Fathers. Later, as he 'moved out of the shadow of . . . liberalism', he returned to the

Fathers and in the summer of 1828 he 'set about to read them chronologically'.[263] His numerous references to the Fathers in his publications reveal how well he knew them and the great respect with which he treated them. In philosophical matters he was particularly influenced by the Alexandrians, Clement and Origen.[264] It is in the thought of the early Church that we find Newman at home; medieval scholasticism and modern rationalism were alien to his mind and he never felt completely at ease when dealing with them. The other really great influence on Newman was Butler's *Analogy*. When asked to select one of Hurrell Froude's books as a keepsake, his first choice was the *Analogy*. Newman first studied the *Analogy* in 1825 and reports that it marked for him, as for 'so many, . . . an era in their religious opinions'. It was 'Butler's doctrine that Probability is the guide of life' that led him 'to the question of the logical cogency of Faith'.[265] But while he often refers to Butler and praises him highly,[266] Newman was also conscious of the difference between Butler's position and his own. In a letter in 1864, he put it that 'Butler tends to reduce certainty to a *practical* certainty' whereas Newman maintained that 'probabilities lead to a speculative certainty legitimately'.[267] While Butler's views were never far from Newman's thoughts about the logic of faith, they posed the problem rather than gave the final answer. It was the conviction of certainty, not the practical probability sufficient for the decisions of day-to-day living, that Newman wanted for faith.

We also find a number of references to Paley in Newman's writings.[268] He described Paley's argument as 'clear, clever, and powerful' but confesses that he has always regarded natural theology 'with the greatest suspicion' and 'could not give it' a 'high place among the arguments for religion'.[269] Paley's arguments were too clear to be convincing and their effect was to make men not humble believers but judges of the evidence for religion. Thus, while he did not 'undervalue' the 'force and serviceableness' of Paley's argument, Newman says that he prefers 'inquiry to disputation in a question about truth'.[270] He might refer to Paley but he is not really indebted to him.

Among the early influences upon his thought, Newman particularly mentions Thomas Scott. He says that Scott convinced him of the doctrine of the Trinity and that as an undergraduate he 'admired and delighted in his writings'.[271] When he became a fellow of Oriel, his friendships with Hawkins and Whately shared significantly in moulding his thought. Hawkins taught Newman to be exact in his thinking and impressed upon him the importance of the Church's tradition.[272] As for Whately, we have already quoted Newman's remark that it was Whately who taught him to think for himself.[273]

Newman's classical studies at Oxford introduced him to Greek philosophy. Though there are several references to Plato in *The Idea of a University*,[274] none of them is important and he is not mentioned at all in the *Grammar of Assent*. Aristotle seems to have exercised a much greater influence and Newman cites him as the authority in matters of logic.[275] Most of his references are to Aristotle's *Nichomachean Ethics* but he also mentions the *Rhetorics*[276] and he wrote an essay about the *Poetics*.[277] Keogh finds this adherence to Aristotle somewhat surprising since he considers that 'by natural temperament and through the influence of the Fathers the set of his mind was largely Platonic.'[278] On the other hand, as Dwight Culler informs us, the 'Noetics' of the Oriel Common Room were deeply indebted to Aristotle in whom 'they found an instrument . . . which precisely suited' their questioning methods.[279] Doubtless their enthusiasm affected Newman, although it is unlikely that Aristotle had any great influence over his thought. Newman defers to him as an authority but he does not appear to have tried to build his own thought on Aristotelian foundations. The position, rather, was that he was happy to refer to Aristotle when their thought coincided.

The only other philosopher whom he seems to have regarded as an authority was Lord Bacon. In the *Grammar of Assent* Newman states that Bacon:

> saw what others before him might have seen in what they saw, but who did not see as he saw it. In this achievement of intellect, which has been so fruitful in results, lie his genius and his fame.[280]

But though he is called 'our own English philosopher',[281] his value to Newman seems to have been mostly in providing illustrations for his ideas. When we turn to the British Empirical School, we find that while Newman knew Locke and Hume and shared their epistemological position, his thought was not consciously based upon them. They provided examples of ideas which he was concerned to advocate or to refute but his own constructive thinking developed independently of them. Apart from Locke's *Essay Concerning Human Understanding* and his *Thoughts on Education* and Hume's *Essay on Miracles*, we have no evidence that Newman read any of the works of these philosophers after his Oxford days. Hume's *Essay on Miracles* is attacked by Newman in his *Essay on the Miracles of Scripture*, in the *Oxford University Sermons* and in the *Grammar of Assent*.[282] As this is the only context in which Hume is mentioned by name, it is unlikely that he exercised any great influence on Newman's thought. Locke was held in high esteem by Newman who speaks of his great 'respect both for the character and the ability of Locke, for his manly simplicity and his out-spoken candour'.²⁸³ Even so, Locke only appears in the *Grammar of Assent* as an opponent whose ideas are contrasted with those of Newman.²⁸⁴ Although Newman says that 'there is so much in his remarks upon reasoning and proof in which I fully concur',²⁸⁵ he never instances Locke as an authority for any of his views. Locke's utilitarian views on education are attacked in *The Idea of a University*.²⁸⁶ When religious rationalism is censored in the *Oxford University Sermons* and in the *Essay on Development*, it is probably Locke's thought which Newman has particularly in mind. While, then, it is clear that Newman was aware of Locke's thought, he chose to respect Locke rather than to follow him. As for Berkeley, although Newman knew that there were apparent similarities in their thought, he was never interested enough to study him—and Zeno has demonstrated that Newman never really held Berkeleyan theories.²⁸⁷

In Newman's private papers we find a few references to other British philosophers such as Mill, Hamilton, Brown, Clarke, Stewart, and Reid, but these references do not indicate that these philosophers significantly influenced Newman.²⁸⁸ There is also a host of passing references in his works to Anglican divines. There are, however, no indications that any of them had any considerable effect on Newman's thought. The question of Coleridge's influence, however, is more debatable. On one occasion Newman stated that he 'never read a word of Coleridge. I was not even in possession of a single work of Coleridge's.'²⁸⁹ This was written when he was aged eighty-three and it is clear that his memory must momentarily have failed him. In an autobiographical note for 1835 he wrote that 'during this spring I for the first time read parts of Coleridge's works; and I am surprised how much I thought mine is to be found there.'²⁹⁰ A letter to R. H. Froude in 1836 describes Coleridge as 'looking at the Church, the Sacraments, doctrines, etc., rather as symbols of a philosophy than as truths'.²⁹¹ Coleridge's achievement in religious philosophy was summarized by Newman in an article in the *British Critic* for April 1839:

> While he indulged a liberty of speculation which no Christian can tolerate . . . he made trial of his age, and found it respond to him, and succeeded in interesting its genius in the cause of Catholic truth.²⁹²

Finally we may refer to Newman's quotation of Coleridge's *Aids to Reflection* in the *Grammar of Assent*.²⁹³ It is not possible to argue from all this that Newman was indebted to Coleridge but it is clear that he must have had a first-hand knowledge of his works.

In the *Stray Essays on Controversial Points* Aquinas is described as 'the greatest of theologians'[294] and in *The Idea of a University* as 'the champion of revealed truth'.[295] Newman's temper of mind, however, was not Scholastic and neither Aquinas nor any of the other Scholastics seem to have been important in the development of his thought. He never refers to the Scholastics for an authoritative opinion on the problems of faith and reason. In some unpublished notes on abstract ideas, Newman refers to the nominalist-realist controversy but admits that he is 'so little versed in the controversy' that he cannot be sure how his own views correspond to it.[296] Keogh holds that this unfamiliarity with Scholastic thought 'was not merely because the great neo-Scholastic revival had not begun in his day' but more 'because he did not feel at home amid the impersonal analyses and with the speculative method proper to Scholasticism'.[297] Newman much preferred the concrete and real to the niceties of notional abstraction.

Newman's knowledge of Continental philosophy and theology was neither great nor direct.[298] He quotes Pascal in 'Taylor's Translation'[299] but only to illustrate something which he had believed for a long time. Descartes is mentioned in the *Grammar of Assent*[300] and his methodology is implicitly rejected when Newman attacks the principle of universal doubt.[301] There are no grounds for supposing that either Pascal or Descartes was the source of any of Newman's ideas. His odd references to Montaigne[302] and to Malebranche[303] do not indicate any real acquaintance with their thought. We have already pointed out that Newman had very little direct knowledge of current German philosophy and theology. In a letter to W. S. Lilly in 1884 Newman wrote that he 'never read a word of Kant.'[304] In spite of the evidence of the partially cut copy of Kant's *Critique of Pure Reason* in Newman's room, we may accept that substantially he is stating the truth.[305] His main sources of information about recent German thought were secondary authorities and it is unlikely that this thought exerted any important positive influence upon Newman.[306]

The conclusion we reach when we try to determine the source of Newman's thought about the logic of faith is that the source is basically Newman himself. Although he was aware of other philosophical works, none of them dominated his thinking. Other philosophers might help to clarify his own thought either by providing illustrations of it or by raising objections which had to be countered, but in the end Newman's thought was indebted to no-one.[307] Keogh's comment on Newman's attitude to Berkeley is true generally of his attitude to other thinkers. Keogh suggests that Newman:

was sufficiently content with his own view of the matter not to wish it complicated by extraneous opinions, however similar; and there was always at the back of his mind a positive determination to avoid being unduly influenced by the theories of others.[308]

Newman was a solitary thinker who preferred to work out his ideas on his own without the encumbrance of the thoughts of others.[309] In the *Grammar of Assent* we are not presented with a system built upon someone else's foundations. The whole structure has been composed by Newman himself and is backed by his authority alone. That similarities can be traced with other thinkers is quite accidental, apart from the one exception of Butler's views on probability and practical certainty. While then, we attempt to determine how far Newman contributed to the nineteenth-century search for theological certainty, we must not be misled into thinking that he was consciously participating in the contemporary debate except in so far as he was drawn into it by his opposition to the 'liberalism' of the day. It so happens, however, that the fundamentally personal questions which Newman faced, and in the *Grammar of Assent* finally tried to answer, concerned the fundamental problem of this debate.

4. THE NATURE OF ASSENT

Contemporary dictionaries indicate that in Newman's time the term 'assent' could signify either abstract agreement to the truth of a proposition or personal commitment to a policy of action. The 1864 edition of *Webster's Dictionary*[310] confines 'assent' to the logical application, distinguishing it from 'consent', but *The Imperial Dictionary* and *A New English Dictionary* agree that the term covers both intellectual agreement to the truth of a proposition and consent of the will.[311] In the *Grammar of Assent* the term emphasizes the element of certainty in belief which interests Newman, for to assent to a proposition is to regard it with that 'unhesitating faith' which characterizes 'a believer'.[312] Before we analyse Newman's conclusions about the nature of belief and determine their significance, we must look briefly at Newman's general understanding of this concept of 'assent'.

Newman regards assent as a natural disposition of the mind which is necessary for thought and action.[313] If a particular assent is erroneous, this is the fault of the individual who gives it, 'and cannot avail to forfeit for him his natural right, under proper circumstances . . . to assent'. The answer to false assents is not to refuse assent but to educate the mind so that it grants its *imprimatur* only when it is correct to do so.[314]

Assent is described as the unconditional acceptance of a proposition as stating the truth.[315] When Newman says that it cannot exist without propositional expression,[316] he seems to have forgotten that while we can be aware of an assent only when it is expressed in a proposition, it is possible for assent itself to exist without linguistic expression. The difficulty is that from the very nature of the case such unexpressable or unexpressed assents cannot be expressed for the purposes of discussion without turning them into propositional form. Thus, although assent is in fact not restricted to what may be apprehended propositionally, our discussion of it is limited to what may be given verbal expression.

In the opening section of the *Grammar of Assent* Newman distinguishes assent from doubt and inference, describing them as the three ways of 'holding propositions',[317] and as expressed in the form of assertions, questions, and conclusions.[318] It is not made clear whether assent is to be regarded as an attitude to a proposition or a mental state expressed by a proposition. The proposition 'x is y' can function either as the object of an assent or as a statement of the assent itself. The difference between my assertion that 'x is y' and my assertion that 'I assent that x is y' concerns my consciousness of my attitude to the proposition, not any change in that attitude itself. In both cases I am stating that it is true that 'x is y', in the second case I am further declaring that I am conscious that I assert this. Thus while the proposition 'x is y' can express an assent, in the statement 'I assent that x is y', 'x is y' does not express my mental attitude at all but the object of it. This ambiguity is not cleared up by Newman but it is usually easy to discern from the context whether a proposition is being used as an assertion, expressing both a description and an assent to its truth, or simply as the object of an assent.

The essence of assent is both the expression of a relationship and the acceptance of it as true. When, for instance, we assent to the proposition 'x is y', we not only describe a relationship between 'x' and 'y' but also announce that this relationship is true. Newman speaks of this 'acceptance of a proposition'[319] as true as 'an act of the intellect'.[320] On the other hand he speaks of complex assent as 'indefectible',[321] suggesting that this form of assent at least has the character of a disposition rather than of a specific act. He does not discuss whether assent is to be classed as an act or as a state. From his description of it, however, it becomes clear that it must be regarded as a state into which an individual decides to enter by an act of the will. Once he has assented, he tends to remain in a state of assent, continuing without further decisions to accept the truth assented to. Initially, though, the assent is the result of a decision which the individual makes. At this point assent is an 'act', whereas later it is more appropriate to talk of it as a 'state' which was entered into by the act. 'Assent' thus denotes an attitude to the truth of a proposition adopted by an individual. Like adoption, it begins with a decision and continues as a state, only our language is too limited to reveal this change.

Assent may be made either to a simple proposition, (and have the form 'I assent that x is y'), or to the truth of a proposition, (and have the form 'I assent that x is y is true'),[322] or to the authority that states a proposition, ('I assent that the authority is true which affirms that x is y').[323] In each case it is the 'absolute reception of propositions as true'.[324] Newman can thus describe assent as:

> the mental assertion of an intelligible proposition, as an act of the intellect direct, absolute, complete in itself, unconditional, arbitrary, yet not incompatible with an appeal to argument, and at least in many cases exercised unconsciously.[325]

The definitive characteristic of assent thus comes out clearly as the unqualified acceptance of a proposition as true. Consequently assent is incompatible with doubt and inquiry for they imply that there is no certainty as to the actual truth. Newman holds, however, that it is perfectly consistent with an assent to investigate its grounds.[326] The reason for this distinction lies in Newman's understanding of the meaning of 'inquiry' and 'investigation'. 'Investigation' is a mental activity which is initiated purely by academic interest. It explores the grounds of the assent without any personal questioning of its truth. 'Inquiry', in contrast, is regarded as a search for support where the validity of a position is in doubt. With this understanding of its meaning, it is obvious that I cannot 'inquire' into what I assent to, for I cannot doubt and assent to the same thing at the same time. The consistency of investigation and the inconsistency of inquiry with assent thus lies in Newman's definition of those terms to describe questionings which arise from very different mental attitudes.[327]

Although certain conditions and antecedents, such as apprehension and reasoning, are required by the act of assent, the act itself is 'in its nature absolute and unconditional' for 'the circumstances of an act, however necessary to it, do not enter into the act.'[328] Just as there are no degrees between truth and falsity, so I either assent or do not assent.[329] Confronted with the proposition 'x is y', there are three possibilities open to me: to assent that 'x is y' is true, to assent that 'x is y' is in some degree uncertain, or to assent that 'x is y' is not true. What I cannot do is to refuse to assent to one of these three. While, then, assent may be given to propositions which express different approximations to the truth, it is not the assent but the truth-value of the proposition to which the assent is given which may vary. Newman puts it that:

> When I assent to a doubtfulness, or to a probability, my assent, as such, is as complete as if I assented to a truth: it is not a certain degree of assent.[330]

Thus 'Opinion' is an assent 'to the probability of a given proposition',[331] having the form 'it is true that it is probable that x is y'. The assent is absolute but the proposition to which it is given can express any approximation to the truth. The different forms of assent which are mentioned by Newman, such as real, notional, simple, complex, profession, credence, opinion, presumption, and speculation, do not mark varieties in the degrees of assent but varieties in the object of the assent. Newman mentions 'dissent' only briefly but what he says indicates that he regards unbelief as having the same logical status as belief.[332]

Newman distinguishes between 'simple' and 'complex' assent. 'Simple' assent is the assertion of a proposition which has the form 'x is y'. When they are first made, simple assents 'are often little more than prejudices'[333] and have behind them no conscious deliberation. If a simple assent is questioned, then the person assenting investigates his simple (but now conscious) assent. The result is either the surrender of the assent or its confirmation. If it is confirmed, the new assent:

> has the strength of explicitness and deliberation. . . . It is an assent, not only to a given proposition, but to the claim of that proposition on our assent as true: it is an assent to an assent, or what is commonly called a conviction.[334]

The form of such an assent is: 'I assent that x is y is true'. Newman calls this second, confirmatory form of assent 'complex or reflex' assent.[335] He holds that certain simple assents can be called 'virtual, material or interpretative' complex assents since only the 'occasion for reflection' is lacking to turn them into proper complex assents.[336] Complex assent is especially interesting to Newman because it is the form of certitude. Indeed, he uses the phrase 'complex assent' and the term 'certitude' synonymously.[337] One characteristic of simple assents is that they are exercised 'unconsciously'. Such assents cover 'our personal likings, tastes, principles, motives, and opinions', for of these the self is not usually explicitly aware. They are the most common type of assent. Complex assent, in contrast, must always 'be made consciously and deliberately'. The consciousness in complex assent does not end with the conciousness of the assent itself, but it extends also to the grounds which make the assent possible. Because complex assent is the confirmation of a previous assent, it is only possible where there are reasons available and known, after consideration of which the assent can be deliberately affirmed.[338] The complex assent of certitude, then, 'is a deliberate assent given expressly after reasoning' and can be described as 'that formal assent' by which I 'seal up the conclusions to which ratiocination has brought me'.[339]

Having described what Newman means by assent, we can now proceed with our analysis of the process by which, according to Newman, we come to assent.

Part III: The Condition of Assent

1. INTRODUCTION

THE preliminaries of any act are of two distinct types, its conditions and its antecedents. The *conditions* of an act are those preliminaries which must be present if the act is to take place at all. Their presence does not mean that the act must take place. They provide the situation which makes the act possible but do not themselves cause the act. The *antecedents* of an act are those motives and forces which, given the conditions necessary for the act, bring it about. We may grasp the distinction more clearly if we examine a specific act. Take, for instance, my decision to go to Church next Sunday for the morning service. Among the conditions which make this decision possible are my beliefs that there is a Church to which I can go and that there will be a morning service there next Sunday. I must believe these things before there can be any possibility of my making the choice. If I did not know that there was such a thing as a Church or if I knew that there was to be no morning service next Sunday, then the decision would be impossible. The conditions necessary for it would not be available. Granted, however, that the conditions are present, the knowledge that there will be a service in the Church next Sunday morning does not mean that I will decide to go to the service. I am no more persuaded to go to a service at Church by the information that there will be one than I am persuaded to go to a Bingo session by the news that one is being held. The antecedents of the act are those pressures and motives which lead me to decide to go. They may be of various kinds. I may decide to go to Church because my wife wants me to go, because I am inquisitive about what will happen, because it is my habit to attend or because I have an obligation to attend. Any of these reasons—or any combination of them—may provide the pressure which will convert the decision from a possibility into an actuality. We may say, therefore, that the *conditions* are those preliminaries which must necessarily be the case if the act is to be possible. They do not, however, bring about its actualization. The *antecedents* are those forces which, the conditions being present, lead to the actualization of the act.

In Newman's analysis of assent, we find that the condition of assent is the apprehension of its object. Before reason and conscience can lead us to assent, we must first understand what it is that we are asked to believe. Accordingly, the first third of the *Grammar of Assent*[1] is devoted to a discussion of the nature of apprehension and of its effects upon assent. The first chapter deals briefly with the 'modes' of 'holding' and 'apprehending' propositions. The second chapter is concerned with the problem of how far apprehension is necessary before assent can be granted. Newman proceeds in the third and fourth chapters to distinguish between 'notional' and 'real' apprehensions and to discuss the differences this makes to our assents. In the final chapter of this section he applies his findings to 'the matter of religion'. Our task now is to examine Newman's thought on these matters. We shall do it under two heads. First we shall discuss his claim that apprehension is a condition of assent. Secondly we shall examine his distinction between 'real' and 'notional' apprehension and its effect on assent.

2. APPREHENSION AS THE CONDITION OF ASSENT

In this section we are to examine Newman's thesis that apprehension is the condition of assent. If this is true, it means that assent, and so faith itself, can only exist where the believer understands what he believes. First we shall describe what Newman means by apprehension and how he understands its relation to assent. We shall then discuss what is implied in such a relationship and make some criticisms of Newman's views on the subject.

a. The Nature of Apprehension

In view of the importance of apprehension as a condition of assent, Newman has surprisingly little discussion of its essential nature. When he states that 'real apprehension is . . . an experience or information about the concrete,'[2] he shows that 'apprehension' can refer to two ways of understanding. It can be used to describe both direct perception ('experience') and the discernment of meaning ('information'). In the former sense the term expresses an immediate recognition of the truth, 'a perception of facts without assignable media of perceiving'.[3] Here 'apprehension' includes such varied mental acts as 'a just view of a man's conduct',[4] the perception of individual things[5] and a child's recognition of God.[6] In the latter sense 'apprehension' expresses the perception of the meaning of words and statements. In either case the significant factor is that the individual understands what is presented to him, whether it be a concrete object or a verbal expression. Since the

Grammar of Assent is mainly interested in assents which can be expressed in the form of statements, we find that Newman generally uses the term 'apprehension' in the sense of 'an intelligent acceptance of the idea or of the fact which a proposition enunciates'.[7] That is, 'apprehension' usually means the discernment of the meaning of a statement.

Newman describes the act of apprehending a statement as 'our imposition of a sense on the terms of which' it is 'composed',[8] or as 'the interpretation of the terms of which it is composed'.[9] We apprehend a proposition when we mentally co-ordinate the combination of words with that to which it refers. The use of the term 'imposition'[10] in this context is unfortunate for it suggests that each individual is responsible for determining what any particular word or combination of words signifies to him. The fact that we can communicate with each other by means of language shows that apprehension is not so arbitrary. Apprehension does, however, have a personal aspect and this is suggested by Newman when he describes it as an 'entering into'[11] the reference of a proposition. His terminology is much to be preferred when he speaks of apprehension as 'interpretation'.[12] When we interpret, we take signs which of themselves are meaningless and discern what they are intended to convey. The signs are media of communication. They have value only so far as the interpretation corresponds to the content to be communicated.

Newman distinguishes between 'apprehension' and 'understanding'. He complains that 'understanding' is a word 'of uncertain meaning' since it may refer either to 'comprehension' or to 'apprehension'.[13] The distinction between these two concepts is very important for his thesis. 'Comprehension' involves a full and complete knowledge of its object whereas 'apprehension' designates only a partial knowledge.[14] We may properly claim to have apprehended a proposition when we have not completely grasped all that it signifies.[15] To claim, therefore, that apprehension is a condition for assent does not imply that I must completely understand the object of my assent before I can assent to it. It is sufficient if I grasp part of its meaning. Assent thus requires only a limited, not a complete, understanding of its object.

This distinction between apprehension and comprehension raises the problem of how far a proposition must be understood before it can be said even to be 'apprehended'. Newman's answer to this question is that we have apprehended a proposition when we have grasped what is expressed in its predicate. He states that:

> in a proposition one term is predicated of another: the subject is referred to the predicate, and the predicate gives us information

about the subject; therefore to apprehend the proposition is to have that information. . . . Therefore I apprehend a proposition, when I apprehend its predicate. . . . The very drift of the proposition is to tell us something about the subject; but there is no reason why our knowledge of the subject, whatever it is, should go beyond what the predicate tells us about it. Further than this the subject need not be apprehended: as far as this it must; it will not be apprehended thus far, unless we apprehend the predicate.[16]

In other words, given the statement 'x is y', of which 'y' is the predicate, Newman holds that we apprehend this statement if we apprehend 'y'. We shall consider the validity of this position later. We shall also suggest that Newman is to be criticized for failing to consider how far the separate constituent terms of a proposition must be individually apprehended before the proposition itself can be apprehended.

b. Apprehension as Necessary for Assent

According to Newman, assent is only possible where its object is apprehended. Although assent is 'absolute and unconditional' in itself, 'it cannot be given except under certain conditions'. One of these 'conditions' is the apprehension of its content.[17] This means that our assent is restricted to those ideas and propositions which we are able to understand in some way or other. The reason for this restriction is that assent is never a blind commitment to an incomprehensible assertion but the deliberate avowal of the truth of a particular proposition. Such an avowal is only possible where there is 'some intelligent apprehension'[18] of the matter under consideration. We cannot assent to a statement until we understand it sufficiently to be able to decide whether or not we consider it to be true.

Newman uses this characteristic of an assent to distinguish it from an assertion. An assent must be 'accompanied by some apprehension of the matter asserted'[19] while an assertion need not be. When we assert, we affirm a proposition without necessarily having any idea what it means. A three-year-old child who has been listening to his older brother doing his homework may repeat '$a^2 = b^2 + c^2$' but not have a clue about what it means. He cannot assent to it until he understands enough mathematics to be able to grasp what it is all about. This need for apprehension also distinguishes an act of assent from an act of inference. An 'inference requires no apprehension of the things inferred'[20] for when we reason we do not need to understand the denotation of the terms involved in our reasoning. We are only concerned with their interrelations. With this minimal knowledge we can manipulate them correctly to achieve a valid conclusion. Newman puts it in this way:

> We cannot give our assent to the proposition that 'x is z' till we are told something about one or other of the terms, but we can infer 'if x is y, and y is z, that x is z', whether we know the meaning of x and z or no.[21]

As we have already noted, Newman considers that we have apprehended a proposition when we have understood its predicate.[22] This does not make it clear how we can assent to the mysteries and paradoxes which are part of religious belief. Newman defines a mystery as 'a proposition conveying incompatible notions, or ... a statement of the inconceivable'. He argues that in such cases we can give assent if our apprehension of the proposition is sufficient to enable us to 'recognize it to be a mystery'. This means that 'the same act ... which enables us to discern that the words of the proposition express a mystery, capacitates us for assenting to it.'[23]

Newman is careful in this respect to point out that he is dealing with mysteries and not with nonsensical groups of words. 'Words which make nonsense, do not make a mystery.'[24] The distinction between a mystery or paradox and nonsense is not, however, simply a matter of our apprehension. Whether we class a statement as a paradox rather than as nonsense does not depend simply upon the difficulty we have in understanding it as a whole. It depends upon whether we believe that we have good reason to take the statement seriously in spite of its difficulty. Consider, for instance, the statement: 'So the Father is God, the Son is God, and the Holy Ghost is God, and yet there are not three Gods: but one God'. If its terms are apprehended at all, we may find that for one person the statement is nonsense, since it is nonsense to say that three Gods are one God, while for another it is the enunciation of a paradox about the divine mystery. What makes the second person treat the statement seriously, i.e. as a paradox, is the fact that he has certain reasons which lead him to believe that the statement refers to some aspect of the being of God. Only for the second person is assent to the statement possible for we cannot properly ascribe truth to what we consider to be nonsense. In his example, then, two people have the same apprehension of a statement but differ in their conclusions about its nature as paradox or nonsense. Assent, therefore, is not made possible simply because the terms of a nonsensical/paradoxical statement are apprehended sufficiently to see that they denote the inconceivable. If this were the case, nonsense statements would be eligible for assent.

Assent to a mystery depends upon the acceptance of reasons which lead us to believe that the statement does refer to something. It is not clear that Newman recognizes this point. When he writes about our apprehending a statement so that we 'recognize it to be a mystery', he may be referring merely to our recognition of the mutual incompatibility of its contents. In this case Newman is wrong in holding that such an 'apprehension' is sufficient to make assent possible. We do not *apprehend* a statement when we realize that it unites 'incompatible notions'[25] but make a *judgement* about it. On this interpretation, Newman's view of the possibility of assent to the divine 'mysteries' is inadequate. On the other hand, Newman may mean that when we apprehend a statement expressing a mystery, we apprehend it not only as uniting incompatible ideas but also as referring to something beyond the limits of our conception. In this case, our 'apprehension' of the 'mystery' not only requires an understanding of its terms but also involves the reasons which lead us to think that it refers to something. If this is what Newman means, then he recognizes that there must be reasons which lead us to take paradoxes seriously and so be able to assent to them. Which interpretation of Newman is correct is not made clear by the *Grammar of Assent*.

c. The Implications of Apprehension being a Condition of Assent

By holding that assent is only possible where its object has been apprehended, Newman shows that while an assent may involve a 'leap', it is never a 'blind leap'. Not only must propositions have meaning but that meaning must be at least partially known to us if we are to be able to assent to them. We cannot assent to such a theological statement as 'the polar character of the ontological elements is rooted in the divine life, but the divine life is not subject to this polarity,'[26] unless this statement has some meaning for us. If it has no meaning for us, we can only assert it uncomprehendingly. Since, therefore, our beliefs are limited to what we can apprehend,[27] we may infer that our assent is confined to the limits of our apprehension. The assent which is given to a particular statement will thus vary according to the various apprehensions of it attained by different people. Take, for example, the case of assent to the statement, 'We worship one God in Trinity, and Trinity in Unity.' We will apprehend this statement differently according to our mental abilities and theological knowledge, and our assents will correspondingly differ. Each of us will assent to what he has apprehended of its meaning.

This leads us to the question whether a person who assents to a statement on the basis of a limited apprehension of its meaning is thereby committed to assent also to all those things it expresses and implies which he has not apprehended in it before his act of assent.[28] Newman holds that a person is so committed. He argues that in making the act of assent the believer gives implicit assent to all that is contained in the proposition concerned, including what may be derived from it by analysis and inference. He states that:

> as regards the Catholic Creed, if we really believe that our Lord is God, we believe all that is meant by such a belief; or, else, we are not in earnest, when we profess to believe the proposition. In the act of believing it at all, we forthwith commit ourselves by anticipation to believe truths which at present we do not believe, because they have never come before us.[29]

This position extends our assent beyond what we have consciously apprehended. First it extends it to cover those elements which are denoted by the proposition but which we have been unable to grasp because of our limited apprehension. Secondly, it includes those elements which are entailed by the proposition but are not contained in its expression. A given proposition may contain ideas 'a, b, c, and d', and these ideas imply 'x, y, and z'. When I assent to a statement expressing the proposition, my assent may be on an apprehension limited to 'a and b' and the implication 'x'. Newman's position is that by assenting to my limited apprehension of the proposition, I am unavoidably committed to holding further that 'c and d' and 'y and z' are true. In religious matters this means that my assent to a dogmatic proposition is implicit assent to all that is included in that proposition and to all that can validly be inferred from it.[30]

At this point Newman has misunderstood the relation between apprehension and assent. Assent is the recognition that what is understood to be the meaning of a proposition is true. This recognition is not an automatic one but a choice made by the individual and directed to what he has understood. If I apprehend a proposition as meaning 'a and b' together with the implication 'x', when I assent to that proposition I decide that 'a and b' and the implication 'x' are true: I do not make any decision about 'c and d' and 'y and z' which are not before me. If I am then confronted with a proposition which I apprehend to contain 'a, b, c, and d' and to imply 'x, y, and z', I am faced with further material about which I must make a separate decision. The fact that the two propositions are expressed in the same form of words only conceals the fact that in the matter of assent they are two propositions. Newman, it seems, believes that in apprehending the first proposition and making a decision about it, I am also deciding about the second proposition. He fails to recognize that in assenting to the proposition which I have apprehended as 'a, b, and x', I assent to what I have understood and that a proposition which I later understand to contain 'a, b, c, and d, x, y, and z' is a different proposition for me to consider. I will assent to that part of it which is contained in my existing assent but I must decide whether or not I will assent to the further material. This explains how a person may withhold his assent to implications which are later drawn out of a statement to which he has previously assented.[31] His refusal to assent to the new material does not mean that he now withdraws his previous assent. I may continue to hold that 'a, b, and x' are true but refuse to accept that 'c and d, y and z' are true. Such withholding of assent is quite proper and consistent when it is accepted that assent is made only to what is consciously apprehended. In the case of implications, there is the additional reason that conclusions reached by inference are themselves 'conditional'. This, as we shall see,[32] is recognized by Newman and means that we are not compelled to assent to the conclusions of reasoning even though we assent to their premises.

Since assent can only be given to what is apprehended, assent is restricted to the objects and ideas of which we are conscious. If we are not conscious of something, we cannot be said to apprehend it. Just as simple assent, however, is assent which we give without being conscious that we have given our assent, so we need not be aware of our apprehension. Apprehension does not demand a self-conscious awareness of its reference, but unless the mind is aware of what it is apprehending, it is nonsense to speak of apprehension. This means that we do not assent to those things of which we are not aware even though we may unconsciously accept them as true in our thought and action. A man may act in accordance with certain precepts and thereby apparently accept them as true, but until he becomes conscious of them he cannot be held to assent to them. One consequence of this is that a person may affirm certain principles in his behaviour but paradoxically refuse to assent to a proposition which expresses them. We are then faced with the situation that while we cannot say that the person assents to the proposition, we can explain his thought and action only on the basis of his unconscious acceptance of their truth. This may appear to be an odd or even a self-contradictory situation, but it is fully consistent with the logic of assent. Assent is not the unexamined or unconscious affirmation of a statement but the deliberate affirmation of its truth. Only by being a conscious act directed towards an object of which we are aware can assent have that element of decision for truth which is its essential nature.

d. Criticism of Newman's View of the Nature of Apprehension and of its Relation to Assent

Our first criticism of Newman is that he does not discuss the problem of how far the separate terms of a proposition must be understood before we can claim to have apprehended the proposition that they form. He limits his exposition to the nature of the apprehension of whole propositions. For instance, in Newman's view, we apprehend the statement, 'Jesus Christ is the Author of our salvation because He was the incarnation of God' if we can apprehend its predicate.[33] But, we may ask, to what degree have we to apprehend the terms 'God', 'salvation', and 'incarnation' before we can claim to have apprehended the predicate which contains them? Is any apprehension of their meaning, no matter how slight and inaccurate, sufficient? Newman does not discuss the problem. This omission suggests that he has not perceived the complexity of the problem which has been raised, the problem of how far we must understand before we can claim to assent or believe. In Newman's defence, however, we may note that his position limits our assent to what we have apprehended. Thus any degree of apprehension is sufficient for assent since it is to that understanding alone that we grant our assent. This means that two people may assent to a particular statement while holding widely divergent interpretations of its meaning. Further to this, we may note that Newman does not investigate the restrictions which are imposed upon our apprehension by our limitations as human beings. In his introduction to the relation of apprehension to assent in religion,[34] he mentions that our apprehension may not extend to all the content of revelation[35] but he does not pursue the matter. This is a pity for the question is important in determining the possible extent of our religious assents. The problem was not unknown to him, however, for in the unpublished papers at the Oratory Newman discusses how far our experience limits our religious understanding.[36]

Our major criticism of Newman's understanding of apprehension concerns his view that we can claim to apprehend a proposition if we apprehend its predicate alone. We cannot accept that this states the minimum required for the apprehension of any proposition. Newman gives two examples in support of his position, namely the statements, 'Trade is the interchange of goods' and 'Lucern is food for cattle'.[37] Significantly, these two statements have the form of definitions. A definition regards the subject as an unknown which is made known by the predicate. Unless the predicate is apprehended, the whole definition is meaningless. If the predicate is apprehended, then at least part of the content of the subject is made known. As this is the purpose of the definition, it can thus be said to be apprehended. So far Newman is correct. Unfortunately he does not seem to recognize that what he has stated to be the condition for the apprehension of propositions is actually only the condition for the apprehension of analytic propositions. To demonstrate this, let us examine two synthetic propositions which have the same subjects as the analytic propositions used by Newman: 'Trade is a method of promoting international co-operation', and 'Lucern produces tender beef in cattle'. According to Newman both these statements can be apprehended so long as their predicate is apprehended. We can test this by substituting 'Jom' and 'Drit' for the subjects of the propositions. We should then be able to apprehend: 'Jom is a method of promoting international co-operation', and 'Drit produces tender beef in cattle'. This is clearly not the case. In neither instance do we grasp what the propositions are trying to express—in the former 'Jom' could refer to 'negotiation', 'fear', or 'war' while in the latter case the subject could be 'turnips', 'milk', or 'grass' for all that the predicate does to specify it. Inability to apprehend the subject of the proposition here prevents the proposition as a whole being apprehended.

Newman in fact has defended his position in terms of the case of analytic propositions. His statement that 'in a proposition . . . the subject is referred to the predicate, and the predicate gives us information about the subject',[38] is true of all propositions but he proceeds to interpret it according to the peculiar pattern of analytic propositions. Here the predicate, as explicatory of the subject, is regarded as an expression which makes the subject known. The abstract form of such a proposition is '$x=y$': where one of the elements is understood, then the meaning of the other is revealed. In a synthetic statement we have a different relationship between the subject and the object which means that such a proposition can be apprehended only when all its elements have been grasped. This is because the meaning of the whole depends upon the interrelation of all the parts. It has the basic form 'y is attributed to x'. Even though 'y' may be known, unless the reference of 'x' is also known, the statement will be meaningless for there will be no way of discovering what is meant by attributing 'y' to 'x'. Accordingly we cannot accept Newman's view that 'I apprehend a proposition, when I apprehend its predicate'[39] as true of all propositions. Its truth is limited to the case of analytical propositions.

If we consider the relationship of apprehension to assent, the validity of this criticism becomes even clearer. Newman holds that when we assent, we grant to be true the information which the predicate gives us about the subject.[40] He also holds that we can do this when the subject is unknown to us. This is to say that we can decide that a predicate gives a true description of something that we do not know. In fact we can assent to a description, i.e. we can be prepared to call it true, only when we can compare that description with what it describes and so judge whether it actually does correspond to it. Thus before we can assent to a statement we must apprehend both its subject and its predicate. Newman has not noticed in the case of his examples[41] that there is an essential difference between the unconditional recognition of a proposition as true and an agreement concerning the meaning that is to be given to a certain word. In the latter case, that of definition, the question of 'truth' is inapplicable because the matter does not concern truth or falsity. When I agree to use a term 'T' as meaning 'm', I do not assent to any synthetic statement which gives information and whose truth may be questioned. All I do is to consent to mean 'm', whose reference I know, every time I use 'T'. Only where the truth/falsity relationship is involved is it relevant to talk about assent. Just as the apprehension of the predicate alone is inadequate for the apprehension of a synthetic proposition, so the apprehension of the predicate alone provides no sufficient basis for assent.

If our criticisms of Newman's understanding of apprehension and its relation to assent are basically correct, then his views about 'indirect assent' are only partly acceptable. Newman holds that 'indirect assent' can be given to a proposition of which neither the subject nor the predicate is apprehended,[42] if that proposition is made the subject of another statement whose predicate is apprehended. For instance, if we apprehend the predicate 'is true', then we can, according to Newman,[43] make an inapprehensible statement the subject of another proposition which is apprehensible since its predicate is 'is true'.[44] Assent which is then given to the composite proposition is 'indirect assent' to its subject because it is 'assent to its truth'.[45] Another form of 'indirect assent' is to make the inapprehensible proposition an explicit assertion of an authority to which we assent.[46] Newman thus holds that we are able to assent indirectly to an inapprehensible proposition by assenting either 'to the truth of the inapprehensible' proposition or 'to the veracity' of the authority which asserts it.[47] This position apparently offers a means of overcoming difficulties of apprehension in matters of belief. If we cannot apprehend an article of faith itself, we can assent to it indirectly when it is made the subject of a statement about its truth or about the authority which asserts it. A 'Catholic' can in this way assent to dogmatic statements which he 'cannot understand' on the basis of his 'implicit faith' in the 'word' of the Church. 'Even what he cannot understand, at least he can believe to be true; and he believes it to be true because he believes in the Church.'[48] An inapprehensible dogma thus becomes for Newman a candidate for indirect assent if it is expressed as an explicit statement of the Church and if 'whatever the Church states is true' is an apprehended proposition. To this understanding of indirect assent we raise no objection, except to point out that the assent is not given to the inapprehensible proposition but to the authority which states it.

We cannot, however, accept what Newman states about 'indirect assent' to the inapprehensible subjects of propositions whose predicate is 'is true'. We cannot in this way avoid the need to apprehend the object of our assent. For us to be able to hold that a statement 'is true', we must be able to understand its meaning and to determine whether or not it is correct. In attempting to distinguish between assent to a proposition and assent to the truth of what it asserts, Newman has failed to recognize the purely formal character of the predicate 'is true'. In the case of the proposition 'P', Newman apparently holds that assent to it can be given in these two forms: i. 'I assent to P', and ii. 'I assent that P is true'. The first case is one of straightforward plain assent which obviously requires the apprehension of 'P'. It can be expressed as 'I hold that P is true.' In the second case our assent has the form 'I hold that it is true that P is true.' In fact the duplication of 'is true' adds nothing to the original proposition except strictly unnecessary emphasis: if something is true, it is true, and to assert that its truth is true is needless repetition. Therefore, since the meaning of 'I assent that P is true' is essentially the same as 'I assent to P', so must its conditions be the same. To assent to the 'truth' of 'P' involves an apprehension of 'P' just as much as plain assent to it. Although the two statements are differently expressed, they basically have the same logical structure.

e. Conclusion

In conclusion, we fully agree with Newman when he holds that assent can only be given to what is apprehended. Unless we can understand a proposition, we cannot judge that it is true. This implies that our assent to the truth of a proposition is limited to what we can grasp of its meaning. We cannot, however, accept Newman's view that we have fulfilled the minimum requirement for apprehension when we have apprehended only the predicate of a proposition. In the case of a synthetic proposition the whole proposition must be apprehended before we can understand it and assent to it. The fact that Newman considers that apprehension is a condition of assent indicates that he is concerned with assent as a personal rather than as a logical matter. Our bare apprehension of a proposition does not influence the assent itself but makes it possible for *us* to assent to it.

3. THE TWO TYPES OF APPREHENSION AND THEIR INFLUENCE ON ASSENT.

In this section we are to examine the distinction which Newman makes between two forms of apprehension. He holds that we can understand a statement either as an 'image' of something we could experience or as an expression of a certain idea.[49] In the former case our apprehension is 'real' and in the latter case 'notional'. After we have discussed these two forms of apprehension and their application to religion, we shall consider the influence they each have upon the act of assent. Finally we shall make some comments on the position maintained by Newman. In brief, we accept the distinction and hold that Newman is correct in pointing out that our mental 'images' of real things generally have far greater influence over us than our notions and ideas.

a. The Distinction between 'Real' and 'Notional' Apprehension

The distinction which Newman draws between 'real' and 'notional' apprehension is based on his understanding of the constitution of reality. He holds that 'all things in the exterior world are unit and individual, and are nothing else.'[50] These 'unit realities' are the objects of our experience.[51] A statement which is 'really' apprehended is one which is understood as expressing such a 'unit reality'. Its 'terms stand for things external to us'[52] and give us information which we interpret in terms of our own experience of reality. A proposition which I 'really' apprehend is thus a proposition which refers to an experiential situation and which I understand in terms of my own remembered experiences.

When Newman talks about the 'real' and about 'experience', he does not restrict himself to the limits of sense-perception. The 'experience' which is the criterion of the 'real' includes that of 'our mental sensations' (as in the aesthetic experience expressed by 'The prospect is charming') as well as that of 'our bodily senses' (as in the visual experience expressed by 'The sun shines').[53] Newman holds that we can have a real apprehension of 'mental acts of any kind, of hope, inquiry, effort, triumph, disappointment, suspicion, hatred and a hundred others'. We can have a 'vivid image of certain anxieties or deliverances', and understand imaginatively the content of ' "lovely", "vulgar" . . . "a catastrophe" '.[54] Again, Newman states that 'facts, causes, effects, actions, qualities' are all 'things'. As such they come within the sphere of what is 'real'.[55]

Newman speaks of real apprehension in terms of 'images'. He considers that a real proposition does not merely describe a situation but evokes in us a mental experience or picture of that situation. What we mentally perceive of the 'unit reality' described by a proposition is our 'image' of it. Newman holds that this real apprehension of a proposition is made possible by the faculty of memory. He writes that:

> memory consists in a present imagination of things that are past; memory retains the impressions and likenesses of what they were when before us; and when we make use of the proposition which refers to them, it supplies us with objects by which to interpret it. They are things still, as being the reflections of things in a mental mirror.[56]

Accordingly, while real apprehension deals with propositions about things and not with the things themselves, it may still be said to be 'an experience or information about the concrete'.[57] It participates through the memory in the immediacy of the direct perception.[58] Without the memory's faculty of re-presenting previous experiences (in the wide sense in which Newman understands the extent of the 'real'), we would be unable to entertain the reference of a proposition as a mental 'image'. Our memory recalls our experience of the real and re-presents it to us when something 'real' is expressed in a proposition. In this way we are able to grasp the reference of the proposition as an object. In the case of an 'image' whose reference could be any one of several experiences (e.g. the image of 'the flavour of a peach' when I have tasted several peaches), the memory does not present us with something which is the common factor of all the relevant experiences. It re-presents either one of the experiences or elements of several of them. All the images produced by our memory are images of what is real.[59]

Real apprehension, however, is not limited to the actual experience of the individual. We can have a real apprehension of propositions which refer to objects we have not experienced and maybe never could experience directly. This is made possible by our ability to construct out of our remembered experiences images of what we have not experienced. These 'new images' are 'mental creations' but 'are in no sense abstractions. . . . They are concrete units' giving us a mental experience parallel to that we have when we remember our actual experiences. This means, for example, that we can have a real apprehension of a unicorn, even though we have seen no pictures of one, if we can be given a description of it in terms of our remembered experiences. The importance of this 'faculty of composition'[60] is seen when we consider the objects of religious faith which can never be apprehended directly.

We now turn to examine what Newman considers to be the other form of apprehension, 'notional apprehension'. In doing this we cannot completely lay aside the 'real', for notions are our 'abstractions and generalizations' from the real. 'The informations of sense and sensation' provide the 'initial basis' of notions.[61] A notion, however, is something which has wider reference than the individual case of unit reality. It expresses what is common to two or more particular cases by the removal of what is particular to each of them. The resulting idea can thus be abstracted from the individual case and be applied in more than one instance. Newman regards our production of notions as arising automatically out of our acts of perception.[62] When we consider an object, we see it not only as itself but as a member of a class, i.e. as it is related to other objects. In this way our experience both contributes to and, at the same time, is controlled by our thought. The categories of class and of relation by which our experience is ordered are produced by abstraction from our experience. We do not, for instance, have a basic idea of what is meant by 'table' and then find that certain objects fit this class. Rather, we note that certain objects have a common shape or use (or both) and denote this common characteristic by the term 'table'. Similarly our idea of the relationship of 'cause' does not come to us *a priori* but is derived from a study of actual relationships.[63] Whenever, then, in our future experience we find objects or relationships which embody these common characteristics, we subsume them under the concepts of 'table' or of 'cause'. Since notions describe what is abstracted from the 'unit realities' of actual experience, Newman holds that they refer to 'ideas existing in our own minds, and . . . nothing outside of them',[64] that is, they refer to 'our own thoughts'.[65] When, therefore, we deal with notions, our 'mind contemplates its own creations instead of things'.[66] This creative activity of the mind is not arbitrary for its notions are created out of the 'real' of experience. A notion does not denote a particular object but it does denote what can be found in a particular object or in a particular relation of objects. It expresses a certain 'real' thing or relation which is found, with individual accidental additions, in different instances.

Notions are essential if we are to understand the world and our experience of it. It is through notions that we are able 'to compare and to contrast' and so to order the diverse content of our experience.[67] Newman's description of notional apprehension as 'to have breadth of mind but to be shallow' is not adverse criticism for this character makes it 'the principle' of the 'advancement' of knowledge. 'Without the apprehension of notions we should for ever pace round one small circle of knowledge'[68]—the circle of what we directly perceive. The possibility of reasoning depends upon notional understanding. Since notions allow our thought to extend beyond the particular, they provide the basis of 'proof, analysis', and 'comparison'.[69] Our acts of inference, so far as they are conducted in words, use notions.[70] When we come later to discuss 'inference', we shall find that Newman is aware of the inadequacies as well as the essential value of notions for reasoning. In the meantime, we must note that just as the process of inference uses notions, so the apprehension of its conclusions must be notional. This is because a conclusion, *qua* conclusion, is considered not for its own sake but in its relation to other ideas. A proposition which expresses a conclusion can, however, also be 'really' apprehended when it is grasped as an 'image', independently of the ideas which have led to it as a conclusion in the act of reasoning.[71]

The distinction which Newman draws between real and notional apprehension refers to our apprehension of a proposition, not to the proposition itself nor to the intention of the person who makes it. Since the distinction lies in the ways we are able to apprehend the statements presented to us, it should not surprise us to find that the same proposition can be interpreted notionally and really by different people.[72] When Newman discusses 'belief in one God',[73] he suggests that 'the notion and the reality' expressed in a statement about God 'are represented by one and the same proposition, but serve as distinct interpretations of it'.[74] Not all propositions can be apprehended either way,—only those whose terms can denote particular things. Propositions whose terms can denote only what is abstract and general can only be notionally apprehended. When a proposition can be understood either way, the possibility of real apprehension is usually limited only by the extent of the experience and imagination of the individual. For instance, whether or not we can 'really' apprehend 'Dum Capitolium scandet cum tacita Virgine Pontifex' depends upon our ability to conjure up 'the living image' of the scene.[75] In other cases,[76] however, the *restriction* of our own experience may give rise to a real apprehension of a proposition which most people would understand as expressing a general or abstract idea. This occurs when we have only one particular experience of the reference of the proposition. Furthermore, because a statement evokes a notional apprehension of its reference at one time, it need not always be notionally apprehended. A Nigerian may find it impossible to 'imagine' what is meant by a description of a cold, frosty morning. Later he may visit the Arctic. He will then be able to have a real apprehension of the description. In this way a notional apprehension is replaced by a real apprehension.[77] What originally was an intellectually recognized truth, an accepted idea, is transformed into a truth which is 'seen' and 'felt'. The change from one mode of apprehension to the other can also happen in the reverse direction: what was formerly imaginatively apprehended comes to be received only notionally. Thus Newman holds that the image of God which a child may possess 'above all mere notions of God', in time can become 'dimmed, distorted, or obliterated'. The original real apprehension then becomes 'almost indistinguishable from an inferential acceptance of the great truth', or dwindles 'into a mere notion of their intellect'.[78]

The distinction between real and notional apprehension is important for assent because real apprehension has a greater effect upon us than notional. The *Grammar of Assent* contains many assertions of this fact. Newman writes that 'of these two modes of apprehending propositions, . . . real is the stronger; I mean by stronger the more vivid and forcible . . . for intellectual ideas cannot compete in effectiveness with the experience of concrete facts.'[79] Real apprehension 'excites and stimulates the affections and passions'.[80] One example of the greater effectiveness of real apprehension is given in a discussion of the proposition 'There is a God'. Newman holds that this statement:

> when really apprehended, is the object of a strong energetic adhesion, which works a revolution in the mind; but when held merely as a notion, it requires but a cold and ineffective acceptance, though it be held ever so unconditionally.[81]

Although real apprehension varies in strength, on the whole it is 'stronger' than any notional apprehension. Newman considers that the superior power of real apprehension stems from its object being regarded as real. 'It is so to be accounted for the very reason that it is concerned with what is either real or is taken for real.' Real apprehension, then, has the greater effect on us because it brings 'facts home' to our minds.[82] Both the *Grammar of Assent* and Newman's other writings demonstrate how the actual case has far more force for him than the general idea. This preference for the 'real', however, is no accident of his individual psychology but is an attitude shared by most people. We see it revealed, for instance, in the way that we often treat the propositions 'X is real' and 'X is true' as equivalent. We see no point at all in disputing a fact of existence and what we apprehend as real carries the force of this unquestioned acceptability. A further contribution to the greater force of real apprehension is the fact that the remembered image of an experience is usually more sharply defined than a notion which has been produced by generalization and abstraction. Since real apprehension is the re-presentation of actual experience, it is more vivid than a notion which has been derived from it. Newman warns us that the vividness of an image 'is no warrant for the existence' of an object corresponding to it.[83] On the other hand, it is clear that we are much more influenced by what is immediate and sharply defined than by what is indirect, vague, and obscure. In so far, then, as the 'real' is also more vivid than the notional, it will exert a greater influence over us.[84]

b. The Application of the Distinction to the Matter of Religion

Before we discuss how the distinction in apprehension between 'real' and 'notional' affects the act of assent, we shall briefly notice how the distinction is applied to the material of religion. First we shall note how certain theological ideas can be apprehended 'really' and others only 'notionally'. We shall then examine the relationship between theology and religion and discuss how far theological inconsistencies may be due to the limitations of our notions. Finally we shall consider whether a real apprehension of God is possible.

Newman gives an example of the difference between real and notional apprehension in a discussion of the doctrine of the Trinity.[85] He suggests that whereas the individual elements of the doctrine can be really apprehended, we can only apprehend the doctrine as a whole notionally. The reason for this is that while we can produce an image of each separate item of the doctrine, we cannot conceive an image of what is meant by the 'Trinity' as such. Newman expresses the position thus:

> though we can image the separate propositions, we cannot image them all together. We cannot, because the mystery transcends all our experience; we have no experiences in our memory which we can put together, compare, contrast, unite, and thereby transmute into an image of the Ineffable Verity.[86]

The doctrine as a whole is not inconsistent with any of the elements which compose it. That the one is notionally while the others may be really apprehended is due to the limitations of our imagination, not to any intrinsic quality of the material which is here presented to us.[87]

The distinction between real and notional apprehension is used by Newman to explain the difference between religion and theology. Religion is concerned with 'the real and . . . the particular', i.e. with what we apprehend as images: theology works with notions, i.e. with what is 'general and systematic'.[88] Where the individual elements of a doctrine are apprehended in images, then they are the objects of religion. When the doctrine as a whole, with all its complex content, is grasped notionally, it is material for theology. As a proposition may be apprehended both notionally and really, so it may be used both theologically and religiously. Indeed, in practice it is impossible to draw a distinct line between the religious and the theological uses of a statement. 'As intellect is common to all men as well as imagination, every religious man is to a certain extent a theologian.'[89] Newman's view that notions are abstracted from the 'real' means that notions cannot ultimately 'be inconsistent'[90] with the real so long as the real is consistent with itself. What is derived from the real cannot contradict the real. Any apparent clash must be due to some error in our understanding. Since Newman holds that religion deals with images and theology with notions derived from the objects of religion, the coherence of the real and the notional provides 'the solution of the common mistake of supposing that there is a contrariety and antagonism between a dogmatic creed and a vital religion'.[91] Because we start with our religious experience and derive our theology from it, there can be no opposition between true religion and true theology. This implies that 'no theology can start or thrive without the initiative and abiding presence of religion.' We begin with 'the witness, first of nature, then of revelation' and proceed to formulate 'our doctrines' by 'the exercise of abstraction and inference'.[92]

There are, however, many cases where it appears that one theological statement contradicts another. For instance, to say that 'our Lord Jesus Christ, the Son of God, is God and Man . . . Perfect God, and perfect Man' is to say two things about Jesus Christ which seem to be contradictory. Newman deals with this problem by reminding us that our notions may be only partially applicable to the concrete instance and that notions derived from our human experience may be most inadequate for expressing truth about God. Since a notion refers to what is common to more than one instance, no notion nor any finite series of notions can ever completely describe an actual concrete instance. As Newman puts it, no 'number whatever of abstractions would, by being fused together, be equivalent to one concrete'.[93] Furthermore, notions may mislead us about the concrete case. We find this when a notion is used in a description of an object and implications are then drawn from the notion which do not apply to the specific object. Although the Duke of Wellington was an Irishman, it would be erroneous to imply from his nationality that he shared the 'national character' and 'must have been impulsive, quarrelsome, witty, clever at repartee'.[94] When we draw out the implications of a concept, we must remember that 'our notion of a thing may be only partially faithful to the original'. In particular we must remember that any one of our finite notions which we apply to God is likely to be very limited in its appropriateness. It may be applicable,

> only to a certain point, in certain cases, but no further. After that point is reached, the notion and the thing part company: and

then the notion, if still used as the representative of the thing, will work out conclusions, not inconsistent with itself, but with the thing to which it no longer corresponds.[95]

This means that in a theological statement, e.g. our description of the nature of Christ or the doctrine of the Trinity, 'the incompatible notions' which the statement contains 'need not each of them really belong to it in that fulness which would involve their being incompatible with each other'.[96] The apparent contradictions of a theological statement may be due to the inadequacy of our ways of expression, not to the impossibility of its reference.

When we turn from theology to religion, from notions to images of the object of our faith, we find that Newman holds that we can have a real apprehension of God. He argues that our conscience provides us with the material which makes this possible. Conscience is 'our great internal teacher of religion' which 'teaches us, not only that God is, but what He is; it provides for the mind a real image of Him'.[97] In the case of our knowledge of objects, Newman holds that what we experience is taken 'instinctively' to be an appearance of what underlies the experience but itself is not experienced. Phenomena are intuitively regarded as providing 'a picture of the things which are perceived through the senses'. Thus while our 'instinct' tells us that our sense-perceptions are of 'a real being', 'the matter or quality' of those sense-perceptions inform us about the nature of the object. Whereas phenomena perceived by our physical senses give us direct information about the created world, our knowledge about the Creator comes only 'indirectly' from our experiences of conscience.[98] Our sense of responsibility, together with our being ashamed and afraid of a bad conscience, implies 'that there is One to whom we are responsible, before whom we are ashamed, whose claims upon us we fear'. Thus, from our experience of our conscience, we can conceive an image of God as 'a Supreme Governor, a Judge, holy, just, powerful, all-seeing, retributive'.[99] This image of God becomes more accurate the more we obey the dictates of our conscience[100] and can be developed 'by means of education, social intercourse, experience and literature'.[101] It always stands, however, under the judgement of theology.[102] Our image of God is not self-authenticating but may have to be modified as a result of our theological reasoning. This means that whereas the notional is totally dependent upon the real, because the 'real' of religion cannot be directly experienced, our images of it are partially controlled by our notional ideas. Newman believes that such a real apprehension of God, constructed primarily out of the experiences of conscience, is possible for every man. He believes that it is just as valid to determine the nature of God from the experience of conscience as it is to infer the nature of an object from its experienced phenomena.[103] This validity is expressed as an 'instinctive certitude'.[104] By this phrase he seems to mean the 'common sense' of statements like: 'It is common sense that things are as we see them.' It is for Newman a basic assumption which is not to be questioned.[105]

c The Difference between Real and Notional Apprehension in the Matter of Assent

We now turn to consider the significance for our acts of assent of the distinction between 'real' and 'notional'. We have already seen that Newman considers 'apprehension' to be a condition of the act of assent. He further holds that the nature of the preceding apprehension 'gives a distinct character' to the assent.[106] If the preceding apprehension is real, then the assent itself is called 'real assent'; if the apprehension is notional, then the assent is 'notional assent'. A real assent is one which 'is directed towards things, represented by the impressions which they have left on the imagination'.[107] Notional assent is assent to 'what the words of the proposition mean' as ideas and generalizations.[108] The distinction between notional and real assent follows the division of apprehension since it is based upon it. In fact, to speak about 'notional' and 'real' *assent* is misleading, for it is not our assent which varies[109] but our understanding of its object.

The respective characteristics of real and notional assent correspond to those of real and notional apprehension. Real assents, being based on real apprehensions, are private and personal. 'They depend on personal experience. . . . Real assent . . . is proper to the individual, and as such, thwarts rather than promotes the intercourse of man with man.'[110] Notional assent, in contrast, shares the common character of notions and is ordinarily of such a public nature that it can be readily shared by different people.[111] This does not imply, however, that different people cannot entertain similar real assents. Just as various individuals can entertain images which are approximately the same, although based upon their own separate and private experiences, so they can give real assents which are the same in all significant respects. Newman is prepared to say that these shared images may be the 'same in all' cases,[112] but this must be qualified. The private character of the experiences from which our shared images are composed means that they can only be held to be similar, approximating to identity but never finally able to achieve it. The fact that different people may entertain what are practically the same images and thus be able to give similar real assents is important for Newman's thesis. Since religious assent (as opposed to theological) is a matter of real assent, the possibility of a common religion depends upon the possibility of substantially the same images being entertained by different people. A belief which is shared by many people,

> is not therefore notional, because it is common, but may be a real and personal belief, being produced in different individual minds by various experiences and disposing causes, variously combined.[113]

Newman goes on to argue that such shared real assents provide a greater bond between the individuals who share them than do notional assents held in common.[114] Hence a shared religion exercises a far greater unifying power than a shared theology. This is because a real assent has far greater force than a notional assent. To this question of the relative 'strengths' of real and notional assents we now turn our attention.

Newman is careful to point out that when he talks about 'strong' and 'weak' assents, it is 'not any incompleteness in the assent itself' which is described.[115] Assent itself admits of no degrees. The variation is in the effective force of our different assents. This effectiveness depends upon the way we have apprehended the object of our assent. As we should expect from our discussion of the difference between real and notional apprehension, real assent is more forcible and effective than notional assent.

> The more fully the mind is occupied by an experience, the keener will be its assent to it, if it assents, and on the other hand, the duller will be its assent and the less operative, the more it is engaged with an abstraction; and thus a scale of assents is conceivable, either in the instance of one mind upon different subjects, or of many minds upon one subject, varying from an assent which looks like mere inference up to a belief both intense and practical.[116]

Accordingly Newman is prepared to assert that 'an act of assent . . . is the most perfect and highest of its kind, when it is exercised on propositions, which are apprehended as experiences and images.' In contrast notional assents 'tend to be mere assertions without any personal hold on them on the part of those who make them'.[117] Just as an image influences us far more than an abstract idea, so our real assents have far more practical force than notional ones. Real assents influence us 'by providing a supply of objects strong enough to stimulate' us into action.[118] Although they do not invariably lead to action, they are far more likely to do so than notional assents.[119] In the case of a real proposition, notional assent to its truth, i.e. certitude, has less force than a simple act of assent to the proposition itself.[120] The function of assent in each case is not to increase the effective force of the image or the notion so much as to validate it by affirming its truth. As we have already mentioned, Newman warns us that the vividness of a real apprehension is not a sufficient reason for us to grant assent to its object. 'We have no right to consider that we have apprehended a truth, merely because of the strength of our mental impression of it.'[121] Nevertheless, the greater force of images is a factor to be considered in any analysis of the act of assent. While an image cannot provide 'the legitimate basis of the assent', it 'may still legitimately act, and strongly act, in confirmation' of the assent.[122] In other words, if a proposition is presented to us for assent, we are more likely to assent to it if we apprehend it as an image rather than notionally.

In the previous section we discussed the distinction between religion and theology which is based on the distinction between real and notional apprehension. In theology, then, we give our assent 'merely to notions of the intellect'[123] but religious assent is given to objects which 'are as present as if they were objects of sight'.[124] On the basis of this distinction Newman considers that theological assent is weak, providing the basis only for a formal religion, while religious assent may be powerful enough to control the whole of a person's life.[125] Since religion is more effective than theology, conversion, i.e. the change from a formal to a living faith, may be understood as the change from notional assent to real assent to a statement of faith.[126] Only when the object of assent is 'addressed to the imagination' can it 'exert that living mastery over the mind' which is true religion. Newman gives an example of what he means in terms of the proposition 'There is a God':

> 'There is a God', when really apprehended, is the object of a strong energetic adhesion, which works a revolution in the mind; but when held merely as a notion, it requires but a cold and ineffective acceptance, though it be held ever so unconditionally.[127]

Thus while we may have a notional or theological apprehension of a dogmatic system and assent to it, our assent will not have the revolutionary effect of a religious conversion until it is directed to an image or series of images. Only when it is based upon what is grasped as real is a faith likely to be living and significant. We may assent to the complexities of a creed or a systematic theology, but to be true believers we must conceive of the objects of our faith not as interrelated ideas but as concrete realities. Religious conversion, therefore, may be interpreted as consisting of four steps: first the notional apprehension of a theological idea, secondly assent to it, thirdly real apprehension of the reference of the idea, and fourthly real assent to it. For Newman popular religion, especially in England, does not go beyond the first two steps. Consequently it persists as a series of pious sentiments; it is not a controlling influence in life.[128] This pattern of conversion is not universal, however, for the object of faith may be presented to the mind straightway as an image and real assent made to it immediately. In such cases the first two steps are by-passed and only appear when the living faith is subjected to theological analysis.[129]

d. Criticism of Newman's View of Real and Notional Apprehension and Assent

The way in which Newman distinguishes between the 'real' and the 'notional' raises the question whether he is to be classed as a nominalist. This school of medieval philosophy held that ' "universals" or common natures—such as *genera* and *species* . . . have no existence beyond our minds where they arise when we think of a number of individual things together and designate them by a common name.'[130] Thus 'universals were merely words, . . . only individuals existed, and . . . the genus or the species corresponded to nothing in the real world.'[131] This seems to be what Newman asserts when, for instance, he holds that 'all things in the exterior world are unit and individual' but 'the mind . . . has the gift, by an act of creation, of bringing before it abstractions and generalizations, which have no existence, no counterpart, out of it'.[132] Here he clearly implies that it is the mind which gives existence (cf. 'by an act of creation') to our notions and that those notions do not denote anything which exists outside the mind.[133] At this point Newman expresses decidedly nominalist views.[134] Furthermore, his restriction of the term 'real' to what is apprehended as an individual object or image (in contrast to the notional which expresses general ideas) follows the nominalist attitude. On the other hand, there are statements in the *Grammar of Assent* which implicitly contradict the nominalist position. As Walgrave points out,[135] nominalism cannot be easily reconciled with Newman's view of 'the objective existence of the Moral Law' and 'our instinctive recognition of the immutable difference in the moral quality of acts, as elicited in us by one instance of them'. Here we have in a single experience a direct perception of an absolute value. Again, Newman's recognition of 'the influence of certain original forms of thinking or formative ideas, connatural with our minds, without which we could not reason at all' contradicts nominalism.[136] Finally, what Newman has to say on several occasions about 'the laws of my nature' is inconsistent with a nominalist point of view.[137] We must not, however, overestimate the amount of material in the *Grammar of Assent* that is incompatible with nominalism. Newman's usual view of notions is in harmony with Ockham's position that ' "a universal is not anything real existing in a subject either inside or outside the soul" but "anything which can be predicated of several things" '.[138]

Some of Newman's critics seek to explain away his apparent nominalism as due to apologetic needs. Boekraad, for instance, holds that Newman used nominalist ideas in order to be understood by his opponents but that at the same time he showed 'his conviction that this view of things is totally insufficient and inadmissable'.[139] Walgrave, similarly, holds that Newman's nominalism is only apparent, arising out of his opposition to the contemporary 'scientism' which 'affirmed that knowledge obtained by the methods of the positive sciences was the sole valid and certain knowledge'.[140] The charge of nominalism, however, cannot be so easily dismissed. D'Arcy[141] and Zeno[142] are nearer the truth when they admit that Newman holds nominalist ideas and attribute them to his educational environment. When Newman was at Oxford, the ideas of Locke, Hume, Berkeley, and Butler exercised a predominant influence. From these authors, and in particular from Locke, whom he greatly respected,[143] he inherited what in effect was 'a nominalist theory of knowledge'.[144] What Newman says in the *Grammar of Assent* about 'common' and 'singular' terms[145] echoes the 'nominalist' position of Whately's *Logic*.[146] Later in the *Logic*, in a section which Newman helped to prepare,[147] the realist position is rejected and an essentially nominalist position is propounded.[148] According to Newman it was Whately who 'opened my mind, and taught me to think and to use my reason' as a young man in Oxford.[149] Furthermore, his familiarity with and preference for Aristotle,[150] together with the Aristotelian interest of the Oriel Noetics, must have led Newman's thought in a nominalist direction.[151]

We must not, however, be too hasty in pinning the label of 'nominalist' onto Newman. Since he was not very well acquainted with Scholastic thought,[152] he was probably not aware of the far-reaching implications of the realist/nominalist controversy. In the *Grammar of Assent* Newman was not concerned with working out a systematic study of 'universals'. He was 'totally occupied with the personal conquest of truth'.[153] The nominalism of his inherited view of knowledge was reinforced by this emphasis on the personal character of assent. I consider, therefore, that Newman's understanding of notions was generally in line with that of the nominalists but that this was an unconscious discipleship. It is an open question whether he would have retained his ideas about the character of notions if he had become fully aware of the issues raised in the controversy over nominalism. As we have pointed out, there are certain views expressed in the *Grammar of Assent* which suggest that if he were pressed to decide, Newman would have supported the moderate realist against the nominalist.[154] We must not forget, finally, that while the nominalist/realist issue is a fundamental one, it does not 'affect vitally the major part of Newman's work'.[155] Whichever label we affix to him, it will not significantly alter our judgement on what he has to say about assent.

Where Newman speaks of the possibility of religious 'images', we must not misunderstand what he means by these 'images' of the real. By 'image' he does not mean a clearly defined visual representation but an awareness of the reality of the object. When, for instance, he states that the objects of religion 'are as present (i.e. to faith) as if they were objects of sight',[156] it is the reality and not the distinctness of those objects which is significant. This explains how Newman can consistently hold both that we can entertain an 'image' of God and that God is transcendent, utterly unlike anything in this world.[157] When elsewhere he claims that we can have a real apprehension of each separate element of the doctrine of the Trinity,[158] he is not claiming that we can construct a clear mental picture of each element.[159] Rather he is asserting that the expression is such that we can be aware of the reality of its references. In this way Newman shows the difference between religion and theology. When we grant theological assent we are merely recognizing the truth of certain ideas. Our religious faith, in contrast, is a commitment to something we recognize to be real and actual.

We may illustrate Newman's understanding of 'image' by reference to the statement: 'John is a brilliant philosopher'. At first my apprehension of this may be purely notional. In this case I have a rough idea who is meant by 'John' and I gather that he is supposed to be very clever, especially with abstract and fundamental ideas. Nevertheless the remark does not arouse any particular interest—it is simply another comment about someone with whom I am not concerned. As time passes, I become increasingly acquainted with John's thought, both through personal contact and through his writings. He stops being just another person and becomes a particular individual. His thought is no longer something to be discussed vaguely in the abstract but something which I know intimately. And the more I know it, the higher is my judgement of its depth and accuracy. If someone at this point now says: 'John is a brilliant philosopher', my apprehension of the statement is very different from my earlier grasp of it. It still conveys to me the notion that a person called 'John' is very clever, but at the same time I am aware of the reality of all that the statement denotes about John and about his thought. It is no longer a rather vague, imprecise remark but a comment that brings to my mind a real and living, complex situation. This is what Newman means when he says that I 'really' apprehend the statement and have before my mind an 'image' of its reference. He does not mean that I have conceived a mental picture or visual representation of its meaning. He signifies instead that the reference of the statement is grasped by my mind as referring to a particular, vivid, and 'real' situation. It is this vividness and particularity which distinguish the 'real'. It is both the determining characteristic of real apprehension and essential to a living faith.

Newman does not consider it necessary to argue that what is really apprehended has far more influence and effect than what is notionally apprehended. He takes it for granted that 'intellectual ideas cannot compete in effectiveness' with images,[160] 'that what is concrete exerts a force and makes an impression on the mind which nothing abstract can rival'.[161] This is, in fact, a matter of general experience. In every part of our thought and activity we are much more moved by real cases than by general ideas. A picture of an emaciated child evokes greater response than the statement that two-thirds of the world's population is starving.[162] To question Newman's view that the real is more powerful than the notional is to challenge the common experience of mankind. Newman is right when he stresses that in actual practice the 'real' is more likely than the 'notional' both to evoke our assent and to affect our actions. In the case of religion, a living and effective faith is much more likely to arise out of our real apprehension of its objects than out of our entertaining theological notions. Newman does not make it clear, however, that the dependence of religion upon 'images' is a practical, not a logical necessity. It is the greater practical force of images upon us that is important.

e. Conclusion

To sum up, then, we accept Newman's distinction between real and notional apprehension and his claim that the 'real' exerts a greater influence upon us than the 'notional'. We agree that we are more likely to assent to what we 'really' apprehend than to what we only grasp as notions and that our real assents influence our behaviour more than our notional assents. When we apply this to religion and theology, we consider that Newman makes a valuable distinction between them on the grounds that refer respectively to the real and to the notional. The importance of the distinction between real and notional apprehension, together with Newman's emphasis on the greater practical force of the real, further indicates that in the *Grammar of Assent* Newman is primarily concerned with the personal character of assent. The fact that the object of assent is real or notional has no logical significance for assent but it is significant for our personal attitude towards it.

Part IV: The Antecedent of Assent

1. INTRODUCTION

IN the last chapter we discussed Newman's view that assent is possible only when we apprehend its object. This implies that no act of faith is a completely blind leap in the dark. We must at least partially understand the object of our faith. In this chapter we are to examine Newman's claim that each act of assent is preceded by some supporting reasoning. This reasoning further reduces the 'blindness' of the leap of faith by indicating the arguments in favour of the assent. Even though it is impossible to 'prove' an article of faith (for then it would be 'known' rather than believed[1]), assent is not an irrational assertion. We can give assent only when we are satisfied that we have sufficient reasons for granting it. This supporting reasoning cannot compel us to assent nor can it modify our assent when it is given. It does not destroy the essential unconditionality of our assent. Its function is to encourage us to assent by demonstrating the justifiability of such an act.

Newman distinguished two types of reasoning, formal and informal. Formal reasoning is explicit and follows recognized rules. Its paradigm is the syllogism and it finds its purest form in the symbolic usages of algebra. The technical name for it is 'Inference, and the science, which is its regulating principle, is Logic', the precise logic of Aristotle. 'Inference' is not restricted to the technical pattern of syllogisms. Newman, for instance, states that 'an enthymeme fulfils the requirements of what I have called Inference' and extends the notion of inference to cover 'verbal reasoning, of whatever kind'. Since logic provides the 'scientific form' of inference, Newman states that 'it will be more convenient here to use the two words indiscriminately, for I shall say nothing about logic which does not in its substance also apply to inference.'[2] When we discuss inference, we shall see that its range is too limited and its method too explicit for it to play any major part as an antecedent of religious assent.

By informal reasoning Newman refers to that type of reasoning which is the activity of our natural ability, developed by experience, to evaluate the force of various subtle arguments. This natural reasoning cannot be adequately expressed in words. The faculty which exercises it is called by Newman the 'Illative Sense'. Its importance for the reasoning which leads to assent lies in its flexibility and its ability to deal with the concrete. Newman thus recognizes that faith is supported not by syllogistic arguments but by a more subtle form of reasoning. We shall use the terms 'inference' and 'illation' to denote respectively the formal and the informal modes of reasoning while 'reasoning' covers both processes. This is not Newman's consistent usage for in the *Grammar of Assent* he sometimes uses 'inference' to include all that we denote here by the term 'reasoning'.³

2. REASONING AND ASSENT

a. The Function of Reasoning as an Antecedent of Assent

In this section we are to examine the significance and function of the reasoning which precedes an act of assent. Newman holds that each act of assent usually has some antecedent reasoning. He states that 'inference is ordinarily the antecedent of assent' and comments that this view is one on which 'surely I need not enlarge'.⁴ His problem is not how to establish the existence of this relationship but how to demonstrate its proper nature. The problem can be expressed as the need to resolve the 'apparent inconsistency' in holding that unconditional assent is given to a proposition as 'the result of its conditional verification'.⁵ The step from accepting the truth of a proposition as a reasoned conclusion to assenting to it is not one of logical implication. No amount of reasoning can logically compel me to convert my acceptance of a reasoned conclusion into an assent to its truth. On the other hand, reasoning and assent are essentially connected in that proper assent is not an arbitrary act but a rationally justifiable one. We can legitimately grant assent only when we have what seems to us reasonable grounds for our action. Newman puts it thus:

> so much is it commonly felt that assent must be preceded by inferential acts, that obstinate men give their own will as their very reason for assenting, if they can think of nothing better; 'stat pro ratione voluntas'. Indeed, I doubt whether assent is ever given without some preliminary which stands for a reason.⁶

What we decide to be true does not depend upon our arbitrary and passing desires but upon what we consider to be the actual state of things. Therefore, we assent to a proposition, i.e. assert its truth, only if we consider that it accurately expresses what really is the case. If, for instance, a person states that 'x is y' but is unable to give any reasons for his assertion, we will generally regard any claim by him that he assents to it as illegitimate. It may be that the proposition does in fact express the truth, but until there are apparently sufficient grounds for holding that it does, we are not prepared to consider its truth and the possibility of assent to it.

The strength of the antecedent reasoning does not affect the strength of our assent but our willingness to assent. The function of this reasoning is to induce us to give our assent. Thus Newman writes that our 'inclination to give assent' is 'greater or less according as the particular act of inference expressed a stronger or weaker probability'.[7] There is, however, no objective standard by which a piece of antecedent reasoning may be judged strong or weak. Such an evaluation depends upon the individual concerned. What is a strong argument for one person may not have any great force for another, while a third may not even be mildly moved by it. Consequently the 'argumentative process necessary' to make different people ready to assent to a particular proposition 'is proportionate to their several capacities'[8] and, we may add, to their individual doubts and problems. Since arguments in support of a proposition incline us to assent to it, arguments which dispute it incline us to withhold our assent although they cannot finally compel us to refuse it. 'Arguments adverse to a conclusion . . . naturally hinder assent.'[9] One result of this is that 'processes of investigation, whether in religious subjects or secular, often issue in the reversal of the assents which they were originally intended to confirm'.[10] It is our readiness to grant assent rather than the assent itself that is weakened by the adverse reasoning; the assent itself is, for Newman, unconditional and independent.

While the function of antecedent reasoning is to incline us to grant assent, it may do this at the cost of weakening the force of our assent. In the first place, our reasoning may lead us to apprehend the object of our assent as a notion rather than as an image. This is particularly the case when the antecedent reasoning is inferential, for an inference 'is the most perfect and highest of its kind, when it is exercised on propositions which are apprehended as notions'. Since assent, as well as apprehension, is strongest when its object is an image, we may well find that 'when Inference is clearest, Assent may be least forcible'.[11] Secondly, our consideration of the reasons which incline us to assent may give rise to 'intellectual hesitations' which will prevent assent.[12] The more we consider the reasons in favour of a particular assent, the more we also become aware of the reasons for not granting that assent. In the end we may develop such a 'habit' of 'questioning' that we are unable to escape from the realm of argument and to give our assent to anything.[13] The need for antecedent reasoning is thus not completely favourable to assent because it may, in certain conditions, diminish its force or even lead us away from it.

Newman recognizes that often we do not clearly distinguish between a conclusion and an assent. Many times we are not conscious of our assent to a proposition. In such cases we are liable to confuse our assent to the proposition with its acceptance as the conclusion of antecedent reasoning. Not having realized that we have granted assent to the proposition concerned but aware that we have demonstrated the probability of its truth by various arguments, 'we are . . . apt to confuse together acts of assent and acts of inference'. This confusion means that we have failed to appreciate the difference between entertaining propositions as conclusions, and therefore 'conditionally', and assent to those propositions 'which unconditionally accepts them'.[14] It is important to distinguish these two ways of holding a proposition. Our assent to a proposition is our absolute recognition of its truth, whereas if we regard that proposition as a conclusion we view it as the result of a process of reasoning and its truth as dependent upon the validity of that reasoning.[15] This does not mean that it is necessarily inconsistent to entertain the same proposition simultaneously as a conclusion and as an assent—'we can at once infer and assent' to a given proposition.[16] This means that our assent to a proposition and our intention to persist with that assent do not prevent us investigating the strength of the argument which supports our assent.

Although assent is normally preceded by reasoning, we must not forget that an assent and a conclusion are essentially distinct.[17] As we have already noticed, Newman considers that antecedent reasoning does not affect the assent itself but our readiness to grant it. That is, the significance of antecedent reasoning is in its influence over us rather than in its purely rational force. The more I can be persuaded that a proposition is likely to be true, the more likely I am to assent to it, but since the granting of our assent is an act of the will, I cannot be induced to give it automatically by any specific degree of conclusiveness in the antecedent reasoning. No amount of reasoning can ever entail the absolute acceptance of assent since the very nature of reasoning means that its conclusions are 'conditional'. Newman recognizes this when he writes that there are:

> very numerous . . . cases, in which good arguments, and really good as far as they go, and confessed by us to be good, nevertheless are not strong enough to incline our minds ever so little to the conclusion at which they point.[18]

On other occasions, however, Newman does not seem to realize that the distinction between 'conditional' conclusions and unconditional assents is a logical one which makes it impossible for reasoning ever to compel assent as a matter of logical necessity. Thus he asserts that there are cases where argument 'forces its way' and may be 'able to command our assent'.[19] In the case of arguments as conclusive and as clearly correct as simple mathematical demonstrations, Newman holds that while:

> assent would not in consequence be the same act as inference, yet it would certainly follow immediately upon it. I allow then as much as this, that, when an argument is in itself and by itself conclusive of a truth, it has by a law of our nature the same command over our assent, or rather the truth which it has reached has the same command, as our senses have. Certainly our intellectual nature is under laws, and the correlative of ascertained truth is unreserved assent.[20]

This develops Newman's earlier statement that 'Inference may also impose on us assents'.[21] It suggests that any reasoning which we consider to be a conclusive demonstration may force us to assent to the proposition which expresses its conclusion. This means that our acceptance of a proposition as a conclusion, i.e. as a statement whose truth depends upon the validity of certain arguments, may entail our acceptance of it as an absolute truth. Newman is here to be criticized on two counts. In the first place he ignores the logical distinction which he recognizes elsewhere between an assent and a conclusion.[22] Assent belongs to the logic of commitment and so ultimately it is a matter of personal choice. It cannot be entailed by reasoning which belongs to the different logic of rational argument. The only 'compulsion' or 'force' that reasoning can exert is practical and personal, not logical. Secondly, Newman has failed in these statements to take into account what he has to say about the 'conditionality' of conclusions and the 'unconditionality' of assents. If a conclusion is necessarily 'conditional', it can never entail something which is essentially 'unconditional'.

When Newman says that the conclusion of an argument is necessarily 'conditional', he is not referring to its logical status. The 'conditionality' of a conclusion does not mean that it is hypothetical or probable. By describing a conclusion as 'conditional' Newman is expressing instead the way in which we entertain a conclusion *qua* conclusion. When a proposition is held to be a valid conclusion, it is held to be true in so far as it is implied by other true propositions. No matter how much we may consider that it has been convincingly demonstrated, we cannot disassociate it, as a conclusion, from those other propositions which implied it. Thus the 'conditionality' of a conclusion refers primarily to the fact that we do not entertain it as true in its own right but because of its dependence on other propositions which imply it. Newman further recognizes that 'a conclusion . . . implies the assumption of premises, and . . . in concrete matter . . . demonstration is impossible.'[23] When we consider a conclusion, then, we are aware that the reasoning which led to it has started from assumptions and these assumptions may or may not be true. In the case of arguments about the real we are also aware of the limitations of images for the processes of reasoning. Basically, however, the 'conditionality' of a conclusion does not refer to our doubts about its conclusiveness but to the fact that whereas a proposition to which we give assent is accepted as true without any reference, conscious or unconscious, to any other proposition, a conclusion is always regarded by us in conjunction with the other propositions which imply it.

Although some passages in the *Grammar of Assent* seem to suggest that reasoning can compel assent, there are other passages which make it clear that this 'compulsion' is not a matter of logical necessity. These passages show that Newman recognizes that there is no direct logical connexion between argument and assent similar to that which exists between the premises and the conclusion of an argument. Thus we read that 'assent' is 'independent of our acts of inference' and it is observed that admittedly good arguments do not always bring about assent. Since an assent is an act of the will, irrational factors such as 'prejudice' can hinder assent to propositions supported by 'the most incontrovertible proofs'.[24] Here Newman recognizes that the essential difference between a conclusion and an assent arises from the fact that they are two distinct ways of accepting a proposition. No degree of conclusiveness can *ipso facto* command our assent. The act of assent is an act of the will, it is a decision to accept something as absolutely true, and no amount of reasoning to show the 'verisimilitude'[25] of its object can require it. When Newman occasionally suggests that reasoning can compel assent, he confuses the issue by failing to distinguish the practical force which a conclusion can exert in persuading us to assent from a logical power to entail assent. The power and function of antecedent reasoning lies in its ability to encourage us to assent by demonstrating the probable truth of the object of assent. The antecedent reasoning cannot, however, require us to accept absolutely as true a proposition whose truth we accept only in relation to other propositions, i.e. as a conclusion. It is the failure to make clear this distinction between the practical and the logical force of reasoning that allows Newman to seem to suggest that a certain degree of reasoning can lead to an assent as a matter of necessary implication. The real situation, in fact, is that a high degree of conclusiveness makes assent so highly justifiable that in practice we are most unlikely not to grant it. The danger of emphasizing the influence of reasoning in our decision to assent is that it tends to obscure the place of our will in the act of assent. In the end, it is our will which determines whether or not assent is granted. The move from antecedent reasoning to assent is a logical type-jump which no degree of conclusiveness can ever entail. Reasoning may exert a tremendous influence upon us but ultimately it can never compel us to assent against our will. Newman admits this when he writes that 'according to the couplet,

> A man convinced against his will
> Is of the same opinion still;—

assent then is not the same as inference'.[26]

Although Newman asserts that some kind of reasoning is a necessary antecedent for an act of assent, he admits that an assent may persist when the antecedent reasoning has been forgotten.

> Assents may endure without the presence of the inferential acts upon which they were originally elicited. . . . We assented to them, and we still assent, though we have forgotten what the warrant was.[27]

Newman does not explicitly deal with the problem of whether an assent can persist when its antecedent reasoning is found to be false. He does say that adverse reasoning cannot compel us to refuse assent any more than favourable arguments can compel us to grant it. This implies that when we have granted assent, the fact that we were encouraged to do so on false grounds will not necessarily lead us to withdraw our assent. In the case of many people, assents which they gave as children and still hold were initially granted upon grounds which they now regard as false. Newman further emphasizes the difference between a conclusion and assent by recognizing that an assent may be withdrawn while its antecedent reasons still hold good.

> Sometimes assent fails, while the reasons for it and the inferential act which is the recognition of those reasons, are still present, and in force. Our reasons may seem to us as strong as ever, yet they do not secure our assent. Our beliefs, founded on them, were and are not.[28]

The persuasive force of antecedent reasoning does not necessarily persist if other conditions change. The function of antecedent reasoning is to incline us to assent, but it cannot ensure that an assent continues any more than it can assure its being granted in the first place.

b. Newman's Criticism of Locke

Newman clearly and consistently holds that the antecedent reasoning does not affect

> the unconditional character of the assent, viewed in itself. The circumstances of an act, however necessary to it, do not enter into the act; assent is in its nature absolute and unconditional, though it cannot be given except under certain conditions.[29]

When we assent to a proposition our assent is 'unconditionally given', 'without reserve or doubt'. Since it is an 'absolute recognition', Newman holds that 'we never say that we give . . . a degree of assent. We might as well talk of degrees of truth as of degrees of assent.'[30] Statements which have the form of qualified assents are misleading. They must be re-expressed to show that it is not the assent which is qualified but the object of the assent, for:

> when I assent to a doubtfulness, or to a probability, my assent as such, is as complete as if I assented to a truth; it is not a certain degree of assent.[31]

The expression 'a probable assent to x' is a misleading way of stating 'an assent that x is probable'. To assent to a proposition is 'to convey to others the impression that we accept it unreservedly, and that because it is true'.[32]

Since he holds that the strength of the antecedent reasoning does not affect the strength of an assent, Newman considers that he is in opposition to the position held by John Locke, a situation in which he feels 'no pleasure' because of his respect for the character and ability of that philosopher.[33] Locke held that assent is the acceptance of a proposition according to the strength of the evidence supporting it. Newman quotes at length Locke's statement that the 'lover of truth' is characterized by:

> the not entertaining any proposition with greater assurance than the proofs it is built on will warrant. Whoever goes beyond this measure of assent, it is plain, receives not truth in the love of it, loves not truth for truth-sake, but for some other by-end. For the evidence that any proposition is true (except such as are self-evident) lying only in the proofs a man has of it, whatsoever degrees

of assent he affords it beyond the degrees of that evidence, it is plain that all that surplusage of assurance is owing to some other affection, and not to the love of truth; it being as impossible that the love of truth should carry my assent above the evidence there is to me that it is true, as that the love of truth should make me assent to any proposition for the sake of that evidence which it has not that it is true.[34]

Newman criticizes Locke on the grounds that has given an arbitrary meaning to the term 'assent' which is 'theoretical and unreal'. Locke is not prepared to accept the actual processes of our mind (which Newman regards as 'natural and legitimate') but propounds:

> his own ideal of how the mind ought to act. . . . Instead of going by the testimony of psychological facts and thereby determining our constitutive faculties and our proper condition, and being content with the mind as God has made it, he would form men as he thinks they ought to be formed, into something better and higher, and calls them irrational and indefensible, if (so to speak) they take to the water, instead of remaining under the narrow wings of his own arbitrary theory.[35]

This is strong criticism, but in fact it is a bogus dispute arising out of the ambiguity of the term 'assent'. In the *Essay concerning Human Understanding* Locke is seeking to determine the sources and limitations of our knowledge. He states that it is his 'purpose to enquire into the original, certainty, and extent of human knowledge, together with the grounds and degrees of belief, opinion, and assent'.[36] This is a logical and not a descriptive task. His interest in discussing our claims to knowledge is to discover what we can justifiably claim to know. When, therefore, Newman criticizes Locke for dealing with the problem on a 'theoretical and unreal' level, he is not making a criticism which would embarrass Locke. Locke is not concerned with describing 'the testimony of psychological facts'[37] but is seeking to provide a critique of our claims to knowledge.

The basic cause of the trouble is Newman's failure to perceive how Locke uses the term 'assent'. Locke nowhere suggests that there are degrees of truth, an idea which Newman rightly rejects as absurd, but he recognizes that our evaluation of the truth of a statement may range from its possibility to its certainty. When Locke talks about giving 'probable assent' to a proposition, he is using a shorthand expression to convey the idea that we accept that it is true that the proposition is probable. Newman has not understood what Locke means by this shorthand expression since he considers that it contradicts his view of assent as the absolute acceptance of a proposition as unconditionally true. In fact the difference between Locke and Newman in the matter of degrees of assent is not material but formal. It concerns the way they use the term 'assent'. Locke writes of possible and probable assents to a proposition where Newman, describing the same situation, must write about assent to the possibility or probability of the proposition. When it is recognized that the two use the term in different ways, this cause of conflict vanishes.

The real difference between Newman and Locke concerns the question of where assent may be legitimately granted, though even here the conflict between them is more apparent than real. Locke does not explicitly define the term 'assent' but his use of it indicates that he means by it something like 'the acceptance of a proposition according to the evidence for it'. With such a definition it is not only consistent but also logically necessary for him to hold that the strength of our assents must vary with the strength of their supporting reasoning. He recognizes that in practice we do sometimes ascribe unqualified truth to statements which we can only demonstrate to be probably true. Following his professed aim in the essay,[38] he challenges the legitimacy of this behaviour, expecially in the chapters 'Of the Degrees of Assent'[39] and 'Of Enthusiasm'.[40] He writes that:

> whatsoever credit or authority we give to any proposition more than it receives from the principles and proofs it supports itself upon, is owing to our inclinations that way, and is so far a derogation from the love of truth as such: which, as it can receive no evidence from our passions or interests, so it should receive no tincture from them.[41]

Thus Locke holds that we act improperly when, in matters belonging to the province of reason, we do not limit our acceptance of a statement to what can be rationally supported. It is important to notice that Locke is here speaking about our assents in matters belonging to the province of reason. In the chapter 'Of Faith and Reason, and their distinct provinces',[42] he recognizes that there are things 'beyond the discovery of our natural faculties, and above reason'[43] where our assent is not governed solely by reasoning. Newman does not notice this in his criticism of Locke nor does he recognize that they are dealing with essentially different problems. Newman is concerned with the problem of how a person may ascribe absolute truth to propositions which cannot be demonstrated. In tackling this problem he deliberately confines himself to a practical and religious issue. Thus, in the *Grammar of Assent*, he tries to determine how people can, do and can be encouraged to believe religious statements. He is not interested in the theoretical and logical question of the propriety of ascribing truth beyond what can be proved to be such. Locke, on the other hand, is concerned with the logical problem of the relationship between claims to truth and what can be known to be true. He is interested not in what makes me commit myself to a proposition but in how far I can assert the truth of a proposition with rational justification. Between Locke and Newman there exists, therefore, a difference of purpose which leads them to make statements which *prima facie* conflict but in fact concern different kinds of problems. Locke's assertion that assent, when truth is the determining consideration, must not be given beyond the limits of what can be rationally justified,[44] means that we must restrict our rational claims to truth to what we can prove. When Newman holds that assent is and should be given beyond the limits of proof, he is stating what is equally acceptable, that in matters of faith we do and should commit ourselves unreservedly to what we believe to be true but cannot prove to be such. There is no real incompatibility between these statements. That Newman believes that there is arises from his failure to understand Locke's problem and how it differs from his own. The dispute between them, at any rate in relation to the view of assent in the *Essay concerning Human Understanding*, is a bogus one. On the other hand, we find in the 'liberalism' of the nineteenth century an attempt to judge all assents and commitments by the criteria of strict rationality. It was against this extension of Locke's position that Newman was really—and rightly—protesting.

c. Religious Belief and Conclusive Arguments

Newman does not only hold that the actual limitations of our reasoning powers require that we give assent in religious matters beyond the range of rational demonstration. In discussing Paley's *Evidences of Christianity*, Newman advances the position that religious faith cannot logically, as well as practically, be founded on conclusive arguments. He considers that the commitment of religious faith must involve a free choice by the individual and that this would be impossible if faith ever became simply the acceptance of the results of a conclusive argument.

> I say plainly I do not want to be converted by a smart syllogism; if I am asked to convert others by it, I say plainly I do not care to overcome their reason without touching their hearts. . . . Some

exertion on the part of the persons whom I am to convert is a condition of true conversion. They who have no religious earnestness are at the mercy, day by day, of some new argument or fact, which may overtake them, in favour of one conclusion or the other.[45]

Newman deplores the lack of any longing for enlightening revelation. Such a longing would stir a man 'to enquire whether a revelation has been given' and would give him a 'just and reasonable anticipation of its probability'.[46] Both active inquiry and the possibility of a decision for faith are killed by conclusive reasoning. In the *Grammar of Assent* Newman quotes from his piece entitled *The Tamworth Reading Room*.[47] The passage makes clear his conviction that religion cannot be simply a matter of inferred conclusions.

> To most men argument makes the point in hand only more doubtful, and considerably less impressive. After all, man is *not* a reasoning animal; he is a seeing, feeling, contemplating, acting animal. . . . Life is not long enough for a religion of inferences; we shall never have done beginning, if we determine to begin with proof. We shall ever be laying our foundations; we shall turn theology into evidences, and divines into textuaries. We shall never get at our first principles. . . . Life is for action. If we insist on proofs for everything, we shall never come to action: to act you must assume, and that assumption is faith.[48]

The limits of antecedent reasoning are here plainly set forth. Both in practice and in theory assent, as absolute personal commitment, can never be compelled by argument. To assent, to have faith, we must choose in the face of uncertainty. The function of reasoning is to make the choice of faith clearer and easier. We now turn to the two forms of antecedent reasoning to see how far the formal and the informal modes, inference and illation, can encourage acts of faith.

3. INFERENCE AND ASSENT

a. The Nature of Inference

By 'inference' Newman means that formal mode of reasoning which relates propositions to each other in order to demonstrate what they imply. Through such reasoning we gain knowledge 'indirectly . . . by virtue of a previous knowledge'.[49] In contrast to the natural and informal ways of reasoning, inference follows established rules of procedure. It is described as 'ratiocination . . . restricted and put into grooves ... and the science, which is its regulating principle, is Logic'.[50] While its paradigm case is the 'Aristotelic syllogism' where the conclusion is related to the premises according to clear and known rules, Newman considers that 'verbal reasoning, of whatever kind, as opposed to mental'[51] is to be regarded as 'inference'. Logic does not provide the actual form of all inferences but gives the 'scientific form' to which in theory they all can be reduced.[52]

Newman outlines the method of inference thus:

> the first step in the inferential method is to throw the question to be decided into the form of a proposition; then to throw the proof itself into propositions, the force of the proof lying in the comparison of these propositions with each other.

In other words, inference:

> does not hold a proposition for its own sake, but as dependent upon others, and those others it entertains for the sake of the conclusion. Thus it is practically far more concerned with the comparison of propositions, than with the propositions themselves.

These statements make it clear why inference is described as 'restricted and put into grooves' for it is limited to what can be demonstrated in a clear and precise manner according to the rules of valid implication laid down by Logic. It is restricted to what can be stated in propositions and, unlike natural or informal reasoning, its procedure must be explicit. Such explicit methods of implication are more easily adapted to exact symbols and to precise notions than to the more vague expressions of what is 'real'. Inference succeeds 'so far as words can in fact be found for representing the countless varieties and subtleties of human thought'. It is liable to fail 'on account of the fallacy of the original assumption' which is the basis of inference, namely, 'that whatever can be thought can be adequately expressed in words'.[53] Newman describes the situation in this way:

> The more simple and definite are the words of a proposition, and the narrower their meaning, and the more that meaning in each proposition is restricted to the relation which it has to the words of the other propositions compared with it,—in other words, the nearer the propositions concerned in the inference approach to being mental abstractions, and the less they have to do with the concrete reality, and the more closely they are made to express exact, intelligible, comprehensible, communicable notions, and the less they stand for objective things, that is, the more they are the

subjects, not of real, but of notional apprehension,—so much the
more suitable do they become for the purposes of inference.
Hence it is that no process of argument is so perfect, as that which
is conducted by means of symbols.[54]

An abstract symbol with an arbitrarily determined reference does not
carry with it the extraneous, subtle, and sometimes only partially
apprehended elements which are involved in terms expressing what is
'real'. Symbols are like notions in having a general reference but are
more useful than notions for inferential processes since their content
may be precisely defined.

In discussing 'Profession',[55] Newman shows that inferences sometimes produce conclusions which are mysterious or 'inconceivable'.
This may happen, for instance, if the notions which form the premises
of an inference are understood to contain elements which were never
intended when those notions were attributed to the matter under consideration. Such a situation may easily arise when a notion denotes
something real but is not really adequate for the purpose.

> Our notion of a thing may be only partially faithful to the original;
> it may be in excess of the thing, or it may represent it incompletely,
> and, in consequence, it may serve for it, it may stand for it, only to
> a certain point, in certain cases, but no further. After that point is
> reached, the notion and the thing part company; and then the
> notion, if still used as the representative of the thing, will work out
> conclusions, not inconsistent with itself, but with the thing to which
> it no longer corresponds.[56]

Inference thus may err while it mechanically follows its established
rules. The source of the error is not the method by which the conclusion is reached but the application of its rules to the particular
situation. Inference requires notions. Thus, when the notions available
do not exactly fit their reference, inference may establish conclusions
which do not correspond to the actual truth. The mechanical exactness
of inference, which gives it such precise accuracy when it deals with
abstract symbols, is a serious handicap when it is used with reference to
the 'real'.

We have already noted, in our examination of the relationship
between apprehension and assent, that in order to infer we do not
need to grasp the meaning of the statements which form the premises
and conclusion of the argument. As Newman puts it, 'we can infer, if
"x is y, and y is z, that x is z", whether we know the meaning of x and
z or no'.[57] What, of course, we must apprehend is the relationships

between the different elements of the argument. Therefore, while 'inference requires no apprehension of the things inferred',[58] inference is impossible unless we apprehend the terms expressing the relationships involved.

What Newman calls the 'conditionality' of a conclusion is undisguised in the case of inferences. This is because the clarity and precision of the processes make the relationship between the conclusion and its premises explicit. For instance, in the case of the inference 'x is y, and y is z, therefore x is z', the conclusion 'x is z', so far as it is regarded as a conclusion, is not entertained as if it had the unconditional character of a self-evident truth. As a conclusion, its acceptance is always clearly related to its premises and their syllogistic connexion.[59] This 'conditionality' is described by Newman at the very beginning of the *Grammar of Assent* when he states that propositions are 'conditional, when they express a Conclusion . . . and at once imply, and imply their dependence on, other propositions'.[60] It does not mean that the conclusion may not be conclusive: in a correct syllogism the conclusion is undoubtedly required by its premises.[61] When Newman speaks of the 'conditionality' of conclusions, he is not referring to their logical relationship to their premises but to the way in which we entertain them. This 'conditionality' is the result of our awareness that all conclusions depend upon other propositions.

Furthermore, while some conclusions are what we call 'self-evident', most conclusions in practice are distinguished from assents because of their 'probable' as well as 'conditional' character. In the case of inference the probability of a conclusion is made clear by the explicit structure of the argument leading to it. It derives from the assumptions upon which the argument rests and upon the process of inference itself. All reasoning is finally based on:

> what are called first principles, the recondite source of all knowledge, as to which logic provides no common measure of minds, —which are accepted by some, rejected by others,—in which, and not in the syllogistic exhibitions, lies the whole problem of attaining to truth. . . . Syllogism, then, though of course it has its use, still does only the minutest and easiest part of the work, in the investigation of truth, for when there is any difficulty, that difficulty commonly lies in determining first principles, not in the arrangement of proofs.[62]

As Newman points out in his discussion of 'Revealed Religion',[63] we may persuade someone of the truth of a religious position if we both 'start from the same principles', for then both of us will agree about what is a satisfactory argument in the case in dispute. If, however, we differ over basic assumptions, there is no possibility of fruitful debate between us. Since these 'principles which govern' reasoning 'are of a personal character',[64] and since they provide the positions from which we reason, their own validity cannot be demonstrated by formal inferences and yet the validity of every inference depends upon them.

Among these non-provable basic assumptions are those which determine what shall be the nature of a satisfactory argument.[65] General agreement concerning the basic forms of inference allows inferential processes to be called 'objective'. They provide a common ground of appeal in disputed cases, a situation which is rarely found in the case of the subjective, undeclared reasoning of the Illative Sense.[66] Thus we find in the forms of inference 'an instrument of reasoning' that is 'less vague and arbitrary than the talent and experience of the few or the common sense of the many' but is 'a common measure between mind and mind . . . a standard such as to secure us against hopeless mistakes, and to emancipate us from the capricious *ipse dixit* of authority'.[67] The systematic statement of these standards by which the validity of inferences can be determined is Logic. The basic principles of Logic, such as that 'a' and 'not a' are incompatible, cannot be proved to be true and so must be assumed, but they are assumed as self-evident truths and it is scrupulous to argue that inferences are probable because of their dependence upon such principles. Other basic assumptions, however, many of which are to be found in religious arguments, are neither so obvious nor command general acceptance, e.g., the assumption that religious experience involves an Other beyond the self and the world, or the assumption that moral values express aspects of the objective structure of reality. Their ultimate dependence upon what are clearly unprovable and often disputable assumptions means that many conclusions are only accepted by us as 'probable'. We must also remember that a conclusion is always the conclusion of a particular argument. Even though its basic assumptions might themselves be true, error could occur in the actual process of inference.

The differences between conclusions and assents is clear and explicit in the case of inferences. In many cases the openness of the argument reveals the 'probable' nature of the inferred conclusion. In every case the explicitness of the argument reminds us that its conclusion is 'conditional', i.e. is entertained not by itself alone but in connexion with other statements. On both counts the conclusion of a process of inference is distinguished from the unconditional and absolute character of assent.

b. The Value of Inference as an Antecedent of Assent

We now turn to the relationship between inference and assent, and in particular we shall be concerned with the importance of inference for the assent of religious faith. We have already noted that the function of any kind of antecedent reasoning is not to 'cause' or 'impose' assent directly but to encourage us to grant our assent. Assent, in fact, is 'independent of our acts of inference'.[68] There is no automatic procedure by which we are forced to step from 'an incontrovertible conclusion' based 'on the condition of incontrovertible premises' to 'absolute recognition . . . unconditionally given'.[69] In other words, no logical necessity exists which requires us to 'follow up our inference of a proposition by giving an assent to it',[70] when by 'assent' we mean our unreserved acceptance of a proposition as true. Newman describes what is essentially the same position from a different point of view when he holds that religious faith must not be regarded as the acceptance of a number of conclusions since its essence is absolute commitment. In his long quotation from his article *The Tamworth Reading Room*, he states:

> no man will be a martyr for a conclusion. . . . No one, I say, will die for his own calculations. . . . Logic makes but a sorry rhetoric with the multitude; first shoot round corners, and you may not despair of converting by a syllogism. . . . Life is not long enough for a religion of inferences; we shall never have done beginning, if we determine to begin with proof.[71]

Religion does not consist of discovering what is the best available hypothesis and deciding to follow out its practical implications because it seems the most likely to be true. Fundamentally religion requires unconditional assent and unquestioning obedience to its dictates. Since this situation can never be characteristic of a group of inferences, we are mistaken if we consider that it is possible to infer beliefs. As the proper function of antecedent reasoning, however, is to encourage us to grant assent, its significance lies in the persuasive force that it can exert upon us. Our problem, therefore, is to determine how far inference, the formal and explicit mode of reasoning, can provide this encouragement. In the *Tamworth Reading Room* article Newman states that 'deductions [sc. inferences, for syllogisms are *par excellence* deductions] have no power of persuasion'.[72] This is too negative for the later views of the *Grammar of Assent* but, even so, inference has little value as an antecedent to assent.

Inference, in reaching a conclusion, attains it through processes which make its 'conditionality', i.e. its essential connexion with other propositions, only too obvious. Since we do not entertain a conclusion for its own sake but in the light of its connexions with other propositions, we are not very likely to regard it as a proposition which should be considered as true absolutely. As a conclusion, its essential connectedness with other propositions, which is clear and explicit in the case of inference, militates against its being given the unconditional acceptance of assent. Furthermore, the explicitness required by inference[73] renders such formal reasoning unsuitable as an antecedent of religious assent since it requires a definiteness which is alien to the subtlety involved in religious statements and reasoning. When the organized thought of theology is applied to religion, it is 'obliged to draw up' long and complicated lists of propositions because of:

> the limitations, explanations, definitions, adjustments, balancings, cautions, arbitrary prohibitions, which are imperatively required by the weakness of human thought and the imperfections of human languages.[74]

As a result of this complexity, theological statements are neither easily nor satisfactorily employed in inferences. They tend to be too diffuse for such simple and straightforward reasoning. The clarity and precision of formal logic thus makes it an unsuitable tool in areas of thought like that of religion where exact definitions are not found. Another consequence of the explicitness of inference, although one that is not mentioned by Newman, is that its conclusions in many cases are so clearly probable that their persuasive force, if any, will be against rather than in favour of assent. The fact that formal argument shows just how probable is its conclusion tends to keep that probability in focus. This tendency hinders us in granting assent to the conclusion because, after considering the grounds for assent, we find it hard to forget the demonstrated probability of the proposition and to treat it absolutely. In these three ways, then, the explicit character of inference contributes to its unsatisfactoriness as antecedent reasoning for assent.

Inference is unsatisfactory as antecedent reasoning for assent, secondly, because it is unable to deal adequately with the 'real'. As we have already remarked, inference works best when it deals with notions and symbols whose meaning is exactly defined whereas assent is most readily given to what is apprehended as real.[75] Now theology, the notional expression of religion, involves statements whose contents are usually far too complex for inference.[76] But if theology is unsuitable, religion is even less satisfactory for inference because religion does not deal with notions but with the 'real' in a part of reality which is at the boundary of our understanding. Any inference which concerns religion must consequently be so weak that it will have little power to incline us to assent. As antecedent reasoning for religious assent, inference fails because it can deal with the 'real' only to a very limited extent.

The value of inference as antecedent reasoning is restricted, thirdly, by the fact that it cannot show, even faintly, the truth of its basic assumptions. Since these assumptions compose the first principles and premises of inference, they are prior to inference and their truth cannot be demonstrated by it. Such assumptions, however, form the core of any religious system and are the source of what often appear to be intractable differences of opinion. 'I cannot convert men, when I ask for assumptions which they refuse to grant me; and without assumptions no one can prove any thing about any thing.'[77] Consequently, in the case of certain fundamental beliefs which are normative for religion, inference must stand by idle and unemployed when we consider whether to grant our assent.

The limited value of inference as antecedent reasoning is finally seen in the matter of the apprehension necessary for assent. Inference itself does not require any apprehension of its conclusion but assent is only possible when its object is apprehended.[78] When, therefore, an inference reaches a conclusion which is not apprehended, that conclusion cannot be regarded in its unapprehended state as a candidate for assent. Furthermore, as Newman points out, even where inference produces conclusions which are apprehended, the inference can weaken our assent to its conclusion by causing us to entertain it notionally rather than 'really'.[79] The 'God' which is produced at the end of an argument is not the 'God' to which a man commits himself in faith but a notional construction. Accordingly, while inference may show the probability of a conclusion, by converting it into a notional proposition it robs it of the power characteristic of religious assent.

It would be a mistake, however, to hold that inference has no value at all as an antecedent of assent. In spite of his assertion in the *Tamworth Reading Room* article that 'deductions have no power of persuasion',[80] Newman does recognize that on occasions inference may both lead to and strengthen an assent. There are cases where inference both 'fortifies and illustrates' our assents and can have the effect of 'a vivid apprehension . . . giving them luminousness and force'.[81] Especially is this true where the conclusion can be so clearly demonstrated on the basis of assumptions generally accepted that its persuasive power in practice is irresistible. Here there is the possibility that the notional assent and the inferred conclusion may be confused.[82] While there is no logical connexion between the conclusion and the assent, we would be hard pressed to refrain from assenting to the demonstrated proposition that 'the three angles of a triangle are together equal to two right angles' when once we had grasped the proof.[83] What so severely restricts the persuasive power of inference as antecedent reasoning is that in practice it is only rarely able to produce such convincing and compelling proofs. Usually all that it can offer is a too clearly 'conditional' and probable conclusion, even when it can apply its methods to the relevant material.

While, then, on odd occasions formal reasoning may lead us to assent, in general it is too limited in its scope and its conclusions too obviously 'conditional' to persuade us to assent. In religious affairs its value is especially restricted by the nature of the objects and the complexity of any statement which hopes adequately to represent them. Inference is not a form of reasoning which is likely to lead to faith and belief. We now turn to the informal mode of reasoning to see if it is more valuable than inference as antecedent reasoning.

4. ILLATION AND ASSENT

a. The Nature of Illation

The term 'illative' appears in the *Grammar of Assent* without any explicit definition. It is an uncommon word which is defined in contemporary dictionaries in terms of 'inference; deduction; conclusion'.[84] Newman may have noticed the word in Locke who writes of 'illation' as the intellectual faculty which 'consists in nothing but the perception of the connexion there is between the ideas, in each step of the deduction'.[85] In this paragraph, the term seems to be used synonymously with 'inference' and 'reason'. The phrase 'illative conjunctions' is found in Whately's *Logic* in a passage which Newman helped to compose.[86] The first time that 'illative' appears in the *Grammar of Assent* it is equated with the 'ratiocinative' and refers to the natural reasoning faculty of the mind.[87] A few pages later Newman describes the 'Illative Sense' as 'right judgment in ratiocination',[88] as the 'power of judging and concluding, when in its perfection'.[89] He explains that 'the word "sense"' is used here 'parallel to our use of it in "good sense", "common sense", a "sense of beauty" etc.'.[90] The faculty may be compared to Aristotle's 'φρονησις' which 'guides the mind in matters of conduct'.[91]

The Illative Sense is very important for Newman's thesis because it is not as restricted as inference. It can reach conclusions and use evidence which are outside the scope of formal reasoning. For instance, in reasoning on any subject whatever, which is concrete, we proceed, as far indeed as we can, by the logic of language, but we are obliged to supplement it by the more subtle and elastic logic of thought; for forms by themselves prove nothing.[92]

This natural reasoning faculty can come to conclusions in matters which are too vague or too complex for the precise, formal methods of inference. It is able to consider matters which cannot be clearly expressed and to solve problems where the relevant considerations are so intricately interrelated that to present them all in writing would be to make the problem too complicated to be grasped. In contrast to inference, the Illative Sense does not follow a procedure which has an explicit form and to which it must demonstrably conform. Often the activity of our Illative Sense can neither be expressed nor verbally analysed but is unconscious and undefined. In such cases 'we reason without effort and intention, or any necessary consciousness of the path which the mind takes in passing from antecedent to conclusion'.[93] Consequently we may not be able to give a comprehensive account of the premises that we have used in reaching a conclusion[94] and yet be convinced that we have good reasons for that conclusion.[95] Newman describes this natural reasoning activity as appearing as:

> a simple act, not as a process, as if there were no medium interposed between antecedent and consequent, and the transition from one to the other were of the nature of an instinct—that is, the process is altogether unconscious and implicit. . . . Our most natural mode of reasoning is, not from propositions to propositions, but from things to things, from concrete to concrete, from wholes to wholes. . . . Not only is the inference with its process ignored, but the antecedent also. To the mind itself the reasoning is a simple divination or prediction. . . . This is the mode in which we ordinarily reason, dealing with things directly, and as they stand, one by one, in the concrete, with an intrinsic and personal power, not a conscious adoption of an artificial instrument or expedient.[96]

Since the process of illation is not explicit, the only elements that are obvious are the conclusion and the sometimes vague indications of the considerations that lead to it. The important activity of relating and balancing the various considerations is executed largely *in camera*. This allows illation to include subtleties which are too fine for inferential treatment. In formal reasoning the premises are related to each other and to the conclusion by certain definite links. This gives a valid inference its 'necessary' character for its conclusion must be demonstrably and undoubtedly entailed by its premises. In an illation, however, the mind is attempting to determine the balance and the degree of probability of a conclusion. In making its estimate all relevant (and often in practice some irrelevant) consideration have their place: anything which bears or seems to bear upon the issue must be evaluated and given its due force in coming to the conclusion. The Illative Sense is thus able to avoid the limitations of formal reasoning which requires 'simplicity and exactness' and thereby is incompetent 'to settle particulars and details'.[97] In illation, in contrast, 'minute but abundant, delicate but effective'[98] considerations can play their part.

The subtle and often unconscious activity of the Illative Sense does not mean that its method is beyond our comprehension. Although we may often not be aware of how we came to a certain conclusion,[99] Newman holds that we can describe in principle the method used in our informal reasoning. It is the method of converging probability. This method works on the basis that while the available evidence may never irrefutably entail a certain conclusion, it may show that this conclusion is so very probably true that in practice we would be foolish to refuse to accept it. We may illustrate this method of reasoning by two examples, one from mathematics[100] and the other from law.[101] The arithmetical series '$1 + \frac{1}{2} + \frac{1}{4} + \frac{1}{8} + \frac{1}{16} + \frac{1}{32} + \frac{1}{64} + \ldots$' carried out to infinity will never exactly add up to '2'. At the infinite degree that sum will still be an infinitely small amount short of '2'. In practice, on the other hand, it would be pressing exactitude to the point of stupidity to deny that the sum of the series is '2'. The sum of the series increasingly approximates to '2' until the difference between the sum and '2' is negligible. For the other example of an argument from converging probability, let us consider the case of a juryman who has to decide whether the accused is or is not guilty of some offence. In the trial he hears reasons why it may be thought practically certain that the man is guilty and he is given other reasons why it might not be thought practically certain. On the one hand, he hears evidence that the accused was recognized in an identity parade, had a sudden increase in wealth, owned a gun of the same type as that used in the crime, and that fibres similar to those of the accused's clothes were found on the scene of the crime. On the other hand, the accused denies that he committed the crime and produces witnesses who give him an alibi. Here there is neither a syllogistic proof nor a single pattern of increasing probability. The juryman must decide if the balance of probability is sufficient to make him practically certain that the man is guilty. In his evaluation the demeanour of the accused and of his friends, his assessment of the trustworthiness of the accused's explanation of his increase in wealth and his own attitude towards scientific evidence, as well as various personal prejudices, will play a part. The decision that is reached will show what the juryman judges the evidence to point to, but in making that decision he will have been influenced by considerations of which he may not be conscious as well as by the evidence given in court.

The method of converging probability used in matters of faith is more akin to the legal than to the mathematical example. It does not work in terms of calculable probabilities but with different factors, each having a different significance, some of which are recognized while others are unconscious. In determining the conclusion which these factors make possible, probable or practically certain, we do not give to each factor a precise plus or minus quantitative value and then add up the figures to find the likelihood of the conclusion. The different elements, together with their composite significance as a whole, are evaluated without any recourse to exact calculations. This does not mean that one piece of evidence will not be granted more weight than another. The juryman, for instance, will be expected to give more weight to the evidence of identification than to shiftiness of the accused's eyes. Since the proportionate significance of the evidence is not mathematically determined, so, when the conclusion is given, it is in general terms. It is given in terms of being 'certain', 'probable', or 'possible that x is y', not that 'it is 93.721 per cent certain that x is y'. The result, then, of reasoning by converging probability in matters like that of faith is not a statistical probability but a personal decision. Newman describes this method of the Illative Sense thus:

> It is the cumulation of probabilities, independent of each other, arising out of the nature and circumstances of the particular case which is under review; probabilities too fine to avail separately, too subtle and circuitous to be convertible into syllogisms, too numerous and various for such conversion, even were they convertible.[102]

In a later passage on the same subject he writes that:

> the conclusion in a real or concrete question is foreseen and predicted rather than actually attained; foreseen in the number and direction of accumulated premises, which all converge to it, and as the result of their combination, approach it more nearly than any assignable difference, yet do not touch it logically, (though only not touching it,) on account of the nature of its subject-matter and the delicate and implicit character of at least part of the reasonings on which it depends. It is by the strength,

variety, or multiplicity of premises, which are only probable, not by invincible syllogisms,—by objections overcome, by adverse theories neutralized, by difficulties gradually clearing up, by exceptions proving the rule, by unlooked-for correlations found for received truths, by suspense and delay in the process issuing in triumphant re-actions,—by all these ways, and many others, it is that the practised and experienced mind is able to make a sure divination that a conclusion is inevitable, of which his lines of reasoning do not actually put him in possession.[103]

From these quotations we can see what Newman understands to be the method of the Illative Sense. It consists of the assessment of probabilities in order to determine to what conclusion, if any, they point.

Illation is not an artificial procedure which we construct and adopt. It is 'our most natural mode of reasoning'[104] and is found 'in what may be called a state of nature, as it is found in the uneducated'.[105] The rules of inference are the result of our deliberate analyses of implication, but our Illative Sense develops unconsciously as we learn how to make decisions about the issues which confront us in everyday life. Illation is not an instinct implanted fully-developed in all men for it is not 'one and the same in all, and incapable of cultivation'. It may be called 'instinctive' only so far as this denotes that it is 'a perception of facts without assignable media of perceiving'.[106] It can, however, be called 'natural' in the sense that it is found in some shape or form in everyone who is capable of reasoning at all, just as 'sight' is natural although its range and capacity vary in different people and in some it does not exist at all. Since in this sense illation may claim to be a 'natural' faculty, Newman believes that there are good grounds for trusting its conclusions and that certainly there are no *a priori* grounds for regarding it as less trustworthy than sense-perception and memory.[107] Indeed, not to hold this is to distrust Providence, whereas Newman, like Amort,[108] holds:

> that since a Good Providence watches over us, He blesses such means of argument as it has pleased Him to give us, in the nature of man and of the world, if we use them duly for those ends for which He has given them.[109]

Newman suggests, therefore, that we must infer wherever possible but that when formal methods are impossible, we are justified in trusting that God will help us find the right answer from the available evidence by informal methods.

In another passage where he seeks to defend our use of our Illative

Sense, Newman argues similarly that we cannot justifiably question the validity of what is given to us in nature. Here the validity of the findings of our Illative Sense does not depend upon direct divine guidance but upon the necessary correctness of any proper use of a natural faculty. This view assumes that what is natural is good and should not be doubted if it is used according to its nature. It is:

> unmeaning in us, to criticize or find fault with our own nature, which is nothing else than we ourselves, instead of using it according to the use of which it ordinarily admits. Our being, with its faculties, mind and body, is a fact not admitting of question, all things being of necessity referred to it, not it to other things. . . . There is no medium between using my faculties, as I have them, and flinging myself upon the external world according to the random impulse of the moment. . . . It is enough for the proof of the value and authority of any function which I possess, to be able to pronounce that it is natural.[110]

This is basically the same as the former defence of illation and differs from it only in that the justification is attributed to 'nature' and not explicitly to the safeguards of a divine Providence. Whether or not we accept Newman's view that our Illative Sense is predestined to discover the truth because of the structure of nature or of the will of God, illation is justified practically as the only method that we can use in the circumstances. There are many occasions when we have to decide what is true in spite of the insufficiency and even the inconsistency of the evidence. All that we can do in such a situation is to determine, as well as we are able, the balance of probability indicated by the available evidence. This is the work of our Illative Sense, in Newman's terminology.

Newman recognizes that the Illative Sense varies with different individuals and subjects and that it develops in each individual as his experience expands. This is why illation cannot be regarded without reservation as natural and instinctive. In embryo it is present in all men, and this is a justification of its validity as a natural faculty, but it has to be developed by experience before it can function with accuracy.

> The intellect admits of an education; man is a being of progress; he has to learn how to fulfil his end, and to be what facts show that he is intended to be. His mind is in the first instance in disorder, and runs wild; his faculties have their rudimental and inchoate state, and are gradually carried on by practice and experience to their perfection.[111]

Although illation is natural, it is still liable to err. This liability declines as our experience and practice increase but it never completely disappears. The practice of illation, therefore, does not confirm Newman's general justification of its validity by reference to its naturalness and to the blessings of divine Providence. At one point Newman restricts the connotation of the phrase 'Illative Sense' to the 'power of judging and concluding, when in its perfection'.[112] The reference to 'perfection' possibly implies that we should only speak of illation where its conclusion is in fact true. This is a tendentious restriction of the meaning of 'illation'. It is not applicable to Newman's general understanding of the term which does allow for its fallibility.

While we speak of 'the Illative Sense' and hold that 'it' has to be developed by experience, Newman is apparently aware that in fact each subject has its own particular illative method.

> The ratiocinative faculty, then, as found in individuals, is not a general instrument of knowledge, but has its province, or is what may be called departmental. It is not so much one faculty, as a collection of similar or analogous faculties under one name, there being really as many faculties as there are distinct subject-matters.[113]

This comes close to a recognition that different subjects have different logics, so that what is a proper method for one subject is inappropriate for another. The recognition, however, is very vague and Newman does not develop the hints contained in this passage. Although he suggests that each subject has its own mode of reasoning, in fact he distinguishes only two modes, the formal and the informal, one employing the method of explicit deduction and the other that of converging probability. Nowhere does he suggest that the illation used in law is not in its essentials the same as that used in mathematics, literary criticism, or theology, although these have four very different subject-matters. Elsewhere the term 'Illative Sense' is used as if it denotes a specific reasoning faculty which operates along identical lines in all cases which are unsuitable for inferential reasoning. What Newman does recognize is that in different subjects different degrees of probability must suffice to show a conclusion.[114]

Our Illative Sense develops in different subjects according to our aptitudes for those subjects and our opportunities to actualize them. Both heredity and environment are involved here. It is not unusual to find one person whose thinking is brilliant on certain matters but who is quite hopeless, no matter how hard he tries, with other subjects, while another person reveals opposite abilities. These individual differences of aptitude often seem to be explicable only in terms of inherited characteristics.[115] Thus a person may be said to be 'naturally' good at physics but 'constitutionally' bad at military strategy. Ability at one thing is no indication of ability at another.

> No one would for a moment expect that because Newton and Napoleon both had a genius for ratiocination, that, in consequence, Napoleon could have generalized the principle of gravitation, or Newton have seen how to concentrate a hundred thousand men at Austerlitz.[116]

'Genius' refers to an exceptional ability to handle and balance particular types of concepts or facts. On the other hand, a latent capacity is of no practical use until it has been actually developed. Newton had to study physics and become conversant with the subject before he was able to use his genius in that field to discover the laws of gravity. Since a person's natural ability in any subject is actualized and improved only by dealing with that subject, experience is necessary for the development of the Illative Sense. A person may have the latent aptitude of a genius in a certain subject but until he has had opportunity to exercise it, it cannot develop into genius.

Since the conclusions of our Illative Sense are not explicity demonstrated, they may be influenced by all kinds of personal considerations. We must not forget that while the method of illation is one of converging probability, its actual employment is controlled by individual judgements in which personal prejudices have their place. Faced by five points of evidence, a, b, c, d, and e, I have first to estimate the validity of each of them and then to decide what conclusion they indicate and with what degree of likelihood. These acts of estimation and decision are open to all kinds of unconscious bias. As I estimate the value of each point in turn, my individual scepticism or gullibility will exert an overall influence while I will be influenced in each particular point by my own experience of the kind of evidence presented. For instance, if I have previously been let down by relying on evidence which resembles that in point 'a', I will tend to devalue it. Again, the subconscious connexion of a piece of evidence with an earlier pleasure may lead me to give undue weight to that point. As for summing up the direction of the evidence and the probability of the conclusion which it indicates, existing prejudices about the conclusion will affect my judgements concerning it. This is partly the reason why 'what to one intellect is a proof is not so to another'.[117] The strength of an illative conclusion depends to some extent upon the self who makes it. The more I desire a certain conclusion, the more likely I am to be satisfied with a little evidence in favour of it, whereas if I intensely dislike a position, only a great weight of evidence will be sufficient to convince me that it is probably true.

There are several passages which show that Newman recognizes the subjective bias of illation but he is sufficiently optimistic not to count it of major importance. His desire to find a way by which articles of faith can receive antecedent reasoning clearly predisposes him to favour the activity of the Illative Sense. The examples which he takes to illustrate its method lead to conclusions which it is hard to conceive of anyone doubting.[118] These well-chosen cases show the Illative Sense reaching conclusions with which we all agree. Here the personal element does not create any significant problems. In fact Newman gives the impression that the activity of the Illative Sense, while being personal, is blessed with an intrinsic natural correctness which is generally undisturbed by the personal prejudices of individuals. In relation to the conclusion 'I shall die one day', he writes that:

> what logic cannot do, my own living personal reasoning, my good sense, which is the healthy condition of such personal reasoning, but which cannot adequately express itself in words, does for me, and I am possessed with the most precise, absolute, masterful certitude of my dying some day or other.[119]

Later he describes illation as 'the true healthy action of our ratiocinative powers',[120] again displaying an optimistic attitude which is not troubled by the possibilities of personal prejudice. The subjectivity is, however, recognized. Newman states that in concrete matters:

> we judge for ourselves, by our own lights, and on our own principles; and our criterion of truth is not so much the manipulation of propositions, as the intellectual and moral character of the person maintaining them, and the ultimate silent effect of his arguments or conclusions upon our minds.[121]

In another passage he makes the following comments upon a metaphysical passage of Coleridge:

> It is plain that, if the passage is worth anything, we must secure that worth for our own use by the personal action of our own minds, or else we shall be only professing and asserting its doctrine, without having any ground or right to assert it. And our preparation for understanding and making use of it will be the general state of our mental discipline and cultivation, our own experiences, our appreciation of religious ideas, the perspicacity and steadiness of our intellectual vision.[122]

An illative 'proof', therefore,

> has always in it, more or less, an element of the personal, because 'prudence' is not a constituent part of our nature, but a personal endowment. . . . We have arrived at these conclusions—not *ex opere operato*, by a scientific necessity independent of ourselves,—but by the action of our own minds, by our own individual perception of the truth in question.[123]

These passages indicate that while illative reasoning is influenced by all kinds of personal prejudice, Newman does not consider that this challenges the general validity of its conclusions. Particular illations may be completely erroneous because of false and misleading prejudices but these are exceptions. In most cases the conclusions reached are to be accepted without question. Whether or not this optimism about the truth-finding qualities of illation is justified, we have to recognize that our powers of understanding are so limited that we have no alternative but to accept illative conclusions if we want reasoned positions where inferences are not possible. With most problems, and certainly with religious ones, the objective certainty of syllogistic reasoning is unattainable: the recognition that illation is influenced by personal factors is the recognition that basically most of our reasoning is affected by subjective forces. One non-evident personal force which Newman recognizes as affecting our illative conclusions is our moral state.[124] We shall see later that moral goodness is considered by Newman to be necessary for making an objectively correct religious assent. Here we are simply concerned to note his view that in religious affairs our moral state is a factor, and sometimes an important factor, in determining the conclusions that we reach by illation. 'In ordinary minds' the Illative Sense may be 'biased and degraded by prejudice, passion and self-interest'.[125] It is the man who really wants to ascertain what is true apart from all personal considerations who is most likely to discover the truth by illation.[126]

b. The Value of Illation as an Antecedent of Assent

Now that we have described what Newman means by the 'Illative Sense', we are to consider its value for the reasoning which is the antecedent of assent. We have already noted that we can assent only where we apprehend the object of our assent. Since inference can result in a conclusion which is not apprehended,[127] it does not necessarily produce a statement which is a candidate for assent. Newman does not discuss the degree of apprehension needed for illation but it is clear from his description of its method that illation is possible only when we have some grasp of the material we are considering and of the conclusion to which it points. We can balance pieces of evidence and estimate the probability of a conclusion only when we understand their reference. Whereas, therefore, inference can sometimes lead to conclusions to which we cannot assent because they are inapprehensible, we can assent to any conclusion reached by illation so far as the apprehension of its meaning is concerned.

Neither the apprehension required by illation nor the method of illation is restricted to notions. On both counts illation can successfully deal with the 'real' and this is its greatest value for assent. In abstract analysis the process of illation may be verbally expressed, but in practice, as we have already mentioned, it usually appears as being:

> not from propositions to propositions, but from things to things, from concrete to concrete, from wholes to wholes. . . . This is the mode in which we ordinarily reason, dealing with things directly, and as they stand, one by one, in the concrete.[128]

Not only can our Illative Sense make full use of the real in its premises, but its 'multiform and intricate process' is able to come to conclusions about 'a concrete fact'.[129] This, often unconscious, reasoning with and about 'real' facts is carried out,

> not by any possible verbal enumeration of all the considerations, minute but abundant, delicate but effective . . . but by a mental comprehension of the whole case, and a discernment of its upshot.[130]

Our Illative Sense is thus able to handle what is individual, existing, and cannot be adequately conceptualized. When, therefore, we consider whether or not to assent to something which is 'real', it will be our Illative Sense which will guide us. In such cases, as with notions which are too vague or too complex for syllogistic methods, inference is too 'restricted'[131] to be of assistance. We need the subtler reasoning of illation to persuade us of the reasonableness of giving our assent. Accordingly it is illation and not inference which is able to handle the material involved in religious assents for these assents concern what is real, complex, and possibly even beyond our conceptual schemes.[132]

Newman believes that our Illative Sense is able to make decisions about the truth or falsity of presuppositions. He holds that:

> it is the mind itself that detects them in their obscure recesses, illustrates them, establishes them, eliminates them. . . . The mind contemplates them without the use of words, by a process which cannot be analysed.[133]

These basic presuppositions are fundamental to any reasoning, whether formal or informal, since all reasoning starts from the assumption of certain basic positions. The assertion 'that we have no right in philosophy to make any assumption whatever' is self-contradictory for it 'is of all assumptions the greatest, and to forbid assumptions universally is to forbid this one in particular'.[134] When we discussed inference, we noted that all formal reasoning depends finally upon presuppositions which themselves cannot be proved by inference.[135] It is equally true that all illation is based upon premises and principles that are assumed. Newman illustrates this by reference to the Protestant assumption 'that Scripture is the Rule of Faith'[136] and the sceptic's assumption of 'the fact of an established order' as an argument against miracles.[137] Every conclusion rests upon some facts and principles whose truth is presupposed. Illation, however, is able to some degree to evaluate these presuppositions—and so to test the bases of our reasonings.

Is Newman justified in claiming that assent, which is normally preceded by reasoning, can be given to these basic assumptions? Can the first principles of our thought be regarded in any way as the conclusions of antecedent reasoning? Newman does not seem to be aware of this problem but some of his statements indicate what his answer to it might be. In his discussion of 'presumptions', which he defines as 'assent to first principles',[138] he mentions, in relation to their origin, 'the aid which from our earliest years we receive from teachers'.[139] So far, then, as we can claim the teaching of 'authority' as an antecedent reason for our assent, we can claim antecedent reasoning for our assent to first principles. In the case of each one of them some authority or other could be instanced. Although authority may not provide very strong motives for granting assent, especially when the authorities themselves do not indicate why we should accept their views as correct, in these fundamental issues it has often in practice sufficient persuasive force. It is most unusual for us to reject the assumptions that are generally accepted in our society and by those who have been responsible for our upbringing. Arguments which appeal to authority, it should be noted, do not deal with the object of assent directly. Their force lies in the fact that some respected person or group have granted their assent in this case. A more direct form of antecedent reasoning for presuppositions, although one that is not expounded by Newman, is possible along the lines of a *reductio ad absurdum*. If the negation of the assumption under consideration leads to apparently absurd implications, we have indications of the likelihood of the original assumption. The force of such an argument would be appreciated by our Illative Sense. It is most probable, however, that our judgement of such a *reductio ad absurdum* would depend upon our existing presuppositions and so ultimately, in the case of presumptions, the argument would be circular.

It is apparent, however, that Newman considers that the basic assumptions which each of us entertains are finally to be traced back to our individual nature. In this case it is irrelevant to speak of reasoning preceding the adoption of our presuppositions for the operative force is not any conscious or unconscious reasoning but the constitution of our individual nature. Our presuppositions are given to us with our very existence and are not within our control, nor can we be held responsible for them.[140] They are described as 'spontaneously issuing out of the state of thought respectively belonging to each'[141] so that everyone 'writes from his own point of view and with his own principles, and these admit of no common measure'.[142] These assumptions:

> reach and affect what is so intimately bound up with the mental constitution of each. . . . Men become personal when logic fails; it is their mode of appealing to their own primary elements of thought, and their own illative sense, against the principles and the judgment of another.[143]

Such 'antecedent reasons . . . are in great measure made by ourselves and belong to our personal character'.[144] This highly personal character which Newman gives to basic assumptions raises the question whether the reasoning activity of our Illative Sense is at all relevant to their acceptance. Newman writes of 'the process of assumption lying in the action of the Illative Sense, as applied to primary elements of thought',[145] but it is doubtful whether he intends this reference to illation to suggest that an assumption is preceded by some form of reasoning, even if unconscious. What seems to be his intention, rather, is to suggest that the Illative Sense makes the assumption and that the assumption itself is derived from the mental constitution of the individual. Our examination of Newman's thought on the question of basic assumptions thus leads us to the conclusion that ultimately he recognizes them as a-rational productions of the individual mind. From the few relevant references in the *Grammar of Assent* we cannot tell whether Newman would regard them as categories of understanding in Kant's sense or simply the contributions of society to our knowledge. What is clear is that he is not, on the whole,[146] prepared to assert that these principles are or can be accepted after a demonstration of their probability. In so far, then, as it is true to say that we 'assent' to basic assumptions, it is an assent without antecedent reasoning, even of the informal kind. On the other hand, if such assents are questioned, we can, as we have suggested, appeal to authority or to a *reductio ad absurdum* for support. Ultimately, nevertheless, such assumptions depend upon our nature: we assume their truth because we are who we are and not because we have any faculty to determine their truth. Thus it is not always true that assent has antecedent reasons, although if we are questioned about our assents to presuppositions, we can support them by reasons which in fact played no part in our original acceptance of them.

Apart from the special case of basic assumptions, there is no need to challenge Newman's view that assent is preceded by some form of unconscious or conscious reasoning. It is here that we see the crucial importance of our Illative Sense in the matter of assent. Not only does this faculty allow us to reason in matters outside the narrow limits of inference but also by this faculty, whose operation is highly personal,[147] we determine both the validity of any reasoning and the force of its conclusion. Even formal reasoning is subject to its judgement for there is no 'ultimate test of truth and error in our inferences besides the trustworthiness of the Illative Sense that gives them its sanction. . . .'[148] When, therefore, we assess the force of any reasoning we use our Illative Sense. The pressure that any antecedent reasoning can exert to persuade us to assent thus depends upon our illative valuation of it.

The judgements of our Illative Sense are personal and practical rather than logical and theoretical. They do not primarily indicate the degree of objective probability of a proposition but suggest how far we should be prepared to accept it as true. When we consider whether or not to grant our assent, we are influenced by these subjectively sufficient conclusions rather than by strictly objective probabilities. This is necessarily the case since we are encouraged to give our assent by what we regard as the real position, not by what is the objectively true situation apart from all personal considerations. Since assent is a personal act of commitment, so the antecedent reasoning which leads to it is that where 'we judge for ourselves, by our own lights, and on our own principles',[149] that is, the reasoning of our Illative Sense. This is true even where the antecedent reasoning is apparently inferential. It is not the formally deduced conclusion that influences us but the conclusion which we accept after a subjective illative assessment of the case. Thus the 'proof' that is relevant to assent 'has always in it, more or less, an element of the personal, because "prudence" is not a constituent part of our nature, but a personal endowment'.[150]

Because he recognizes this personal element in antecedent reasoning, Newman appreciates the significance of personal testimony when we turn to religious assent. Since the issues that are involved in such assents are so complex and often based upon disputed assumptions, they are necessarily material for the Illative Sense. When we are questioned about our religious beliefs, we cannot claim that they are demonstrably true in any objective way. We can offer only the arguments which have seemed relevant and important to us. The individual, as Newman puts it,

> brings together his reasons, and relies on them, because they are his own, and this is his primary evidence; and he has a second ground of evidence, in the testimony of those who agree with him. But his best evidence is the former, which is derived from his own thoughts; and it is that which the world has a right to demand of him; and therefore his true sobriety and modesty consists, not in claiming for his conclusions an acceptance or a scientific approval which is not to be found any where, but in stating what are personally his own grounds for his belief in Natural and Revealed Religion—grounds which he holds to be . . . sufficient.[151]

We advocate our faith most effectively as we state what has convinced us of its truth and trust that as these reasons have satisfied us, so they will satisfy others.

The greater value of illation in contrast to inference for antecedent reasoning lies in its implicit as well as in its personal character. As we have pointed out, inference is essentially explicit and its procedure clear and public. As a result, inferred conclusions are so obviously 'conditional' that they tend to hinder rather than to encourage our assent to them. Illation, however, is implicit and, in consequence, the conditionality of illative conclusions is not so obvious.[152] This obscurity has value in the matter of assent. If we are not aware, or only slightly aware, of the 'conditionality' of a conclusion, then we are much more likely to grant assent to it than if we were highly conscious of its 'conditionality'. Thus the obscurity of illations is an advantage for antecedent reasoning.

We shall later discuss in detail what Newman has to say about certainty and certitude in order to examine the view that the *Grammar of Assent* is concerned with the psychological rather than the logical character of faith. Before we close this section, however, we must pay some attention to Newman's view that our Illative Sense may present us with conclusions which we may regard as certain, and legitimately so. Newman does not use the word 'certain' in its logical sense of 'necessarily true' (as when we say 'it is certain that x is z if x is y and y is z') but to refer to the state of being personally convinced of the truth of something (as when, on looking out of the window, I say 'I am certain that Mrs. Green is walking up the road'). In his discussion of illation, Newman states that by it a person may come to:

a conclusion of which he can be certain, and ought to be certain, and that he will be incurring grave responsibility, if he does not accept it as certain, and act upon the certainty of it.[153]

This does not contradict his view that every conclusion, *qua* conclusion, is conditional but reminds us that a conclusion can, in practice, seem so convincing to us that we are prepared to regard it as certain and to describe it as 'morally certain'. Newman claims correctly the support of John Locke for this view that the conclusions of sufficiently strong arguments can be regarded as certain for all practical purposes.

> That there are cases, in which evidence, not sufficient for a scientific proof, is nevertheless sufficient for assent and certitude, is the doctrine of Locke, as of most men. He tells us that belief, grounded on sufficient probabilities, 'rises to assurance'; and as to the question of sufficiency, that where propositions 'border near on certainty', then 'we assent to them as firmly as if they were infallibly demonstrated'.[154]

But whereas Locke 'seems to think' that these moral certainties are 'few in number', Newman believes that there are very many of them. He holds that 'moral certitude' is the most 'that we can attain, not only in the case of ethical and spiritual subjects, such as religion, but of terrestrial and cosmical questions also' and gives examples from astronomy and mathematics.[155]

At this point Newman seems almost to be on the point of ignoring the logical difference between an assent and a conclusion. In the end, however, we find that he distinguishes between the result of the reasoning and the certitude which it evokes. He describes the mental process in reaching certainty as passing from 'the proof to an act of certitude about it'.[156] Again, he writes that 'from probabilities we may construct legitimate proof, sufficient for certitude.'[157] In all these cases he has left room, even if only just,[158] for a personal decision between the reasoning process and the acceptance of its conclusions as certain. Not even the most convincing illative reasoning can logically entail assent or certitude. We may, nevertheless, regard a conclusion as so highly probable that we consider ourselves morally obliged to assent to it and to act as if it were objectively certain. In all but the simplest matters, it is only our Illative Sense which is able to produce such powerful conclusions.

c. Conclusion

Our discussion of the Illative Sense shows that if any form of reasoning is generally going to be able to persuade us to assent, it will be this informal mode. Its implicit and hidden procedure allows it to deal with the 'real' as well as the 'notional' and to give due weight to subtle considerations. By it we can reach conclusions on every kind of subject. Its method of reasoning may be largely unconscious and subjective but its results express our own estimation of the matter. By this faculty we determine the force of an argument and the degree to which we are influenced by it. It is on the basis of such personal judgements that we consider whether or not to grant our assent. Although illative conclusions are still conclusions, and therefore 'conditional', their 'conditionality' is not as obvious as those of inference. In consequence this quality of 'conditionality' in the case of illative conclusions does not hinder our decision to assent. If assent must have antecedent reasoning, then what Newman calls our 'Illative Sense' is the faculty which will offer it. But is this 'Illative Sense' anything more than what we usually call our 'common sense'?[159]

Part V: The Act of Assent

In the previous chapters we have studied the condition and the antecedent of assent. Assent is only possible when its object is apprehended. Normally it is also justified by some form of supporting reasoning which makes clear the probability of the object of assent. This reasoning encourages us to assent but it cannot compel us for its conclusions are 'conditional'. There remains the problem of how we bridge the gap between the conclusion of antecedent reasoning and the actual assent itself. This gap marks the boundary between the conditional and the unconditional acceptance of a proposition as true. To this gap we now turn our attention. First we shall discuss the rôle of conscience in the act of assent, then we shall review the whole process of an act of assent, attempting to connect its various elements. Finally we shall consider what Newman has to say about certainty and certitude. This will confirm the view that the primary aim of the *Grammar of Assent* is not to determine the logical status of faith but to describe the way by which we come to assent. Newman's problem is the nature of commitment, and in this both logical and psychological factors are involved.

1. ASSENT AND CONSCIENCE

In view of the fact that Newman is conscious of the 'conditional' character of a conclusion and the absolute nature of an assent, he gives surprisingly little space to discussing the question of how we move from the one to the other. It is this, rather than anything which he explicitly states, which gives the impression that he does not consider that the gap between a strong illative conclusion and an assent is a significant one. The information Newman does provide about the actual act of assent indicates that it is an act of the will which comes under our moral judgement. This act of assent is bound up with our conscience, a faculty which Walgrave suggests is 'always the primary factor . . . in Newman's thought'.[1] Newman himself states that:

> Conscience has a legitimate place among our mental acts; as really so, as the action of memory, of reasoning, of imagination, or as the

sense of the beautiful; that, as there are objects which, when presented to the mind, cause it to feel grief, regret, joy, or desire, so there are things which excite in us approbation or blame, and which we in consequence call right or wrong.[2]

Since this faculty is a normal and natural constituent of the human mind,[3] its dictates are as significant as those of our other faculties. The same truth-value and authority is attributed to the faculties which provide our moral and aesthetic judgements as to our reason and memory. Conscience is distinguished from faculties such as reason, memory, and taste in that it is not concerned with mental or physical 'objects in themselves' but:

> with persons primarily, and with actions mainly as viewed in their doers, or rather with self alone and one's own actions, and with others only indirectly and as if in association with self.[4]

Since it works on a personal level, it is misunderstood if its dictates are regarded as purely abstract and objective. Its activity concerns an individual and is primarily concerned with his behaviour: the judgements of my conscience are essentially concerned with my policies of action and they express my understanding of my obligations. Even in its critical aspect the judgements of my conscience indirectly concern my future duties, for to pronounce an act wrong implies among other things that I would be wrong to commit such an act on a future occasion. We cannot then properly talk about 'conscience' without talking about persons and personal activity.

Newman considers, however, that the judgements of conscience have also some objective quality. He writes that

> conscience does not repose on itself, but vaguely reaches forward to something beyond self, and dimly discerns a sanction higher than self for its decisions, as is evidenced in that keen sense of obligation and responsibility which informs them.[5]

Here he distinguishes it from taste. Aesthetic judgements do not relate to any objective standard whereas the feeling aroused by conscience always implies . . . the recognition of a living object, towards which it is directed.[6] The assumption that conscience has an external correlate is for Newman a basic assumption of the same order as our assumption that the sensations of sight provide us with information of independently existing objects.[7] Conscience is thus regarded as a cognitive faculty, providing us with knowledge of part of external reality. Nevertheless, Newman recognizes that the demand of a particular judgement of conscience is primarily directed to the person who is confronted with it.

It is misleading to speak of conscience as if it were something whose judgements and activity were invariably the same in all cases. Though conscience is found in all men,[8] its decisions vary with the individual. Each person has his own peculiar conscience which is binding upon him and upon him alone. For each individual its decisions are final because they are his own personal judgements on the matter in hand.

> Conscience is a personal guide, and I use it because I must use myself; I am as little able to think by any mind but my own as to breathe with another's lungs. Conscience is nearer to me than any other means of knowledge.[9]

Conscience thus resembles the Illative Sense. The activity both of illation and of conscience are often not explicit and in many cases there is no stated or even statable connexion between the evidence and the judgement. The mental procedure of each is peculiar to the individual and produces results which bind him alone. Finally, both conscience and the Illative Sense have ultimate authority with the individual because they are his only way of reaching a decision in their respective spheres. While illation judges the rational quality and force of a conclusion, conscience judges its moral quality and implications. Our conscience functions both magisterially and critically. On the one hand it expresses 'a sense of duty', commanding us to obey its directions and telling us of our obligations. This function of conscience, which tells us what we ought to do, plays an important part in leading us to grant assent. The other aspect of conscience is its 'moral sense'.[10] This judges the ethical quality of an act, bestowing upon it moral approval or condemnation. It can judge after the event that an act of assent was justifiable or obligatory but it has no part in leading us to grant assent.

Just as the Illative Sense improves in accuracy with experience and use, so obedience and use reduce the liability of error in conscience. Newman puts it that conscience:

> is so constituted that, if obeyed, it becomes clearer in its injunctions, and wider in their range, and corrects and completes the accidental feebleness of its initial teachings.[11]

The more we follow our conscience, the more likely it is to give us correct information. Just as a baby improves its focus with practice in the use of its eyes, so a person improves his recognition of ethical standards by obedience to the reports of his conscience. At the basis of this understanding of the moral faculty is Newman's assumption that it is a cognitive faculty which can and does provide objective knowledge.[12]

In the end, however, our conscience is not infallible although it is binding upon us. Like our other faculties, it is liable to err no matter how much it is trained and developed. It can 'be biassed by personal inclinations and motives'[13] and produce distorted decisions. These variations do not

> interfere with the force of its testimony and of its sanction: its testimony that there is a right and a wrong, and its sanction to that testimony conveyed in the feelings which attend on right or wrong conduct.[14]

That is, we may recognize theoretically that our understanding of our duty may be objectively wrong, but we cannot evade our moral obligation to fulfil that duty as we understand it. What is right in the circumstances is what our conscience dictates. If we feel ourselves obliged to grant assent to a particular proposition, the fact that our self-understanding may not be justified by some unknown external standard cannot be advanced as a justifiable reason for not making the act of assent.

In our discussion of real apprehension, we noticed Newman's view that the feelings of conscience provide us with materials from which we can discover the nature of God and construct an 'image' of Him.

> If the cause of these emotions does not belong to this visible world, the Object to which his perception is directed must be Supernatural and Divine; and thus the phenomena of Conscience, as a dictate, avail to impress the imagination with the picture of a Supreme Governor, a Judge, holy, just, powerful, all-seeing, retributive, and is the creative principle of religion. . . .[15]

Just as conscience improves in accuracy with obedience and practice, so do its indirect declarations of the nature and reality of God.[16] This function of conscience, while it is primarily concerned with the apprehension of the 'Object' of religion, is also involved in the granting of assent in religious matters since it is the basis of our judgements on the validity of assertions about God. Conscience, for Newman, is the final authority in religious issues. No statement about God which conflicts with the feelings of conscience can be granted an assent which is morally justified since these feelings are both the primary source of our apprehension of God and normative of our understanding of Him.

> I take our natural perception of right and wrong as the standard for determining the characteristics of Natural Religion, and I use the religious rites and traditions which are actually found in the world, only so far as they agree with our moral sense. . . . No religion is from God which contradicts our sense of right and wrong. . . . A

religion which simply commanded us to lie, or to have a community of wives, would *ipso facto* forfeit all claim to a divine origin.[17]

This means that in religious matters our conscience wields a veto which is able to prevent us granting assent. No matter how much evidence may be produced in favour of a certain doctrine, that doctrine must be in harmony with the picture of God which corresponds to the feelings of our conscience if it is to be a serious candidate for our assent. As the ultimate standard of truth and error in religious issues, our conscience thus controls our acts of assent. Newman's position here rests upon his assumption that conscience tells us about the objective structure of reality. He implicitly rejects the view that our conscience may have been determined by what we have been taught about God. He believes rather that our knowledge of God is dependent upon the dictates of our conscience.

Our conscience has a further important rôle in the matter of assent. A mind that is prejudiced and biassed will be unable to be fair in its treatment of the material presented to it. An open mind concerned only to establish the truth is necessary for an accurate determination of the force of a conclusion. Such a moral requirement is of greater importance in religious than, say, in astronomical thinking because its 'subject matter' is the less 'clear and simple'. Whoever, therefore, seeks the truth in religion must be, in the words of Butler quoted by Newman,

> as much in earnest about religion, as about their temporal affairs, capable of being convinced, on real evidence, that there is a God who governs the world.[18]

An irrational credulity which is prepared to grant authority to the slenderest of evidence in order to find reasons for a desired conclusion is as reprehensible as an irrational scepticism which is predisposed to doubt any conclusion, no matter what evidence can be adduced in its favour. Assent is an act of the will which we can morally justify only if we have tried as far as possible to accept nothing but what we honestly consider to be the truth of the matter. In this way conscience has some control over our assent by its criticism of our attitude towards the supporting evidence. We will not feel justified in granting assent when we are condemned for unwarranted credulity or scepticism. Assent is a matter of the will, and we can usually grant it only when we have a clear conscience on the matter: doubts about the moral justification of our act prevent us from giving the unreserved commitment which is the essence of assent.

If different persons are given conflicting judgements by their respective consciences, these judgements cannot both be objectively correct although they are each subjectively binding. Both consciences cannot be completely correct, while it may be the case that both are partially or totally in error. Newman does not provide any external criteria by which we may distinguish objective truth from error in the reports of conscience. He seems to be convinced that the feelings of his own conscience are sufficient evidence for others as well as for himself! When he mentions that others, presumably on the basis of their own consciences, disagree with the picture of God presented by his conscience, he does not regard their objections very seriously but asserts that they are due to their failure to understand the nature of God. He claims that his view of the 'retributive justice' of God is 'the very attribute under which God is primarily brought before us in the teachings of our natural conscience'.[19] In other words, the consciences of those who cannot accept that God is a God of vengeance and punishment are not 'natural' but have failed to reach their proper fully-developed state. This is no argument at all but simply an assertion of personal authority—a mode of appeal which Newman elsewhere recognizes as following a breakdown in reasoning.[20]

Although conscience has what may be called an illative function, since it influences our judgement of the probability of propositions, its most important function in relation to assent is its exertion of moral pressure to bring us to assent. By reasoning, whether formal or informal, we determine the truth-value of a proposition. In the case of some inferences this can be precisely determined but usually our reasonings only result in an approximate estimation of probability. Confronted with the proposition whose probability we have now estimated, we still have to decide how we will treat it. As Newman recognized in his article *The Tamworth Reading Room* and states again in the *Grammar of Assent*, 'man is not a reasoning animal; he is a seeing, feeling, contemplating, acting animal'.[21] When we have reasoned our way to a conclusion, we still have to decide how far we shall allow the conclusion to influence our thought and behaviour. We can choose to ignore a conclusion with a high degree of likelihood and we can decide, if we so wish, to base our thought and action on a proposition whose probability is extremely slight. In such decisions our reasoning is not the final determining factor: we are not controlled by the relative truth-value of our ideas. Ultimately we choose as individuals how we will act and upon what bases. Because it is a decision about our will, moral considerations are involved and our conscience clearly has an important rôle.

When we discussed the Illative Sense, we noted that illation can, according to Newman, lead us to moral certainty. We now examine this idea more closely for it illustrates the way in which conscience bridges the gap between conclusions and assents. By illation a person may come to a conclusion which he judges:

> that he ought to accept . . . as true in his case; . . . that this is a conclusion of which he can be certain, and ought to be certain, and that he will be incurring grave responsibility, if he does not accept it as certain, and act upon the certainty of it.[22]

The evidence in such cases is said to be 'sufficient proof of a fact or a truth'[23] or to be 'sufficient for certitude'.[24] In these statements it is significant that the evidence is not said to 'demonstrate' or 'entail unavoidably' that the conclusion is a logical certainty. The language that is used is much more indefinite. It indicates that the individual's will or choice has the final decision to make. When evidence is described as 'sufficient' for a certain position, it is implied that the evidence does not logically compel that position (as 'all a is b, all b is c' logically compels the conclusion 'all a is c'), but is of such a strength that it justifies the adoption of that position. The justification involves both logical and moral considerations. It could be expressed in a statement such as 'he had good reasons for his action'. Logic is involved because it is the strength of the reasoning that provides the justifying factor, but the defence of the specific act is itself a matter of morality. Here logic and morality meet. The moral validity of the action depends both upon the rational determination of the strength of the reasoning and upon the judgement of conscience that this strength of reasoning is sufficient to justify the decision to act. If we turn to astronomy, we find Newman holds that 'moral evidence and moral certitude are all that we can attain' in this subject.[25] By this he means that in astronomy we are compelled to work on the basis of more or less accurate approximations to the truth since the truth itself cannot be precisely determined. The phrases 'moral evidence' and 'moral certitude' thus describe evidence and certitude which we are justified in using although they lack complete cogency. When, for instance, we say that we are 'morally convinced' that the sun is 97 million miles away, then we announce that we consider ourselves justified in thinking the sun is this distance away. We declare that this estimation is so well attested that we would not feel morally guilty if we acted upon it and it was later discovered to be false. The term 'morally' shows that we believe that there is sufficient evidence for the position for ethically good action to be based upon it. Newman further suggests that 'in the case of ethical and spiritual subjects, such as religion', we are restricted to 'moral evidence and moral certitude'.[26] Here the use of the term 'moral' is more significant than in the case of astronomy because ethical considerations play a more important part. In a passage which we have already quoted, Newman makes it quite clear that the conclusion of a theological argument may place a person under a moral obligation to think and act in a certain way. The evidence is not only 'sufficient' for certainty but also leads the person to consider that 'he ought to be certain' of the conclusion 'and will be incurring grave responsibility, if he does not accept it as certain, and act upon the certainty of it'.[27] 'Moral certitude' is here a certainty which we are not only morally justified in accepting but also are under moral pressure to accept. Our conscience has judged that a particular conclusion is practically certain and that it is our duty to receive it as unconditionally true.

The gap between the reception of a proposition as having demonstrated probability and an unconditional assent to that proposition is one that we cannot bridge by reasoning. It is a gap which divides the logic of reasoning from the logic of personal commitment. It is bridged by our decision to move from the one logical sphere to the other. As an act of the will it comes under ethical judgement and may arouse either the approval or the condemnation of our conscience. With subjects such as astronomy, the activity of conscience is restricted to a passive judgement of justifiability, but in the case of faith conscience may urge the act of assent upon us. Here it performs an active rôle, pressing us to assent and warning us of moral condemnation if we fail to assent. In face of the gap between regarding a proposition as probably true and as unconditionally true, we may be aware of a moral demand to leap from estimated truth-value to commitment. Thus Newman holds that there are some conclusions of which we consider that we 'ought to be certain'. In such situations our conscience functions as persuasive force, urging us to leap from the sphere of reasoning and conclusions to that of commitment and unconditional assents. Such activity is regarded as unnecessary with subjects like mathematics when 'strict logical demonstration',[28] arriving at conclusions strong enough for practical certainty, is possible. It is, however, a 'dictate of nature' that:

> we are not justified, in the case of concrete reasoning and especially of religious inquiry, in waiting till such logical demonstration is ours, but on the contrary are bound in conscience to seek truth and to look for certainty by modes of proof, which, when reduced to the shape of formal propositions, fail to satisfy the severe requisitions of science.[29]

Hence Newman claims that in subjects such as religion, we are obliged by our conscience to treat as 'certain' what reasoning can only show to have some degree of probability. The gulf between what can be demonstrated to be probable and the acceptance of it as unconditionally true is bridged by an act of the will, following the bidding of conscience.

It will be obvious from our scattered references to the *Grammar of Assent* that Newman nowhere provides any extended, systematic discussion of the function of conscience in the act of assent. What can be said of his views on this matter has to be culled from brief comments at odd places. The function of conscience, however, is of major importance in understanding the act of assent. Even after we have apprehended a proposition and determined its probability, it receives our assent only by an act of our will. There is an essential difference between a conclusion and an assent.[30] Only when we choose to commit ourselves do we move from the one position to the other. As an act of our will, the move comes under the judgement of our conscience. It may be both urged upon us as a moral duty and afterwards approved as morally justified. In either case, moral considerations are a significant factor in the act of assent.[31]

2. THE DECISION TO ASSENT

We have now considered individually what Newman regards as the conditions and antecedents of assent. Our task in this section is to discuss the relationship between these different elements. In doing this we hope to show what Newman understands to be the nature of this act and to make it clear that his problem in the *Grammar of Assent* is not purely logical but also involves psychological factors. By a 'logical problem' we mean one which has to do with the structure of knowledge as it is based upon reasoning. A 'psychological problem' deals with personal attitudes and positions which ultimately are not determined by reasoning processes although they are influenced by them.[32] The question which is answered by Newman does not primarily concern the purely rational and objective truth-value of assents in general and religious ones in particular. This is Locke's problem in his *Essay concerning Human Understanding*. Accordingly Locke produces a critique of knowledge which is undisturbed by personal considerations and which seeks to show the positions that people ought to adopt if they are to entertain only rationally known truth-values. Nor is Newman attempting to provide objective proof for unqualified faith. Newman's problem in the *Grammar of Assent* is to discover how we come in practice to commit ourselves absolutely to the truth of certain matters. His work is concerned with the phenomenology of assents and not simply with the rational demonstrability of their truth-value. Logical issues do enter into this discussion. As we have seen, reasoning is an antecedent which encourages us to assent. This raises the logical problems of the force of conclusions and the possibility of reasoning outside syllogistic forms and notional concepts. It also raises the question of the relationship between thought and action, between reasoned conclusions and personal activity concerning those conclusions. The discussion of assent, however, shows that assent does not belong to the logic of reasoning but to that of unconditional personal commitment. At times Newman may seem tempted to assume that assent is little or nothing more that the strong conclusion of an illation but his emphasis elsewhere on what he calls the 'conditionality' of conclusions and the 'unconditionality' of assents reveals that these two belong to different logics. In this way Newman provides, albeit unconsciously, a solution to a logical problem by placing 'assent' and 'religious faith' in the category of commitment.

In our first chapter we indicated how the problem of the status of religious statements was bequeathed by Hume and Kant to the theologians of the nineteenth century. On the Continent several attempts were made to solve the problem by propounding different interpretations of the nature of faith and of theology. English theology was somewhat ignorant of this work and generally suspicious of it when its ideas were published in this country. In our second chapter we suggested that Newman himself had little direct knowledge of this field and the questions that it was trying to solve. His own personal doubts, however, led him along similar tracks. His treatment of faith in the *Grammar of Assent* makes it clear that he would attempt to answer the problem of faith by regarding its logical status as one of personal commitment. Newman does not attempt to reinterpret the content of faith-statements but accepts that such assertions refer to an external objective reality in the same way that empirical statements refer to objective realities. At the same time Newman recognizes that faith-statements are peculiar in that we accept them as absolutely true in a way that is ultimately independent of any reasoning or evidence concerning them. This means that religious statements have a logical status which distinguishes them from what is strictly empirical and demonstrable. They express what we unconditionally accept as true about elements of some objective reality but they finally rest on personal acts of commitment which go beyond the conclusions of investigation and reasoning. Faith belongs to the sphere of personal decision and not to that of the purely rational determination of truth-values.

This suggests that a distinction between theology and religion may be made on the basis of their logical positions rather than on the basis of our apprehension of their contents. In our earlier examination of real and notional apprehension, we discussed Newman's view that theology deals with notions while religion is directed towards images. From this it might be inferred that the only change which occurs when we move from a theological to a religious position is that our grasp of its objects becomes real instead of abstract. Such a view is misleading because it ignores the element of personal commitment which is essential for religion but need not be present in a theological affirmation. When we make theological affirmations which express notionally our religious assents, then the only difference between this theology and our religion does lie in the apprehension involved. This is true, however, only of an individual's own beliefs. A theological statement need not be the notional form of an assent actually given by anyone at all. Even if someone does assent to their real apprehension of what it expresses, that assent, which is essential to religion, is not contained in the change to an imaginative grasp of its content. Confronted by a theological dogma, my apprehension of its content may change from notional to real and I may consider it to be the conclusion of valid theological arguments, but I am still faced with the choice of whether I assent to that proposition or not. Only if I assent to it does it become a statement of my faith.

The term 'religious' thus has two uses which can be easily confused. It can refer to what is really apprehended or to what has been granted assent. Real apprehension and assent are distinct matters. Newman may be correct when he holds that the assent of faith is granted only to what is imaginatively apprehended but the fact that something is grasped as an image is no sure indication that it is or will be granted assent. The nature of religious apprehension must not be allowed to obscure the fact that whereas a theological position may be reached as a conclusion of certain reasoning, a religious position always comes under the logic of commitment. Their different positions on the logical map mean that it is improper to place general theological conclusions and religious beliefs in the same logical class. For example, if any of the arguments for the existence of God were logically acceptable, their theological conclusions could still not be regarded as statements of religious belief. Even if a person could construct an image of the content of such a conclusion, as a conclusion it would still not come under the logical class which includes religious beliefs. Between either the notional or the real apprehension of the conclusion of a theological enquiry and religious belief in the content of that conclusion stands the act of personal commitment. It is by this act and this act alone that the object comes under the logic of assent.[33]

This problem of the logical status of belief is not Newman's real problem in the *Grammar of Assent*. While we can find a logical status for religious belief in his description of assent, we must remember that it is not given explicitly by Newman but is only implied by his ideas. The *Grammar of Assent* is primarily concerned with the phenomenology of religious belief. It seeks to describe both the actual nature of faith and the way by which in practice people come to it, thereby showing how it may be attained by others. This interest in the source and existence of a personal attitude is concerned with its objective status only so far as this is relevant to the actual act of assent. Newman himself does not seem to be aware that the problem of the certainty of faith involves psychological as well as logical factors. At times he apparently wants to show that faith can have objective as well as subjective unconditionality, failing to realize that the very logic of faith means that its objective validity can never be rationally deduced. Our next section will show how much Newman is confused on this score in the matter of certainty. Here we hope to demonstrate that the relationship which Newman understands to exist between assent and its condition and antecedents shows that faith is finally a matter of personal decision and not simply one of logical implication.

The claim that Newman is interested in the actual character of assent rather than in defending its validity is illustrated by his acceptance of it as a natural attitude of the mind. In the course of his attack on Locke, Newman shows clearly that he is dealing with assent as it is found in practice, not with assent as it may be rationally justified. He is aware that day-to-day thought and action are based upon attitudes whose truth can never be conclusively demonstrated:

> Assent on reasonings not demonstrative is too widely recognized an act to be irrational, unless man's nature is irrational, too familiar to the prudent and clear-minded to be an infirmity or an extravagance. None of us can think or act without the acceptance of truths, not intuitive, not demonstrated, yet sovereign.[34]

The act of assent is 'natural to the mind' and in making it 'we are not violating the laws of our nature . . . but are acting according to . . . its legitimate constitution'.[35] Since both life in general and religion in particular require for their normal existence commitments which extend beyond what is demonstrably true, it is as ridiculous to question the validity of the act of assent as it is to dispute the propriety of moral duty. The existence of assent in practice is for Newman sufficient justification of its rationality. He is interested in what this state actually consists of and how it is attained.

The essence of assent is unconditional commitment in which the truth of a proposition is accepted without any qualifications whatsoever. It is the 'absolute reception of propositions as true',[36] 'the mental assertion of an intelligible proposition'.[37] It belongs to the logic of personal decision and not to that of reasoned conclusions. Although assent has certain conditions and antecedents, these concern our activity in granting assent: they do not modify the assent itself.

> Neither apprehension nor inference interferes with the unconditional character of the assent, viewed in itself. The circumstances of an act, however necessary to it, do not enter into the act; assent is in its nature absolute and unconditional, though it cannot be given except under certain conditions.[38]

Newman is concerned that this unconditionality should not be understood to imply arbitrary irrationality. By examining its conditions and antecedents he seeks to minimize the necessarily undemonstrable element in assent and to show how far an act of faith can be rationally justified. There is always a gap between the acceptance of an apprehended proposition and assent to it but Newman is intent on narrowing the gap as far as possible. The conditions and antecedents all tend to diminish the significance of the rôle of our will in assent. The hope seems to be that ultimately the conclusion will be so strong that the difference between conclusion and assent will be in practice negligible.

We have already noted that apprehension is the condition of assent. We are now to consider the effect that this condition has upon the act of assent which it makes possible. The limitation of assent to what we apprehend means that the leap of faith is never into the totally unknown but is always to what is at least partially known. Psychologically we find it much easier to decide to jump a gap when we can see the other side than when we are blindfolded and cannot tell what the other side is like. Because apprehension is a *sine qua non*, assent is never a blind leap. Thus the condition of assent itself helps to diminish our reluctance to grant it. Furthermore, since real apprehension has more influence over us than notional, we are more likely to assent to what we grasp 'really' than to what we entertain only as an abstract idea. Indeed, Newman is so convinced of the potential power of an 'image' that he warns his readers that vividness alone is 'no warrant for the existence of the objects which those images represent'.[39] Thus, by making known to us the object of our assent and by presenting it to us sometimes as an 'image', apprehension, which is the condition of assent, narrows the gap that we have to cross in the act of assent.

As for the antecedents of assent, they have very definite leap-reducing functions. The purpose of antecedent inference and illation is not to produce assent to a proposition with the Q.E.D. finality of a geometrical proof[40] but to encourage and even to press us to assent by demonstrating its probability. The more we are persuaded of the likelihood of what we are asked to assent to, the more willing we are to grant our assent. Since the function of this reasoning is to encourage us to assent, its significance lies in the pressure that it can exert upon us. The conclusions of inferences are less satisfactory in this respect than those of methodologically obscure illations because the 'conditionality' of its conclusions is more obvious with the explicit procedure of formal reasoning. What matters for assent is not so much the objective truth-value of the conclusion as its convincingness to each of us. In some cases we may judge a conclusion to be so strong that there is a temptation to equate our acceptance of it as a conclusion with assent to it. The force of the reasoning makes the leap of faith seem insignificant. Indeed, Newman himself seems at times to be so impressed with the force of certain conclusions, especially with those of the Illative Sense, that he is inclined to suggest to the unwary that reasoning alone can occasionally produce assent.[41] Thus in his long final chapter on 'Inference and Assent in the Matter of Religion', he offers what are for him some 'of the arguments adducible for Christianity' which suggest 'its divine origin'. These arguments create 'a certitude of its truth' by reasoning which is 'too various for direct enumeration, too personal and deep for words, too powerful and concurrent for refutation'.[42] Nevertheless, even though these arguments are very powerful for him personally, they do not themselves entail assent but only lead him to grant it. Newman cannot avoid recognizing that while reasoning can reduce the gap which faith has to leap, it can never finally eradicate it.

The final factor in the act of assent is conscience as it exerts pressure upon us to make the leap of faith. No matter how strong may be the conclusions of our antecedent reasoning, no assent is made without some moral consideration. In most cases there is an appreciable difference between the convincingness of our supporting reasoning and the absolute character of an assent. The probability and 'conditionality' of their conclusions are often only too obvious when trains of reasoning are presented as arguments for our assent. In such circumstances conscience is the decisive factor. It may urge us to assent to the conclusion because it judges that assent is here a moral duty even though the available evidence is rather slight. On another occasion conscience may overrule our unwillingness to assent by judging that it is due to a morally unjustifiable demand for extreme degrees of proof or to other illegitimate motives. In most cases our conscience urges us to assent simply on the grounds that we ought not to remain uncommitted but should commit ourselves to whatever position seems to us to have the strongest support. The activity of conscience is particularly important in the case of religious belief because conclusive demonstrations of its truths are notoriously unattainable.

It is important to realize that not one of the elements of the act of faith nor any combination of them can alone produce assent. A proposition is presented to me for my assent. I grasp what it means and apprehend its reference as a distinct image. My reasoning powers, formal and informal, convince me that this proposition is very likely to be true. My conscience approves of the arguments and pronounces that it is my moral duty to assent. In spite of all this pressure, the decision to assent is left to me and to me alone. If I so choose, I can entertain the proposition merely as expressing what is highly probable or, if I so determine, I can commit myself unreservedly to its truth. In this latter state alone do I assent. The condition of apprehension, the force of antecedent reasoning, the influence of conscience, each contribute to easing the leap of faith. In spite of all this, there is a gap and, according to Newman, I must choose whether or not to leap across it. This leap is the act of faith. It follows the fulfilment of its conditions and antecedents but it is not the end-point of a continuous process of which they mark the stages. The act of commitment is a distinct act complete in itself. If it were simply the result of a process leading up to it, it would have the same 'conditionality' as a reasoned conclusion. It is important to insist upon this point. Although Newman makes the distinction between absoluteness and 'conditionality' the principle of the differentiation between assents and conclusions,[43] the *Grammar of Assent* tends to leave the impression that this distinction is not very significant. The emphasis is upon the conditions of assent and its reasonableness rather than upon the intrinsic nature of the act itself. This criticism of the *Grammar of Assent* is only a warning that its consideration of the preliminaries rather obscures the essence of faith. Apprehension, reasoning, and conscience influence the decision to believe but the actual act of assent is a leap across a logical gulf which these factors can never bridge.[44] Newman's examination of its circumstances must not make us forget that the act of assent is not causally produced by them.

Since assent belongs to the logic of personal commitment, the factors which bring us to assent are important for their subjective as well as for their purely rational force. The need for apprehension indicates the personal aspect of assent. By formal argument we may reach a conclusion which we cannot understand: to such an unknown result we cannot assent. We cannot unreservedly commit ourselves to a complete blank. Reasoning can be a mechanical and impersonal activity but our decision to commit ourselves is rational only if it is restricted to what we have grasped. The personal aspect of assent is, secondly, revealed in the fact that it is more readily given to what is imaginatively than to what is notionally apprehended. The objective truth-value of a conclusion is not increased by its being grasped as real rather than as notional. It is because of our psychological make-up that we are attracted more by images than by notions. Thirdly, the fact that assent is independent of its supporting reasoning shows that it is not simply a matter of objective reasoning. A conclusion varies in force according to the weight of evidence supporting it but an assent is unvarying whatever its antecedents. It cannot, therefore, be regarded as a type of conclusion which belongs to the logic of reasoning. The personal basis of assent is further revealed by the fact that the value of any antecedent reasoning is affected by our individual prejudices. In the final chapter of the *Grammar of Assent* Newman shows us what sort of factors might influence his own decision to assent but the description is mainly of biographical interest. A fourth indication of the personal element in assent is given when it is contrasted with the 'conditionality' of a conclusion. This 'conditionality' is not the logical conditionality of an hypothesis but a psychological 'conditionality' which arises from the fact that the conclusion is entertained in connexion with its premises. The absolute or unconditional character of assent is not the direct result of a conclusive, indisputable deduction. It describes the consequence of a personal commitment to what is thereby recognized as true. The personal nature of assent is revealed, fifthly, by the function of conscience in the act of assent. If assent were merely a logical matter, the function of conscience would concern only the antecedent reasoning, judging whether the processes had been free from unjustifiable prejudices, but the activity of conscience does not end here. It further appraises the justifiability of assent and even commands us to assent as a moral duty. Such ethical judgements cannot concern a purely logical position. When I state that 'all a is b, and all b is c, *must* imply that all a is c', I use a logical and not a moral 'must'. The fact that the granting of assent can be urged on by moral 'musts' shows again that assent belongs to the logic of personal activity and not to that of reasoned conclusions.

It has been necessary to embark on this prolonged exposition of the act of assent in order to make clear its essentially personal nature. Once he has disposed of the question of the condition of assent, Newman becomes engrossed in its rational antecedents. The element of 'leap' in faith is not given any treatment of its own but is mainly to be discerned through the contrasts made between conclusions and assents. In consequence we are liable to regard faith as a matter for the reason rather than for the will. In the next section this is illustrated by the confusions contained in Newman's understanding of certainty and certitude. In this analysis of the parts played by the different elements of the act of assent, it has become clear that they are relevant and important in so far as they make possible an act of the will by which we commit ourselves absolutely. We shall see in the next section, however, that it is not at all clear if Newman realized that his view of the assent of faith essentially involves a leap made on our individual decision. At times he seems to want to place assent in the logic of reasoning although ultimately he must regard it as dependent upon an act of the will. We cannot be coerced to assent by any force of argument: finally our act of assent is a matter of personal decision.

3. CERTAINTY AND CERTITUDE

In this section I intend to examine the distinction between objective 'certainty' and subjective 'certitude'[45] to illustrate the thesis that the *Grammar of Assent* is really concerned with faith as personal commitment. Newman's failure to perceive this distinction leads him mistakenly to consider his problem to be one of reasoning and objective truth. The English language lends itself to confusion at this point because the one word 'certain' is used to describe both objective and subjective states. It is used 'subjectively' when it refers to our unreserved commitment to a proposition while it is used 'objectively' when it expresses the fact that something actually is true, whatever people may think about it. The former usage refers to a state which properly belongs to the logic of personal commitment while the latter usage belongs to the logic of reasoning. There is no necessary connexion between these two uses of the word. It is possible for a person to be (subjectively) certain of what is in fact false and for another to withhold agreement from what really is (objectively) certain. We must not allow the ambiguity of the word 'certain' to blind us to the difference between its two meanings.[46] At the same time we are faced with the fact that Newman does not make any consistent distinction between these meanings. Sometimes he distinguishes between 'certainty' and 'certitude' in the same way as Tennant but at other times the meaning of either term can be found only by examining its context. The use of the adjective 'certain' is never differentiated.

The consideration of 'certitude' is important because it is what Newman calls 'complex assent'.[47] In contrast to 'simple assents' which are usually granted unconsciously, complex assent:

has the strength of explicitness and deliberation. . . . It is an assent, not only to a given proposition, but to the claim of that proposition on our assent as true; it is an assent to an assent. . . .[48]

While this type of assent is the reaffirmation of a previously granted simple assent,[49] it is a form which is valuable for analysis since it is made deliberately. It is presumed that the same processes which lead us to conscious assent to an assent are involved in our unconscious simple assents, although only in the case of complex assents can we discern these processes. As a complex assent certitude requires the characteristic conditions and antecedents of assent,[50] and, since it is 'a natural and normal state of mind', it has 'a legitimate place among our mental constituents'.[51] The possibility of error is reduced by experience[52] while the existence of error is no proof 'that certitude itself is a perversion or extravagance' of our 'nature'.[53] Certitude is always a notional assent because it has the form of assent to the truth of a simple assent.[54] Thus Newman describes the assent of certitude.

On a few occasions Newman does distinguish between the subjective and the objective aspects of being 'certain'. In one passage, for instance, he says that where a proposition is 'objectively true as well as subjectively' then 'the conviction' that it is true may be called 'a *certitude*' and 'the proposition or truth a *certainty*'.[55] The passage does not, however, indicate whether Newman would allow us to speak of certitude being given to what was later found to be false since he draws the distinction with reference to a proposition which is assumed to be objectively true. The objective/subjective differentiation of certainty and certitude is suggested by three other passages. In contrast to certainty, certitude is defined in terms of 'nothing more than the relation of the mind towards given propositions'.[56] Certainty is connected with proof and demonstration but certitude is 'a state of mind'.[57] Finally Newman says that 'certitude is a mental state: certainty is a quality of propositions.'[58] These are clear and precise distinctions. They place certitude in the logic of personal commitment while certainty belongs to the logic of objective truth-values. Unfortunately Newman does not stick to these distinctions and so we find in the *Grammar of Assent* various confusing and misleading statements about certainty. For example, in his discussion of 'Informal Inference', he says 'that the certainty of a proposition, does properly consist in the certitude of the mind which contemplates it'.[59] If we interpret this statement on the basis that certainty is objective and certitude subjective, it asserts that the objective truth of a proposition depends upon its being regarded as such. The context of the statement, however, indicates that Newman is not here proposing an unusual view of objective truth. He is using 'certainty' here to express the state of being held to be certain. In this sense when I speak about the 'certainty' of 'x', I am referring to the fact that I hold 'x' to be 'certain'. 'Certitude' is presumably used here with its usual reference to the state of mind of being certain. In the end, then, Newman is really saying that 'My view that "x" is certain consists in my state of mind of being certain of "x"',[60] i.e., I ascribe certainty to 'x' because I am personally certain of it. What Newman has done here is to make the concept of 'certainty' as well as that of 'certitude' depend on personal attitudes rather than on objective states. Because he does not seem to have been at all clear about the meaning of the terms, he probably was not aware that he had used 'certainty' in a different sense than elsewhere.

Newman generally prefers to talk about 'certitude' rather than about 'certainty'. His use of this term is riddled with confusion because of his failure to make a constant and clear distinction between logical and psychological issues. To start with, we find that certitude is claimed both to be restricted to the objectively true and to be capable of error. We read that certitude 'is the perception of a truth with the perception that it is a truth'.[61] This claim that certitude is by definition restricted to what is objectively correct is made even more explicitly a few pages later when Newman writes that:

> It is the characteristic of certitude that its object is a truth, a truth as such, a proposition as true. There are right and wrong convictions, and certitude is a right conviction; if it is not right with a consciousness of being right, it is not certitude.[62]

Certitude may thus be described absolutely as 'the attainment of what is true'.[63] There is no suggestion in these statements that certitude is an act of commitment which may in fact be wrong. It is asserted without any qualification that certitude is confined to the objectively true and another term, 'conviction',[64] is used of states which appear to be those of certitude but actually are directed to what is false. The unsatisfactory nature of this view of certitude becomes clear when it is realized that there are no testing procedures by which we can determine whether what appears to be a certitude does in fact express the truth or is merely a false conviction.

> No line can be drawn between such real certitudes as have truth for their object, and apparent certitudes. No distinct test can be named, sufficient to discriminate between what may be called the false prophet and the true. What looks like certitude always is exposed to the chance of turning out to be a mistake.[65]

A possible test may be offered along the lines that since certitude is about the truth and since the truth always remains the same, so certitude should be distinguishable from false conviction by its immutability.[66] This is theoretically correct and we find that Newman stresses the 'indefectability' of certitude. In fact, however, Newman recognizes that 'any conviction, false as well as true, may last; and any conviction, true as well as false, may be lost'.[67] The test of immutability, while theoretically good, can provide no definite indication in practice.

We turn now to the statements in the *Grammar of Assent* which assume that certitude can be objectively false. These are not found in a separate part of the *Grammar* but come from the same sections as the passages we have just referred to and are intermingled with them. When it is claimed that 'there are far fewer instances of false certitude than at first sight might be supposed',[68] it is unavoidably implied that 'false certitude' can and does actually happen. The contrast between 'wrong ... convictions' and 'genuine certitudes' in the following passage has the same implication:

> Certitude is at most nothing more than infallibility *pro hac vice*. ... That I am certain of this proposition today, is no ground for thinking that I shall have a right to be certain of that proposition tomorrow; and that I am wrong in my convictions about today's proposition, does not hinder my having a true conviction, a genuine certitude, about tomorrow's proposition.[69]

We read that though a person is 'balked by false certitudes a hundred times in the course of his experience',[70] error in one certitude about a particular situation is not to prevent a further different certitude about it.[71] In this latter passage, we are even presented with examples of changes of certitude. There is no reason to believe that any one of these certitudes is not a full certitude. Newman is describing a situation where certitude is not 'indefectible' but where one certitude may be given up in favour of another. Only a few pages later we read the contrary assertion that 'certitudes indeed do not change'.[72]

How are these contrary views of certitude to be explained? Why does Newman assert both that certitude is directed only to the objectively true and that it can be false, without making any distinction between different meanings of the term? The confusion is due to his failure to distinguish between the logical and the psychological forms of being certain. He did not thoroughly appreciate the distinction between certainty and certitude which we have discovered in some passages in the *Grammar of Assent*. Instead he allowed the two notions with their incompatible implications to be conflated in his mind. Where he asserts that certitude necessarily refers to the objectively true, he is dealing with it in terms of logical certainty. To speak of certitude here is to make a statement about the actual state of things apart from any recognition of them. The essential factor is not what we know or believe but what actually is the case. The statements which contradict this position, allowing for false certitudes and changes of certitude, are derived from a personal or psychological understanding of the term. In these cases 'certitude' describes a personal belief about what is true. Though each individual considers that his certitude expresses the objectively true, here it is the personal belief and not its objective correctness which is the determining factor.

When Newman suggests that certitude necessarily reflects what is objectively correct he shows that he has not fully grasped the proper logical status of assent. While he recognizes that certitude is a form of assent, he wants to treat it as if it were concerned with objective truth-values instead of with the truth-values which the individual ascribes. Accordingly he tries to place the essence of certitude in the nature of its object rather than in personal commitment. Such a view wrongly implies that certitude, and therefore assent, of which it is a form, does not belong to the logic of commitment. The other statements in the *Grammar of Assent* which contradict this view show that Newman also thinks of certitude on the lines of personal commitment to what the individual holds to be true. When certitude is treated basically as a personal act of commitment, it properly belongs to the logic of assent and of faith.

This confusion of personal and logical certitude is further reflected in what Newman has to say about the 'indefectibility' of certitude. The second half of his chapter on 'certitude' is devoted to an extended discussion of this issue.[73] Defining certitude as 'a right conviction', he argues thus:

> Now truth cannot change; what is once truth is always truth; and the human mind is made for truth, and so rests in truth, as it cannot rest in falsehood. When then it once becomes possessed of a truth, what is to dispossess it? but this is to be certain; therefore once certitude, always certitude.[74]

Here we have the immutability of certitude derived from the objective truth-value of its object; our certitudes do not change because they are directed towards the truth which does not change. The position is clinched by the claim that we have a natural faculty for recognizing the truth when it is presented to us. This is an epistemological assumption which is contradicted by Newman himself on the next page when he admits that we may give up true as well as false convictions.[75]

Newman is mistaken when he deduces the necessary immutability of certitude from the unchangeability of truth. If certitude by definition essentially reflects what is objectively true, this argument cannot be denied. What Newman is talking about here, however, is not the logical status of a proposition but our personal attitude to a proposition. The indefectibility of certitude thus depends upon our infallibility in recognizing the truth as such and error as such in particular cases. The fact that even Newman talks about false certitudes and false convictions shows that such an infallible faculty does not exist. What is not recognized, and being unrecognized is the source of confusion, is that while logical certainty is necessarily unchangeable, psychological certitude, being a personal attitude arising from a personal decision, is fallible. The truth as such cannot change, but our grasp of it can change—and very clearly does on occasions.

A further example of the confusion produced by the failure to distinguish between logical and psychological certitude—or certainty—is afforded by the following passage:

> Truth need not be universal, but it must of necessity be certain; and certainty, in order to be certainty, must endure; yet how is this reasonable expectation fulfilled in the case of religion? On the contrary, those who have been most certain in their beliefs are sometimes found to lose them, Catholics as well as others; and then to take up new beliefs, perhaps contrary ones, of which they become as certain as if they had never been certain of the old.[76]

Newman attempts to answer this problem on the grounds that what are given up are not real certitudes because our real certitudes persist through our conversion. He recognizes, however, that such an answer is open to the charge of 'quibbling'.[77] In fact Newman is here attempting to find an answer to a bogus question. The use of the word 'certainty' in the quotation is ambiguous and the problem arises because it is used equivocally. The 'certainty' which 'must endure', if this 'must' is a logical 'must', is the certainty entailed by objective truth being unchangeable, but the believer's 'certainty' reflects his personal decision that something is true. There is no real problem here for there is no conflict between the fact that the truth itself is always the same and the fact that personal decisions about what is true are fallible and changeable.

The confusion in Newman's view of certainty is also seen in a passage where he deals with the argument that certainty is improper in matters where there is no universal agreement. He replies:

> Surely a truth or a fact may be certain, though it is not generally received; we are each of us ever gaining through senses various certainties, which no one shares with us; again, the certainties of the sciences are in the possession of a few countries only, and for the most part only of the educated classes in those countries; yet the philosophers of Europe and America would feel certain that the earth rolled round the sun, in spite of the Indian belief of its being supported by an elephant with a tortoise under it.[78]

Both the problem that is being tackled and the answer to it reflect the confusion. There is a problem only because the universality that necessarily belongs to objective truth is applied to the certitude of a deliberate act of personal assent. Since this ascription of universality to personal certitude is unwarranted and unnecessary, the problem is a bogus one. In the passage we have just quoted, the logical certainty of a fact and the personal certainty of individuals are not distinguished. It seems that Newman believes he is talking about the same thing when he mentions the certainty of 'a truth or a fact' and when he deals with the certainties which we 'feel' and possess. He moves from one to the other without any indication that he is moving from one logic to another. Here again he fails to recognize the proper logical status of certitude, and presumably of assent.

What Newman has to say about the 'certainty' of religious belief further demonstrates this confusion in his thought. He does not recognize that the certainty which is required for a living religion is not the logical certainty of its objective truth. What he says about the attitude needed for religious faith is undoubtedly correct. The depth and persistence of commitment which mark out a living faith are not to be found in merely *ad hoc* assents.

> Assents may and do change; certitudes endure. This is why religion demands more than an assent to its truth; it requires a certitude, or at least an assent which is convertible into a certitude on demand. Without certitude in religious faith there may be much decency of profession and of observance, but there can be no habit of prayer, no directness of devotion, no intercourse with the unseen, no generosity of self-sacrifice.[79]

With this we have no quarrel. In many matters we do not require the complex assent of certainty as a foundation for our behaviour. We are prepared to act on the basis of probability. With living religion, however, the issue is different. Here we are faced, as Tillich would say, with matters of 'ultimate concern'.[80] The absolute self-commitment at a fundamental level which is required by real religion can only be made to what we are certain of. As Newman is aware,[81] I cannot base my faith on what I assent to simply as a working hypothesis. Pascal's wager is shown at this point to be religiously irrelevant as well as irreverent. My real faith is in what I am certain of and therefore in what I am committed to without any qualifications or limitations at all. Where we quarrel with Newman is in his understanding of what this demand for certainty implies. He suggests that such a position can only be based on the objectively true:

> The initial truths of divine knowledge ought to be viewed as parallel to the initial truths of the secular: as the latter are certain, so too are the former. . . . In both the one and the other the primary principles, the general, fundamental, cardinal truths are immutable. In human matters we are guided by probabilities but, I repeat, they are probabilities founded on certainties.[82]

Here it is not the individual who is certain and his commitment which is immutable, it is the truth itself which is described as 'certain' and 'immutable'. This is the language of objectivity, not that of personal commitments.

In this same section there are other statements which indicate what we consider to be the correct position, namely, that a living faith must be based upon absolute personal commitment. Thus we read that the elements of true faith 'presuppose a real hold and habitual intuition of the objects of Revelation, which is certitude under another name'. Such an all-embracing, absolute faith:

> may be ruled by the world to be a perverseness or a delusion; but as long as it exists it will pre-suppose certitude as the very life which is to animate it.[83]

This is a recognition that what faith is based upon is not necessarily the objectively true but an unreserved personal certainty that its foundation is the objectively true. It is personal or psychological certitude, not logical certitude, which is required. Religion is a state of complete personal commitment to what is believed to be absolutely certain. The demand for certainty at the heart of religion does not destroy the need for a leap of faith. The fact that Newman confuses logical and psychological certitude in his understanding of religion shows his failure to discern consistently the proper character of assent in religious matters.

In this section we have tried to show that Newman's treatment of the complex assent of certainty or certitude suffers from the same basic confusion as does his understanding of assent in general. He does not distinguish between the objectively logical and subjectively personal references of these terms but moves from the one to the other without any indication that he is committing a logical type-jump. The result is that sometimes objective characteristics are erroneously ascribed to religious assent and Newman makes statements which imply that faith belongs to the logic of reasoning. This failure to grasp fully the proper structure of faith prevents Newman from presenting a wholly consistent treatment of the problem of faith.

Part VI: Conclusion

THIS concluding chapter is concerned with two questions. First, how successfully does Newman answer his problem of faith in the *Grammar of Assent*? Secondly, how valuable is his work for the theology of his day and ours?

Before we can judge how far Newman has answered his problem, we must decide what that problem was. When he finally published his understanding of the nature of belief, Newman chose to concern himself primarily with the practical aspects of the problem. He states that his intention in the *Grammar of Assent* is to provide a phenomenological analysis of assent:

> My object in the foregoing pages has been, not to form a theory which may account for those phenomena of the intellect of which they treat, viz. those which characterize inference and assent, but to ascertain what is the matter of fact as regards them, that is, when it is that assent is given to propositions which are inferred, and under what circumstances. . . . How it comes about that we can be certain is not my business to determine; for me it is sufficient that certitude is felt. That is what the schoolmen, I believe, call treating a subject *in facto esse*, in contrast with *in fieri*. Had I attempted the latter, I should have been falling into metaphysics; but my aim is of a practical character.[1]

In accordance with this statement by Newman, most commentators interpret the *Grammar of Assent* as a work of practical psychology. Walgrave writes that 'in adopting a psychological standpoint based entirely on an analysis of what goes on in the mind, Newman took pains not to pass beyond it.'[2] Similarly, Zeno holds that in the *Grammar* Newman 'wanted to show the psychological basis of an act of faith',[3] thereby giving us 'a phenomenological analysis of the art of thinking'.[4] According to Keogh, Newman's 'method was not speculative analysis, but psychological, and to a large extent what is today called phenomenological description. His object was not knowledge displayed in an objective system, but knowledge seated in the individual mind.'[5] Thus

Newman 'confined himself rigorously . . . to describing experience' and produced 'a work of natural phenomenology' which must be judged 'solely' by 'experience'.[6] In opposition to the 'a priori elaborations of objective reason, he marshalled the testimony of concrete facts': he tried to show how in fact 'the mind . . . *does* reason' against the rationalist attempts to show how it 'ought to reason'.[7]

These statements undoubtedly describe Newman's main intention in the *Grammar of Assent*, but to limit his work to phenomenological description is an inadequate appraisal. Boekraad points out that although Newman was primarily interested in 'personal certainty', with the result that his 'immediate problem is concerned with the reaching of certainty regarding supernatural faith, we must always remember that at bottom there lies a truly philosophical question'.[8] This metaphysical question concerns the possibility of our subjective certitude corresponding to objective truth.[9] Newman answers it by showing that the reasoning processes which precede our assents are rationally valid and by asserting that what our faculties indicate to be objectively true, we must accept as such. This latter assertion if not merely the recognition that we are limited to the informations of our faculties because we have no other way of discovering the truth. It is linked with a metaphysical or theological claim that 'nature' or 'God' guarantees the objective accuracy of those faculties if they are properly used.[10] Thus Newman states that for him 'it is enough for the proof of the value and authority of any function which I possess, to be able to pronounce that it is natural'.[11] First, then, we must consider Newman's success both in describing the phenomenology of assent and in providing a rational justification for acts of assent. In our evaluation we must remember that Newman did not regard his work as a definitive treatise. He called it *An Essay in Aid of a Grammar of Assent* and never claimed that it was comprehensive.

The metaphysical basis of Newman's thought is an assumption which can hardly be challenged. As Newman states:

> we are what we are, and we use, not trust our faculties. To debate about trusting in a case like this, is parallel to the confusion implied in wishing I had had a choice if I would be created or no. . . . We are as little able to accept or reject our mental constitution, as our being. We have not the option; we can but misuse or mar its functions.[12]

Later, in a section on 'The Sanction of the Illative Sense', Newman makes the same point:

> Such as I am, it is my all; this is my essential standpoint, and must be taken for granted; otherwise, thought is but an idle amusement,

> not worth the trouble. There is no medium between using my faculties, as I have them, and flinging myself upon the external world according to the random impulse of the moment, as spray upon the surface of the waves, and simply forgetting that I am. I am what I am. . . . I cannot avoid being sufficient for myself, for I cannot make myself any thing else, and to change me is to destroy me.[13]

This is a useful protest against those who question our claim that what we hold to be the truth corresponds to the truth itself, that what is known corresponds to the thing-in-itself. Newman does not deny that the question is possible but he questions whether it is answerable. Since we can determine the truth only through our faculties, to ask whether our faculties give us the objective truth is to ask a question which we cannot answer except by using them. If we accept that a question is only 'meaningful' if we can designate a way to find its answer, then the question is probably 'meaningless'. What the question does show is that our use of the phrase 'objectively true' must either be purely theoretical, as we may say that discussions of Kant's 'noumena' are theoretical, or be restricted to what can be known through our cognitive faculties. In this latter case, the distinction between subjective and objective truth is ultimately relative.

It is difficult to see how we can justifiably refuse to accept that our faculties provide us with knowledge of the truth, even though we may reject the theological and natural guarantees Newman finds for them. The only alternative to such an assumption seems to be a complete scepticism about the possibility of knowing the truth. Even to assert that we are correct in doubting the possibility of knowing the truth is to affirm the assumption! When we grant the assumption, the problem that remains for us is the degree to which our faculties can justify our assents, especially our assents in matters of religious faith. Newman holds that while we cannot secure a complete justification, both because of the essential distinction between conclusions and assents and because of the inconclusiveness of the available evidence, we can find a certain measure of support for our assents. This is what he seeks to demonstrate in his discussion of the Illative Sense. He shows that valid arguments are not restricted to syllogistic modes but that conclusions reached by converging probability are philosophically respectable as well as practically necessary. His rejection of the view that syllogisms are the only proper forms of logical reasoning is fully justified. What is not so clear is the degree to which even illative reasoning can show the probability of items of religious faith. Reasoning, however, is not the end of the matter.

While it may determine that the object of our assent is more or less likely, our assent is finally a personal act which goes beyond the limits of what is demonstrated. Even so, our assents are not arbitrary decisions but acts of commitment to objects whose probability we have ascertained to some extent.

When we try to evaluate Newman's description of the phenomenology of faith, we are on personal grounds. We can judge his success or failure only by comparing his description with our own experience of faith and others' descriptions of their experience. Since this is a highly personal procedure, there seems to be no value in pursuing it here. Each of us must finally decide for ourselves whether Newman's description of the empirical nature of faith tallies with our own self-awareness. What I intend to do is to suggest where Newman seems to succeed and where he seems to fail in his work.

Newman's first success is his perception that apprehension is a condition of assent. If we are asked to believe a proposition which we do not understand, we must first be told what it means. Until this has been done, we cannot even consider granting assent. It is demanding the impossible to ask us first to believe and then, through believing, to discover the meaning of theological doctrines. Attempts to explain the meaning of religious statements by suggesting that they form part of a sphere of meaning which can only be understood from the inside break down at this point.[14] As no one can believe what he does not apprehend, so no one can enter the religious sphere unless he has some understanding of its contents. This does not preclude the possibility that we may enter the religious sphere through inadequate or unsatisfactory apprehensions which are later altered and developed by a more accurate understanding which comes from religious and theological activity. What is necessary is that we have some understanding of the object before we assent. It is only so far as we apprehend it that we assent to it. In view of the fact that apprehension is a condition of assent, it is amazing that Boekraad can write a book entitled *The Personal Conquest of Truth according to J. H. Newman* without once dealing with the subject of apprehension, while in Zeno's *John Henry Newman, Our Way to Certitude* it receives only the very briefest mention.[15] Newman has appreciated this aspect of the problem better than some of his critics!

Newman succeeds secondly when he points out that what we apprehend as 'real' has a far greater effect upon us than what we understand notionally. H. D. Lewis comments on this:

> I may not doubt at all the truth of a report of a railway disaster of which I read in the papers, but the horror of the incident does not

overwhelm me as it might if someone I loved were involved in it—or if I were given an exceptionally harrowing description of the scene of suffering and death.[16]

The use of illustrations in sermons and of particular cases in charitable appeals further reminds us of the truth of this claim. It is a matter of general experience that we are more affected by the concrete than by the abstract. One implication of the distinction between 'real' and 'notional', and one which Newman well draws out, is that an assent which is to have the full force of a religious belief must be a 'real' assent. A living faith is a commitment to something particular, not merely the acceptance of a set of general principles.

A third achievement of the *Grammar of Assent* is its demonstration that our reasoning produces significant conclusions even though its processes can rarely be expressed in syllogistic forms. We commonly argue by converging probability, although we would often be at a loss to give a formal description of our method. A juror may not be conscious of the way in which he comes to his verdict as he weighs up the evidence, but this does not deny the validity of his verdict. The fact that we cannot present our theological arguments in syllogistic forms does not mean that they are valueless. Through experience and common sense we learn to reach accurate conclusions even from most miscellaneous collections of evidence. Newman shows that we must not despise our illative methods. They are a thoroughly valid way of reaching conclusions and have a vital rôle in religious thinking.

Fourthly, in spite of certain vacillations, Newman shows that assent, and so faith, is essentially a personal matter. He does this in various ways, —by making apprehension a condition and real apprehension (in itself a private matter) a stimulus for assent, by revealing that the antecedent reasoning is usually of a personal nature, and by indicating the function of the individual's conscience and will in the act of assent. The personal character of assent is most marked in the distinction made between conclusions and assents which shows that we can never be forced to assent. While other people's arguments and explanations may help to lead us to faith, in the end our faith is something which is characteristic of ourselves.

At this point we become aware of one of Newman's failings in the *Grammar of Assent*. Even though our faith is our own and reveals something of our character, it is not at all clear that our assent is finally to be regarded as a leap made by an act of will. Newman's view that faith is partly an act of the will is backed by good authority. Aquinas, for instance, says that:

The act of believing is an act of the intellect assenting to the Divine truth at the command of the will moved by the grace of God, so that it is subject to the free will in relation to God.[17]

Can this view be sustained? A certain conclusion may seem to me to be very probably true, my conscience may tell me that I am morally obliged to act on the basis that it is true, but, even so, can I really choose to assent to it? It seems to me that there is an essential difference, which Newman does not recognize, between consciously deciding to act *as if* something were true and actually accepting it as true without any qualifications at all, conscious or unconscious. So far as I can tell, I can only decide to think and act *as if* something were true,[18] whereas 'assent' describes a state where I accept something as true without any doubt or reservation at all. This is a state in which I find myself rather than a state into which I choose to enter. For example, Tillich speaks of faith as 'the state of being *grasped* by an ultimate concern'[19] and I. T. Ramsey views faith-statements as 'disclosure models' through which the 'light dawns' and I become aware of reality at a deeper level.[20] In neither case do I control what reveals itself to me. Thus I consider that Newman's understanding of faith in the *Grammar of Assent* is inadequate because it fails to recognize that 'assent' refers to a state more akin to that of captivation or fascination, which I suddenly find myself experiencing without any decision to experience it, than to that of being polite which I can choose to adopt. Just as I cannot decide to be captivated by something, so I cannot decide to entertain something absolutely as true. All I can decide is to do certain things which will make it more or less likely that I will have the experiences involuntarily at some time or other.[21] What I can choose in relation to faith is to hold a proposition *as if* it were true. As a result of holding it in this way I may find at some later time that I now accept it as true unconditionally, without any awareness of an 'as if' situation. Newman's failure to give an adequate treatment of the function of the will and conscience in the act of assent may be due to an implicit recognition of the inability of the will to bring about a state of absolute assent. His views on this topic have to be culled from various scattered passages in the *Grammar of Assent*. It is obvious, however, from what he does say that he considers that assent is made by an act of the will which is in part under the control of conscience. This means that for Newman assent is basically the willed state of accepting something as if it were unconditionally true rather than the unwillable state of accepting it without reservation.[22]

Our second major criticism of the *Grammar of Assent* concerns its failure to determine how we can assent to presuppositions. We have discussed this already and there is no need to repeat our argument that in the case of these basic assumptions or first principles, assent cannot be preceded by any really significant reasoning. Since they express the fundamental convictions upon which our thought rests and in terms of which our reasoning is carried out, these beliefs are the norms of all our intellectual activity.[23] When we appeal to them, we appeal to that behind which we, at any rate, cannot go. How we assent to these basic assumptions, or 'presumptions', is never made clear by Newman. What is clear is that assent to them cannot have any significant antecedent reasoning. Furthermore, if assent is regarded as an act of the will, it is hard to envisage how we can be said to 'assent' to presuppositions when they provide the basis of our decisions and choices. Our acceptance of these first principles seems to originate elsewhere than in what Newman regards as the 'act' of assent. They are dispositions and normative attitudes which we do not 'decide' to accept so much as 'find' ourselves possessing. What Newman describes is how we come to accept secondary beliefs. These are the beliefs which are derived in part from our basic assumptions. Take, for instance, the problem whether I should believe that Gwyneth's attitude to Arthur was the best in the circumstances. If I assume as a first principle that love is the highest moral value, I examine the case to determine whether, in view of all the facts, the attitude was the best possible expression of love. If I judge that as far as I can tell, it was such an expression of love, I have antecedent reasons for assenting that Gwyneth's attitude to Arthur was the best. What is not questioned at all in my deliberations about the secondary belief is my primary belief that love is the highest moral value, i.e., is 'best'. This is assumed and I am committed to it beyond all possibility of its being questioned. How we come to accept such primary presuppositions does not receive any significant treatment in the *Grammar of Assent*—Newman merely suggests that in some indeterminate way it is connected with the Illative Sense.[24] This failure to determine how we can assent to presuppositions means that what Newman has to say concerns mainly our secondary beliefs while the crucial question for faith is how we come to and can justify our primary beliefs.

A third major criticism, and one which we have already discussed, is Newman's failure to distinguish consistently between the logical and the psychological aspects of faith and assent. This is particularly seen in his confusion about certainty and certitude. The aim of the *Grammar of Assent* is not simply to determine the logical status of faith-statements but also to describe how we come to make them. In this treatment of the phenomenology of commitment both logical and psychological factors are involved. Unfortunately Newman did not realize this at all clearly and at times failed to perceive the proper logical status of the matters before him. For instance, when he is really dealing with certitude, to use Tennant's distinction, Newman sometimes makes statements which belong to the logic of certainty as if they concerned the same problem. Since we have pointed out cases of this as they have occurred in our discussion of the *Grammar* there is no need to labour the point further.

Finally we consider that Newman is to be criticized for restricting his treatment of faith to assent to propositions. Faith is not just assent to a series of statements about God but also involves a direct relationship with God. As Herrmann states in his discussion of Ritschl's view of faith, faith is only partially understood when it is regarded as 'holding for true doctrines and narratives offered us with divine authority, and thenceforth depending upon them', for 'the longing of our souls after true life will not be stilled by receiving a doctrine about God, but only by finding God Himself'. Real faith stems from an experience of and 'unconditional submission to a Power which a Christian distinguishes from his own inner life'.[25] Tillich describes the essence of faith similarly:

> Faith is not a theoretical affirmation of something uncertain, it is the existential acceptance of something transcending ordinary experience. Faith is not an opinion but a state. It is the state of being grasped by the power of being which transcends everything that is and in which everything that is participates.[26]

Newman never seems fully to appreciate this aspect of faith although his treatment of 'real' assent may imply a faint recognition of it. He viewed faith basically in terms of doctrines, not of personal relationships—he described his conversion in terms of 'a great change of thought' and receiving 'a definite Creed'.[27] Consequently, while the *Grammar of Assent* helps us to understand how we can believe the articles of faith, it is not so much help if we seek faith as a living, personal relationship.

The one question that remains to be answered concerns the value of the *Grammar of Assent* for the theology of Newman's day and ours. Reviewing the *Grammar* in the *Quarterly Review* for July 1870, J. B. Mozley welcomed it as a vindication of 'the claims of Christianity generally upon human belief' which 'has filled up a vacant place in Christian apologetics'.[28] Mozley was right when he stated that the book was not denominationally biased, but can his judgement on the value of the book be sustained, both in relation to the thought of the nineteenth century as it experienced a fundamental crisis for faith and in relation to the theological thought of our day which is still trying to meet that crisis? As we have indicated, Newman's work on faith should not be regarded as a deliberate reply to any particular theological or philosophical system. It would be misleading, for instance, to try to relate his thought to each of the different positions discussed in our first chapter as they led to the crisis for faith. Rather we must see Newman's work on faith primarily as a personal attempt to combat the fundamental principles of that 'liberal' attitude which underlay the various elements in the crisis for faith. From this point of view we judge the value of his work.

By dealing with faith, Newman went to the heart of the religious and theological problem of the nineteenth and twentieth centuries. He saw that the answer to the crisis for faith was not to be found by attempting to reply piecemeal to the many and various philosophical, ethical, scientific, literary, historical, and 'democratic' ideas that currently were disturbing faith. Such replies might patch up specific cracks in the structure of faith but the real problem was that people wondered if it was a structure that was worth trying to repair. What Newman called the 'liberal' attitude, and which today more commonly appears as the popular understanding of the 'scientific' attitude, was consciously or unconsciously challenging the propriety of preserving any edifice which used 'faith' for its foundations. The demand of the age was for 'knowledge'—and knowledge was what could be conclusively demonstrated by experience and reason on generally agreed principles. Religion seemed to many to be supportable only by the use of experience, reasoning, and principles which were highly disputable. Newman's work on faith is important because it attacks this 'liberal', 'rationalistic', or 'scientific' attitude by showing, first, that we all have in practice to live by faith as well as by sight, whether we like it or not, and secondly, that the assent of faith is not a completely a-rational, arbitrary matter. It is an assent which can be backed on occasions by considerable supporting reasoning. Although we have to make a leap of faith at some point or other, there is no need for that leap to be totally 'blind'. Indeed, it cannot be totally 'blind' since we must always have some prior apprehension of the position to which we are being committed by it. Newman's work, then, is valuable both for his day and ours in that it makes it clear that we cannot do without faith. Existing faith-positions may be threatened but to live we need some faith-position or other. The question is, what faith-position is the right one?—and how do we decide that it is such?

In the *Grammar of Assent* Newman also indicates lines along which this latter question might be solved. While he was one of the few theologians in the nineteenth century who recognized that apprehension was a condition for belief, he did not manage to do more than show that we must understand before we can believe. For contemporary theology his important contribution lies not here but in the way he suggested a possible logical status of faith-statements. Newman did not attempt to answer the Kantian question of faith by reinterpreting its statements in terms of what we might call some 'non-religious' reality or position. He regarded the statements of faith as statements about an objectively existent God, not as disguised statements which were really about limiting concepts, or metaphysics, or morals, or man (ideal or actual). Such interpretations, which were and still are offered in various forms, avoid rather than solve the problem of faith as Newman understood it. For Newman, statements of faith involve some kind of factual claim which is partly derived from our empirical experience and partly accepted in the commitment of faith. By distinguishing between assents and conclusions, he indicates that faith-statements are not to be classed as conclusions but as statements which describe personal commitments to what is held to be the truth. These commitments involve claims about what is factually true but they can never be completely justified or compelled by reasoning alone. These commitments are also personal matters which reflect the fundamental attitudes of the individual.[29] Any analysis of the logical structure of faith-statements, therefore, will find that they essentially involve a combination of factual descriptions, normative attitudes, and personal commitments.

Newman thus indicates in the *Grammar of Assent* a way in which we might construct a model by which we could synthesize the different and apparently disparate elements in the understandings of faith expounded, for instance, by Schleiermacher and by Kierkegaard. The usefulness of this model will be greatly enhanced if we add a third element which has been located in faith-commitments by I. T. Ramsey. Newman, then, offers a model of the structure of faith which may allow us to give due weight both to the investigations and arguments classically pursued by natural theology and to the understanding of faith propounded by existentialist thinkers. On this model natural theology in its various forms functions as the agency which suggests to us both the meaning of faith-statements and reasons why we might accept such faith-statements as likely to be true. Natural theology thus fulfils the necessary condition of faith by making its objects apprehensible and also provides the reasoning which is an essential antecedent to faith. Its significance is that it makes faith possible and encourages us to adopt the stand of faith. The commitment of faith, however, cannot be unavoidably entailed by such reasoning. There is a gap left which no amount of reasoning can bridge—and no amount of moral exhortation can compel us to leap. Arguments may shrink the gap and moral pressures may encourage us to risk the jump but the gap is still there. This is the element of faith which existentialist thought emphasizes. It is a characteristic of faith which is especially noticeable when we consider those fundamental beliefs which provide the assumptions, standpoints, and attitudes from which the rest of our thought and action is derived, though even here some kind of supporting reasoning may be possible.[30] At this point we have to break company with the model that is suggested by the *Grammar of Assent*. Newman seems to hold that the gap is bridged by an act of the will. Certainly such an act of will is involved in our choice to think and act 'as if' something were true but, as we have already suggested, this does not reflect what happens in the full commitment of faith. Our faith cannot be adequately described in terms of our choice to act 'as if' a certain thing were true, our faith expresses our total commitment to that thing as true. We believe it because we believe that it is true, not simply because we consider that it is a good basis for thought and action. Although we talk about 'decision' and 'choice' in matters of faith, in the end the situation seems to be more akin to what I. T. Ramsey calls a 'disclosure situation'. In religious circles this element in assent is often attributed to the work of divine grace. If we do not want to involve ideas of supernatural forces working upon us in our understanding of faith, we may simply have to say that the situation is as little within our conscious control as when a pattern or a system finally 'clicks' into shape in our minds or as when a particular truth 'comes home to us' and authenticates itself to us in a way that we find irresistible.

To sum up, by various kinds of natural theology we may apprehend what a particular doctrine means and be given reasons which encourage us to believe that it is true. At the same time we may be conscious that there is a gap—in religious matters often a noticeable gap—between what our reasoning can demonstrate and the commitment that is asked of us. We may also be conscious of three other things: first, that we must live by some faith or other; secondly, that the antecedent reasoning gives us good grounds for the particular faith-position presented to us; and thirdly, that the reasons given make the position morally proper and even obligatory for us to adopt. On this basis we can then choose to live by that faith—to live, that is, *as if* it were true. As we do this, however, we may find that the faith-position, suddenly or gradually, 'comes home' to us not as an hypothesis by which we live but as a truth which has grasped us, convincing us by some inherent power that it is the truth. At this point we enjoy the unreserved, absolute assent of faith. By offering suggestions which lead to this model of faith, Newman makes an important contribution to the theological debate of his day and ours. In the end, however, we may take comfort from the words of St. Ambrose which Newman used as a motto for this work, words which may cheer a believer as he struggles to establish his faith:

'Non in dialecticâ complacuit Deo salvum facere populum suum'.

Appendix I

NEWMAN'S CLASSIFICATION OF THE TYPES OF ASSENT

IN the *Grammar of Assent*[1] Newman suggests how the various types of assent are to be divided according to his distinction between real and notional assent. He includes in the class of real assent those assents which 'are sometimes called beliefs, convictions, certitudes',[2] while 'Profession, Credence, Opinion, Presumption and Speculation'[3] are said to be notional assents. In this appendix we are to examine this classification of the different types of assent and we start with what Newman considers to be the forms of real assent.

Certitude is a reflex or complex assent, being 'the perception of a truth with the perception that it is a truth'.[4] It has the basic pattern 'I assent to my assent to P'. Later in the *Grammar of Assent* Newman holds that such a proposition can only be apprehended notionally and so can be given only notional assent.

> The reflex or confirmatory assent of certitude always is given to a notional proposition, viz., to the truth, necessity, duty, &c., of our assent to the simple assent and to its proposition. Its predicate is a general term, and cannot stand for a fact, whereas the original proposition, included in it, may, and often does, express a fact.[5]

Newman thus contradicts his later judgement when he calls certitude a real assent. His mistake may have been occasioned by a combination of his conviction that real assent is superior to notional in power and influence with a desire to class certitude among the more powerful group of assents. While he considers that reflex assents are made only when simple assents are challenged,[6] he also holds that certitudes are so powerful that when they have been made they are 'indefectible'.[7] He may, on the other hand, have erred in his classification of certitude because he confused 'P is true' (which in fact is another way of expressing the simple assent 'I assent to P') with 'I assent that P is true' (which is complex and essentially notional). Whatever may have been the reasons which led Newman to his view that certitude is a real assent, that view cannot be reconciled to the way he distinguished between the real and the notional.

A similar criticism must be levelled against Newman's assertion that *conviction* is a form of real assent. In the *Grammar of Assent* the concept does not play a large part[8] but where it is used it expresses a reflex assent. Newman writes of complex assent that 'it is an assent, not only to a given proposition, but to the claim of that proposition on our assent as true, it is an assent to an assent, or what is commonly called a conviction.'[9] The difference between a conviction and a certitude is that whereas the former can be objectively either true or false, the latter is sometimes regarded as a reflex assent solely to what is objectively true.[10] Since a conviction is a reflex assent, it must be notional. Its classification as real may again be due to the strength of assent which Newman finds in conviction. He holds that a conviction is the opposite of 'light and casual . . . assent'.[11] If it is consistent, it involves a 'magisterial intolerance of any contrary assertion'.[12] But although it is such a powerful assent, its form as 'an assent to an assent'[13] means that it must be notional. Newman errs in describing it as a form of real assent.

The third, and most important form of assent which Newman classifies as real, is *belief*. At times in the *Grammar of Assent* it seems that belief is synonymous with real assent. For instance, we read 'Real Assent, or Belief, as it may be called', 'acts of Belief, that is, of Real Assent', and 'Real Assent or Belief'.[14] The equivalence of the terms is confirmed by the assertion that belief is 'concerned with things concrete, not abstract'.[15] There are passages in the *Grammar of Assent* where 'belief' is used as equivalent to assent as such[16] without any definite connexion with images, but 'belief' is never explicitly directed towards notions. In the matter of religion and theology, Newman uses the term 'faith', which he regards as having wider reference than belief,[17] to cover both real and notional assents and he appears to confine the use of the term 'belief' to cases where its object is really apprehended.[18] This is possibly not a conscious distinction, because Newman never enunciates it as such, but it is a consequence of his view that belief is a real assent. As religion has to do with images, religious assent is belief and theological assent faith. This restricted use of 'belief' does not follow common usage. Generally 'belief' and 'faith' can be applied indiscriminately to what is notionally and to what is really apprehended. The restriction is probably connected with Newman's preference for the real. Since our beliefs are recognized to be a dominant influence over us, so they come to be viewed as real. In those passages[19] where he apparently uses 'belief' simply as conterminous with assent as such, Newman follows common usage, but we must not forget that elsewhere he explicitly identifies belief with real assent. Thus, while 'belief' always expresses an assent, the context of that assent must be examined before we can be sure that a specifically real assent is involved.

We now turn to the forms of notional assent mentioned by Newman.[20] *Profession* does not play any part in the thought of the *Grammar of Assent* although it is included in the list of notional assents.[21] Its defining characteristic is that it is an assent 'so feeble and superficial as to be little more than' an assertion. It includes 'assents made upon habit and without reflection' and 'the assents of men of wavering restless minds'.[22] Newman does not indicate why 'profession' can only be a notional assent. Any weak assent made to an image would fit his description of profession as well as any weak notional assent. He presumably calls profession a notional assent because he assumes that real assent is powerful. Otherwise there is no reason why weak real assents should not be classed as professions.

Newman explicitly states that *credence* is a notional assent[23] and yet he includes within it assent to 'professed facts' as well as to 'opinions'.[24] It is the 'otiose and passive' assent given to those things 'which are ever presenting themselves to us without any effort of ours, and which we commonly take for granted'[25] without examination, 'the principles, doctrines, sentiments, facts'[26] of contemporary thought. The only reason for describing credence as a notional assent seems to be the superficiality of the assent in such cases.[27] Newman's restriction of this form of assent to notions must be questioned, for, as he recognizes, it can be granted to 'facts'. There is thus no decisive reason why real assents which we take for granted and which do not evoke any especially powerful response, should not be called 'credences'. As an example of such a weak real assent we may instance our assent to the proposition 'King Charles hid in an oak tree.' Newman's analysis of this form of assent does not show why the 'informations' which it spontaneously accepts must be regarded as essentially notional.[28]

Opinion is undoubtedly to be classed as notional for in Newman's usage it is 'an assent to a proposition, not as true, but as probably true, that is, to the probability of that which the proposition enunciates'.[29] It is essentially notional since it is both a reflex assent and an assent to a probability, an abstract concept.[30] Newman recognizes that opinions largely direct our thought and activity in daily life.[31] Their influence, therefore, is considerable although they are notional assents.

Presumptions are notional assents which are even more powerful. They express the basic and normative assumptions of thought and action, being assents to:

> first principles . . . with which we start in reasoning on any given

subject matter. . . . They are all of them notions, not images, because they express what is abstract, not what is individual and from direct experience.[32]

Whether we agree with Newman that these presumptions are derived from experience or believe that some of them at least are *a priori*, it cannot be denied that they are only notionally apprehensible. Nevertheless, these notional assents may be entertained as certain,[33] and as first principles they exert tremendous influence since they control the nature and validity of our activities.

Newman's other type of notional assent is *speculation*.[34] This form of assent is regarded as the 'most direct, explicit and perfect' notional assent, being 'the firm, conscious acceptance of propositions as true'.[35] Newman does not say much about its objects but those which he does list may all be regarded as notional. They include:

> all reasoning and its conclusions, . . . all general propositions, . . . all rules of conduct, . . . all proverbs, aphorisms, sayings, and reflections on men and society . . . mathematical investigations and truths . . . legal judgments and constitutional maxims . . . the determinations of science . . . the principles, disputations, and doctrines of theology.[36]

Since Newman defines 'speculation' in terms of 'mental sight, or the contemplation of mental operations and their results as opposed to experience, experiment or sense',[37] it cannot be applied to real assents. Speculation, in fact, is a strong form of notional assent.

This discussion of Newman's examples of real and notional assents suggests that while the distinction between real and notional may be fairly clear in itself, his application of it to the types of assent is anything but clear and satisfactory. Newman seems to be led astray by his awareness of the superior power of the real. As a result of this awareness, he seems tempted to class all strong assents as real and to belittle the power of notional assents.

Appendix II

NEWMAN'S LIST OF HIS UNPUBLISHED ATTEMPTS TO WRITE ON FAITH AND REASON

In a note dated October 30, 1870,[1] in *The Journal 1859–79*, Newman describes some of his attempts to write the *Grammar of Assent*:

> Since I published my Essay on Assent last March, I have meant to make a memorandum on the subject of it. It is the upshot of a very long desire and effort—I don't know the worth of it, but I am happier to have at length done it and got it off my hands. . . . The book itself I have aimed at writing this twenty years;—and now that it is written I do not quite recognize it for what it was meant to be, though I suppose it is such. I have made more attempts at writing it, than I can enumerate. However, I actually have manuscripts remaining, to prove the following distinct separate beginnings:
>
> 1. June 17. 1846. St. Thomas's view of faith as 'cogitare cum assensu'.[2]
> 2. March 5. 1850. My letters to Dr. Errington about Gerdil, and the inquiries out of which they arose.[3]
> 3. February 1851. 'On a view of the conclusion greater and distincter and higher than that of the premisses'. This is a problem long in my mind, e.g. in University Sermons—go through my attempts historically. . . . 'Against historical religion. 1st. We cannot suppose etc.'. . . . 'Fluctuations of human opinion. . . .' 'On certainty etc. . . .'[4]
> 4. September 25. 1851. 'A defence of the Catholic Religion'.[5]
> 5. (Without date) On certainty etc.[6]
> 6. May and June 1853. Fr. Edward Caswall's notes of my Lectures on Faith and certainty—And my own notes of the same.[7]
> 7. March 1857. 'In festo S. Gregorii' 'Opus magnum' (as it was to be).[8]
> 8. July and September 1857. 'What God is personally TO 'US.[9]

9. January 1859 and February. Lectures to Scott etc. on Logic. 'Whether religious certitude may be legitimately produced by probable arguments etc.' 'Whether words stand for ideas or things'.[10]
10. 1859–60. Letters to Dr. Meynell—(about Mansel's theory?).[11]
11. January 5. 1860. 'On the popular, practical, personal evidence for the truth of Revelation'.[12]
12. January 12. 1860. 'The Evidences of Religion'.[13]
13. January 1861. 'The Holy Trinity in connection with the early Fathers and the Disciplina Arcani'.[14]
14. September 1. 1861. 'I find my dear—, that you are both interested etc.'—'On the senses'.[15]
15. October 12. 1861. At Ventnor. 'Schema totius operis etc'.[16]
16. September 22. 1863. Doctrine of the Holy Trinity.[17]
17. December 12. 1863. Doctrine of the Holy Trinity. §1. begins: 'The knowledge, which is most intimately our own, and directly personal to us, lies in our experience etc. and so on, what afterwards became 'Imaginative and notional apprehension'.[18]
18. August 11, 1865. On certitude—intuition—instinct.[19]

These attempts, though some of them close upon others, were, I think, all distinct. They were like attempts to get into a labyrinth, or to find the weak point in the defences of a fortified place. I could not get on, and found myself turned back, utterly baffled. Yet I felt I ought to bring out what my mind saw, but could not grasp, whatever it was worth. I don't say it is worth much, now that it has come out, but I felt as if I did not like to die before I had said it.

This list of attempts is not exhaustive. Newman's book of *Sundries*[20] or private memoranda contains several entries which are concerned with the problem and there are some other papers and fragments on the subject preserved at the Oratory. Among these loose notes are some entitled

'Ultimate Resolution of certainty of Faith'.[21]
'(On the Nature and Cause of Faith)',[22]
'April 30, 1853',[23]
'May 13, 1853: 'Analysis of Religious Inquiry according to the foregoing Rules',[24]
'December 16, 1853. On the Certainty of Faith',[25]
'June 26, 1865. Certainty not inconsistent with probable evidence',[26]

'20 July, 1865. (*Essay on Certitude*)',[27]
'September 25, 1865. (*Meaning of Certitude*)',[28]
'Chapter iii §1. On apprehension and assent through the imagination considered in reference to the being of a God'.[29]
'(Believing what we do not understand)',[30]
'§ 3 Certitude',[31]
'§ On Counterfeit Intuitions'.[32]

Appendix III

SIXTEEN EXTRACTS FROM NEWMAN'S UNPUBLISHED PRIVATE MANUSCRIPTS CONCERNED WITH HIS THOUGHT ABOUT THE LOGIC OF FAITH

(These are printed by the kind permission of the Fathers of the Oratory, Edgbaston, Birmingham. The copyright of this material belongs to that Oratory. It is hoped that eventually Newman's private manuscripts on theology and philosophy will be published in full.)

1.

17 June 1846 *On St. Thomas's view of Faith as cogitare cum assensu.* [This is in packet B.9.11 and deals with Newman's comments on Aquinas's Commentary on 3 Sent. d.23 q.2 a.2.]

... (2) An act (operatio) of intellect is either a simple apprehension (intelligentia or formatio) or a judgment, i.e. here an assent ... An assent of the intellect is either
(i) from sense or intuition (intellectus or visio)
(ii) from strict reasoning into principles known (scientia)
(iii) from faint reasoning supported and carried through by will.
... This last assent is the assent of faith.
(3) Therefore faith is *cogitare cum assensu,* for intelligens per se (which is the first above mentioned) has not *cogitatio.* Sciens (which is the second) has cogitatio as well as assent, but not cogitatio cum assensu sed ante assensum.

(This is *precisely* my main distinction in my University Sermons: on which I insisted and hammered so much, that the fault of Protestant theories of faith is that they say, '*reason comes first,* and *then* comes the will and *faith*', against which I speak of *presumption* supported by the *will* being the proof—or cogitatio and assensus going together.)

It must be observed, however, that assensus does not stand for *will,* but the act of the intellectus—this act, says St. Thomas, is not determined by the cogitatio that is weak, but by the will, which obliges the assensus to *anticipate* the cogitatio, i.e. while the cogitatio is going on and the process of proof is not perfect, the will obliges the intellect to receive the conclusion . . .

2.

Ultimate Resolution of certainty of Faith (Easter 1848). [Drawn up at Maryvale, found in Packet B.9.11.]

. . . The *difficulty* is this:—Faith is conceived to be inconsistent with *doubt*. How then can it be the result of *reasoning*? for no reasoning, in moral subjects, leads to an indubitable conclusion. . . .

Now a state of certainty of mind takes place when we think the conclusion *ought* to be believed. We say to ourselves: this or that objection indeed may be made; perhaps we cannot answer it; but it is not enough to affect the certainty of the conclusion. The evidence is quite enough for conviction; the conclusion is *fide dignum* or *credibile*. Let this be well observed—we are brought into that state of mind which we call certainty, not when we think a proposition proved beyond all logical exception or certain as a conclusion, but when we think it so proved that it ought to be believed, or *fide dignum* or *credibile*.

It seems then that a person is certain, not when he can pronounce a conclusion certain, but when he can pronounce it *credibile*. . . .

. . . Hence there is an act of the mind/reason prudenter or reasonably determining that what has such and such evidence ought to be believed. This prudentia depends on this principle, that it is impossible to have an equally clear process, i.e. equal evidentia in all subject matters, that in mathematics indeed we have the evidentia veritatis, but in moral subjects we cannot commonly have anything beyond the evidentia credibilitatis. Now observe a process such as the above, is necessary even in metaphysical certainty, or mathematics—for the mind may doubt its own right to be certain, its power of intuition, &c. Thereupon the will comes in in every case.

Now let us consider what is the action of the mind when under the influence of that state which we called certainty or conviction with regard to any fact.

This: viz. it drops altogether the logical considerations which led to that conclusion which it felt to be dignum fide or credibile, and which issued in the state of certainty; but having arrived at the state of certainty, it takes and uses that conclusion as a first principle, absolutely true. . . .

On the proof constituting a conclusion fide dignum or credibile.

The objective proof of revelation, (or the corpus of Evidences as they are called in English) is most abundant, varied, and consistent, as being one whole with many parts. . . .

3. What is the actual proof or measure of proof which makes revelation credible to one is not the same as that which makes it credible to another; or in other words, what is credible varies with the individual mind.

4. Yet, since the objective proof of revelation is consistent, the proof which one man has more or less implies the proof which presents itself to another.

5. Hence an apparently slender proof may be sufficient to an individual from its implicit bearings.

6. Hence we cannot limit the apparent exiguitas/slenderness of the proof sufficient for the conviction of an individual.

7. The test of the validity of a proof for credibility, (or to speak briefly, the test of a credible proof) is that it leads the mind *prudently* to receive the conclusion for certain.

On probability

8. A probable argument, leading from the nature of the case, only to a probable conclusion, can never in itself be sufficient in prudence for certainty.

9. Yet a probable argument may be such merely in its mode of stating, and as involving other arguments implicitly in itself, may in that sense be sufficient for certainty.

10. Two probable arguments form an argument of greater probability than one.

11. As probabilities cumulate, the resulting probability rises, and the limit of increasing probabilities is credibility in the conclusion and certainty in the mind.

12. A proof made up of probable arguments is not necessarily a probable proof.

13. The point at which it ceases to be such, depending on the implicit weight of each probability as held in individual minds, varies with the individual. . . .

15. It follows that a conclusion with probabilities for and against is not necessarily a mere proof of the greater or overbalancing probability.

16. Arguments of slender probability may under strong verisimilitudes (Gerdil Vol 1, p. 221) i.e. antecedent probabilities, be raised into a credible proof.

17. No proof of credibility is greater than that which is cumulative from verisimilitude and probabilities.

3.

(*On the Nature and Cause of Faith.*) [Paper in B.9.11, with 'Papers on Faith 1848' written on the front of folder. A note in Newman's hand reads: 'All this, I think, is embodied in my last paper at Maryvale.' This is the paper dated Easter 1848 and called *Ultimate Resolution of certainty of Faith*.]

§ On the nature of Faith.

Faith is a *firm assent* to the word of God *obscurely revealed*.

Therefore it is at once *certus* and *inevidens*:—*certus*, because its assent is without doubt or fear; *inevidens*, because its method of proof is imperfect.

It is no cognitio, or

It is an assent stronger than is warranted by the motiva or discursus/reasons which lead to it.

Therefore its assent does not really depend on those motiva, for no conclusion can be more certain than the premisses from which it is drawn.

In other words, it is not resolvable into its motiva.

In a word it is not discursive.

Such an assent is, from the nature of the case, supernatural, and a divine gift. The mind moves forward to believe, as it moves forward to love; in one case on hearing His word about Himself, in the other on perceiving His goodness.

And it holds the things to which it assents, not as conclusions from premisses, but as revealed truths, independent of all previous knowledge except the veracity of God.

Such is divine faith; on the other hand when it is resolvable into its premisses and depends on them, that is, when it is discursive and doubtful, it is but human faith, or fides acquisita. . . .

[The intervening section deals with the object of faith.]

§ On the motiva (which precede) Faith.

The reasons or motiva which precede Faith are conditions not causes of Faith.

They are the means of applying or duly/sufficiently proposing or recommending the Object of faith to the mind. . . .

They commonly result in human or acquisita fides, prior to the act of divine faith itself.

Acquisita fides, while concurring in the conclusions which are received, though not as conclusions, by divine faith, differs from it in this:—that what divine faith receives as *certain*, acquisita or human faith has already received as not more than credible, because depending on the truth of certain premisses and the cogency of a certain logical process. . . .

By 'credible' is not meant merely capable of belief, but morally (or practically) certain, though not without doubt and fear; or highly probable, or prudent to believe; or sufficient in itself, but not sufficient considering the great importance of the subject. . . .

§ On the proximate (?) cause of Faith.

Since the motiva, or reasons which precede faith, do not absolutely lead to conviction, but are only motiva credibilitatis, the real cause of faith is not any constraint upon the reason from the laws of reasoning, but the free exercise of the will. When the motiva are credibilia, the will commands the reason to believe what otherwise it would not believe.

The will cannot and does not make arguments of greater force than they are.

The will commands the intellect, whenever there is a desire of the things which are the objects of faith.

From a sense of the prudence of believing.

The virtue which causes this pia motio voluntatis is, as some say, love; as others, prudence, (de Lugo); as others studiositas. . . .

4.

The Oratory, Birmingham, August 20, 1866. From Fr. Edward Caswall's notes on Lectures with the Father 1853. [Packet B.7.4. In the margin there is a note in Newman's hand: N.B. I seem to have given these lectures here reported with my Paper of Easter 1848 before me.]

. . . Certainty then 1st is a state of mind, an adhesion or persuasion, 2nd it does not admit of degrees.

As a state of mind it is more properly called *certitude* than certainty. There are two other meanings of the word certain: 1st as it is applied to premisses, 2nd as applied to conclusion. Thus we have three certainties. 1st That of the state of mind or subjective certainty

That of the premisses viewed apart or formal certainty

That of the conclusion viewed apart or objective certainty.

But formal certainty or that of the premisses cannot really be distinguished from objective or that of the conclusion.

This leaves us then only two certainties.

   1st Subjective   2nd Objective.

Certainty Proper is Subjective certainty

Certainty Improper is Objective certainty. It is not truly certainty. . . . Further Subjective certainty or certainty proper is indivisible and admits of no degrees. But Objective certainty or certainty improper is divisible and admits of degrees. . . .

. . . When subjective certainty is the result of a truth it is called certainty.

When subjective certainty is the result of error it is called obstinancy.

The two states of mind are different in God's sight, but there is no human criterion for distinguishing them to the individual within the mind itself of the individual. We must look to the general effect in multitudes through a course of time. . . .

5.

May 13, 1853: *'Analysis of Religious Inquiry according to the foregoing Rules'*. [Found in 3 packets: B.9.11; A.18.11; A.30.11.]

[Sheet 1 in B.9.11.]

. . . 1. An *argument* is an inducement made to the reason to judge a certain proposition to be true.

An argument, which induces the reason to judge it true, is a *proof*.

An argument, which tends to induce the reason to judge it true, is a *probability*.

An argument, which proposes to induce the reason to judge it true, is a likelihood.

2. An *inference* is the judgment following on that inducement.

An inference which follows on a proof, is a conviction.

An inference which follows on a probability, is an *opinion*.

An inference which follows on a presumption, is a *view*.

3. *Assent* is the acceptance of a proposition as true.

Assent is either *absolute* or *conditional*. Absolute assent is such as certainty, persuasion, prejudice, unbelief.

Conditional assent is such as belief, doubt, conjecture, suspicion, scruples, etc.

4. Assent follows inference, and that *by an act of the will*, which determines whether it shall be absolute or conditional, whether it shall be withheld, or whether it shall be given to the contradictory. . . .

5. Absolute Assent naturally follows on a conviction, and is then called *certainty*.

Conditional Assent naturally follows on an Opinion, and is called Belief; and on a View, and is then called *Surmise*.

6. Absolute Assent, by a mere act of the will, follows on an Opinion or on a View, and is then called *Persuasion*.

Conditional Assent, by a mere act of the will, follows on a Conviction, and is then called *Doubt*. . . .

9. And thus we have ten intellectual feelings, or postures of mind towards, or modes of receiving, a true proposition, of which six are the natural and legitimate correspondents of certain reasoning processes under (not without) the determination of the will; and four are the creation solely of that determination; viz.

Certainty, Belief, Surmise, Disbelief, Suspicion, Suspense,
Persuasion, Doubt, Prejudice, Ignoring . . .

... 12. Since every natural appointment is right, the former six are right which are according to nature, and the latter four wrong, which are against nature;—and morally right or wrong respectively, according and so far forth as, in each particular case, the will acts as a moral agent. [Sheet 2 in A.18.11.]

1. As each of these ten postures of mind really depends on the will, each can be lost or reversed by the will.

2. As each presupposes as a sine qua non an antecedent act of reason of a definite kind, none of them is simply created by an act of the will. ...

6.

December 16, 1853 *On the Certainty of Faith* [Packet B.7.4.]

§ On the two modes of apprehending or holding truth, the Evidentia Veritatis, and the Evidentia Credibilitatis.

We may
      1. *see* that a proposition is true
    or 2. *feel* that it is true. ...

(4.2.) Under the head of things which we feel, are those which are in contingent matter and recommended to us on what is called probable/ *moral* grounds; those which are gained not by syllogism, but by induction, those which are reached, not by one direct simple and sufficient proof but by a complex argument consisting of accumulating and converging probabilities. Here I hold the analysis of the proofs of induction as I have laid down in my third University Discourse, and not as it is described by Whewell or by Mill. viz. I do not think that induction is a necessary proof or demonstration. [Marginal note: Enlarge 1. on converging probabilities—question—whether they can make up a proof sufficient for *feeling*. I have no doubt of it. 2. on induction. ...]

5.1. The first class of truths, then, are those which are *demonstrable,* that is, which can be made sure, be proved or which are the subject matter of proof, i.e. can be proved true—or which are *known.* [Marginal note: To *see* and to *feel* are to *know* and to *believe.*]

5.2. The second class of truths are those which are credible, or rather *credificative,* that is, which can be proved believable, or have credentials, and are then subject matter for faith, or which are *believed.* ...

6. It follows, as a corollary, from what I have said, or rather has been already said, that whereas in truths which we see, the truth is evident, so in truths which we feel, though their truth is not evident, yet the grounds for thinking their truth, that is, for believing them, are evident. That is, the one has *evidentia veritatis,* the other, the *evidentia credibilitatis.*

7. The proof that a proposition is credible may be/is as complete and sufficient as the proof that it is true; or referring to our original language, we are as rational when we feel as when we see a truth. . . .

§ On the contrast in the process of apprehension between the Evidentia Veritatis and the Evidentia Credibilitatis in the two modes above set down.

. . . What is evidentia (of a truth) to one man is not evidentia to another, or a truth may be evidens, and known, to one and not to another. . . .

2. The principles or existing truths or premisses in one subject matter are not the same as those in another. . . .

[Newman goes on to discuss the Evidentia Credibilitatis and says this about it:]

On the whole, then, it differs from the evidentia veritatis, first, in its proving the truth apprehended, not true but credible or to be held as really true; next that it proves its credibility, not by any scientific proof resting on generally received principles and drawn out in exact syllogisms, but on the action of the individual mind, which knows what others may or may not know, and acts not necessarily by rule, but by practical expertness. . . .

§ On the Office of a judgment or Prudentia as the arbiter of/in determining the Evidentia Credibilitatis.

. . . The mental faculty which sees, furnishes, dispenses/uses and applies the premisses of the Evidentia Credibilitatis is called Prudentia or Judgment. . . . This Prudentia is partly a natural endowment common to all, or a special gift to certain persons, partly the result of experience; and it varies in its worth and preciousness, and its rarity with the subject matter in which it is employed. . . .

[Marginal notes: Prudentia also decides between its own method/way or science—which is to be used: empiricism or the rule of the thumb; or the rule of Laputa.

Further than this Prudentia is a sovereign judge what subject matter or cases admit of proof of truth and what do not, and how many, and what arguments are necessary in each varying case to prove credibility. . . .]

§4. On the propagation of truths apprehended on the Evidentia Credibilitatis.

. . . How then are we to propagate truth, that is to cause its reception by others as well as ourselves, when it is apprehended on the evidentia credibilitatis?

I answer: we offer/give others two ways of gaining it: either

1. by gaining that Prudentia, (in the particular subject matter in which

the Quaestio lies,) which discerns, seizes, and applies the premisses or principles. or

2. by using the Prudentia of those who are already versed in that particular subject matter.

Of these two modes the latter is the more common, on the principle Cuique in sua etc. Life is not long enough to obtain prudentia in every subject matter. . . .

§5. Application of the foregoing doctrine to the instance of revealed/ religious truth.

1. Since we are saved, not by knowledge, but by faith, Revealed Religion has the evidentia credibilitatis, not veritatis.

2. And since that evidentia is level to the intellect of children and of the illiterate, as well as others, it must be gained, not in the way of science, but by the exercise of prudentia. (At the same time, since it must be a real evidentia, it must imply a rational proof.)

3. Moreover, since it is intended for very various classes of persons, for all ages and stations, the Evidentia must be variously gained, that is, it must appeal to a variety of grounds, reasons or motiva, each of which is capable of creating it. . . .

§6. On certainty

Certainty is an act (or habit) of the intellect reflecting on, recognizing, and ratifying its existing apprehension of a truth, whether known or believed. Since, according to this definition, certainty is a judgment, and a judgment is the assent of the intellect, and again, an apprehension of a truth is a judgment and assent, therefore certainty is the judgment of a judgment, or an assent of the intellect to an assent, e.g. Proposition enunciated by the apprehension: 'C is A'. Proposition enunciated by the certainty: 'I apprehend C is A'.

2. This account of certainty implies that it is a natural and ordinary but not a necessary consequence of apprehension. . . .

. . . 4. . . . Certainty, it seems, is an assent of the mind to an apprehension of a truth accompanied with a reference to the grounds or motivum of that apprehension, e.g. first, whether it is a truth known or believed, next, what the reasons are, &c. That is, it is a recognition, not simply of an apprehension, but at least improperly and accidentally of the motiva and consequently the evidentia of that apprehension. [Marginal note: That is, it contemplates and recognizes the truth *in* its formal proof.]

5. If certainty is a recognition of an apprehension of a truth, it is a recognition of a truth; for we cannot apprehend falsehood. Hence (from its very definition) certitudini non potest subesse falsum. If it is not a truth, we do not call it certainty.

6. Since an assent does not admit of degrees, neither does certainty; but since it is a recognition, not only of the apprehension itself, which is also an assent, but of the motiva and consequent evidentia which does admit of a more or less, it follows that though we cannot be more or less *certain* of the truth, we can be certain of it with more vigour, keenness, and directness according to the quality of the motiva/evidentia in the particular case. . . .

[Newman next discusses the certainty that follows logical arguments but notes in the margin that it is 'not satisfactorily analysed'. He then outlines the different kinds of certainty and the criteria for certainty.]

§9. On the process of supernatural faith, and the portion of it which is supernatural.

Every step of the process, from the very first up to the assent to the credibilitas of the supernatural revelation *inclusive*, is natural. Every step then of that process, including the judgment of the prudentia declaring the credibilitas of the revelation may be mastered by a mind destitute of the grace of Christ. . . .

The process is as follows:

A body of proof exists for the credibilitas of Revelation which makes that credibilitas evidens, and which viewed as one is the motivum credibilitatis to the individual.

This body of proof is substantially the same to all men, but it is variously represented, with various relative prominences of its portions to various minds.

This body of proof is the formal cause of the conclusion, or the shape in which the conclusion comes to us.

It consists of all the facts and truths of the case, each in its right place, as the prudentia sees and arranges them, conspiring to the conclusion of the credibilitas of Revelation.

It exists and is present to the mind of every one who has prudentia; it is not present to those who have not.

This prudentia is simply a natural acquisition, in the subject matter of revelation, as well as in the subject matter of medicine and farming.

This prudentia not only arranges and forms the body of proof, or motiva of the credibilitas of Revelation, but carries on the mind to a distinct judgment of, or assent to, that credibilitas, [but only an assent with *fear—in Margin*].

And this assent to, or speculative evident judgment of, the credibilitas of Revelation is followed by the act of reflexion upon, or recognition of that assent, which I have called certainty.

The whole of this is within the power of natural reason. An infidel may get as far as this. A mind which gets as far as this does not yet believe. It only sees that Revelation is credible.

The steps which follow are rational, according to human reason, but supernatural also, or require grace. They consist of:

1. A practical judgment, as it is called, accompanying the speculative—viz. an assent to the proposition that it is right and fitting and excellent to believe what is credible.

2. A pia affectio, or voluntas credendi, determining and commanding the intellect to believe.

3. The act of faith, in the intellect, thus commanded; the object being at once Revelatio and the Res Revelata, viz. that God has spoken and that He has spoken thus. . . .

7.

In festo S. Gregorii. 1857. *Opus Magnum. In nomine P.F. et S.S.* [Packet A.23.1. Here Newman is concerned with the limitations of our knowledge and our need to recognize them.]

. . . There is then an infinity of things unknown and to be revealed to us.

3. And Unknown classes of things as well as things—unknown laws, etc. On the narrowness of saying that all things must be on the analogy of things seen. . . .

So far then we have got to this:—that strangeness is the characteristic of revelation? if *made*.

1. Next on the great strait we are in, from the impossibility of there being nothing more to be known—or of our state being one of scepticism. It is as difficult to acquiesce in that we are made for nothing, or that there is no end of our being, as to believe the dogmas of a revelation. . . .

(This is but the beginning of a large work which is to go on to defend the Church and its position in the world in the nineteenth century as confronted with, and as against the penetrating knowledge, learning and ability of the scientific men and philosophers of the day.)

8.

January 12 1860. *The Evidences of Religion* [Packet A.30.11. On January 5th Newman had started to write about this subject but had not managed to do more than pose the problem.]

There are few religious questions of more importance practically in a day like this, than that of the grounds on which the mass of men believe in Christianity, or in other words, the relation of faith, viewed in the concrete as a habit or act of the mind, towards reason. . . .

It is as long ago as the year 1832, that I began Sermons on the subject in the Oxford University Pulpit, which I continued down to the year 1843, when I published them. I shall proceed on the basis of those Sermons, in what I have to say, but I shall attempt to speak with a distinctness which for two reasons they had not; first because I was feeling my way and had not found it; next because, conscious of this, I had not the requisite confidence in my own train of thought. . . .

The reason why I think the subject/it of great importance just now is this: because just now a scepticism is on foot, which throws on the individual believer the *onus* probandi, in a way never *contemplated*, or at least recognized before. Hitherto a man was allowed to believe till it was logically brought home to him that he ought not to believe: but now it seems tacitly to be considered, that a man/he has no liberty to believe, till he can state/show cause distinctly, or at least till others can do it for him, why he has a right to do so. [Alternative reading given by Newman: till it has been brought home to him in a rational form, that he has a right to do so.]

Occasion of/Reason for considering and investigating the assurances

The question then to be considered takes the shape of an objection, and that objection is of the following form:—Faith, which is not based upon rational grounds, is a superstition, or a prejudice, or a fanaticism, or some kind or other of unreality. What are the grounds on which the great mass of religious persons believe? . . .

. . . Though the real source and cause of religious faith is beyond nature and actual reason, still reason is its antecedent, and cause *sine quâ non,* and it is in this aspect of it that it falls to me to consider it. . . .

I would maintain that faith must rest on reason, nay even in the case of children and of the most ignorant and dull peasant, wherever faith is living and loving; . . .

(1) Next I observe, since the grounds are to be such as apply to all classes of men, they must lie deep in the constitution of our nature. . . .

(2) And further they must be obvious and not abstract; of a nature to be intelligible and to arrest the attention of all, and to touch them and of a natural persuasiveness/come home to them, and work upon them.

(3) And moreover since they apply to all men, ignorant as well as learned, they must not require books, or education, or an array of facts, or the like, but they must be portable, like the philosophia of the Latin orator, which peregrinatur nobiscum, etc. . . .

APPENDICES 217

9.

September 1863. Chapter II [Packet A.30.11. In this fragment Newman is concerned with the problem of the meaning of statements about God in an attempt to meet the objection that they mean nothing although they are presented as having vital significance. At the end of the passage is the date December 1 1863.]

. . . from the nature of the case, all our language about Almighty God, so far as it is affirmative, is analogical and figurative. We can only speak of Him, whom we reason about but have not seen, in the terms of our experience. When we reflect on Him, and put into words our thoughts about Him, we are forced to transfer to a new meaning ready made words, which primarily belong to objects of time and place. We are aware, while we do so, that they are inadequate, but we have the alternative of doing so or doing nothing at all. We can only remedy their insufficiency by confessing it. We can do no more than put ourselves on the guard as to our proceeding and protest against it while we do it. We can only set right one error of expression by another, by this method of antagonism we steady our minds, not so as to reach their objects, but to point them in the right direction; as in an algebraical series we might add and subtract in series, approximating little by little, by saying and unsaying to a positive result we lay down that the Supreme Being is omnipresent *or* everywhere, and yet nowhere; that He is everlasting, yet not for age after age; He is infinitely one yet He is exuberantly manifold. We draw lines which seem to us parallel, because the point at which they meet is so distant that we do not ever see that they do meet in it, we only know by calculation that they must.

Such is the character of our knowledge in this world about the Supreme Being altogether; the knowledge of Holy Trinity, given us by revelation is the same in kind as this, (1) as determinate and as obscure (2) as logical and as inconceivable (3) as dogmatic and as mysterious. . . .

10.

§2 The Conceivable [Packet A.30.11. Probably written between 3rd and 12th December 1863[

. . . 1. The Inconceivable is not the same as the self-contradictory in terms. . . . 2. Nor is inconceivable equivalent to illogical, and the conceivable to logical. . . . 3. Nor are conceivable and inconceivable the same as the possible and impossible, though the words are often used for each other. . . . 4. Nor are they the same as true and false, that is, as fact and not fact. . . .

Applying what I have said to the question of revealed religion, I would observe, what I suppose is very plain, that a strong antecedent argument against it is its strangeness, or inconceivableness. . . . When Hume, for instance, speaks of its being against experience and therefore not verisimilar, he uses a fair objection, which has to be met; but its real force is upon the imagination, not upon the reason, viz. that the revealed truths are not simply unlikely, but that they are inconceivable. It is easy to reply that the Supreme Being and His providence are so far above us, that we cannot determine ourselves what is likely and what unlikely as regards His dealing towards us. This is unanswerable to the objection as such, and covers the whole ground; but it does not touch the distress occasioned to the imagination by the particular doctrines revealed. The persons in question find their minds recoil from them as so strange, so alien to the whole current of their experience, and the structure of their thoughts, so inconceivable, when confronted point by point in detail.

Apparently to meet this difficulty, Butler wrote his great work on the Analogy of Religion; the word analogy being in fact a denial that the doctrines of Revelation were inconceivable, for what is analogous is not inconceivable, and he has succeeded in a still remarkable way in quieting the imagination than in convincing the reason, though of course I am not denying the argumentative power of his Treatise. . . .

The case would really seem to stand thus: so far as revealed doctrine is after the analogy of our natural experience, so far it is inconceivable. It is partly the one, and partly the other; but, whether the one or the other, its truth is independent of either. . . .

11.

(*A Comparison of the Moral Sense and Certitude. 1865.*) [The fragment is numbered p. 17. It is in Packet A.30.11.]

. . . I consider then:

(1) that certitude is a faculty or disposition of mind natural to us, and that never to exercise it would be most unnatural; rather I should say, simply impossible, constituted as we are. . . .

(4) That certitude is not the compulsory effect of any process of argument as its proper cause, or anything else that we have in common with others, but a free act (to speak generally), just as the acts of conscience are free and depend upon our will.

(5) That, while certitude has truth for its object, what we thus take to be truth, may be falsehood, as what our moral sense tells us is right may in fact be wrong; that in such cases it is not really certitude that is exercised, but persuasion or delusion, but still, since no direct available

test exists by which we can at once discriminate between truth and falsehood, it may for convenience be called by the general name of certitude.
(6) That not to have certitude, i.e. to make assent to a proposition or its contrary as true, when there is a call of duty on us to have it, because we have before now assented to falsehood instead of truth, is a parallel fault to that of not listening to one's moral sense because we have before now mistaken vice for virtue. . . .
(8) That when there is a duty to be certain, we must do our best to fulfil the duty, and the way of fulfilling the duty lies in the use of our best judgment.
(9) That the judgment or sense is not of a scientific character, any more than is the practical judgment by which we determine points of conscience, that is, it is not capable of being exhibited, and thereby superseded, by a series of principles, arguments, conclusions and rules, but is a habit of mind which acts *pro re natâ*. . . .
(13) That even mere persuasions and delusions, if the result of our best judgment under a sense of duty, are more consistent with our nature and our position in the world than a simple suspense of assent.
(14) That a man who has made acts of certitude on his best judgment is in a state of mind more favourable to the attainment of true certitude and more consistent with his nature, than he who in such a case has, if it be possible, abstained from any act of certitude, real or false, altogether.

12.

June 26, 1865. Certainty not inconsistent with probable evidence [Packet A.30.11.]

We all know what is meant by saying that we are sure of a thing. When we say that we are sure that Queen Victoria is alive or Prince Albert is dead, we mean that we do not admit the idea that Prince Albert is not dead, that we cannot even admit the idea without an effort of mind. . . .

. . . When this sureness or certainty of mind has for its subject what is true, we are accustomed to call it a conviction; when its subject is not true, we call it a persuasion or a fancy.

I know of no test sufficient in concrete matters for discriminating between a conviction and a persuasion. . . .

. . . The mere feeling of certainty then brings no test of truth, we are left to distinguish conviction from persuasion by the event, permanence being an attribute of conviction rather than of persuasion, though of course this is far from sufficient to constitute a characteristic difference between them.

But if this be so, what right have we ever to indulge the feeling of certainty? It never is its own evidence: it may after all be nothing more than a persuasion of that which really is not true. And from this it would seem to follow that we ought in all concrete matters to cherish a reserve of doubt, taking care that an hypothesis of possible error should underlie all our beliefs, and even speaking, as it were, under correction. Pursuing this train of thought, we shall come to see that nothing has a claim to be believed and acted upon as absolutely true, but simply as probable, and as safe to hold and to follow, as (for instance) we might attend to an alarm of fire, though we had no proof that it was well-grounded. This is what is called by Catholics a 'practical certainty';

[The fragment ends here]

13.

20 July 1865 (*Essay on Certitude*) [Packet A.23.1.]

Certitude is an assent, deliberate, unconditional, and conscious, to a proposition as true. . . .

A first and essential characteristic, then, of certitude is, that it cannot co-exist with hesitation or doubt, or with the admission into the mind of the very supposition in any shape that it is misplaced as to its object. On this follows close a second. Such a state of mind, it is plain, cannot be immediately dependent on the reasons which are its antecedents, and cannot rightly be referred back to them as its producing cause. . . . Certitude does not admit of a more or less, but is a state of mind, definite and complete, admitting only of being and not being. To fancy that it may be strengthened, is to imply that it never has been attained. Conclusions indeed may be strengthened by the adduction of fresh arguments, and strengthened without limit: but certitude, being already a full assent, and nothing short of it, for that reason cannot be any thing beyond it. This being the case, it is plain that it does not rest on sense, reason, authority, or any other informant of the mind, as its proper and intrinsic cause. . . . Certitude then is not to be measured by the logical force of the premisses; the very arguments which create certitude in one mind, fail to do so in another. . . .

It does not then come under the reasoning faculty; but under the imagination. . . . Sense, logic, authority, testimony, belong to the process; the result is beyond them and independent of them, and stands by itself, as long as I choose, created and dependent on myself as an individual and free agent.

14.

September 25, 1865. (*Meaning of Certitude*) [Packet A.23.1.]

... I observe that by certitude of mind I mean the state of being certain; and that, like other states or habits of mind, it is a disposition or adaptation of the mind towards certain acts, which acts are the evidence of its existing/existence. And, as other habits, it is created, in the first instance, by means of these acts; and therefore, viewed as a habit, admits of growth and of being stronger and weaker. The word may also be used to express the abstract type and generalization of the acts in which the habit manifests itself; in which sense of course it does not admit of degrees, as it does when viewed in the concrete. So much in general.

Next, what is an act of certitude? It is an unconditional assent to a proposition as true; by an assent to a proposition as true, I mean the assertion of my intellect, that what it is contemplating subjectively, has an existence outside of me. Further, the propositions to which I give the assent of certitude, are, as falling under the particular category of 'true', are necessarily of a complex character, being of the form, not of 'a is b' but of 'that a is b is true'.

Moreover, the act of the mind in certitude is reflex; for, as being the assertion of a correspondence between what is without and what is within me, it involves a recognition of myself. Thus it differs from knowledge which is the simple contemplation of truth as objective. Hence we speak of having knowledge and feeling certain.

Lastly, it an unconditional assent; that is, it is more than a belief, an opinion, or a judgment, but such, that we reject from our minds, as out of the question, the very notion of our being mistaken. And thus viewed in its acts it is as exclusive of degrees as it is in its abstract idea, though it admits more or less when viewed as a habit, for a habit may be but practically formed enabling it to act only now and then, or in some cases not in others.

15.

Chapter iii §1. On apprehension and assent through the imagination considered in reference to the being of a God. April 26/68, again May 5/68, again September 7/68. [A pencilled note adds: On concrete apprehension and real assent in relation to the   Packet A.30.11.] [This fragment deals with the relation of real and notional apprehension to the matter of inference and assent. On a similar sheet of paper and folded together with the sheet on which this note is written are notes by Newman about abstract truths and ideas. From this second note come the quotations given.]

If abstract truths, (or what nominalists call 'generalizations' from experience) are objective, (as realists would hold), therefore they are objects—what *is* the *object*? Beautifulness, for instance,—*what* does the mind see when it contemplates this abstraction?—is it God? if not, is it one of the Platonic everlasting ideas external to God? if not, can it be anything at all, and are we not driven to agreement with the school of Locke and of sensible experiences?

I dare say there is some simple refutation at once of the following answer, which has this only recommendation, that I have held it these forty years strenuously—on the other hand I am so little versed in the controversy, that I am not sure that it is not inconsistent with the elementary conditions to which both parties in it agree before engaging in it, or resolvable at once into some perfectly known doctrine belonging to one party or the other.

I do not allow the existence of these abstract ideas corresponding to objective realities with Locke—but then, I do not pass over the experiences gained from the phenomena of mind so lightly, as I fancy the school of Locke is apt to do. I should argue as follows:

There is a right and a wrong—a true and a false—a better and a worse —We have a sense of these as realities. We have a sense of duty, of virtue, of justice, of beautifulness;—Have we (what is often called) an *intuition* of these? do we see them with the mind's eye as objects, as we see with the bodily eye colours and forms and the phenomena of material things generally?

What I think our mind really has as parts of its nature is certain sensations, that is, a property of being affected in a certain way by certain concrete sensible objects or experiences—A certain class of sensible objects produce on our palate an effect which to the sentient mind is what it calls sweetness—and other certain things, individual and sensible, create the feeling of pain, when they are applied to the nerve. Thus I get the idea of sweetness or of painfulness—it is the quality of a feeling. I do not need, nor do I believe there is, any object which my mind sees and calls sweetness or painfulness. The idea conveyed in these words is/ are my mode of apprehending a quality.

Now to proceed to experiences not sensible. A danger is impending over me; it continues days and months; in consequence I have a sensation of mental pain, continual and wearing. It is a pain perfectly distinct from other pain—e.g. from the pain of bereavement, of disgrace, of self-discipline. I give it a name—I call it 'anxiety'. I have a clear idea of what I mean by anxiety. Nor is it an abstract word—it denotes a *mode* of mind. It does not denote a generalization or universal on the one hand, or an intuition of some extra-mental object on the other. I contemplate anxiety, not as a thing, yet it has its *root* in that which is a thing.

16.

§ On Counterfeit Intuitions [No date. Packet A.30.11.]

. . . According as these ideas have a corresponding object external to the mind, they are called true or false, and the assent to them is called right or wrong. And this is to be said of simple and complex assents.

But the question at once arises, how can these ideas, whether simple or complex, be so compared to their objects, as to enable us to determine whether they are true or false? In other words, are there objects, and are they like our ideas of them? From the nature of the case it is an impossibility. In this difficulty of obtaining a criterion for our purpose, the nearest approach to one would be, a universal general agreement in the assent in all minds. For instance were there a universal agreement among all nations that each individual man in his present and separate personality would/or would not continue in being, and that without termination, after/though death had destroyed his visible body, this might be considered a conclusive ground for holding that assent (or dissent) to be right, and the idea or doctrine true. But in matter of fact such assents are not to be found.

However, all men, I suppose, would agree in this principle itself, though it may not admit of application; and such agreement is something. They would assent, I say, to the principle that a universal assent must be right, and the thing assented to true. But *why* would they assent to this principle? Because, I suppose, what all men whatever display is a characteristic of human nature; and a universal idea is a true idea, because it is natural to us. . . .

Notes

NOTES ON PART I: THE PROBLEM OF FAITH: PAGES I-59

1 John Robinson, *Observations Divine and Morall*, 1625, p. 82f.
2 Cf. Charles Hartshorne, *Reality as Social Process*, Glencoe, Illinois, and Boston, Massachusetts, 1953, p. 164: 'The entire life of man, including quite especially his intellectual life, is the expression of faith or trust. . . . To look for evidence is to express one's trust in the value of evidence. . . . Even suicide expresses the trust that to die is, in certain cases at least, better than to live.'
3 Cf. Paul Tillich, *Systematic Theology*, Vol. III, London, 1964, p. 138: 'Faith, formally or generally defined, is the state of being grasped by that toward which self-transcendence aspires, the ultimate in being and meaning. In a short formula, one can say that faith is the state of being grasped by an ultimate concern.'
4 Augustine, *Confessions*, Everyman, 1907, p. 100f.
5 Examples of such generally held faith are faith in the uniformity of nature, faith in the existence of objects corresponding to our perceptions, and faith in the trustworthiness of our rational powers.
6 Aquinas, *Summa Theologica*, Part I. Qu. 2, Art. 2.
7 Ibid., Part I, Qu. 12, Art. 12.
8 Ibid., Part I, Qu. 1, Art. 1.
9 Ibid.
10 William Paley, *Natural Theology*, Collected Works, London, 1837, Vol. IV, p. 291; cf. p. 356: 'These points being assured to us by Natural Theology, we may well leave to Revelation the disclosure of many particulars, which our researches cannot reach, regarding either the nature of this Being as the original cause of all things, or his character and designs as a moral governor; and not only so, but the more full confirmation of other particulars, of which, though they do not lie altogether beyond our reasonings and our probabilities, the certainty is by no means equal to the importance.'
11 Cf. William Paley, *Evidences of Christianity*, Collected Works, London, 1837, Vol. III, p. 1ff.
12 Cf. ibid., pp. 398ff.
13 *Natural Theology*, p. 290.
14 Ibid., p. 268.
15 Ibid., p. 271: cf. p. 276.

16 Ibid., pp. 295ff.
17 Immanuel Kant, *Prolegomena to Any Future Metaphysic*, London, 1889, p. 1ff.
18 Immanuel Kant, *Critique of Pure Reason*, London, 1958, p. 29.
19 Immanuel Kant, *Religion within the Limits of Reason Alone*, New York, 1960, p. 151; cf. *Critique of Pure Reason*, p. 650.
20 *Critique of Pure Reason*, p. 646. What Kant calls 'conviction' we shall call 'certitude' using Newman's terminology.
21 Paley, *Moral and Political Philosophy*, Collected Works, London, 1837, Vol. I, pp. 290–298.
22 Ibid., p. xv. His *Evidences* were 'a set-book for Little-go at Cambridge until early in the twentieth century'.—; A. R. Vidler, *The Church in an Age of Revolution*, Penguin Books, 1961, p. 39. Cf. also, J. D. Boulger, *Coleridge as Religious Thinker*, Yale, 1961, p. 20f.
23 Ford K. Brown, *Fathers of the Victorians*, Cambridge, 1961, p. 1.
24 G. M. Young, *Victorian Essays*, Oxford, 1962 pp. 117–122.
25 E. Steane, (editor), *The Religious Condition of Christendom, exhibited in a series of papers prepared at the instance of . . . the Evangelical Alliance. . .* , London, 1852, p. 154, cf. p. 148.
26 Ibid., p. 149.
27 Ibid., p. 77. This paper was entitled *On the Aspects of Infidelity* and was given by the Professor of Moral Philosophy at Aberdeen.
28 L. E. Elliott-Binns, *English Thought 1860–1900*, London, 1956, pp. 9f; Cf. *Essays and Reviews*, London, 1861, pp. 150f.
29 Cf. W. T. Stace, *Religion and the Modern Mind*, London, 1953, p. 47 for 143ff., and *passim*.
30 Kant, *Critique of Practical Reason*, London, 1909; Memoir of Kant by T. K. Abbott, p. xxxiv f.
31 R. G. Smith, *J. G. Hamann*, London, 1960, p. 244; H. Heine, *Religion and Philosophy in Germany*, Boston, 1959, p. 109.
32 D. Hume, *A Treatise of Human Nature*, Book 1, London, 1962, p. 40.
33 Ibid., p. 42.
34 D. Hume, *Dialogues concerning Natural Religion*, New York, 1948, *passim*.
35 D. Hume, *An Inquiry concerning Human Understanding*, New York, 1955, p. 117 et seq.
36 D. Hume, *The Natural History of Religion*, reprinted in *Hume on Religion*, London, 1963, cf. pp. 54, 62f., 85ff.
37 *An Inquriy concerning Human Understanding*, p. 118. This position was stated by Locke in his *Essay on Human Understanding*, Book 4, Chapter XVI, and is criticized by Newman in the *Grammar of Assent*—cf. p. 132ff., *infra*.
38 Paley, writing after Hume, does not refute Hume so much as assert what Hume denied. Paley does not seem to have recognized, for instance, that Hume had shown the impossibility of arguing from miracles by demonstrating that either the evidence was insufficient to trust the miracle-report or the evidence required a new understanding of the

laws of nature. Either way there was no miracle left to argue from.
39 *Prolegomena*, p. 2.
40 *Critique of Pure Reason*, p. 22.
41 Ibid., p. 524, cf. pp. 500ff.
42 Ibid., p. 531.
43 Ibid., pp. 487ff.
44 Ibid., p. 492.
45 *Critique of Practical Reason*, p. 222; cf. p. 230.
46 Ibid., p. 222f.; cf. *Critique of Pure Reason*, p. 527: 'The moral laws do not merely presuppose the existence of a supreme being, but also, as themselves in a different connexion absolutely necessary, justify us in postulating it, though, indeed, only from a practical point of view.'
47 *Critique of Pure Reason*, p. 90.
48 *Critique of Practical Reason*, pp. 219, 196f.
49 Cf. *Prolegomena*, p. 127f.
50 *Critique of Practical Reason*, p. 235f.
51 *Prolegomena*, pp. 125ff.; cf. Heine, op. cit., p. 115: 'God, according to Kant, is a noumen. . . . Kant shows that we can know nothing regarding this noumen, regarding God. . . . The words of Dante, 'Leave all hope behind!' may be inscribed over this portion of the *Critique of Pure Reason*.'
52 *Critique of Pure Reason*, p. 29.
53 Cf. what Kant says about the transcendental ideal in the *Critique of Pure Reason*, the postulates of practical reason in the *Critique of Practical Reason*, and the idea of God in *Religion within the Limits of Reason Alone*.
54 Cf. the testimony of Barth to the importance of Schleiermacher in Barth, *From Rousseau to Ritschl*, London, 1959, pp. 306f.
55 F. Schleiermacher, *On Religion, Speeches to its Cultured Despisers*, New York, 1958, pp. 16f.; cf. pp. 53, 87f., 93f.
56 Ibid., p. 36.
57 F. Schleiermacher, *The Christian Faith*, Edinburgh, 1928, pp. 16ff.
58 Ibid., p. 5; cf. p. 5ff.
59 S. Kierkegaard, *Fear and Trembling*, New York, 1955, p. 41. In the religious stance, according to Kierkegaard, the ethical is 'suspended'. A 'sacrifice' is an offering made to God in obedience to God's command.
60 Cf. S. Kierkegaard, *Training in Christianity*, Princeton, 1944, pp. 132f.
61 S. Kierkegaard, *Attack upon Christendom*, Boston, 1956, p. 271.
62 S. Kierkegaard, *Concluding Unscientific Postscript*, Princeton, 1941, pp. 99–107.
63 Ibid., pp. 183, 306.
64 Cf. S. Kierkegaard, *Philosophical Fragments*, Princeton, 1936, pp. 31ff.
65 *Concluding Unscientific Postscript*, pp. 115f.
66 Ibid., p. 182; cf. *Fear and Trembling*, p. 131, where faith is described as 'the highest passion in a man'.
67 Cf. S. Kierkegaard, *Sickness unto Death*, New York, 1955, pp. 214ff.
68 *Concluding Unscientific Postscript*, pp. 188, 290; cf. *Training in Christianity*,

pp. 79–144 where Kierkegaard discusses at length the problem of finding God in Jesus Christ when the appearance seems to contradict the actuality.
69 Cf. *Philosophical Fragments*, pp. 84ff.; *Training in Christianity*, pp. 68ff.
70 The other was Bentham. This passage is quoted from Mill's *Dissertations and Discussions* by B. Willey in his *Nineteenth Century Studies*, Penguin Books, 1964, p. 9.
71 F. D. Maurice, *The Kingdom of Christ*, London, 1959, Vol. 1., p. 6.
72 S. T. Coleridge, *Biographia Literaria*, London, n.d., pp. 70ff.
73 S. T. Coleridge, *Aids to Reflection*, Edinburgh, 1896, p. 365.
74 Ibid., pp. 305ff.
75 Cf. S. T. Coleridge, *Notes, Theological, Political and Miscellaneous*, London, 1853, pp. 347f.; cf. also Boulger, op. cit., pp. 20–36.
76 *Aids to Reflection*, p. 222.
77 *Notes, Theological. . .* , p. 381.
78 *Biographia Literaria*, pp. 96f. Newman, we shall see, held very similar views about the way to faith.
79 *Aids to Reflection*, pp. 152f.; cf. pp. 120f.
80 Ibid., p. 147.
81 *Notes, Theological. . .* , p. 380; cf. p. 367. These statements illustrate the Kantian influence on Coleridge's thought.
82 *Aids to Reflection*, p. 124; cf. pp. 129f.
83 E. J. Whately, *Life and Correspondence of Richard Whately, D.D.*, London, 1866, Vol. 2., p. 155.
84 *Notes, Theological. . .* , p. 368.
85 *Aids to Reflection*, p. 178.
86 *Notes, Theological. . .* , p. 129.
87 Cf. Maurice, op. cit., Vol. 1., p. 15.
88 Cf. Kant's statement in the Preface to the Second Edition of the *Critique of Pure Reason* which we have quoted and Philo's statement quoted at the end of Hume's *Dialogues concerning Natural Religion* (op. cit., pp. 94f.,)—this passage is probably ironic but claims that since man cannot trust natural reason in matters concerning God, he must be prepared to accept revelation in faith.
89 Sir W. Hamilton, *Discussions on Philosophy and Literature, Education and University Reform*, London, 1852, pp. 12f. For Mansel's regard for Hamilton, see his Bampton Lectures, *The Limits of Religious Thought*, Oxford, 1858, p. viii f.
90 H. L. Mansel, *Metaphysics or the Philosophy of Consciousness*, Edinburgh, 1860, p. 382–386. This volume is a republication of an article Mansel wrote for the *Encyclopaedia Britannica*.
91 Ibid., p. 398.
92 *The Limits of Religious Thought*, p. ii.
93 Ibid., p. 24; cf. pp. 27ff.
94 Ibid., p. 50, 47; cf. pp. 47ff., 58f.
95 Cf. ibid., pp. 69, 94.

96 Ibid., p. 59; cf. pp. 67f., 182f.
97 Ibid., p. 96; cf. pp. 198f.
98 Cf. ibid., pp. 113–122.
99 Ibid., pp. 127, 131; cf. pp. 143ff.
100 Ibid., p. 141.
101 Ibid., p. 146; cf. pp. 149f., 229ff., 259ff.
102 Ibid., pp. 257, 265; cf. pp. 234ff.
103 Cf. A. M. Ramsey, *F. D. Maurice and the Conflicts of Modern Theology*, Cambridge, 1951, pp. 72ff. Maurice wrote about Mansel's Bampton Lectures, 'I can only say if they are true, let us burn our Bibles, let us tell our countrymen that the agony and bloody sweat of Christ, His cross and passion, His death and burial, His resurrection and ascension, mean nothing.' (Ibid., p. 78.)
104 *Letters of the Rev. J. B. Mozley, D. D.*, edited by his sister, London 1885, p. 240.
105 Cf. correspondence between Newman and Meynell between December 20th, 1859 and May 19th, 1860. The correspondence is preserved at the Oratory, Edgbaston. We refer to it later—cf. p. 83 *infra*.
106 Cf. J. M. Robertson, *A History of Freethought in the Nineteenth Century*, London, 1929, pp. 210ff.
107 Cf. ibid., pp. 213ff.; A. M. Ramsey, op. cit., p. 75.
108 M. St. J. Packe, *The Life of John Stuart Mill*, London, 1954, p. 443f.; *Autobiography of John Stuart Mill*, New York, 1960, p. 193.
109 G. W. F. Hegel, *The Positivity of the Christian Religion*, printed in *On Christianity, Early Theological Writings by Friedrich Hegel*, translated by T. M. Knox, with an introduction by R. Kroner, New York, 1961, p. 68; cf. pp. 86, 98.
110 G. W. F. Hegel, *The Phenomenology of Mind*, London, 1910, pp. 779–783.
111 G. W. F. Hegel, *Philosophy of Mind*, Oxford, 1894, pp. 155ff.; Hegel wrote that 'Religion is the very substance of the moral life itself' (p. 156).
112 Ibid., p. 182.
113 G. W. F. Hegel, *Lectures on the Philosophy of Religion*, London, 1895, Vol. III, p. 10; cf. pp. 10ff.
114 Ibid., Vol. II, p. 328.
115 Quoted in A. O. J. Cockshut, *The Unbelievers*, London, 1964, p. 144 from *Robert Elsmere*.
116 L. Feuerbach, *The Essence of Christianity*, New York, 1957, p. 12.
117 Ibid., pp. 60, 63; cf. p. 73.
118 This is Marx's estimate of Feuerbach's work—cf. Marx's *Theses on Feuerbach*, in *Marx and Engels On Religion*, Moscow, 1957, p. 71; cf. also Feuerbach's preface to the second edition of his *Essence of Christianity* where he says that his intention is to 'show that the true sense of Theology is Anthropology'—op. cit., p. xxxvii.
119 Cf. Robertson, op. cit., pp. 240f.
120 Quoted in Cockshut, op. cit., p. 46; for this reappraisal of the meaning of Christian beliefs, cf. Cockshut, op. cit; H. C. Sheldon, *Unbelief in the*

Nineteenth Century, London, 1907; and the lively but tendentious account in Robertson, op. cit., pp. 187–266.
121 Cf. Cockshut, op. cit., pp. 113f., 128f., 145, 150ff., 181ff.; H. G. Wood, *Belief and Unbelief since 1850*, Cambridge, 1955, pp. 101ff.
122 Report of a conversation with F. W. Myers quoted in Willey, op. cit., p. 214.
123 J. S. Mill, *Three Essays on Religion*, London, 1874, pp. 97, 110f.; cf. p. 89ff.
124 J. S. Mill, *Utilitarianism*, New York, 1957, pp. 10, 37; cf. *Autobiography*, op. cit., pp. 45ff.
125 Cf. Cockshut, op. cit., pp. 28f., 154ff.
126 Cf. Sheldon, op. cit., pp. 96f.; Cockshut, op. cit., pp. 77ff.
127 H. Spencer, *First Principles*, London, 1937, p. 12f.; cf. pp. 37, 87f. Spencer refers to Hamilton and Mansel in connexion with his view of the essential incomprehensibility of the object of religious belief.
128 Ibid., pp. 358f., 456; cf. Sheldon, op. cit., pp. 98ff.
129 Cf. J. Martineau, *Types of Ethical Theory*, Oxford, 1885, Vol. II, pp. 335ff.
130 Quoted in Cockshut, op. cit., p. 175.
131 Thus T. H. Huxley, in his *Evolution and Ethics* (The Romanes Lecture for 1893), criticized the attempt to use scientific evolutionary theories in ethics.
132 Huxley stated that 'Social progress means a checking of the cosmic process at every step and the substitution for it of another, that may be called the ethical process.' T. H. Huxley, *Evolution and Ethics and other Essays*, London, 1895, p. 81.
133 Mill, *Three Essays*, p. 76.
134 Cf. *The Portable Nietzsche*, edited by W. Kaufmann, New York, 1954 p. 652 where Nietzsche holds that Christianity condemned the culture of Islam because Islam stood for 'noble . . . male instincts, because it said Yes to life', and p. 655 where Nietzsche holds that Christianity has 'turned every value into an un-value'.
135 Cf. Cockshut, op. cit., pp. 114, 158, 175.
136 A. Sabatier, *Religion and Modern Culture*, a lecture delivered in Stockholm in 1897 and printed in his *The Doctrine of the Atonement and Religion and Modern Culture*, London, 1904, pp. 163ff.
137 A. N. Whitehead, *Science and the Modern World*, New York, 1948, p. 9.
138 J. S. Mill, *A System of Logic*, London, n.d., p. 191; cf. Whitehead, op. cit., pp. 2f.; Stace, op. cit., p. 3–68; A. Richardson, *The Bible in the Age of Science*, London, 1961, pp. 9–31.
139 This was the real problem between Galileo and the Inquisition. It was a case of Galileo's ideas being rejected because they did not fit in with the established world-view.
140 Whitehead, op. cit., p. 13.
141 Cf. H. Butterfield, *The Origins of Modern Science*, London, 1950, pp. 59, 105.
142 Cf. Derham, *Physico-Theology*, London, 1712; Paley, *Natural Theology* and *Evidences of Christianity*; J. Dillenberger, in *Protestant Thought and*

230 THE WAY TO FAITH

Natural Science, London, 1961, p. 152, tells us that two books appeared in the eighteenth century entitled *Insecto-Theologie* and *Wasser-Theologie*.

143 Cf. T. Chalmer's Bridgewater Treatise which is entitled *On the Power Wisdom and Goodness of God as manifested in the Adaptation of External Nature to the Moral and Intellectual Constitution of Man*. The Earl's will desired works to be published 'On the Power, Wisdom, and Goodness of God, as manifested in the Creation; illustrating such work by all reasonable arguments—as for instance the variety and formation of God's creatures in the animal, vegetable, and mineral kingdoms; the effect of digestion, and thereby of conversion; the construction of the hand of man, and an infinite variety of other arguments. . .'. (Quoted in Chalmers, London, 1853, p. xxxv).

144 Cf. Stace, op. cit., pp. 79–129.

145 Cf. Kierkegaard, *Sickness unto Death*, p. 216 and *Concluding Unscientific Postscript*, p. 188.

146 Tennyson, *In Memoriam*, liv, 4.

147 *Notes, Theological. . .*, p. 399.

148 Cf. F. D. Maurice, *Theological Essays*, London, 1957, p. 40, where he speaks of human history as one of 'six thousand years' experience of Evil'.

149 Quoted in Robertson, op. cit., p. 4; cf. p. 114ff.

150 Cf. O. Chadwick, *The Victorian Church*, London, 1966, Part 1, p. 559. Usher's chronology gave Creation at 4004 B.C. but other dates were advanced. Historians of Chinese and Egyptian life argued that the Creation must have been not earlier than 6000 B.C.

151 Cf. Dillenberger, op. cit., pp. 215f.

152 Cf. Chadwick, op. cit., pp. 561f.

153 Cf. Vidler, op. cit., p. 114; Dillenberger, op. cit., pp. 215, 226. Gosse was a scientist and asserted this in 1857.

154 J. Pye Smith, *The Relation between the Holy Scriptures and some parts of Geological Science*, London, 1852, pp. 280–282.

155 *Essays and Reviews*, pp. 209–223; cf. pp. 250ff.

156 Ibid., Preface entitled 'To the Reader'.

157 Cf. Chadwick, op. cit., pp. 563ff.

158 W. H. Pinnock, *An Analysis of Scripture History*, Cambridge, 1848, pp. 17 and 248.

159 Robertson, op. cit., p. 313.

160 Cf. ibid., pp. 127f., 314f. Robertson claims the date of 1840 for *The Vestiges of the Natural History of Creation*.

161 Cf. Robertson, op. cit., pp. 315f.; Chadwick, op. cit., pp. 565f.

162 Cf. Robertson, op. cit., pp. 319f.; Vidler, op. cit., pp. 117ff.; Dillenberger, op. cit., pp. 219–235; Darwin himself wrote in 1879: 'In my most extreme fluctuations I have never been an atheist in the sense of denying the existence of a God. I think that generally . . . an agnostic would be the more correct description of my state of mind.'—quoted in Sheldon, op. cit., p. 97.

NOTES

163 *Essays and Reviews*, p. 250.
164 *In Memoriam*, iii.
165 Ibid.
166 Mill, *Logic*, pp. 208, 504; cf. p. 509.
167 Cf. Whitehead, op. cit., pp. 78ff.
168 *In Memoriam*, liv, lv.
169 Cf. Cockshut, op. cit., pp. 96f.
170 Cf. Mill, *Three Essays*, pp. 176-195; R. H. Hutton wrote: 'Men ask how an omniscient mind which knows precisely what is wanted can set Nature groping her way forward as if she were blind, to find the path of least resistance. And again, they ask how, if bad only becomes good by steady starvation of the worse, it is possible to see in this process the cherishing love of a divine Creator?'—quoted in Wood, op. cit., pp. 52f.
171 Cf. Hume, *Dialogues*, especially Parts X and XI.
172 Cf. Sheldon, op. cit., pp. 154-167; Elliot-Binns, op. cit., pp. 53ff.
173 Letter to J. B. Mozley, in *Letters of J. B. Mozley*, p. 260. The letter was written in 1864.
174 Schleiermacher, *The Christian Faith*, p. 72; cf. Dillenberger, op. cit., pp. 198ff.
175 Mill, *Logic*, pp. 364-366; cf. T. H. Huxley, 'Scientific and Pseudo-Scientific Realism', printed in his *Science and the Christian Tradition*, London, 1894.
176 Maurice, *Kingdom of Christ*, Vol. 2, pp. 156-159.
177 R. C. Trench, *Notes on the Miracles of our Lord*, London, 1878, pp. 15, 21.
178 J. B. Mozley, *Lectures and Other Theological Papers*, London, 1883, p. 23—from a lecture of 1868 on 'Physical Science and Theology'.
179 John Henry Newman, *An Essay in Aid of a Grammar of Assent*, London, 1870. The edition used for this book is that edited by C. F. Harrold and published in 1947. It will be referred to as G.A. The page numbers in brackets are those of the 1898 edition. Here the quotations are from G.A. 62 (81).
180 *Essays and Reviews*, p. 110; cf. p. 114.
181 Cf. ibid., pp. 142ff.
182 Huxley, op. cit., pp. 243, 246, 310, 27.
183 *In Memoriam*, Prologue.
184 S. Freud, *The Future of an Illusion*, London, 1962, p. 52.
185 *Essays and Reviews*, p. 211.
186 Cf. Elliot-Binns, op. cit., pp. 40ff.
187 Cf. Aubrey Moore's protest in *Lux Mundi*, edited by C. Gore, London, 1904, p. 75—he speaks of the 'imperious' and 'increasingly confident' demands of science in matters which are properly theological.
188 Whitehead, op. cit., p. 98.
189 Sabatier, op. cit., p. 174; cf. pp. 168ff.
190 Cf. Cockshut, op. cit., pp. 136-143, for this position in relation to Carlyle and Hale White.

191 Cf. Elliott-Binns, op. cit., pp. 93–174 for the contribution of critical scholarship to belief.
192 Cf. *Essays and Reviews*, p. 151: 'The influence of this foreign literature (sc. of German Biblical criticism) extends to comparatively few among us. . .'. (Comment of H. B. Wilson).
193 R. W. Mackay, *The Tübingen School and its Antecedents*, London, 1863, p.x.
194 *Essays and Reviews*, p. 211; cf. p. 24, *supra*.
195 H. P. Liddon, *The Divinity of Our Lord and Saviour Jesus Christ*, London, 1868, pp. 44ff.
196 Mozley, *Lectures* . . . , p. 74.
197 Cf. *Life and Correspondence of Whately*, Vol. 1, pp. 379ff. Whately says that the right to teach anything 'I can confirm from Scripture' allows the individual to teach almost anything, for 'I can hammer out of the Bible (or any other book) . . . any assignable amount of tradition or of conjectural speculation.'
198 Both Tractarians and Evangelicals accepted the inerrancy of the Bible but differed greatly about what was to be found in the Bible.
199 *Life and Correspondence of Whately*, Vol. 1, p. 375.
200 *The Religious Condition of Christendom*, pp. 95–98.
201 Toland, *Christianity Not Mysterious*, 1696, quoted in C. R. Cragg, *The Church and the Age of Reason*, Penguin Books, 1960, pp. 77f.
202 *Notes, Theological*. . . , pp. 326f.
203 S. T. Coleridge, *Confessions of an Inquiring Spirit*, London, 1956, pp. 43, 51f., 55, 57, 75; cf. J. Tulloch, *Movements of Religious Thought in Britain during the Nineteenth Century*, London, 1885, pp. 24–30.
204 Robertson, op. cit., p. 140.
205 The work did not in fact achieve great popularity—it was reprinted only in 1841 and 1871. Robertson suggests (p. 141ff.) that there was a conspiracy of silence among believers to prevent it being widely read!
206 Cf. Willey, op. cit., pp. 217ff.
207 Cf. ibid., p. 230ff.; also Robertson, op. cit., pp. 150ff.; Sheldon, op. cit., pp. 263ff.
208 Cf. Mackay, op. cit.
209 Quoted by Sheldon, op. cit., p. 275 from *Kritik der evangelischen Geschichte der Synoptiker*, §91.
210 Cf. Mozley's *Letters* pp. 247ff.; Wood, op. cit., pp. 63ff.; Vidler, op. cit., p. 123ff.
211 *Essays and Reviews*, cf. pp. 52f., where Williams suggests that among English scholars 'the explicitness of truth is rare', and p. 63.
212 Ibid., p. 53–80.
213 Ibid., p. 60; cf. p. 77.
214 Ibid., p. 93; cf. p. 434.
215 Ibid., p. 337; cf. pp. 330–337.
216 Ibid., p. 337; cf. pp. 337, 342ff.
217 Ibid., pp. 418ff.
218 Ibid., p. 343.

219 Ibid., p. 154; cf. pp. 155, 161.
220 Cf. ibid., pp. 175ff.; 185ff.; 201.
221 Vidler, op. cit., p. 128; it was said that the Lord Chancellor 'dismissed Hell with costs, and took away from orthodox members of the Church of England their last hope of everlasting damnation'. The judgement was given in February 1864.
222 Cf. Robertson, op. cit., pp. 134ff.
223 H. H. Milman, *The History of the Jews*, London, 1866, Vol. I, p. iv, ix, xiii f., xxxii.
224 Ibid., Vol. I, p. xi, 306; cf. p. iv f.
225 Cf. Robertson, op. cit., p. 144ff.; Tulloch, op. cit., pp. 80ff.
226 Cf. S. C. Carpenter, *Church and People, 1789–1889*, London, 1959, pp. 442ff., 504f.
227 This reversal of order had already been suggested by Vatke at Berlin and Reuss at Strasbourg. It had been made famous by Duhm in 1875.
228 The German edition had appeared in 1878.
229 Cf. Vidler, op. cit., pp. 170ff.
230 Cf. *Lectures and Essays of William Robertson Smith*, edited by J. S. Black and G. Chrystal, London, 1912, pp. 133ff., 229ff. Robertson Smith wrote that we 'must regulate all our exegesis and all our criticism by the great principle that we are to seek in the Bible, not a body of abstract religious truth, but the living personal history of God's gracious dealings with men . . .' (p. 229).
231 S. R. Driver, *An Introduction to the Literature of the Old Testament*, Edinburgh, 1891, pp. xiv, xix; for the cautious attitude of Driver cf. pp. xi f.
232 *The Times*, Saturday, 12 March, 1892.
233 Matthew Arnold, *God and the Bible*, London, 1888, p. xxvii.
234 Matthew Arnold, *St. Paul and Protestantism*, London, 1887, pp. 164ff.; cf. *God and the Bible*, xxv ff.
235 Matthew Arnold, *Literature and Dogma*, London, 1876, pp. xxvii, xxxi; cf. pp. xxxi f., 400.
236 Cf. *God and the Bible*, pp. xii ff.
237 Cf. F. D. Maurice, *Theological Essays*, pp. 223–245; *Kingdom of God*, Vol. 2, pp. 149ff.
238 Cf. also B. F. Westcott's *The Gospel of Life* which had appeared the previous year. Sanday's Bampton Lectures were published in 1894 under the title *Inspiration*.
239 Westcott and Hort's text appeared in 1881 and was accompanied by a separate volume of 'Introduction' which discussed the need for and the methods used in textual criticism. Dean Burgon in a series of articles, later reprinted in 1883 as *The Revision Revised*, defended the Received Text—the Greek basis of the Authorised Version, cf. Elliott-Binns, op. cit., pp. 170f.
240 *Lux Mundi*, p. vii.
241 Ibid., pp. 260ff.

242 Cf. A. Schweitzer, *The Quest of the Historical Jesus*, London, 1954; A. M. Fairbairn, *The Place of Christ in Modern Theology*, London, 1902; W. Sanday, *The Life of Christ in Recent Research*, London, 1908.
243 C. Hennell, *Inquiry Concerning the Origin of Christianity*, London, 1838, p. 152.
244 cf. p. 34, supra.
245 This is stated in the Preface to the first edition of the *Life of Jesus*.
246 This was stated in his book *The Old Faith and the New, A Confession*.
247 E. Renan, *The Life of Jesus*, London, 1935, p. xi states that 60,000 copies were sold in the first six months after publication and that it went through twenty-three editions in twenty years. The English translation first appeared in 1864—a year after the book's appearance in France.
248 Cf. ibid., pp. 6, 13, 16–20.
249 Ibid., p. 104.
250 Ibid., p. 166.
251 Cf. ibid., pp. 184f.
252 Ibid., p. 211.
253 Ibid., p. 35; cf. p. 220.
254 Cf. Wood, op. cit., pp. 122ff.; Sheldon, op. cit., pp. 298ff.
255 J. R. Seeley, *Ecce Homo, A Survey of The Life and Work of Jesus Christ*, London, 1890. The work was originally published anonymously in 1865. Before its true authorship was known, it had been attributed, *inter alia*, to J. S. Mill and J. H. Newman!
256 Ibid., p. xxvi.
257 Cf. ibid., pp. 49ff.; (Horton Davies is misleading when he speaks of Seeley's 'unmiraculous Christ' in his *Worship and Theology in England, 1850–1900*, London, 1962, p. 183, cf. p. 293).
258 Ibid., p. xxvi.
259 In 1882 Seeley published *Natural Religion* but it did not deal with this issue. It expressed a very liberal view of religion and stated that 'you may speak of the truth of a philosophy, of a theory, of a proposition, but not of a religion, which is a condition of the feelings'—p. 212.
260 *Ecce Homo*, p. xxvi.
261 Ibid., p. 361.
262 Fairbairn, *Place of Christ*, pp. 3f.; cf. p. 20f.
263 A. Harnack, *What is Christianity?*, New York, 1957, p. 31.
264 Quoted in Schweitzer, op. cit., pp. 228–231.
265 Ibid., pp. 397, 399.
266 One point at which the two disciplines overlapped concerned Jesus' view of the Old Testament. It seemed from the Gospels that Jesus had held certain views about the Old Testament which Biblical scholarship regarded as erroneous. Some believers used Jesus' attitude to defend the traditional view of the Bible. They preferred an infallible Jesus to a fallible critic (cf. Liddon, op. cit., p. 468ff.). Others felt compelled to surrender their theological belief in the infallibility of the historical Jesus. Thus Dale (cf. R. W. Dale, *Christian Doctrine*, London, 1895, p. 286ff.),

Driver (op. cit., p. xviii f.), and Gore (*Lux Mundi*, p. 263ff.) suggested that the incarnate Christ, i.e. the historical Jesus, was limited to contemporary ideas about matters of fact, including historical facts about the Old Testament. Such views horrified traditional believers like Liddon and Pusey and led Robert Elsmere in Mrs. Humphrey Ward's novel to give up his faith in the divinity of Jesus Christ.

267 Cf. O. Chadwick, *From Bossuet to Newman, The Idea of Doctrinal Development*, Cambridge, 1957, pp. 1-95.
268 Cf. G. W. F. Hegel, *Reason in History*, New York, 1953, pp. 68f.
269 Hegel, *Philosophy of Religion*, Vol. I, p. 79.
270 Ibid., Vol. III, p. 1; cf. pp. 1ff.
271 Ibid., Vol. III, p. 124.
272 Mark Pattison wrote to Newman on April 5th, 1878, 'Is it not a remarkable thing that you should have first started the idea—and the word—Development, as the key to the history of church doctrine, and since then it has gradually become the dominant idea of all history, biology, physics, and in short has metamorphosed our view of every science, and of all knowledge?'—quoted in O. Chadwick, *Bossuet to Newman*, p. x.
273 Cf. J. H. Newman, *An Essay on the Development of Christian Doctrine*, London, 1890, p. 10.
274 J. H. Newman, *Fifteen Sermons preached before the University of Oxford*, London, 1872, pp. 320, 327.
275 Cf. *Development*, p. 169ff.
276 Ibid., p. 31.
277 Cf. Tract 85, reprinted in J. H. Newman, *Essays Critical and Historical*, London, 1890, Vol. II, pp. 1-73 and entitled *Catholicity of the Anglican Church; Development*, pp. 75-92; J. H. Newman *Apologia pro Vita Sua*, Boston, 1956, p. 193; G. A. pp. 385ff. (495ff.).
278 Cf. O. Chadwick, *Bossuet to Newman*, p. 164ff.; cf. also the article by D. Nicholls, *Developing Doctrines and Changing Beliefs*, in *Scottish Journal of Theology*, 19, 4, September 1966.
279 Although Newman attacked the 'liberalism' of the day (cf. pp. 60, 65f., *infra* and especially points 6 and 7 in his note on liberalism in *Apologia*, p. 276), it must not be forgotten that he was influenced by and largely accepted the critical historical approach that was part of the 'liberal' attitude.
280 Cf. Dale, op. cit., pp. 306f.
281 Cf. Fairbairn, *Place of Christ*, pp. 32ff.
282 Ibid., p. 35.
283 Ibid., p. 296.
284 Cf. ibid., pp. 293ff., 355, 377ff., 476ff.; cf. also his *The Philosophy of the Christian Religion*, London, n.d., *passim*.
285 E. Hatch, *The Influence of Greek Ideas and Usages upon the Christian Church*, (edited by A. M. Fairbairn), London, 1892, p. 1. These Hibbert Lectures had been delivered in 1888.
286 Ibid., p. 351.
287 Harnack, op. cit., p. 299.

288 Ibid., p. 184; cf. p. 176ff.
289 Mozley, *Lectures* . . , p. 74.
290 Hastings Rashdall, *Doctrine and Development*, London, 1898, p. vii–ix.
291 *Lessing's Theological Writings*, edited by H. Chadwick, London, 1956, p. 53. Lessing himself talked about the doctrines of faith in terms of 'necessary truths of reason' but his point applied to any belief which was both held as 'certain' and was based upon historical judgements.
292 Ibid., p. 54.
293 Chadwick states in his introduction to *Lessing's Theological Writings* that 'the questions that he asked have dominated, perhaps even haunted, modern theology' (p. 48). He was widely read in Germany but only his *The Education of the Human Race* was translated into English. Coleridge studied him in German (ibid., p. 32) and Chadwick sees his influence in Newman's *Development of Doctrine* (ibid., p. 32) and in *Essays and Reviews* (ibid., p. 48). Lessing had an important influence on Fichte and on Kierkegaard (ibid., p. 32, 48).
294 Cf. *Life and Correspondence of Whately*, Vol. 1, p. 442—letter of December 12, 1839.
295 Cf. *Essays and Reviews*, pp. 98, 110ff., 132, 138.
296 Kierkegaard, *Philosophical Fragments*, p. 87.
297 *In Memoriam*, xxxvi.
298 *Lux Mundi*, p. 172.
299 W. E. H. Lecky, *The Rise and Influence of the Spirit of Rationalism in Europe*, London, 1873, Vol. II, pp. 137f.
300 Ibid., Vol. II, p. 225.
301 An analysis of The Revelation in John Wesley, *Explanatory Notes upon the New Testament*, London, 1950, p. 1051.
302 Quoted in D. Thompson, *England in the Nineteenth Century*, Penguin Books, 1950, p. 76.
303 Five of the six points were in fact part of the British constitution by 1919.
304 T. Carlyle, *Chartism and Past and Present*, London, n.d., p. 237.
305 Cf. Packe, op. cit., pp. 405f.
306 Cf. A. M. Fairbairn, *Religion in History and in Modern Life*, London, 1894, p. 26ff.
307 Lecky, op. cit., Vol. II, p. 129.
308 K. Marx 'Anti-Church Movement, Demonstration in Hyde Park', published in *Neue Oder-Zeitung*, 28 June, 1855, and reprinted in *Marx and Engels on Religion*, p. 126.
309 Fairbairn, *Religion in History*, pp. 29f.
310 Carlyle, op. cit., p. 26.
311 Willey, op. cit., p. 174; cf. Packe, op. cit., pp. 402ff.
312 Cf. W. H. J. Campion in *Lux Mundi*, pp. 321ff., who suggested that Christianity can be compatible with an authoritarian establishment.
313 Cf. Fairbairn, *Religion in History*, pp. 23, 30f.
314 Cf. A. W. W. Dale, *The Life of R. W. Dale*, London, 1899, pp. 254ff.
315 Chadwick, *The Victorian Church*, p. 438.

316 Cf. J. H. Newman, *On Consulting the Faithful in Matters of Doctrine*, (edited by J. Coulson), London, 1961, pp. 63, 77ff.
317 Ibid., pp. 103f.; Coulson comments that 'if the Church had a duty to consult the faithful, then it also had a duty to manifest itself fully as a *conspiratio* of priests and laity, as distinct from the existing practice of acquiescing in a laity which was either superstitious or indifferent, and capable of a merely notional assent in matters of faith' (p. 33). Newman's emphasis in the *Grammar* on the need for 'real' and not merely 'notional' assent and his attempt to show how every believer can have a 'certain' faith further reflect the views he expressed in this article first published in the *Rambler* for July, 1859.
318 Chadwick, *The Victorian Church*, p. 438.
319 Cf. Fairbairn, *Religion in History*, p. 46: 'Men who once knew no story but the *Pilgrim's Progress* now read Thackeray and Dickens, Walter Scott and George Eliot; or those whose only history book was the Old Testament, now read Carlyle and Froude, Gardiner and Lecky; or those whose only poetry was Watts' or Wesley's Hymns, now study Tennyson and Browning, Arthur Hugh Clough and Matthew Arnold.'
320 Ibid., p. 18, 22; cf. p. 6.
321 For the Church-State relations of the Church of England, cf. Chadwick, *The Victorian Church*, passim.
322 Lecky, op. cit., Vol. II, p. 120; cf. pp. 120ff.
323 Compton Rickett, Chairman of the Congregational Union, quoted in A. B. D. Alexander, *The Shaping Forces of Modern Religious Thought*, Glasgow, 1920, p. 372.
324 S. C. Neill, *A History of Christian Missions*, Penguin Books, 1964, p. 358.
325 Lecky, op. cit., Vol. II, p. 131; cf. p. 133.
326 K. Marx and F. Engels, *Manifesto of the Communist Party*, Moscow, 1954, pp. 43, 104.
327 Cf. ibid., pp. 57ff.
328 Fairbairn, *Religion in History*, pp. 37-40.
329 Sabatier, op. cit., p. 163ff.; cf. pp. 168-174.
330 Cf. Heine's story of a mechanical robot without a soul, Heine, op. cit., p. 105f.
331 Robert Browning, *Easter Day*, I & II.

NOTES ON PART II: THE BACKGROUND TO THE *Grammar of Assent*: PAGES 60-96

1 J. Pieper, *Belief and Faith*, London, 1964, pp. 7f.
2 Sermon entitled *The Infidelity of the Future*, preached on 2 October, 1873, and printed in *Catholic Sermons of Cardinal Newman*, edited by C. S. Dessain, London, 1957, p. 122f.
3 It is interesting, for instance, to speculate on what Thomas Arnold

junior, the brother of Matthew Arnold, might have told Newman about literary and historical criticism of the Bible when he came from teaching English Literature in the Irish University to be a schoolmaster at the Oratory School. He was there from 1862 until 1865 when he left after 'a bad attack of doubts, brought on by the Pope's publication of the Syllabus of Errors' (Meriol Trevor, *Light in Winter*, London, 1962, p. 369).

4 For Newman on Paley, cf. A. Dwight Culler, *The Imperial Intellect*, Yale, 1955, pp. 267f.

5 *Development*, pp. 193, 201f.

6 First printed in 1835, reprinted in *Essays Critical and Historical*, Vol. I, pp. 30ff., and entitled *On the Introduction of Rationalistic Principles into Revealed Religion*. Newman says that the 'fundamental principle' of Erskine's *Internal Evidence* is the claim that 'the human mind may criticize and systematize the Divine Revelation' and may limit its uses to its 'workings through our own reason and affections' (ibid., p. 72). Abbott's *Corner Stone* follows the same principle, according to Newman, and is 'really a specious form of trusting man rather than God, . . . is in its nature Rationalistic, and . . . tends to Socinianism' (ibid., p. 95). In a note appended to this essay, Newman adds that he wrote the essay because of his 'deep and increasing apprehension, that the religious philosophy' underlying the works of Erskine and Abbott, 'was making its way into Oxford, and through Oxford among the clergy, by the writings of Dr. Whately, Dr. Hampden's Bampton Lectures, and Mr. Blanco White's (then) recent publications' (ibid., p. 101). In his essay, *Apostolical Tradition*, dated July 1836, printed in the *British Critic* and reprinted in *Essays Critical and Historical*, Newman continued his attack on Hampden (cf. ibid., Vol. I, p. 114f.).

7 Ibid., Vol. I, pp. 96ff.

8 Cf. Zeno, *John Henry Newman, Our Way to Certitude*, Leiden, 1957, p. 80. Zeno refers to G. A. p. 49 (64) but Newman here refers to no authority for his views. Unless the reader already knew that these views had been expressed by Kant, there would be nothing in the text to make him consider that Newman was expressing Kantian views and not simply views that he had worked out for himself.

9 For Hume, cf. J. H. Newman, *Two Essays on Scripture Miracles and on Ecclesiastical*, London, 1870, *passim*; *Oxford University Sermons*, pp. 185, 195, 231; J. H. Newman, *The Idea of a University*, New York, 1959, pp. 78, 93, 297, 302, 430; *Apologia*, p. 23; G.A. 62 (81) 232f., (306f.). It has been suggested that Newman was greatly influenced by Hume but these references do not show how much of Hume Newman may have read apart from Hume's *Essay on Miracles*. He may have acquired other Humean ideas from current thought without recognizing their Humean source.

For Coleridge, cf. p. 90 *infra*. Newman refers to the *Aids to Reflection* in G.A. 231f., (305).

For Hamilton, cf. Cardinal Newman, *Stray Essays on Controversial Points*, (Privately Printed), 1890, pp. 94f., where Newman quotes from Hamilton. This essay, however, was written in 1886 and we do not know what Newman knew of Hamilton earlier in his life and thinking. In his correspondence with Meynell about the draft of the G.A., we find that Meynell mentions Hamilton six times but Newman does not give any indication that he knows Hamilton's philosophy for himself,—cf. the correspondence printed in Zeno, op. cit., pp. 226–270.

10 Newman also published three volumes of *Historical Sketches* which include essays on The Turks, Cicero, Benedictine Schools, Northmen and Normans, and Medieval Oxford.
11 Cf. p. 46, *supra* where we mention the place of Newman's *Development of Doctrine* in the crisis for faith.
12 Cf. J. H. Newman, *The Arians of the Fourth Century*, London, 1883; *Development*; J. H. Newman, *Discussions and Arguments on Various Subjects*, London, 1891; *The Idea of a University*; G.A.
13 Cf. G.A. 283 (373), 368 (483).
14 Cf. Culler, op. cit., pp. 262f.
15 Cf. ibid., p. 249.
16 Reprinted in *Essays Critical and Historical*, Vol. II, p. 188. Milman is also mentioned in the *Development*.
17 Cf. Culler, op. cit., p. 195.
18 Cf. John Henry Newman, *Autobiographical Writings*, edited by H. Tristam, London, 1956, pp. 44, 54, 167f. (The note that is scribbled partly in pencil is probably based on Buckland's views.); Culler, op. cit., pp. 15, 24f.
19 *The Idea of a University*, p. 124.
20 Cf. ibid., *passim;* Culler, op. cit., p. 245ff.
21 *The Idea of a University*, p. 399ff.
22 *Stray Essays*, pp. 2, 32.
23 *Discussions and Arguments*, p. 398. The review is reprinted from the *Month*, June, 1866.
24 The first was published in the *Nineteenth Century* for February, 1884; the second was written in reply to criticisms of the first and was circulated privately by Newman. They are reprinted in *Stray Essays*.
25 Cf. *Stray Essays*, p. 23ff.
26 Ibid., p. 12; cf. Culler, op. cit., p. 316, n.70. In *Development* p. 147ff. Newman suggests that Scripture is too unsystematic to be a standard for faith.
27 Cf. the admirable edition of Newman's letters by C. S. Dessain, *The Letters and Diaries of John Henry Newman*, London. The index to each volume lists the places where Newman is dealing with reason, faith, and probability.
28 Cf. letters of 11 December 1845, and 7 October 1853.
29 Cf. p. 83f., *infra*.

30 *Letters and Correspondence of John Henry Newman*, edited by A. Mozley, London, 1891, Vol. II, p. 300.
31 Quoted in Culler, op. cit., p. 267 and notes.
32 For Mill, cf. notes dated 27 January 1859 and 5 January 1860, mentioned in A. J. Boekraad, *The Personal Conquest of Truth according to J. H. Newman*, Louvain, 1955, pp. 187–190, 268f.
For Kant, cf. notes dated 1 December 1859, 9 February 1860 and 2 May 1860;—cf. also Boekraad, op. cit., pp. 269f., and Zeno, op. cit., pp. 63, 80 n., 275.
33 *Apologia*, p. 34.
34 Cf. Boekraad, op. cit., pp. 26–29 where he criticizes Nédoncelle.
35 *Apologia*, p. 34; Boekraad, op. cit., pp. 97ff.; *Oxford University Sermons*, p. 8, 14f.
36 *The Idea of a University*, p. 352; cf. p. 104ff., 352ff.; 368ff.; 391ff.; 413ff. In this volume the term 'liberal' is also applied by Newman to 'education' in a way that is quite free from overtones of criticism or disvalue. 'Liberal education' is a praiseworthy thing—cf. Culler, op. cit., pp. 173–181, 194, 219, 262, but contrast pp. 206f., 258. Newman also contrasts 'liberalism' with the proper and praiseworthy attitude of men of a truly 'philosophic habit'—ibid., pp. 190, 263.
37 *Apologia*, pp. 65f., 246.
38 Ibid., p. 271.
39 Ibid., p. 275; cf. Zeno, op. cit., p. 59f.
40 *Catholic Sermons*, p. 122.
41 Quoted in Trevor, *Light in Winter*, pp. 567–570.
42 *The Journal, 1859–79*, note dated 14 October 1874; printed in *Autobiographical Writings*, p. 271f. Cf. E. A. Sillem, *Cardinal Newman, A New Discovery*, in *The Wiseman Review*, 495, Spring 1963, p. 76, where it is said that William Froude asked Newman in 1860 to write a book on the act of faith and show how he would defend its reasonableness. Sillem holds that the *Grammar* was Newman's answer to this request. Newman himself does not seem to think that the Grammar was such a direct response according to the evidence of his *Journal*. Cf. Boekraad, op. cit., p. 161ff.
43 Newman was then fifteen and according to the *Apologia* the experience was so well defined that he could date its first and last days as 1 August and 21 December 1816—*Apologia*, p. 24 n.2; cf. M. Trevor, *The Pillar of the Cloud*, London, 1962, p. 17; J.-H. Walgrave, *Newman, The Theologian*, London, 1960, p. 29f.
44 *Apologia*, p. 24; cf. p. 34.
45 Cf. Walgrave, op. cit., p. 30, n.5; A. J. Boekraad, op. cit., p. 90.
46 *Apologia*, p. 24ff.
47 *Early Journals: Book 1*, note dated 10 October 1819; published in *Autobiographical Writings*, p. 161.
48 Note dated 6 January 1821; ibid., p. 179f.
49 Note dated 1 June 1821; ibid., p. 166f.

50 Note dated 4 August 1821; ibid., p. 174.
51 Note dated 15 May 1874, referring to material of 1820-21; ibid., p. 149f.
52 Note dated 2 June 1822; ibid., p. 186.
53 Note dated 21 February 1824; ibid., p. 196f.
54 *Apologia*, p. 31; cf. p. 31f.
55 Ibid., p. 33f.; cf. Newman's letter to Monsell, published in Boekraad, op. cit., p. 91ff. The letter is dated 10 October 1852.
56 *Oxford University Sermons*, p. 1.
57 Ibid., p. 3f.
58 Ibid., pp. 7ff.
59 Ibid., pp. 14f.
60 Ibid., p. 8.
61 Ibid., p. 17.
62 Ibid., p. 18; cf. pp. 18ff.
63 Ibid., p. 27.
64 Ibid., pp. 21ff.
65 Ibid., pp. 54ff.
66 Ibid., p. 55.
67 Ibid., p. 57; cf. pp. 58ff., 68ff.
68 Ibid., pp. 65ff.
69 Ibid., pp. 66, and n.4.
70 'Personal Influence, The Means of Propagating the Truth', preached on 22 January, 1832; ibid., p. 75ff.
71 Cf. ibid., p. 90.
72 Ibid., p. 79.
73 Ibid., p. 84f.
74 Cf. ibid., p. 122 and p. 132, (preached on 27 May 1832); cf. also p. 149 from Newman's next sermon.
75 Ibid., pp. 121ff., 127.
76 Ibid., p. 156, from the sermon 'Wilfulness, The Sin of Saul', preached on 2 December 1832.
77 Cf. ibid., p. 171f.
78 *Apologia*, p. 50.
79 *The Arians*, p. 9.
80 Ibid., p. 33.
81 Ibid., p. 87, cf. pp. 110, 136f. Newman's view that heresy and moral evil go together is illustrated in his description of the character of Arius (p. 237ff.) and his description of the ill-treatment of Athanasius and all his followers by the heretics (p. 327ff.).
82 Ibid., p. 143ff. This is another expression of Newman's view that a 'real' rather than a 'notional' apprehension is needed for a dynamic faith.
83 Ibid., p. 221; cf. pp. 110, 136f., 221ff.
84 *Essays Critical and Historical*, Vol. I, p. 31; cf. p. 60.
85 Ibid., p. 33ff.; cf. p. 54, and p. 91 where the rationalistic 'spirit of the age' is described as 'that scornful, arrogant, and self-trusting spirit'.

86 Ibid., p. 35.
87 Ibid., p. 40. Cf. 'No revelation can be complete and systematic, from the weakness of the human intellect; *so far as* it is not such, it is mysterious.' "Revelation" refers to what is clear in a religious doctrine, "mystery" to what is not clear in the same doctrine,' ibid., p. 41; cf., p. 66.
88 Cf. ibid., p. 32; cf. Kant's claim quoted on p. 9 *supra*.
89 Ibid., p. 52.
90 Cf. ibid., pp. 51f., 54.
91 John Henry Newman, *How to Accomplish It*, March 1836, reprinted in *Discussions and Arguments*, p. 1ff.
92 John Henry Newman, *Apostolical Tradition*, July 1836, reprinted in *Essays Critical and Historical*, Vol. I, p. 115.
93 Cf. ibid., p. 104.
94 Ibid., p. 103; cf. p. 107; cf. *Dr. Pusey's Tracts on Holy Baptism*, 11 January and 3 March 1837, reprinted in John Henry Newman, *The Via Media of the Anglican Church*, London, 1877, Vol. II, p. 189: 'I consider I am but speaking what the Catholic Fathers witness to be Christ's Gospel. I am exercising no private judgement on scripture. . .'.
95 *Via Media*, Vol. II, p. 193.
96 *On the Mode of Conducting the Controversy with Rome*, 1836, reprinted in *Via Media*, Vol. II, p. 132.
97 Ibid., p. 95; cf. p. 101ff., where it is stated that our arguments must not be 'radically unreal or rhetorical or sophistical' but 'such as are likely to convince serious and earnest minds who are really seeking for the truth'. Thus our arguments 'must not only be true and practical, but we must see that they are not abstract arguments and on abstract points'.
98 *Lectures on the Prophetical Office of the Church*, 1837, reprinted in *Via Media*, Vol. I., p. 1f.; cf. p. 22.
99 Ibid., p. 2f.
100 Ibid., p. 85f.; cf. pp. 87f., 135f.
101 Ibid., pp. 86f.; cf. John Henry Newman, *Parochial Sermons*, Second Edition, London, 1839, Vol. IV, p. 263 where a distinction is drawn between accepting something as a conclusion and believing it.
102 *Via Media*, Vol. I, p. 109.
103 Cf. ibid., p. 130.
104 Cf. ibid., p. 131ff. Our 'internal means of judging' include 'common sense, natural perception of right and wrong, the sympathy of the affections, exercises of the imagination, reason, and the like' (ibid., p. 131; cf. p. 15, p. 109; cf. the role of the 'illative sense' and of conscience in the *Grammar of Assent*) while the 'external are such as Scripture, the existing Church, Tradition, Catholicity, Learning, Antiquity, and the National Faith' (ibid., p. 131; cf. pp. 132ff.). We are to employ as many of these means as possible in coming to our decisions about faith.
105 Ibid., p. 189; cf. pp. 268, 272f., and see pp. 153–167 for the application of this to the interpretation of Scripture.
106 Cf. ibid., pp. 135f., 189.

107 Cf. John Henry Newman, *Lectures on the Doctrine of Justification*, Third Edition, London, 1874, pp. 224ff., 255ff., 293.
108 Ibid., p. 224.
109 Ibid., p. 258.
110 Cf. ibid., pp. 224, 258, 263f. The distinction made here between mere faith and justifying faith is the same as that made between opinion and faith in *Via Media*, Vol. I, p. 86f., (cf. note 104 *supra*).
111 Cf. ibid., pp. 252, 269 and cf. also *Parochial Sermons*, Vol. IV, pp. 228, 338.
112 *Lectures on Justification*, p. 267; cf. pp. 269f.
113 John Henry Newman, *Holy Scripture in its Relation to the Catholic Creed*, September 1838, reprinted in *Discussions and Arguments*, pp. 109ff.
114 Ibid., p. 199f.
115 Cf. ibid., p. 249ff.; cf. *Parochial Sermons*, Vol. IV, p. 322ff.
116 Cf. *Discussions and Arguments*, pp. 213f.; cf. *Parochial Sermons*, Vol. IV, p. 341.
117 These sermons are entitled, 'Faith and Reason, Contrasted as Habits of Mind', 'The Nature of Faith in Relation to Reason', 'Love the Safeguard of Faith against Superstition', 'Implicit and Explicit Reason'.
118 *Oxford University Sermons*, p. 183; cf. p. 182f.
119 Cf. ibid., p. 270; cf. also *The Catholicity of the Anglican Church*, reprinted in *Essays Critical and Historical*, Vol. II, p. 12 for a similar view in an essay published in January 1840.
120 *Oxford University Sermons*, p. 183; cf. pp. 183f., 225, 253ff., 262.
121 Cf. ibid., pp. 266f., 277.
122 Ibid., p. 207; cf. pp. 206, 256.
123 Ibid., p. 208; cf. p. 204.
124 Cf. ibid., pp. 209ff.
125 Ibid., pp. 199f.; cf. pp. 190, 222f., 231, 271.
126 Ibid., p. 187; cf. pp. 185ff.
127 Ibid., p. 230; cf. pp. 230f.
128 Ibid., p. 213; cf. pp. 213ff.
129 Ibid., p. 215; cf. pp. 188, 219ff., 224.
130 Ibid., p. 233; cf. pp. 232ff.
131 Ibid., p. 234; cf. p. 238.
132 Ibid., p. 236; cf. pp. 235ff.
133 Cf. ibid., pp. 216ff.
134 Ibid., p. 216; cf. pp. 218, 266f.
135 Ibid., p. 257.
136 Ibid.
137 Cf. ibid., p. 257f.
138 Ibid., p. 258.
139 Cf. ibid., pp. 258f.
140 Ibid., p. 259.
141 Cf. ibid., pp. 259f., 271f.
142 Ibid., p. 274; cf. pp. 274ff., 277.

143 Ibid., p. 191; cf. pp. 191ff.
144 Ibid., p. 193; cf. pp. 193ff., 203, 226f.; cf. also *The Theology of St. Ignatius*, reprinted in *Essays Critical and Historical*, Vol. I, p. 223f.
145 *Oxford University Sermons*, p. 229.
146 Ibid., p. 226.
147 Ibid., p. 239; cf. also John Henry Newman, *Parochial and Plain Sermons*, London, 1891, Vol. V, p. 197.
148 *Oxford University Sermons*, p. 193; cf. p. 208.
149 Ibid., p. 237; cf. p. 237ff.
150 Ibid., p. x. This is in the Preface to the Third Edition of 1872.
151 *Milman's View of Christianity*, January, 1841, reprinted in *Essays Critical and Historical*, Vol II, p. 230f.
152 *The Tamworth Reading Room*, printed in *The Times* in February 1841, and reprinted in *Discussions and Arguments*, pp. 254ff.
153 Ibid., p. 261.
154 Ibid., p. 268.
155 Ibid., p. 262; cf. p. 268.
156 Ibid., p. 270; cf. p. 272ff.
157 G.A. p. 70ff. (92ff).
158 *Discussions and Arguments*, p. 294.
159 Ibid., p. 293.
160 Ibid., p. 295; cf. p. 296.
161 Ibid., p. 292.
162 Ibid., p. 302; cf. pp. 292f., 298ff., 302f.
163 Ibid., p. 304.
164 *Essays Critical and Historical*, Vol. II, p. 338; cf. p. 336f.
165 Ibid., p. 342; cf. pp. 341ff.
166 Ibid., p. 353; cf. p. 355.
167 Ibid., p. 353; cf. pp. 353f., 367.
168 These sermons are entitled 'Wisdom, as Contrasted with Faith and with Bigotry', preached in June 1841, and 'The Theory of Developments in Religious Doctrine,' preached in February 1843.
169 *Oxford University Sermons*, p. 280; cf. pp. 279, 281. cf. J. H. Newman, *Sermons Bearing on Subjects of the Day*, Second Edition, London, 1844, pp. 388f.
170 Ibid., p. 281.
171 Ibid., pp. 292f.
172 Ibid., p. 297; cf. p. 299.
173 Ibid., pp. 297f.
174 Cf. ibid., pp. 313, 317, 320, 351.
175 Cf. ibid., pp. 294f, 317.
176 Cf. ibid., pp. 320f, 323, 327f.
177 John Henry Newman, *An Essay on the Development of Christian Doctrine*, Seventh Edition, London, 1890, p. 123; cf. pp. 109, 122f.
178 Ibid., p. 190—this 'moral perception' is a kind of intuitive awareness; cf. pp. 190f, 383f.

179 Ibid., p. 191; cf. p. 383.
180 Ibid., p. 325.
181 Ibid., p. 327.
182 Ibid., p. 327f., where Newman quotes from Locke, *Essay concerning Human Understanding*, Book IV, Chapter 18; cf. also *Development*, pp. 357f.
183 Cf. p. 46 *supra*.
184 *Apologia*, p. 227.
185 See Appendix II for a list of these attempts. A great number of Newman's private papers are preserved at the Oratory, Edgbaston. I was given the opportunity to consult them through the kindness of Fr. Stephen Dessain. They will be described as 'Or. MSS.' and the reference after them will denote the packet where they are kept in Newman's room at the Oratory. Extracts from sixteen of them are given in Appendix III.
186 *The Journal, 1859–79*, note dated October 30, 1870; reprinted in *Autobiographical Writings*, p. 269.
187 J. H. Newman, *John Keble*, June, 1846; reprinted in *Essays Critical and Historical*, Vol. II, p. 451ff.
188 Cf. ibidem; letter to Mrs. William Froude on 27 June 1848, printed in *Letters and Diaries*, Vol. XII. Newman here holds that 'there is really no medium between scepticism and Catholicism' and that 'directly you have a conviction that you *ought* to believe, reason has done its part, and what is wanted for faith, is, not proof, but *will*. . . . The simple question is, whether you *ought*' (p. 227f.).
189 Or. MSS. B. 9. 11. '17 June 1846. On St. Thomas's view of Faith as cogitare cum assensu'.
190 Ibidem.
191 Letter to W. G. Penny on 13 December 1846, printed in *Letters and Diaries*, Vol. XI, p. 293; cf. letters of 8 February 1846 (where Newman says that the arguments that led him to become a Catholic cannot be presented abstractly and detachedly for 'moral proofs are grown into, not learnt by heart') and of 1 June 1846 (where Newman states that God gives to each person arguments 'sufficient for his guidance' in coming to a decision and we must act on this basis). In a letter to Dalgairns in December 1846 Newman states that while he is accused 'of denying moral certainty and holding . . . that we cannot get beyond probability in religious questions', this accusation is due to a misunderstanding of his position for 'I use "probable" in opposition to "demonstrative" and moral certainty is a *state of mind*, in all cases however produced by probable arguments which admit of more or less—the measure of probability necessary for certainty varying with the individual mind' (ibid., p. 289 —cf. also C. S. Dessain's comment that Newman uses Dugald Stewart's definition of 'probable'—ibidem.).
192 Published in *Catholic Sermons of Cardinal Newman*, p. 23. The sermons in question are seven in number and were preached between 30 January and 26 March 1848.
193 Cf. ibid., pp. 21ff.

194 Cf. ibid., pp. 57ff. and especially p. 61.
195 Ibid., p. 62.
196 Ibid., p. 88.
197 Ibid., pp. 77f.; cf. pp. 75ff.
198 Ibid., p. 63.
199 Or. MSS. B.9.11. 'Ultimate Resolution of certainty of Faith (Easter 1848)'; cf. letters of 27 June and 12 October 1848, in *Letters and Diaries*, Vol. XII, p. 227ff., 289.
200 Or. MSS. B.9.11. '(On the Nature and Cause of Faith)'. This paper is dated at this time because it is in the folder marked 'Papers on Faith, 1848', the piece itself is not dated. Newman notes on the paper 'All this, I think, is embodied in my last paper at Maryvale'—presumably referring to 'Ultimate Resolution of certainty of Faith' mentioned in n. 199 *supra*.
201 Ibidem; cf. John Henry Newman, *Certain Difficulties felt by Anglicans in Catholic Teaching*, London, 1888, Vol. I, pp. 269f., where the same view is expressed. The volume first appeared in 1850.
202 John Henry Newman, *Loss and Gain, The Story of a Convert*, London, 1962, (the volume was first published in 1848), p. 195; cf. p. 207: 'Reason has gone first, faith is to follow.'
203 Ibid., p. 218.
204 Ibid., p. 187; cf. pp. 166, 208, 211; cf. also *Certain Difficulties felt by Anglicans*, Vol. I, p. xii, 'Faith depends upon the will, not really upon any process of reasoning, and . . . conversion is a single work of divine grace'.
205 Or. MSS. A.18.11. 'February 1851. For a Preface (say) to a new volume.' Or. MSS. A.30.11. 'September 25, 1851. An Argument for the Catholic Religion'.
206 Or. MSS. B.7.4. 'The Oratory, Birmingham, August 20, 1866. From Fr. Edward Caswall's notes on Lectures with the Father, 1853'.
207 Ibid.; marginal note in Newman's own hand.
208 (i) Or. MSS. A.23.1. 'April 30, 1853'.
(ii) 1st sheet now in Or. MSS. A. 18.11 (it was in B. 9. 11.); 2nd sheet in Or. MSS. A. 18.11; 3rd and 4th sheets in Or. MSS. A. 30. 11. 'May 13, 1853: "Analysis of Religious Inquiry according to the foregoing Rules" '.
(iii) Or. MSS. B. 7. 4. '16 December 1853. On the *Certainty* of Faith'.
209 In the *Grammar of Assent* Newman holds that assent is invariably unconditional and absolute.
210 Newman gives both words in his manuscript.
211 All the above quotations are from the paper dated 'May 13, 1853'. cf. note 208 *supra* for details.
212 Cf. Newman's claim in *The Idea of a University*, p. 61–126 *passim*, that theology is a science.
213 In the G.A. this is the 'Illative Sense'.
214 Or. MSS. B. 7. 4.; cf. letter dated 7 October 1853 in *Letters and Diaries*, Vol XV, pp. 456f.

215 Or. MSS. A. 23. 1. 'In festo S. Gregorii. 1857. *Opus Magnum*. In nomine P. F. et S. S.'.
216 Cf. *The Idea of a University*, p. 66: The being of God is 'inferred by an inductive process, brought home to us by metaphysical necessity, urged on us by the suggestions of our conscience'; and John Henry Newman, *Sermons Preached on Various Occasions*, 6th edition, London, 1887, pp. 64f. (The first edition was published in 1857).
217 *Book of Sundries*, preserved at the Oratory, Edgbaston; *Proof of Theism*, 7 November, 1859.; cf. the article on this *Book of Sundries* by E. A. Sillem, *Cardinal Newman, A New Discovery*. Newman was working at this time on a metaphysics of religion to meet the challenge of rationalist liberalism. He never finished the work.
218 Ibidem; cf. *Book of Sundries*, note dated 'July 15 1860' where Newman rejects proofs of the existence of God from the material world: 'I cannot comprehend how anyone can deduce the Being of God from the visible world, taken by itself, for this reason, that (putting aside the difficulty of assuming design because there is order) order has only reference to form, not to matter, and if order proves Mind, phenomena quite as forcibly prove Matter. In other words, the visible world leads to a dualism—for where do we learn from the visible world that Mind can create Matter?'
219 H. L. Mansel, *The Limits of Religious Thought*, cf. p. 15f., *supra*.
220 Ibid., p. v.
221 Ibid., p. 126; cf. p. 67f., 94ff., 142ff.
222 Ibid., p. 127; cf. p. 143.
223 Correspondence between Newman and Meynell between 20 December 1859 and 19 May 1860. Preserved at the Oratory, Edgbaston, are letters from Newman dated 20 December 1859; 23 January 1860; 9 May 1860; and one marked 'not sent'; and letters to Newman dated 'No date' (reply to Newman's letter of 20 December 1859); 22 January 1860; 11 May 1860, 19 May 1860.
224 The reference is to Newman's *Oxford University Sermons*, letter dated 20 December 1859.
225 Letter dated 23 January, 1860.
226 (i) Or. MSS. A. 30. 11. 'January 5. 1860. On the popular, practical, personal evidence for the truth of Revelation'.
(ii) Or. MSS. A. 30. 11. 'Jan. 12. 1860. *The Evidences of Religion*'.
227 Or. MSS. A. 30. 11. 'January 5. 1860 . . .'
228 Or. MSS. A. 30. 11. 'Jan. 12. 1860 . . .'
229 Letter dated 9 May 1860.
230 Letter from Meynell dated 19 May 1860.
231 *Book of Sundries*, note dated 'Sept 17, 1861'.
232 Or. MSS. A. 18. 11. 'Ventnor Oct. 12. 1861. Schema totius operis'.
233 *Book of Sundries*, note dated 'July 7, 1863'. This was written on the left hand page opposite the note dated 'Sept 17, 1861' quoted above.
234 Or. MSS. A. 30. 11. 'Sept. 1863. Chapter II'. The date in this heading is written in pencil and the note closes with the date 'December 1, 1863'.

235 Note dated 30 October, 1870 in *The Journal, 1859–79*.
236 Or. MSS. A. 30. 11. 'Decr. 12. 1863'.
237 Or. MSS. A. 30. 11. 'Decr. 3. 1863'. This was rewritten in the papers referred to in the note 236 *supra* and the note 238 *infra*.
238 Or. MSS. A. 30. 11. '#2 The Conceivable'. This is an expanded rewriting and development of the last two paragraphs of the paper of 3 December, 1863, (see note 237 *supra*) and is presumably the second section of the paper whose first section is dated 12 December, 1860 (see note 236 *supra*).
239 Ibidem.
240 Cf. *Apologia*, pp. 65f., 246, 269ff.
241 Ibid., p. 65.
242 Ibid., p. 66.
243 Cf. John Henry Newman, *An Internal Argument for Christianity*, June 1866, reprinted in *Discussions and Arguments*, pp. 364f.; and *Books of Sundries*, note dated 'March 21, 1861'.
244 *Apologia*, p. 66; cf. *Autiobiographical Memoir* written by Newman in 1874 and revised in 1876 and published in *Autobiographical Writings*, p. 81.
245 *Apologia*, p. 169; cf. pp. 168f., and p. 103 where Newman writes, 'who can know himself, and the multitude of subtle influences which act upon him?'
246 Ibid., p. 193.
247 Ibid., p. 194.
248 Ibidem.
249 Ibid., p. 206; cf. pp. 207, 217, 219f.
250 Ibid., p. 227.
251 Cf. ibid., p. 228, pp. 233ff., where he defends belief in the infallibility of the Church.
252 Or. MSS. A. 30. 11. '(A Comparison of the Moral Sense and Certitude. 1865)'. The fragment itself is numbered 'p. 17'.
253 Or. MSS. A. 30. 11. 'June 26, 1865. Certainty not inconsistent with probable evidence'; cf. *An Internal Argument for Christianity*, reprinted in *Discussions and Arguments*, p. 371.
254 Or. MSS. A. 23. 1. '20 July 1865. (*Essay on Certitude*)'.
255 Or. MSS. A. 23. 1. 'September 25, 1865 (*Meaning of Certitude*)'.
256 *The Journal. 1859–79*, note dated 30 October, 1870, published in *Autobiographical Writings*, p. 270.
257 Cf. ibid., pp. 271ff., where, in a note dated 'October 14, 1874', Newman says that it took him four years to write the *Grammar of Assent*.
258 *Book of Sundries*, note dated 'January 28, 1867'; cf. note dated 'January 24, 1867'.
259 Or. MSS. A. 30. 11. 'Chapter iii § 1. On apprehension and assent through the imagination, considered in reference to the being of a God. April 26/68, again May 5/68, again Sept. 7/68.' There is a note added in pencil 'On concrete apprehension and real assent in relation to the'.

NOTES

260 Letter to Meynell on 2 July, 1869. The whole correspondence is published in Zeno, op. cit., pp. 227-270.
261 *The Journal. 1859-79*, note dated 'October 14, 1874', published in *Autobiographical Writings*, p. 272; cf. p. 67 and n. 42 *supra*.
262 C. B. Keogh, *Introduction to the Philosophy of Cardinal Newman*, Université Catholique de Louvain, 1950. There is a copy of the thesis at the Oratory, Edgbaston.
263 *Apologia*, pp. 27, 45.
264 Cf. ibid., p. 45f.
265 Ibid., p. 31; cf. Boekraad, op. cit., pp. 103ff.
266 Cf. *Essays Critical and Historical*, Vol II, p. 57: 'What a Note of the Church is the mere production of a man like Butler, . . . and how strange it is, if it be as it seems to be, that the real influence of his work is only just now beginning!' Butler's *Analogy* is referred to in *Development of Doctrine*, *The Idea of a University* and G.A.
267 Letter to Canon Walker dated 24 October, 1864 and printed in Boekraad, op. cit., p. 288; cf. also letters of 8 December, 1846 and 7 October, 1853, in *Letters and Diaries* where Newman reveals his difference from Butler —see also G.A. 179f. (237).
268 Paley is mentioned in *Essays Critical and Historical, Discussions and Arguments, Justification, Development of Doctrine, The Idea of a University* and G.A.
269 These quotations are from G.A. p. 323 (425); *The Idea of a University*, p. 140; and *Stray Essays*, p. 105.
270 G.A. p. 323f., (425ff.).
271 Cf. *Apologia*, pp. 25f.
272 Cf. ibid., pp. 29f.
273 Cf. ibid., pp. 31f.; quoted on p. 68 *supra*.
274 Cf. *The Idea of a University*, pp. 101, 128, 136, 263, 275, 278, 295, 310, 366, 392f.
275 Cf. G.A. pp. 200 (263), 202 (266), 257 (338), 259 (341), 268ff. (353ff.), 314f. (414f.); *The Idea of a University*, pp. 135f.
276 *The Idea of a University*, pp. 135f., 373, 379.
277 J. H. Newman, *Poetry with reference to Aristotle's Poetics*, January 1829, reprinted in *Essays Critical and Historical*, Vol. I, pp. 1-26.
278 Keogh, op. cit., p. 22.
279 Culler, op. cit., p. 36.
280 G.A. p. 282 (372); cf. p. 274 (361); *The Idea of a University*, pp. 190, 227, 258.
281 G.A., p. 266 (350); cf. *The Idea of a University*, p. 302.
282 J. H. Newman, *The Miracles of Scripture Compared with Those Reported Elsewhere, as Regards Their Nature, Credibility and Evidence*, first published in *Encyclopaedia Metropolitana*, 1826, and republished in *Two Essays on Scripture Miracles and on Ecclesiastical*, London, 1870, *passim*; *Oxford University Sermons*, pp. 185, 195, 231; G.A. 62 (81), 232f. (306f.).
283 G.A. p. 122 (162); but cf. *The Idea of a University*, p. 302: 'Locke is scarcely an honour to us in the standard of truth.'

284 Cf. G.A. 121ff. (160ff.); Newman made similar criticisms of Locke in *Development of Doctrine*, p. 327ff.
285 G.A. 122 (162).
286 *The Idea of a University*, pp. 176ff.
287 Cf. *Apologia*, p. 39; Zeno, op. cit., p. 60–63.
288 Cf. *Letters and Diaries*, note by C. S. Dessain to a letter of 8 December 1846 which suggests that Newman used Dugald Stewart's definition of the term 'probable'. We also know from Newman's private papers that he had studied Mill's *Logic*—cf. note 32 *supra*.
289 Letter to W. S. Lilly in 1884, quoted by Keogh, op. cit., p. 28.
290 Quoted by A. E. Baker, *Prophets for an Age of Doubt*, London, 1934, p. 35. It is described as being part of 'the Chronological Notes for 1835'; cf. *Oxford University Sermons*, p. 23, n.2.
291 Letter to R. H. Froude on 28 January 1836, found in A. Mozley, *Letters and Correspondence of John Henry Newman*, London 1891, pp. 154ff.
292 *The British Critic and Quarterly Theological Review*, article *State of Religious Parties*, April 1839, No. L; reprinted in *Essays Critical and Historical*, Vol. I, pp. 263ff., as *Prospects of the Anglican Church*, p. 269.
293 G.A. p. 231f.(305); cf. also Culler, op. cit., pp. 176, 181, for further evidence.
294 *Stray Essays*, p. 55.
295 *The Idea of a University*, p. 354.
296 Or. MSS. A.30.11. 'On apprehension and assent through the imagination considered in reference to the being of a God. April 26/68, again May 5/68, again September 7/68'.
297 Keogh, op. cit., p. 26f.
298 Cf. *Via Media*, Vol. I, p. 20; *Development of Doctrine*, pp. 192ff., 201ff.
299 G.A. p. 234ff. (307ff.); cf. *Parochial and Plain Sermons*, Vol. IV, p. 286.
300 Ibid., p. 218 n.1 (287 n.1).
301 Ibid., p. 286 (377).
302 Ibid., p. 236f. (311f.).
303 *The Idea of a University*, p. 430.
304 Letter to W. S. Lilly in 1884, quoted by Keogh, op. cit., p. 28; cf. p. 62 and n. 8 *supra*.
305 Cf. S. C. Carpenter, *Church and People* . . . p. 140 where it says that Newman 'only read' Kant 'in his extreme old age'. This could have been after 1884 and, in any case, there is no reason to believe that Kant was a source for any of Newman's ideas.
306 Cf. p. 61f., *supra* for secondary authorities used by Newman which would have provided him with some knowledge of German thought.
307 Newman is happy to acknowledge where others hold the same views, —for example, see his remarks about Aquinas (Or. MSS. B. 9. 11. 'On St. Thomas's View of Faith'), about Coleridge (quoted p. 90 *supra*) and about Butler (as in the letter dated 7 October 1853).
308 Keogh, op. cit., p. 318.
309 Cf. the comment of S. C. Carpenter, op. cit., p. 140, that Newman

'was not constructive in the sense of knowing and using all that was being said by his contemporaries. Lord Acton said of him as late as 1884 that he knew "what he might have known in the time of Waterland and Butler"... He lived all his life in a certain degree of intellectual isolation'. We have argued, however, that this is not wholly true—Newman knew what others were saying but did not try to develop his thought directly from or counter to their ideas. Primarily his thought on faith was concerned with his own problems. Cf. also E. A. Sillem, *Cardinal Newman's Grammar of Assent on Conscience as a Way to God*, in *The Heythrop Journal*, Vol. V, No. 4, October 1964, pp. 308f., which speaks of Newman's suspicion of metaphysics.

310 *Complete Dictionary of the English Language*, edited by Webster, revised by Goodrich and Porter, London, 1864.
311 *The Imperial Dictionary*, edited by J. Ogilvie, revised by C. Annandale, 1883; *A New English Dictionary*, edited by Murray, Oxford, 1901.
312 G.A. p. 5 (6); cf. pp. 144ff. (190ff.).
313 Ibid., p. 135 (179).
314 Ibid., p. 6 (7); cf. p. 176 (232f.).
315 Ibid., p. 197 (259).
316 Cf. ibid., p. 90f. (119f.).
317 Ibid., p. 4 (5).
318 Cf. ibidem. This use of the term 'assertion' is not pursued by Newman who later uses the term to describe situations where we claim that a proposition is true which we do not apprehend—'assent is more than assertion just by this much, that it is accompanied by some apprehension of the matter asserted'—p. 11 (13).
319 Ibid., p. 197 (259).
320 Ibid., p. 142 (188); cf. p. 4 (5).
321 Ibid., pp. 167ff. (221ff.).
322 Cf. ibid., p. 13 (15).
323 Cf. ibid., p. 34 (43).
324 Ibid., p. 135 (179); cf. pp. 12(14), 13(16).
325 Ibid., p. 142 (188).
326 Cf. ibid., pp. 144f. (191f.).
327 The distinction in fact is the same as that between real doubt and methodological doubt, a distinction which Newman does not make: cf. P. Flanagan, *Newman, Faith and the Believer*, London 1946, p. 128.
328 G.A. p. 119 (157); cf. pp. 11 (13), 45 (59), 130 (172), 133 (176).
329 Cf. ibid., pp. 7 (8), 30 (38), 119 (157), 131 (174).
330 Ibid., p. 132 (175).
331 Cf. ibid., pp. 45f. (58f.).
332 Cf. ibid., p. 5 (6).
333 Ibid., p. 146 (194).
334 Ibid., p. 147 (195).
335 Ibid., p. 142 (189).
336 Ibid., p. 161 (212).

337 Cf. ibid., p. 148 (196), 159 (210).
338 Cf. ibid., p. 142f. (188f.).
339 Ibid., p. 173 (229).

Notes on Part III: The Condition of Assent: Pages 97–124

1 G.A. pp. 3–115(3–153).
2 Ibid., p. 19(23); cf. p. 195ff. *infra*, for a discussion of the distinction between 'real' and 'notional' apprehension.
3 Ibid., p. 254(334); cf. Newman's quotation from Scott's *Peveril of the Peak* that the heroine 'felt "an instinctive apprehension that all was not right" ' (254/335) and his reference to a person's 'apprehension of sacred objects' (255/336).
4 Ibid., p. 16 (20).
5 Ibid., p. 84f. (111f.).
6 Ibid., p. 87 (114f.).
7 Ibid., p. 16f. (20).
8 Ibid., p. 7 (9).
9 Ibid., p. 11 (13).
10 Ibid., p. 7 (9).
11 Ibid., p. 17 (20).
12 Ibid., p. 11 (13).
13 Ibid., p. 16 (19). Newman also notes that the term 'understanding' can stand for 'the faculty or act of conceiving a proposition' (p. 16/19) but this usage is not significant for his thesis.
14 Cf. the distinction made between the terms in *Complete Dictionary of the English Language*, edited by Webster, revised by Goodrich and Porter, London, 1864. Here it is said that '*Apprehend* denotes the *laying hold* of a thing mentally, so as to understand it clearly, at least in part. *Comprehend* denotes the embracing or understanding it in all its compass and extent. We may *apprehend* many truths which we do not comprehend.' A similar distinction is found in *The Imperial Dictionary*, edited by J. Ogilvie, revised by C. Annandale, 1883.
15 Newman refers to the incompleteness in apprehension when he states that 'it is possible to apprehend without understanding' (G.A., p. 16/19). As an example he cites a situation where the mind gathers what is meant by each individual part of a complex relationship and yet is unable to grasp the relationship as a whole (ibid. 16/19f.).
16 Ibid., pp. 11f. (14).
17 Ibid., p. 119 (157); Locke makes a similar point in his *Second Vindication of the Reasonableness of Christianity*; cf. *Works*, London, 1768, Vol. III, pp. 146bff.
18 Ibid., p. 7 (8).
19 Ibid., p. 11 (13).
20 Ibid., p. 68 (90).
21 Ibid., p. 7 (8); cf. p. 68f. (90); cf. also Richard Whately, *Elements of Logic*,

Eighth Edition, Revised, London, 1844, pp. 31f., where the same view is expressed. It appears from a letter written by Newman to Monsell on 10 October 1852 that Newman wrote this passage as it now stands—for the letter see Boekraad, op. cit., p. 91f.
22 Cf. G.A. 11f. (14).
23 Ibid., pp. 35f. (45f.).
24 Ibidem.
25 Ibid., pp. 35f. (46).
26 P. Tillich, *Systematic Theology*, Vol. I, London, 1953, p. 269.
27 It follows from this that the contemporary enquiry into the meaning and logic of theological statements is a crucial one for religious faith. Our religious assents (i.e. beliefs) depend upon the possibility and nature of our understanding the meaning of theological statements.
28 Cf. D. Nicholls, op. cit., S.J.T., September 1966, p. 287 for criticism of this view.
29 G.A. p. 114 (151).
30 Cf. ibid., pp. 113ff. (150ff.).
31 Thus those who left the Roman Catholic Church after the Vatican Council of 1870 were logically justified in refusing to accept *de fide* implications of previous, particular doctrinal beliefs. The fact that Newman rejects this position may be due to ecclesiastical concerns which have prejudiced his logical perception. The case of the Roman Catholic's assent to the truth of what the Church says is a different matter. This is not an assent to the particular doctrines of the Church but an assent to what the Church as such says is true. If this assent is made, nothing that the Church says can logically affect it. On the other hand, the individual making it only gives indirect assent to what the Church says: his assent is to the truth of the dictates of the Church, not to the content of those dictates.
32 Cf. p. 129f. *infra*.
33 Cf. G.A. p. 12f. (15).
34 Ibid., pp. 75ff. (98ff.).
35 Ibid., p. 76 (100).
36 Cf. Newman's correspondence with Charles Meynell between 20 December 1859 and 19 May 1860. Here Newman writes that 'I do not say *truth* is contradictory to *truth*—this is absurd, but transcendent truths may admit of but *partial* communication to us—and that under the images of earthly things, which are on the one hand the only possible means of conveying such a truth to our minds, yet on the other *because* they are earthly are not true representations in the fulness of their meaning. . . . And so Justice, as we see it exercised on earth and by men, is inconsistent with Mercy, as we witness it here—and therefore we think still more that *Infinite* Justice is opposed to Infinite Mercy—but All-mercifulness, as it exists in God, or All-Justice, is not compounded of exactly *our* idea of mercy or justice, and our idea of infinity. . . . The very word "*contradiction*" has reference to *language*, not to *fact*.' (Letter dated 9 May 1860).

Also cf. the unpublished paper headed 'Sept. 1863. Chapter II' (Or. MSS. A.30.11.).
37 G.A. 12 (14f.).
38 Ibid., pp. 11f. (14).
39 Ibidem.
40 Cf. ibidem.
41 Cf. ibid., pp. 12f. (14f.).
42 Ibid., p. 13 (15).
43 Cf. ibid., pp. 13f. (15ff.).
44 Newman does not recognize that 'is true' is not a normal descriptive predicate but has the same peculiar logical function as predicates about existence. The phrase 'is true' in the statement that 'x is y is true' does not describe anything about 'x' and 'y' but concerns the logical status of the phrase 'x is y'.
45 G.A. p. 13 (15).
46 Cf. ibid., pp. 13f. (15f.).
47 Ibid., p. 14 (16); cf. p. 34 (43f.).
48 Ibid., p. 113 (150); cf. pp. 187f. (247f.); cf. also *Via Media*, Vol. I., pp. 255ff.
49 Cf. ibid., pp. 7f. (9f.).
50 Ibidem; cf. p. 19 (22) where Newman states that 'all things that are, are units'. Later, (pp. 120ff.), we shall discuss whether Newman is a nominalist.
51 Ibid., p. 8 (9). A meson, an atom, a molecule, a leg, and a table would all be proper objects of real apprehension so long as and so far as each of them could be related to actual experience. Thus the 'unit-ness' or individuality of the contents of 'the exterior world' is, for Newman, not the absolute unity of what cannot be further subdivided but the separateness of what are correlates of different experiences. We cannot be sure if Newman considers that we have a direct-apprehension of a table as such or whether he holds that such a direct-apprehension of a unit-reality is composed out of various experiences, which are put together in the mind to produce the object that is apprehended.
52 G.A. p. 8 (10); cf. p. 17 (20); pp. 18f. (22f.).
53 Ibid., p. 19 (23).
54 Ibid., p. 21 (25f.).
55 Ibid., p. 17 (20). An extensive list of what Newman considers to be included in the 'real' is given incidentally in the section devoted to the comparison of real and notional assents, (cf. pp. 68ff./89ff.). Here, under the description of 'real objects of whatever kind', are placed 'motives and actions, character and conduct, art, science, taste, morals, religion', while the title of 'things concrete' is used to cover, *inter alia*, 'objects' which have 'moral . . . properties' (cf. p. 67/87 where Newman writes of 'the moral experiences which perpetuate themselves in images'), and 'what is beautiful, useful, admirable, heroic; objects which kindle devotion, rouse the passions, and attach the affections' (p. 69/90). The wide reference which Newman gives to the concept of the 'real' means

that although he has the empiricist preference for the real against the notional, he can be called an 'empiricist' only if the term 'empirical' is extended to cover all the self's responses to external stimuli and is not restricted to physical sensations. For the position which Newman holds, the statement 'The picture is blue and beautiful' describes more of what is *real* than the statement 'The picture is blue'. Aesthetic, moral and valuative statements, provided that they have a specific reference, are thus to be held as 'real' as the description of something that has been seen and touched. All the self's feelings and experiences are for Newman a record of the nature of objective reality as directly perceived by it.

56 Ibid., p. 19 (23).
57 Ibidem.
58 Newman asserts that in memory we 'create nothing' but 'see the facsimiles of facts', (p. 20/24) but he later recognizes that memory is fallible. In this later passage he holds that it is not to be trusted universally but only in terms of specific acts of memory which themselves may be wrong, (cf. p. 47/60f.).
59 Cf. ibid., p. 20 (24f.).
60 Cf. ibid., pp. 21f. (26f.).
61 Ibid., p. 8 (9); 27 (34).
62 Cf. ibid., pp. 24f. (30f.).
63 Thus on p. 49ff. (64ff.) Newman argues that our 'presumptions' or 'first principles' are 'abstractions . . . in consequence of our particular experiences of qualities in the concrete'. Basic value terms (moral and aesthetic) are held to be derived from experience—in Newman's extended idea of experience.
64 Ibid., p. 7 (9); cf. p. 19 (22).
65 Ibid., p. 17 (20).
66 Ibid., p. 57 (75).
67 Ibid., p. 24 (30).
68 Ibid., p. 28 (34).
69 Ibid., p. 91 (119); cf. p. 10 (12).
70 Cf. ibid., p. 215 (283); p. 25 (31).
71 Cf. ibid., p. 32 (40).
72 Cf. ibid., p. 8 (10).
73 Ibid., pp. 77ff. (101ff.).
74 Ibid., p. 91 (119).
75 Ibid., p. 8 (10).
76 Cf. ibid., p. 9 (11).
77 Cf. ibid., pp. 57ff. (75ff.).
78 Ibid., p. 88 (115f.).
79 Ibid., p. 9 (11f.).
80 Ibid., p. 10 (12); cf. p. 29 (36f.).
81 Ibid., p. 95 (126); cf. p. 61 (80); pp. 353ff. (464ff.).
82 Ibid., pp. 9f. (11f.); cf. p. 29 (36).
83 Ibid., p. 61 (80).

84 According to Newman the vividness and force of a real apprehension vary according to the sense or senses that are involved in producing the image. In general Newman finds that 'the impress . . . of the experiences which come to us through our other senses' are 'not so vivid' as those which come to us through our sense of sight, (p. 20/24); cf. p. 29 (36f.).
85 Cf. ibid., pp. 94ff. (124ff.).
86 Ibid., pp. 98f. (130).
87 Cf. ibid., p. 99 (131) where Newman expresses a similar view in relation to the doctrine of God: 'Our image of Him never is one, but broken into numberless partial aspects. . . . We know one truth about Him and another truth—but we cannot image both of them together'.
88 Ibid., p. 106 (140).
89 Ibid., p. 75 (98).
90 Ibid., p. 27 (34).
91 Ibid., p. 91 (120).
92 Ibid., p. 75 (98f.); cf. p. 87 (115) where a child is said to have 'an image of the good God. . . . before it has been reflected on, and before it is recognized by him as a notion'.
93 Ibid., p. 27 (33); cf. p. 215 (282).
94 Ibid., p. 26 (32).
95 Ibid., p. 36 (46f.).
96 Ibid., p. 39f. (50); cf. note 36 *supra*.
97 Ibid., p. 296 (389f.); cf. E. A. Sillem, *Cardinal Newman's Grammar of Assent on Conscience as a Way to God*, pp. 377ff.
98 Ibid., pp. 78f. (102ff.). There is no argument here from appearance to existence: it is a basic assumption that the phenomena are of 'things' and that from the phenomena we learn not only the being but also the quality of what lies behind them.
99 Ibid., pp. 83f. (109f.).
100 Cf. ibid., pp. 88f. (115ff.); pp. 92f. (122ff.).
101 Ibid., p. 88 (116).
102 Cf. ibid., p. 92 (121).
103 Cf. ibid., p. 85 (111f.); pp. 48ff. (62f.).
104 Ibid., p. 78 (102).
105 The fact, however, that he speaks of a 'certitude' shows that there is a possible doubt about the relation between our experiences and what they are of. Newman admits (cf. p. 71/93) that we only say we are 'certain' after we have been faced with a doubt.
106 Ibid., p. 15 (18).
107 Ibid., p. 57 (75); cf. p. 68 (89); p. 90 (119).
108 Ibid., p. 90 (119); cf. p. 57 (75).
109 Cf. ibid., p. 30 (37).
110 Ibid., p. 64 (83).
111 Cf. ibid., pp. 63f. (83f.).
112 Ibid., p. 66 (87).

113 Ibid., p. 66 (86).
114 Cf. ibid., pp. 66f. (87f.).
115 Ibid., p. 30 (37).
116 Ibid., p. 28 (35); cf. pp. 14ff. (16f.); 30f. (38).
117 Ibid., p. 32 (40).
118 Ibid., p. 63 (82).
119 Cf. ibid., p. 68 (89).
120 Cf. ibid., p. 162 (214f.).
121 Ibid., p. 61 (80).
122 Ibid., p. 160 (212).
123 Ibid., p. 78 (102).
124 Ibid., p. 43 (55).
125 Cf. ibid., p. 105 (138f.).
126 Cf. ibid., p. 61 (79f.).
127 Ibid., p. 95 (126).
128 Cf. ibid., pp. 43ff. (55ff.); 95 (126).
129 In *Appendix I* we examine Newman's classification of the different types of assent into real and notional assents.
130 C. C. J. Webb, *A History of Philosophy*, London, 1915, p. 126.
131 G. Leff, *Medieval Thought*, Penguin Books, 1958, p. 104.
132 G.A. pp. 7f. (9f.); cf. p. 19 (22f.).
133 Cf. ibid., p. 57 (75).
134 Cf. J. H. Walgrave, op. cit., pp. 83f.; Zeno, op. cit., pp. 69ff.; M. C. D'Arcy, *The Nature of Belief*, Dublin, 1958, pp. 102ff.
135 Walgrave, op. cit., pp. 85ff.; cf. Zeno, op. cit., p. 65.
136 G.A. p. 49f. (64f.).
137 Cf. ibid., p. 264 (347). A list of other texts expressing this idea is to be found in Boekraad, op. cit., p. 185, n.198.
138 Leff, op. cit., p. 284, from Ockham, *Sentences*, I, 2, 7; cf. *Summa Totius Logicae*, I, xv.
139 Cf. Boekraad, op. cit., pp. 182ff.
140 Walgrave, op. cit., pp. 84ff.
141 D'Arcy, op. cit., p. 102.
142 Zeno, op. cit., p. 68f.
143 Cf. G.A. p. 122 (162).
144 D'Arcy, op. cit., p. 102.
145 G.A. p. 8 (9f.).
146 Cf. R. Whately, op. cit., p. 134.
147 Cf. Boekraad, op. cit., p. 91 where he quotes from an unpublished manuscript of Newman which is preserved at the Oratory, Edgbaston.
148 Cf. Whately, op. cit., pp. 276ff.
149 *Apologia*, p. 31.
150 Cf. p. 89 *supra*.
151 Cf. A. Dwight Culler, op. cit., p. 36.
152 Cf. Zeno, op. cit., p. 64; cf. also Or. MSS. A.30.11., 'Chapter iii, §I. On Apprehension. . . .'

153 Boekraad, op. cit., pp. 184, 187.
154 Cf. ibid., pp. 187f.; Zeno, op. cit., pp. 65f.
155 D'Arcy, op. cit., p. 103.
156 G.A. p. 43 (56).
157 Cf. ibid., p. 77 (101) where God is said to be 'like Himself, unlike all things besides Himself'.
158 Cf. ibid., p. 96 (127f.); p. 102 (135).
159 Such a distinct picture is impossible because we find the meaning of each part of the doctrine in relation to all the other parts. Thus the terms 'one', 'three', and 'person' cannot have their everyday meaning in the doctrine of the Trinity, for otherwise the doctrine would be a nonsensical self-contradiction. The terms are used in this doctrine with peculiar meanings which only approximate to their everyday meanings. This means that what the terms of the individual elements of the doctrine picture in everyday situations is not what they picture when they are used in the doctrine of the Trinity.
160 G.A. p. 9 (12).
161 Ibid., p. 29 (36).
162 A poetic expression of this is to be found in Tennyson's *In Memoriam*, xxxvi,

>   For Wisdom dealt with mortal powers,
> Where truth in closest words shall fail,
> When truth embodied in a tale
>   Shall enter in at lowly doors.

Commenting on this, Horton Davies writes 'Deeds beget deeds, but dreams only provoke reveries', (Horton Davies, *Worship and Theology in England*, Vol. IV, Oxford, 1962, p. 179).

NOTES ON PART IV: THE ANTECEDENT TO ASSENT: PAGES 125–160

1 Cf. the distinction in F. R. Tennant, *The Nature of Belief*, London, 1943, p. 17.
2 Cf. G.A. p. 200 (263); cf. R. Whately, op. cit., p. 6 which sees logic as 'begun and completed' by Aristotle. This is in a passage which was written up by Newman.
3 Cf. G.A. pp. 125f., (167f.); p. 251 (331); p. 261 (343); p. 273 (359); and the use of the phrases 'informal inference' and 'natural inference'.
4 Ibid., p. 119 (157). Here Newman uses 'inference' in our sense of 'reasoning'.
5 Ibidem. We shall examine later what Newman means by describing the conclusion of a reasoning process as 'conditional'.
6 Ibid., p. 129 (171f.).
7 Ibidem.

8 Ibid., p. 160 (212).
9 Ibid., p. 129 (171).
10 Ibid., p. 145 (192).
11 Ibid., p. 32 (40).
12 Ibid., p. 164 (216).
13 Cf. ibid., pp. 164ff., (216ff.).
14 Ibid., pp. 142f., (188f.).
15 Cf. ibid., p. 143 (190); p. 125 (166).
16 Ibid., p. 6 (6); cf. p. 144 (190f.).
17 Cf. ibid., p. 130 (172).
18 Ibid., p. 127 (169).
19 Ibid., p. 128 (170). In the second quotation Newman actually says that argument 'is not always able to command our assent'. That this implies that it is sometimes 'able to command our assent' is shown by the way Newman develops the theme on p. 128 (170).
20 Ibidem.
21 Ibid., p. 35 (45).
22 Cf. ibid., pp. 130f., (172f.).
23 Ibid., p. 7 (8).
24 Ibid., p. 127 (169).
25 Ibid., p. 197 (259).
26 Ibid., p. 128 (169).
27 Ibid., pp. 125f., (167).
28 Ibid., p. 126 (167f.).
29 Ibid., p. 119 (157).
30 Ibid., pp. 130f., (172ff.).
31 Ibid., p. 132 (175).
32 Ibidem.
33 Ibid., p. 122 (162).
34 Ibid., pp. 122f., (162f.); (from Locke, *Essay concerning Human Understanding*, Book 4, Chapter XIX, Section 1.)
35 Ibid., p. 124 (164).
36 Locke, *Essay concerning Human Understanding*, Book 1, Chapter I, Section 2.
37 G.A. p. 124 (164).
38 Cf. Locke, *Essay concerning Human Understanding*, Book 1, Chapter I, Section 2, quoted *supra*.
39 Locke, *Essay concerning Human Understanding*, Book 4, Chapter XVI.
40 Ibid., Chapter XIX.
41 Ibid., Chapter XIX, Section 1.
42 Ibid., Chapter XVIII.
43 Ibid., Chapter XVIII, Section 7.
44 Ibid., Chapter XIX.
45 G.A. p. 323 (425).
46 Ibidem.
47 Originally letters published in *The Times* in February 1841 and afterwards published as a pamphlet and reprinted in *Discussions and*

Arguments. The letter quoted was entitled 'Secular Knowledge not a Principle of Action'; cf. *Discussions and Arguments*, pp. 292ff.
48 G.A. p. 72 (94f.).
49 Ibid., p. 198 (260).
50 Ibid., p. 200 (263); cf. Locke's criticism of 'inference' in op. cit., Book 4, Chapter XVII.
51 Ibidem.
52 Ibidem. For Newman logic is essentially that of Aristotle, cf. p. 125 and n. 2 *supra*; Boekraad, op. cit., p. 155f.; Zeno, op. cit., pp. 34f.
53 G.A. pp. 200f., (263f.).
54 Ibidem; cf. pp. 10 (12); 31f. (39f.); 203f. (267f.); 211 (277f.); p. 215 (283).
55 Ibid., pp. 33ff., (42ff.).
56 Ibid., pp. 33ff., (42ff.).
57 Ibid., p. 7 (8).
58 Ibid., p. 68 (90).
59 Cf. ibid., p. 197 (259f.); p. 201 (264f.).
60 Ibid., p. 3 (3).
61 Cf. ibid., p. 130 (172) where Newman writes about 'an incontrovertible conclusion on the condition of incontrovertible premisses'; cf. also R. Whately, op. cit., p. 29. This is in a passage which was written up by Newman. Newman does not contradict this in the *Grammar of Assent*.
62 G.A. p. 205 (269f.).
63 Ibid., pp. 313f., (413).
64 Ibidem.
65 Cf. ibidem.
66 Cf. ibid., p. 275 (362).
67 Ibid., p. 199 (261f.).
68 Ibid., p. 127 (169).
69 Ibid., p. 130 (172).
70 Ibid., p. 131 (173).
71 Ibid., p. 71f. (93ff.).
72 Ibid., p. 70 (92).
73 Cf. ibid., pp. 200ff., (263ff.).
74 Ibid., p. 99 (131f.).
75 Cf. R. Whately, op. cit., p. 246 where it is stated that 'no *matter of fact* can be mathematically demonstrated.' This is in a passage which was written up by Newman.
76 Cf. G.A. p. 99 (131f.).
77 Ibid., p. 312 (410). This follows Aquinas, *Summa Theologica*, Part I, Qu. 1, Art. 8.
78 Cf. G.A. p. 7 (8).
79 Cf. ibid., p. 164 (217).
80 Ibid., p. 70 (92).
81 Ibid., p. 218 (287).
82 Cf. ibid., p. 31 (39).
83 Cf. ibid., p. 128 (170).

84 Webster, *Complete Dictionary of the English Language*, 1864; also Murray, *A New English Dictionary*, 1901.
85 Locke, *Essay concerning Human Understanding*, Book 4, Chapter XVII, Section 2.
86 R. Whately, op. cit., p. 28.
87 G.A. p. 251 (330).
88 Ibid., p. 260 (342).
89 Ibid., p. 268 (353).
90 Ibid., pp. 262f., (345).
91 Ibid., p. 268 (353f.).
92 Ibid., p. 272 (359); cf. Locke, op. cit., Book 4, Chapter XVII.
93 Ibid., pp. 197f., (260); cf. Locke, *Essay concerning Human Understanding*, Book 4, Chapter XVII, Section 4, where this natural reasoning capacity in man is described and evaluated. It is also called 'illation'.
94 Cf. ibid., p. 253 (333).
95 Cf. ibid., p. 222 (291f.).
96 Ibid., pp. 250f., (330f.); cf. p. 222 (291f.); p. 229 (301f.).
97 Ibid., p. 216 (284).
98 Ibid., p. 222 (291).
99 Cf. ibid., p. 229 (301f.); pp. 273f., (360f.).
100 Cf. ibid., p. 244 (320f.).
101 Cf. ibid., pp. 246ff., (324ff.).
102 Ibid., p. 219 (288); cf. p. 221ff., (291ff.).
103 Ibid., p. 244 (321).
104 Ibid., p. 251 (330).
105 Ibid., p. 198 (260); cf. p. 251f., (331f.).
106 Ibid., p. 254 (334); cf. p. 198 (260).
107 Cf. ibid., p. 196 (260).
108 Cf. Amort, *Ethica Christiana*, p. 252.
109 G.A. p. 313 (412).
110 Ibid., pp. 263f., (346f.).
111 Ibid., p. 176 (233); cf. p. 253f., (332f.).
112 Ibid., p. 268 (353).
113 Ibid., p. 257 (339).
114 Cf. ibid., p. 272 (358f.).
115 To some degree they can also be traced to bad early teaching which gives rise to misconceptions about the significance of basic ideas.
116 G.A. p. 257 (339); cf. p. 272 (359); cf. also *Oxford University Sermons*, pp. 217f., for the use of military strategy to illustrate the illative sense.
117 Ibid., p. 223 (293).
118 The conclusions given are that Great Britain is an island, (pp. 223ff./294ff.), that Virgil, Terence, Horace, Livy, and Tacitus wrote the books generally ascribed to them (pp. 225ff.,/296ff.), and that I shall die (pp. 227ff.,/298ff.).
119 G.A. p. 228 (300f.); note that the activity of the Illative Sense is that of '*good* sense'.

120 Ibid., p. 241 (317).
121 Ibid., p. 230 (302).
122 Ibid., p. 232 (305f.).
123 Ibid., pp. 241f., (317f.); cf. p. 250 (329); p. 256 (337f.).
124 Cf. ibid., p. 230 (302); p. 243 (320).
125 Ibid., pp. 251f., (331).
126 Cf. ibid., p. 313 (412).
127 Cf. ibid., p. 7 (8).
128 Ibid., p. 251 (330f.).
129 Ibid., p. 219 (288); cf. 219ff., (288ff.); pp. 273f., (360f.).
130 Ibid., p. 222 (291); cf. p. 229 (301); pp. 243-250 (320-329).
131 Cf. ibid., p. 200 (263).
132 Cf. ibid., pp. 295-311 (389-408); p. 326 (428f.).
133 Ibid., p. 274 (361).
134 Ibid., p. 286 (377).
135 Cf. ibid., pp. 204f. (269f.).
136 Ibid., p. 288 (379).
137 Ibid., pp. 290f. (382).
138 Ibid., p. 46 (60).
139 Ibid., p. 49 (64).
140 Cf. ibid., pp. 313f. (412f.).
141 Ibid., p. 277 (364).
142 Ibid., p. 279 (367).
143 Ibid., p. 280 (368f.); cf. p. 314 (413).
144 Ibid., p. 289 (381).
145 Ibid., p. 282 (371).
146 Cf. statements apparently to the contrary quoted *supra* from p. 274 (361).
147 Cf. ibid., p. 262 (345); p. 268 (353).
148 Ibid., p. 273 (359).
149 Ibid., p. 230 (302).
150 Ibid., p. 241 (317).
151 Ibid., p. 293 (385f.).
152 Cf. op. cit., pp. 222f., (292f.).
153 Op. cit., p. 221 (291).
154 Op. cit., pp. 240f., (316); the references to Locke are to the *Essay concerning Human Understanding*, Book 4, Chapter XVI, Section 6, and Book 4, Chapter XV, Section 2.
155 Cf. ibid., p. 242ff. (318ff.).
156 Ibid., p. 250 (329).
157 Ibid., p. 312 (411).
158 Cf. ibid., pp. 228f. (300f.).
159 Cf. ibid., p. 217 (285); p. 225 (296); p. 241 (317); cf. also Newman's letter to Meynell on 17 November 1869 when he writes, 'You will be sadly disappointed in my "illative sense"—which is a grand word for a common thing.' This letter is published in Zeno, op. cit., p. 263; cf. also Zeno, op. cit., pp. 2f., 19f.

Notes on Part V: The Act of Assent: pages 161–185

1 Walgrave, op. cit., p. 25.
2 G.A. p. 80 (105).
3 Cf. ibid., p. 177 (233f.).
4 Ibid., pp. 81f., (105).
5 Ibid., p. 82 (107).
6 Ibid., p. 83 (109).
7 Cf. ibid., pp. 48f., (62f.); pp. 84f., (110f.).
8 Cf. ibid., p. 177 (233f.).
9 Ibid., p. 296 (389f.).
10 Ibid., p. 80 (105).
11 Ibid., p. 296 (390).
12 Cf. ibid., pp. 84f., (110f.).
13 Ibid., p. 177 (234).
14 Ibid., p. 81 (106).
15 Ibid., p. 84 (110); cf. the article by Edward A. Sillem, *Cardinal Newman's Grammar of Assent on Conscience as a Way to God*, pp. 377ff.
16 Cf. G.A. pp. 88f., (110ff.); pp. 92f., (122ff.).
17 Ibid., pp. 318f., (419); cf. S. Kierkegaard's discussion of religious and ethical principles in *Fear and Trembling*: Newman's position here expresses the moral rather than the religious viewpoint since it is the moral which is primary and normative. Alternatively, Newman can be held to be affirming what Kierkegaard calls the Religion of Immanence in contrast to the (authentically Christian) Religion of Paradox.
18 Ibid., p. 243 (320); Butler, *Analogy of Religion*, ed. 1836, p. 278.
19 Ibid., p. 319 (420).
20 Cf. ibid., p. 280 (369).
21 Ibid., p. 72 (94).
22 Ibid., p. 221 (291).
23 Ibid., p. 250 (329); cf. pp. 240f., (316).
24 Ibid., p. 312 (411).
25 Ibid., p. 242 (318).
26 Ibidem.
27 Ibid., p. 221 (291).
28 Ibid., p. 313 (412).
29 Ibidem. Thus Newman speaks of the preaching which leads to conversion as 'the moral instrument' of belief (p. 353/464). It is through his conscience that man makes his religious assents.
30 Cf. ibid., pp. 125ff., (166ff.).
31 In the *Grammar of Assent* Newman is primarily concerned to analyse the logic of acts of assent in general and not simply the case of the acts of assent of religious faith. Because of this he does not discuss the 'supernatural' aspect of faith in this book. His other published and unpublished writings, however, show that Newman considered that there was some aid of divine grace in the assent of faith. It is primarily at this

point of the urgings of conscience that divine grace plays its part in bringing us to the assent of faith.
32 E.g. my assents are not purely arbitrary. Even though they go beyond what reason can demonstrate, reason is taken into account before I grant them.
33 A practical example of this distinction can be found in the discussion of Douglas Hyde's religious pilgrimage in the article *The Faith Ladder* by B. E. Jones, in the *Expository Times*, May 1961.
34 G.A. p. 135 (179).
35 Ibid., p. 6 (6f.); cf. p. 176 (232).
36 Ibid., p. 135 (179); cf. p. 7 (8); p. 197 (259).
37 Ibid., p. 142 (188).
38 Ibid., p. 119 (157).
39 G.A. p. 61 (80).
40 Cf. ibid., pp. 119ff., (157ff.).
41 Thus Zeno, op. cit., mistakenly holds that Newman views certitude as a consequence of illation; cf. pp. 26f., 45, 101, 158, 173, 193.
42 G.A. p. 374 (491f.).
43 Cf. ibid., pp. 125ff., (166ff.).
44 Cf. ibid., p. 11 (13); p. 45 (59); p. 119 (157).
45 Cf. F. R. Tennant, *Philosophical Theology*, Cambridge, 1928, Vol. I., pp. 290ff.; also F. R. Tennant, *The Nature of Belief*, p. 5ff., for this distinction.
46 Cf. A. R. Vidler in *Objections to Christian Belief*, London, 1963, p. 66, where he says 'All I need point out here is the distinction, which is often overlooked, between the logical certainty of propositions and the psychological certitude of persons: between saying "it is certain" and "I am certain".'
47 G.A. p. 154 (203f.); cf. p. 159 (210); p. 164 (216).
48 Ibid., p. 147 (195); cf. p. 142 (188f.).
49 Cf. ibid., p. 164 (216).
50 For reasoning as an antecedent to certitude, cf. ibid., p. 173 (229); p. 179 (236); pp. 223ff., (292ff.); p. 228 (300f.); p. 240 (316); pp. 249f., (327ff.); p. 312 (411); and p. 374 (492).
51 Ibid., p. 158 (209); cf. p. 177 (234); p. 262 (344).
52 Cf. ibid., pp. 173ff., (228ff.).
53 Ibid., p. 176 (233).
54 Cf. ibid., p. 162f., (214f.).
55 Ibid., p. 148 (196).
56 Ibid., p. 172 (288).
57 Ibid., p. 246 (324).
58 Ibid., p. 262 (344).
59 Ibid., p. 223 (293).
60 Cf. Boekraad, op. cit., p. 199 n.236.
61 G.A. p. 149 (197).
62 Ibid., p. 167 (221).

63 Ibid., p. 154 (204).
64 Cf. ibid., p. 167 (221).
65 Ibid., p. 168 (222).
66 Cf. ibid., p. 194 (256).
67 Ibid., p. 168 (222).
68 Ibid., p. 148 (196).
69 Ibid., p. 172 (227).
70 Ibid., p. 173 (228).
71 Cf. ibid., pp. 175ff., (231ff.).
72 Ibid., p. 184 (243).
73 Ibid., pp. 167-196 (221-258).
74 Ibid., p. 167 (221); cf. p. 194 (256); p. 270 (355).
75 Cf. ibid., p. 168 (222).
76 Ibid., p. 184 (242f.).
77 Ibid., p. 191 (252).
78 Ibid., p. 183 (242).
79 Ibid., p. 167 (220).
80 P. Tillich, *Dynamics of Faith*, Harper, New York, 1958, pp. 1-4.
81 Cf. G.A. p. 180 (237f.).
82 Ibid., pp. 180f., (237ff.).
83 Ibid., pp. 180f., (238f.).

NOTES ON PART VI: CONCLUSION: PAGES 186-197

1 G.A. pp. 261f., (343f.). In this passage 'inference' is used in terms of what we have called 'reasoning' in general.
2 Walgrave, op. cit., p. 74.
3 Zeno, op. cit., p. 13.
4 Ibid., p. 86.
5 Keogh, op. cit., p. 60.
6 Ibid., p. 37.
7 Ibid., p. 58f.; cf. our discussion of Newman's criticism of Locke, p. 132ff. *supra*.
8 Boekraad, op. cit., p. 33.
9 Cf. ibid., p. 11f.
10 Cf. G.A. pp. 263ff., (346ff.); p. 313 (412).
11 Ibid., p. 264 (347).
12 Ibid., p. 47 (61).
13 Ibid., p. 263f., (347).
14 Cf. the article *The Logical Status of Religious Belief* by A. MacIntyre in *Metaphysical Beliefs, et al.* by A. MacIntyre, London, 1957.
15 Zeno, op. cit., p. 49 n.112 and p. 125.
16 H. D. Lewis, *Our Experience of God*, London, 1959, pp. 25f.
17 Aquinas, *Summa Theologica*, Pt. II-II, Qu. 2, Art. 9.

18 This is the position described in William James, *The Will to Believe*, cf. especially pp. 29ff., in the Dover Publications edition, 1956.
19 P. Tillich, *Systematic Theology*, Vol. 3, p. 138,—the italics are mine.
20 Cf. I. T. Ramsey, *Models and Mystery*, London, 1964, *passim*; cf. also Ramsey's article, *The Beatles as a Cosmic Disclosure*, in the *Guardian* newspaper for 10 September, 1964, where he writes that 'religious belief arises as such a response to a striking feature of some particular situation, when we talk of the "light dawning", the "ice breaking", the "penny dropping". . . . All such phrases as these point to the kind of situation I have called a 'disclosure".'
21 Thus I can choose to regard a painting seriously and to try to understand it. In this way I deliberately adopt a right frame of mind for it to 'captivate' me.
22 Newman does not discuss in the *Grammar of Assent* the distinction between *fides humana*—which we may choose to have—and *fides divina* —which is an absolute assent regarded as a work of divine grace; cf. n. 31 in Chapter V for the reason for this.
23 Cf. G.A. p. 46 (60), p. 205 (270).
24 Cf. ibid., p. 282 (371).
25 Wilhelm Herrmann, *Faith as Ritschl Defined It*, printed in *Faith and Morals*, London 1904.
26 P. Tillich, *The Courage to Be*, London, 1962, p. 168.
27 *Apologia*, p. 24.
28 Mozley, *Lectures* . . . , pp. 275, 300.
29 Cf. the logic of arguments which try to support faith-statements suggested in the attempt to prove the existence of the 'gardener' in J. Wisdom, *Gods*, reprinted in *Logic and Language*, (First Series), edited by A. Flew, Oxford, 1955, pp. 187ff.
30 For instance, when Kierkegaard examines the content and implications of the various stances which it is possible to adopt—the aesthetic, ethical, religion of immanence and religion of paradox stances—he suggests a possible way in which we might argue about them for we could compare the adequacy of these standpoints as a basis for a full life (though would this be ultimately to examine them in terms of the aesthetic stance?); cf. also H. A. Hodges, *Languages, Standpoints and Attitudes*, Oxford, 1953, for a discussion of how we can compare, judge, and change our standpoints and basic attitudes.

NOTES ON APPENDIX I

1 G.A. pp. 33ff. (42ff.).
2 Ibid., p. 67 (87).
3 Ibid., p. 33 (42).
4 Ibid., p. 149 (197).

5 Ibid., p. 162 (214).
6 Ibid., pp. 146f. (194f.).
7 Ibid., pp. 167ff. (221ff.).
8 Cf. ibid., p. 45 (58); p. 67 (87); pp. 147f. (195f.); p. 150 (198f.); pp. 167f. (221f.).
9 Ibid., p. 147 (195).
10 Cf. ibid., p. 148 (196); 167f. (221f.).
11 Ibid., p. 45 (58).
12 Ibid., p. 150 (199).
13 Ibid., p. 147 (195).
14 Ibid., p. 68 (89f.).
15 Ibid., p. 69 (90).
16 Cf. ibid., p. 5 (6); p. 144 (190f.); p. 146 (193f.).
17 Cf. ibid., p. 76 (99f.).
18 Cf. ibid., p. 76 (99f.); pp. 95f. (126f.).
19 Cf. ibid., p. 5 (6); p. 144 (190f.); p. 146 (193f.).
20 Cf. ibid., p. 33 (42).
21 Ibidem. It is used also on p. 177 (234).
22 Ibid., p. 33 (42).
23 Ibid., p. 41 (53); p. 42 (54).
24 Ibid., p. 41 (53).
25 Ibidem.
26 Ibid., p. 42 (54).
27 Cf. ibid., p. 42 (55).
28 Cf. ibid., p. 45 (58).
29 Ibidem.
30 Cf. ibid., p. 46 (59).
31 Cf. ibid., p. 179 (237).
32 Ibid., p. 46 (60).
33 Cf. ibid., pp. 179f., (236ff.).
34 This term is only found in the *Grammar of Assent* in the list of notional assents on p. 33 (42) and its exposition on pp. 56f., (73f.).
35 Ibid., p. 56 (73).
36 Ibid., pp. 56f., (73).
37 Ibidem.

Notes on Appendix II

1 *The Journal, 1859–79*, printed in *Autobiographical Writings*, p. 269f.
2 Or. MSS. B.9.11.
3 These cannot be found. Gerdilius was a Cardinal in the eighteenth century. Newman refers to him in his 'Lectures on Faith' recorded by Fr. Caswall (Or. MSS. B.7.4.) and in his paper 'Ultimate Resolution of certainty of Faith'. (Or. MSS. B.9.11.).

4 The first part of this is found in a note 'February 1851. For a Preface (say) to a new volume'. Or. MSS. A.18.11.
5 Or. MSS. A.30.11. Here it is entitled 'An Argument for the Catholic Religion'.
6 It is not possible to identify this for certain but there is a paper 'December 16, 1853. On the *Certainty* of Faith' (Or. MSS. B.7.4.) which may be what Newman is referring to. Alternatively there is a paper entitled 'Ultimate Resolution of certainty of Faith' of Easter 1848 (Or. MSS. B.9.11.).
7 Or. MSS. B.7.4. 'The Oratory, Birmingham, August 20. 1866. From Fr. Edward Caswall's notes on Lectures with the Father 1853'. These are not in Newman's hand-writing but in the margin there is this note in his hand: 'N.B. I seem to have given these lectures here reported with my paper of Easter 1848 before me'.
8 Or. MSS. A.23.1.
9 This cannot be found.
10 Or. MSS. A.18.11. contains pp. 1–12, 17–24 of these. These sections deal only with logic.
11 These letters are at the Oratory. There are eight of them in all, four to Newman and four from Newman, one of which he did not send according to a note in his own hand. They stretch from 20 December 1859 to 19 May 1860.
12 Or. MSS. A.30.11. It is unfinished.
13 Or. MSS. A.30.11. It is unfinished.
14 Or. MSS. A.28.1. It deals with the tradition of the Church in the transmission of doctrine.
15 Or. MSS. A.46.3a. It deals with the problem of sense-perception.
16 Or. MSS. A.18.11.
17 This cannot be located for certain but there is a fragment which is headed 'Sept. 1863 [in pencil] Chapter II' (Or. MSS. A.30.11.). It deals with the problem of the meaning of statements about God and ends with a brief reference to the doctrine of the Trinity. The fragment closes with the date 'December 1, 1863'.
18 Or. MSS. A.30.11. This passage was first drafted on 3 December, 1863. The draft is also found in Or. MSS. A.30.11. The rewritten passage is in two parts, Part I beginning as quoted by Newman, Part II is headed 'The Conceivable'.
19 This may be the fragment numbered 'p. 17 (A Comparison of the Moral Sense and Certitude)' found in Or. MSS. A.30.11.
20 *Book of Sundries,* preserved at the Oratory; cf. notes dated 24 February 1859; 7 November 1859; 4 December 1859; 28 February 1860; 15 July 1860; 21 March 1861; 2 July 1865; 7 July 1861 (cf. 17 September 1861); 10 October 1864; 13 March 1866; 24 January 1867; notes on the page opposite the entry dated 27 October 1867; and 7 November 1877.
21 Or. MSS. B.9.11. This was drawn up at Maryvale, Easter 1848. Accord-

ing to a note by Newman it formed part of his lectures recorded by Fr. Edward Caswall (cf. note 7 *supra*).
22 Or. MSS. B.9.11. It is untitled. Newman has added a note that 'All this, I think, is embodied in my last paper at Maryvale.' The folder in which it is contained has 'Papers on Faith, 1848' written on the cover—but the origin of this description is unknown.
23 Or. MSS. A.23.1. This paper distinguishes between opinion, doubt, certainty, and persuasion.
24 This paper is on four sheets. Sheet 1 was originally kept in B.9.11. but is now to be found in Or. MSS. A.18.11; Sheet 2 is in Or. MSS. A.18.11; Sheets 3 and 4 are in Or. MSS. A.30.11.
25 Or. MSS. B.7.4.
26 Or. MSS. A.30.11. This is only a fragment.
27 Or. MSS. A.23.1.
28 Or. MSS. A.23.1.
29 Or. MSS. A.30.11. This is dated 'April 26/68, again May 5/68, again Sept. 7/68'.
30 Or. MSS. A.30.11. This is an undated fragment.
31 Or. MSS. A.30.11. This is an undated fragment.
32 Or. MSS. A.30.11. This is an undated fragment.

Index of Subjects

absolute assent, 210
Absolute, the, 15
Absolute Spirit, 45, 56
act of faith, 175
aesthetic judgements, 162
agnostic, agnosticism, 15, 16, 26, 29, 230
antecedents of an act, 97
antecedent probabilities, 74
anthropomorphism, 9
apologetics, 10, 15, 16, 18, 22
Apostolic Tradition, 71, 72
apprehension, 75, 84, 94, 98–123, 143, 153, 154, 161, 171, 173, 175, 176, 189, 190, 195, 203, 204, 205, 241, 252, 256
arguments for the existence of God, 4, 7, 8, 9
Argument from Design, 26
articles of belief, 30
articles of faith, 1, 11
Articles, Thirty-nine, 37
assent, 1, 12, 13, 60, 70, 72, 77, 80, 86, 87, 92–177, 193, 198, 204, 210, 237, 254
assertion, 100, 125
assumptions, 130, 139, 140, 143, 155, 156, 157, 188, 192, 196
atheism, 46
Atonement, 20, 26
authority (Bible, Church, etc.), 31, 32, 48, 51, 52, 53, 54, 55, 66, 71, 72, 107, 155, 156, 163, 164, 166
autonomy of man, 58
autonomous ethic, 20, 57

behaviour, 1, 19
Being, Moral, 13
belief, believe, believer, 2, 4, 6, 7, 11, 13, 15, 16, 18, 19, 20, 21, 22, 23, 25, 26, 27, 29, 32, 35, 36, 37, 38, 39, 40, 41, 48, 60, 68, 71, 72, 75, 76, 80, 98, 118, 133, 172, 175, 183, 188, 190, 192, 198, 199, 210, 211, 215, 221
Bible, 23, 24, 25, 31, 32, 33, 34, 35, 36, 37, 38, 39, 40, 41, 48, 63, 64, 68, 70

captivation, 191, 196, 266
cause, 2, 7, 9, 15, 22, 27
certain, certainty, 1, 4, 29, 55, 57, 59, 64, 66, 67, 68, 69, 71, 74, 77, 78, 79, 80, 81, 82, 83, 84, 85, 86, 88, 92, 133, 147, 153, 158, 159, 172, 177–185, 192, 193, 202, 203, 206, 208, 209, 210, 213, 214, 219, 237, 264
certitude, 4, 6, 78, 79, 86, 95, 96, 117, 118, 158, 159, 177–185, 192, 193, 198, 203, 204, 209, 218, 219, 220, 221, 256, 264

Christ, 4, 14, 26, 34, 35, 36, 38, 40, 41, 42, 43, 45, 47, 48, 64, 105, 115, 116
Christianity, 3, 7, 12, 14, 16, 17, 20, 21, 23, 26, 33, 34, 35, 36, 43, 47, 50, 57, 64
Christology, 47
Church, 31, 34, 35, 37, 41, 48, 52, 53, 54, 55, 56, 63, 69, 70, 76, 82, 85, 88, 90, 107, 253
commitment, 73, 100, 129, 135, 136, 141, 161, 165, 168, 169, 170, 171, 172, 174, 175, 176, 177, 178, 179, 181, 183, 184, 189, 190, 192, 195, 196
complex assent, 177, 178, 198
composition, 110
comprehend, comprehension, 99, 252
concept of God, 84, 116, 119, 122, 143, 164, 165, 217, 218, 226, 230
conclusion, 78, 79, 80, 104, 112, 126, 128, 129, 130, 136, 137, 138, 139, 140, 141, 145, 146, 153, 158, 161, 173, 174, 190, 181, 206
conclusive arguments, 135
conditional assent, 80, 128, 129, 141, 161, 210
conditional conclusion, 144, 159, 160, 161
conditionality (of conclusions etc.), 129, 130, 139, 140, 142, 158, 174, 175
conditions of an act, 97
conscience, 13, 14, 53, 69, 70, 74, 80, 83, 85, 98, 116, 153, 161–169, 174, 176, 190, 191, 211, 215, 218, 242, 245, 247, 263
conscious assent, 95
consensus fidelium, 54
contradictions, 115, 253, 258
converging probability, 146, 147, 151, 188, 190, 207, 211
conversion, 67, 119, 120, 193
conviction, 4, 69, 78, 80, 95, 179, 180, 181, 182, 198, 206, 210
Convocation, 37
'Copernican revolution' of Kant's philosophy, 8
cosmological argument for the existence of God, 7, 8
Court of Arches, 37
credence, 95, 198, 200
credibility, 78, 79, 81, 82, 206, 207, 208, 211, 214, 215, 245
credificative, 81
critical philosophy, 3, 11, 12, 14, 15, 16, 40, 44
critics (Biblical, historical, literary, etc.), 6, 31, 35, 40, 44, 50, 61, 63, 64

deism, 23, 24
democracy, democratic age, democratic ideas, 6, 51, 52, 53, 54
demonstration, 1, 3, 12, 13, 22

INDEX OF SUBJECTS

dependence, 10, 11
design, 3
development, 44, 45, 46, 47, 48
'disclosure models', 191, 196
doctrines, 10, 11, 12, 13, 15, 16, 17, 18, 20, 26, 31, 32, 33, 34, 35, 44, 46, 48, 60, 66, 70, 73, 90, 116
dogma, 7, 14, 43, 67, 71
doubt, 4, 5, 6, 16, 68, 77, 78, 79, 80, 91, 93, 94, 95, 132, 165, 206, 210, 220
Dutch school of theology, 32
duty, 8, 14

education, 55, 75, 149, 240
effects, 2
empiricism, 7, 13, 89, 235
ens realissimum, 8
epistemology, 89
essence of God, 2
ethics, 7, 11, 18, 19, 20, 21, 47
Evangelical Alliance, 5, 32–33
Evangelical Revival, 6
everlasting punishment, 20
evolution, 19, 20, 25, 26, 49, 62, 65
existence of God, 2, 4, 7, 12, 15, 83, 85, 171, 226, 247
existentialism, 12, 195, 196
experience, 8, 10, 105, 109, 111, 115, 117

faith, 1, 2, 3, 4, 5, 6, 7, 8, 9, 10, 11, 12, 13, 14, 15, 16, 17, 18, 19, 20, 21, 22, 23, 24, 25, 26, 27, 28, 29, 35, 43, 45, 46, 49, 59, 60, 61, 63, 65, 66, 67, 68, 69, 70, 71, 72, 74, 76, 76, 77, 78, 79, 83, 84, 86, 88, 134, 170, 175, 185, 188, 193, 196, 199, 213, 243, 253
faith as a direct relationship with God, 193
faith-statements, 9, 10, 195
Fall of Man, 26
feel, feeling, 162, 211, 234
fideism, 14
finite, 15
Flood, 23, 24, 25
foreign missions, 56f
formal assent, 96
formal reasoning, 125, 144, 155
freedom, 53

genius, 151
geology, 24, 25, 63, 65
gnosticism, 35
God, 1, 2, 3, 4, 7, 8, 9, 10, 11, 12, 13, 14, 15, 16, 17, 18, 19, 20, 22, 23, 24, 25, 26, 28, 29, 30, 31, 33, 36, 37, 39, 40, 41, 50, 56, 64, 65, 71, 76, 83, 103, 105, 112, 143
Gospel, the, 26, 37, 47, 48, 71
Gospels, 34, 36
grace, 68, 74, 75, 76, 78, 79, 80, 82, 87, 191, 196, 208, 214, 215, 263, 266

Hegelian philosophy, 12, 35, 41
historians, 46, 62
historical credibility, 50
  criticism, 6, 31
  ideas as challenge to faith, 194
  Jesus, 42, 43, 44, 48, 50, 64, 235
  judgements, 50
  movement, 49
  research, 48
  studies, 48
  techniques, 33, 34, 35, 37, 39, 40
historicity of the Bible, 40, 41, 43
history, 45, 46, 49
Holy Spirit, 40, 45, 49, 75
hypothesis, God as an, 9

illation, 'Illative Sense', 70, 74, 76, 81, 84, 85, 126, 136, 140, 144–160, 163, 170, 173, 174, 188, 190, 192, 212, 213, 219, 242, 262, 264
image, 70, 84, 85, 109, 110, 117, 118, 119, 120, 122, 127, 130, 171, 176
imagination, 220
imaginative apprehension, 203
implicit assent, 103, 104
implicit faith, 253
Incarnation, 17
indefectibility of certainty, 219
indefectibility of certitude, 180, 181, 182, 198
indirect assent, 107, 108
infallible authority, 77
infallible R.C. Church, 48
inference, 75, 93, 100, 112, 118, 125, 126, 128, 129, 130, 131, 136–144, 154, 155, 157, 158, 173, 174, 210
infidelity, 4, 5, 6
infinite, 15
informal reasoning, 144ff.
inquiry, 61, 72, 76, 94
inspiration of the Bible, 24, 34, 37, 39, 40, 64
intellect, 13, 14, 33, 65, 89, 94, 119
interpretation of faith, 58
interpretation of the Bible, 36
intuition, 9
investigation, 94, 128, 170

judgements, aesthetic, 162

kenosis, 47
Kingdom of God, 49
knowledge, 1, 2, 3, 4, 7, 8, 9, 10, 11, 12, 15, 16, 72, 75, 77, 82, 83, 125, 133, 135, 163, 169, 186, 188, 194, 211, 213
knowledge of God, 2, 14

laity, 54
law of our nature, 172
liberal education, 240
liberalism, 43, 46, 60, 62, 66, 67, 71, 85, 87, 92, 135, 194, 235, 247
liberty, 51, 63
literary effect of Bible, 40
literary ideas challenging faith, 194
literary techniques, 33, 34, 35
logic, 14, 30, 74, 89, 137, 140, 141, 145, 179
logic of faith, 9, 30, 66, 91
logic of science, 30
logical certainty, 181, 182
logical certitude, 180, 184
logical positivism, 7, 30
logical system, 12

Mark's Gospel, 35
mathematics, 7, 38
memory, 110
Messiah, 41, 42, 43

INDEX OF SUBJECTS 273

metaphysics, 3, 7, 9, 15, 17, 19, 34, 43, 47, 49, 186, 187, 195
miracles, 3, 4, 7, 28, 29, 38, 41, 42, 43, 66, 78, 225

natural philosophy, 7
natural reason, 2
natural religion, 7, 164
natural theology, 3, 8, 9, 10, 11, 12, 88, 195, 224
nature, 148, 149, 150, 151, 152, 162, 172, 187, 188, 218
nature of man, 172
nominalism, 91, 120, 121, 122, 221
notional, 69, 70, 72, 84, 91, 95, 189, 190, 255,
notional apprehension, 84, 98, 109–124, 138, 173, 189, 203, 221, 222, 241
notional assent, 72, 98, 117–120, 124, 178, 198–201, 237, 254
notions, 84, 85, 87, 111, 112, 121, 123, 137, 138, 142, 143, 154, 160, 171, 176
noumena, 8, 9

ontological argument for the existence of God, 7, 8
opinion, 1, 4, 71, 95, 133, 198, 200, 210, 221, 243

paradox, 101, 102, 115, 116, 253
Pauline epistles, 32
Pentateuch, 36, 37, 38, 64
perception, 77, 111
persuasion, 80, 210, 219
philosophy, 14, 33, 34, 35, 48, 61, 62, 65, 69, 89, 238
philosophers, 82, 88, 89, 90, 91, 122
practical certainty, 92, 146, 147, 168, 208, 220
practical probability, 88
practical reason, 8, 9, 13
pragmatism, 30
prejudice, 130, 151, 152, 153, 164, 165, 210
presumptions, 73, 74, 76, 77, 95, 192, 198, 200, 215, 255
presuppositions, 75, 78, 154, 155, 156, 157, 191, 192, 266
private judgment, 71, 72, 76
probability, 88, 92, 95, 127, 132, 134, 136, 139, 142, 143, 146, 147, 148, 149, 150, 156, 161, 174, 183, 184, 188, 189, 190, 210, 211, 219, 245, 250
probable, 74, 78, 79, 133, 140, 144, 157, 203, 207
profession, 95, 138, 198, 200
proofs for the existence of God, 4, 9
progress, idea of, 49
prophecy, 4, 39
prudence, 153, 157, 172, 206, 207, 209, 212, 213, 214
psychological certitude, 180, 182, 184, 186
psychological factor, 169, 175, 176
psychology, 169, 172, 173, 175, 176, 179, 187, 192
pure Gospel, 47, 48

ratiocination, 96, 136, 144, 150
rational religion, 13
rational theology, 13, 14, 15, 16
rationalism, rationalist, 5, 61, 62, 64, 66, 71, 72, 73, 76, 77, 90, 104, 238, 247

rationalistic attitude, 194
real, 69, 70, 91, 95, 109, 115, 117, 121, 122, 130, 137, 142, 143, 154, 160, 183, 189, 190, 193, 237, 254, 255
real and notional assent, 117–120, 193, 254
real apprehension, 84, 98, 109–124, 138, 164, 173, 189, 190, 221, 222, 241, 256
real assent, 193, 198–201, 237
reality, 109
reason, reasoning, 1, 2, 3, 4, 8, 13, 14, 15, 36, 60, 65, 68, 69, 70, 71, 72, 73, 74, 75, 76, 78, 85, 86, 98, 104, 111, 120, 125, 130, 131, 145, 160, 161, 169, 170, 174, 175, 177, 190, 195
reasoning powers in matters of faith, 73
reasons for belief, faith, 73, 76, 77, 78, 80, 81, 125ff., 130, 141, 208
reductio ad absurdum, 155, 156
Reformation, 6
relationship of real and notional apprehension/assent, 123
relative effectiveness of real and notional apprehension, 113
relative strengths of real and notional assents, 118
religion, 3, 4, 5, 6, 14, 16, 17, 18, 19, 20, 21, 22, 25, 30, 31, 45, 57, 67, 68, 69, 70, 75, 76, 88, 98, 114, 115, 116, 118, 119, 122, 135, 136, 141, 142, 144, 153, 154, 158, 164, 165, 169, 170, 171, 172, 183, 184, 188, 190, 194, 199, 213, 217
religious experience, 115
Renaissance, 6
revelation, 2, 3, 10, 11, 15, 16, 24, 26, 32, 33, 40, 41, 45, 46, 48, 63, 66, 69, 82, 105, 136, 203, 213, 215, 224, 242

sacraments, 90
salvation, 2
scepticism, 7, 65, 82, 165, 188, 215, 245
scholasticism, 88, 91, 120, 121
science, 6, 7, 39, 50, 63, 69, 75, 76, 82, 121, 194
scientific advance, 21–31
secularization of life, 57
simple assent, 95, 177, 178
speculation, 8, 95, 198, 201
speculative certainty, 88
speculative philosophy, 12
speculative reason, 8, 13
speculative theology, 16
speculative thought, 17
Spiritual Community, 45
substance, 7
summum bonum, 8
supernatural, 42
syllogism, 74, 76, 125, 137, 139, 141, 146, 147, 153, 154, 188, 190, 211, 212

teleological argument for the existence of God, 7, 8
teleology, 23, 24
'Tendenzkritik', 35
text of the Bible, 40
theism, 20, 26
theistic belief, faith, 7, 18, 57
theologians, 40

theological doctrines, 13, 15, 17
  knowledge, 16
  statement, 11
  truth, 2
theology, 2, 13, 14, 37, 43, 45, 46, 47, 49, 51, 57, 91, 114, 115; 116, 118, 119, 122, 123, 142, 150, 168, 170, 171, 195, 199
  rational, 14, 15, 16
transcendental ideal, 8
Trinity, doctrine of, 17, 32, 88, 102, 114, 116, 203, 217, 258
unbelief, 5, 68, 73, 80, 95, 210
uncertainty, 2, 59, 72, 136

unconditional, 139, 140, 141, 168, 170, 173, 191, 220, 221
unconditionality of assent, 125, 128, 129, 132, 134, 170, 172
understanding, 99, 117
unit realities, 111, 120
universals, 120, 121

will, 13, 14, 77, 78, 80, 82, 86, 92, 93, 126, 128, 130, 131, 136, 159, 161, 165, 166, 168, 169, 175, 176, 177, 190, 191, 196, 205, 209, 210, 211, 215, 218, 245, 266

Index of Books, Names, and Places

Abbott, J., 62, 238
Abbott, T. K., 225
Aberdeen, 225
Abraham, 11, 36, 37, 40
Adam, 24
'Adam Bede', 18
Aids to Reflection (Coleridge), 90, 227, 238
Albert, Prince, 25, 219
Allies, 63
Ambrose, St., 85, 197
Amort, 148
Analogy of Religion (Butler), 88, 263
Analysis of Scripture History (Pinnock), 230
'Anti-Church Movement, Demonstration in Hyde Park' (Marx), 236
Apocalypse, 22, 35
Apologia pro Vita Sua (Newman), 65, 67, 77, 85, 235, 238, 240, 241, 249, 257
Apostles, 31
Apostolical Tradition (Newman), 242
Aquinas, St. Thomas, 2, 77, 91, 202, 205, 224, 260, 265
Archbishop of Canterbury, 22
Arctic, 112
Arians of the Fourth Century, The, (Newman), 62, 70, 239, 241
Aristotle, 7, 89, 125, 144
Arnold, Matthew, 39, 233, 237
Arnold, Dr. Thomas, 64
Arnold, Thomas (junior), 237
Attack upon Christendom (Kierkegaard), 226
Augustine, St., 224
Austerlitz, 151
Authorized Version, 40
Autobiography of John Stuart Mill, 228, 229

Bacon, Lord, 89
Baden Powell, 29, 36, 50
Bampton Lectures, 15, 40, 64, 83, 227, 228
Barth, Karl, 226
Baur, 35, 45
'Bede, Adam', 18
Belief and Faith (Pieper), 237
Belief and Unbelief since 1850 (Wood), 229
Bell, 18
Bentham, 19, 227
Berkeley, 15, 90, 91, 121
Bernard, T. D., 40
Bible, 39, 40, 41, 44, 48, 55, 63, 64, 68, 70, 71, 72, 78
'Bible': Article by Robertson Smith in the *Encyclopaedia Britannica*, 38–9
Bible in the Age of Science, (Richardson) 229
Biographia Literaria (Coleridge), 13, 227

Birmingham, 78
Birmingham, see Oratory
Bishop of London, 22
Boekraad, 65, 121, 187, 189, 240, 249, 264
Book of Sundries (Newman), 82
Boulger, J. D., 225
Boyle, 22
Brabant, Dr., 34
Bridgewater, Earl of, 22
Bridgewater Treatises, 22, 230
British Critic, 63, 90, 238
Brown, 90
Brown, Ford K., 5, 225
Browning, Robert, 59
Buckland, 24, 63
Bunsen, Baron, 36
'Bunsen's Biblical Researches', 36
Burgon, 233
Butler, Bishop, 62, 64, 71, 88, 92, 121, 165, 263
Butterfield, H., 229

Cambridge, 5, 22, 25, 39, 225
Campbell, McLeod, 20
Campion, H. J., 236
Canterbury, Archbishop of, 82
Carlyle, 49, 51, 53, 64, 232, 236
Carpenter, S. C., 233
Caswall, Fr. Edward, 79, 80, 202, 209
Catholic Sermons (Newman), 240
Chadwick, Owen, 53, 230, 235, 237
Chalmer, T., 230
Chalybäus, 61, 65
Charles, King, 200
Chartism Past and Present (Carlyle), 236
Chillingworth, 71
Christ and Modern Theology (Fairbairn), 47
Christian Doctrine (Dale), 235
Christian Faith (Schleiermacher), 10, 225, 231
Christianity Not Mysterious (Toland), 232
Church, R. W., 16, 26, 28
Church and People, 1789–1889 (Carpenter), 233
Church in an Age of Revolution (Vidler), 225
Clarke, 90
Clement of Alexandria, St., 88
Clinton, 63
Cockshut, A. O. J., 228, 229, 231, 232
Colenso, Bishop, 37, 38, 61
Coleridge, 13, 14, 23, 33, 34, 62, 90, 152, 227, 236
Coleridge as Religious Thinker (Boulger), 225
Colossians, Epistle to, 35
Comte, 18
Concluding Unscientific Postscript (Kierkegaard), 12, 226, 230

INDEX OF BOOKS, NAMES AND PLACES

Confessions of an Inquiring Spirit (Coleridge), 33, 34
Confessions of St. Augustine, 224
Copernicus, 21
Corinthians I and II, 35
Corinthians, First Epistle, 74–5
Corner Stone (Abbott), 238
Coulson, J., 237
Critiques (Kant), 3, 6
Critique of Practical Reason (Kant), 9, 225, 226
Critique of Pure Reason (Kant), 4, 9, 61, 91, 225, 226, 227
Culler, Dwight, 89, 238, 239, 257
Cyprian, St., 72

D'Arcy, 121
Dale, R. W., 46, 53, 235, 237
Daniel, 36, 40, 64
Dante, 226
Darwin, 19, 25, 26, 65, 230
David, King, 37, 64
Davies, Horton, 234, 258
Derham, 22, 229
Descartes, 91
Descent of Man (Darwin), 26
Deuteronomy, 40
Development of Doctrine, see *Essay on the Development of Christian Doctrine*.
'Developing Doctrines and Changing Beliefs' (Nicholls), 235
Dewar, 62
Dialogues concerning Natural Religion (Hume), 227, 231
Dillenberger, J., 229, 230, 231
Discussions and Arguments on Various Subjects (Newman), 239, 242, 243, 244
Discussions on Philosophy and Literature, Education and University Reform (Hamilton), 227
Dissertations and Discussions (Mill), 227
Divinity of Our Lord and Saviour Jesus Christ (Liddon), 232
Doctrine and Development (Rashdall), 236
Doctrine of the Atonement and Religion and Modern Culture (Sabatier), 229
Drey, 44
Driver, S. R., 39
Dublin, 63
Duhm, 233
Duke of Wellington, 115
Duns Scotus, 6

Easter Day (Browning), 237
Edgbaston, see Oratory
Education of the Human Race (Lessing), 236
Ecce Homo, A Survey of The Life and Work of Jesus Christ (Seeley), 43, 63, 234
Either/Or (Kierkegaard), 11
Elijah, 36
Eliot, George, 18, 19, 34, 35
Elliott-Binns, 6, 225, 231, 232, 233
Encyclopaedia Britannica, 227
Engels, 57
England in the Nineteenth Century (Thompson), 236
English Thought 1860–1900 (Elliott-Binns), 225
Ephesians, Epistle to, 35
Errington, Dr., 202
Erskine, 62, 238

Essay Concerning Human Understanding (Locke), 89, 133–135, 144, 169, 225, 245, 259, 260, 261, 262
Essays Critical and Historical (Newman), 235, 238, 239, 241, 243, 244, 249
Essay in Aid of a Grammar of Assent, 60, 63, 67, 70, 72, 73, 74, 75, 76, 77, 81, 84, 85, 86–7, 90, 91, 92, 93, 98, 99, 102, 113, 120, 121, 122, 124, 126, 130, 134, 136, 139, 141, 144, 156, 158, 161, 166, 169, 170, 171, 172, 175, 176, 177, 178, 180, 181, 186, 187, 189, 191, 192, 193, 194, 195, 196, 198, 199, 200, 202, 225, 231, 237, 240, 263, 266, 267
Essay on Certitude (Newman), 204
Essay on the Development of Christian Doctrine (Newman), 46, 62, 63, 76, 90, 235, 236, 238, 239, 244, 245, 250
Essay on Miracles (Hume), 89, 238
Essay on the Miracles of Scripture (Newman), 89
Essays and Reviews, 24, 25, 29, 32, 35, 37, 38, 61, 225, 226, 231, 232, 236
Essence of Christianity (Feuerbach), 16, 228
Essene, 41
Evangelical Alliance, 5, 32
Evidences of Christianity (Paley), 135, 224, 229
Evolution and Ethics (Huxley), 229
Ewald, 61
Explanatory Notes upon the New Testament (Wesley), 236

Fairbairn, 43, 47, 52, 53, 57, 234, 235, 236, 237
Fathers of the Victorians (Brown), 5, 225
F. D. Maurice and the Conflicts of Modern Theology (Ramsey), 228
Fear and Trembling (Kierkegaard), 11, 226, 263
Feuerbach, 18, 228
Fichte, 236
First Principles (Spencer), 229
France, 52
Freud, 30, 231
From Bossuet to Newman, The Idea of Doctrinal Development (Chadwick), 235
From Rousseau to Ritschl (Barth), 226
Froude, Hurrell, 88, 90
Future of an Illusion (Freud), 231

Galatians, Epistle to, 35
Galilee, 47
Galileo, 21, 229
Geddes, 37
Genesis, 32
Geneva, Lake of, 86
Gerdil, 202, 207
German Protestantism (Dewar), 62
German Rationalism (Pusey), 62
Gibbon, 48, 62, 63
Glion, 86
God and the Bible (Arnold), 233
Goodwin, C. W., 24, 25, 26, 32, 36
Gore, Charles, 40, 231
Gospel of Life (Westcott), 233
Gospels, 39
Gosse, 24, 230
Grammar of Assent, see *Essay in Aid of a Grammar of Assent*
Gray, Asa, 26

INDEX OF BOOKS, NAMES AND PLACES   277

'Gray', fictional character of Mrs Humphrey Ward, 17
Greek Text of the New Testament, Westcott and Hort's version, 40
Green, 49
Gregory, 72
Grote, 63

Hamann, 7
Hamilton, Sir William, 14, 16, 62, 90, 227, 229, 239
Hampden, 71
Harnack, 43, 47, 234, 236
Harrold, C. F., 231
Hartshorne, Charles, 224
Hatch, Edward, 47, 235
Hawkins, 68, 88
Hebrews, Epistle to, 35
Hegel, 17, 45, 228, 235
Hegelians, 12, 34, 41
Heine, H., 7, 225, 237
Hennell, 34, 41, 234
Herder, 7
Herrmann, 193
Hibbert Lectures, 47, 235
Historic Doubts respecting Napoleon Buonaparte (Whately), 49
Historical Sketches (Newman), 239
Historical Survey of Speculative Philosophy from Kant to Hegel (Chalybaüs), 65
History of Christian Missions (Neill), 237
History of Christianity (Milman), 87
History of the Church of Christ (Milner), 87
History of Freethought in the Nineteenth Century (Robertson), 25, 228
History of Israel to the Death of Moses (Ewald), 61
History of the Jews (Milman), 37, 63, 64, 233
Hoadley, 71
Hobbes, Thomas, 37
Holy Spirit and Inspiration (Gore), 40
Homerton College, 24
Hort, 26, 40
Hume, David, 3, 6, 7, 8, 9, 14, 22, 28, 29, 48, 62, 89, 121, 170, 218, 225, 227, 231, 238
Hunt, Leigh, 18
Hutton, R. H., 231
Huxley, T. H., 18, 20, 25, 28, 29, 229, 231

Idea of a University (Newman), 63, 65, 89, 90, 91, 238, 239, 240, 246, 249, 250
Ignatius, St., 72
Imperial Dictionary, 92, 251, 252
Imperial Intellect (Culler), 238
In Memoriam (Tennyson), 230, 231, 236, 258
'Infidelity of the Future' (Newman: Sermon), 237
Influence of Greek Ideas and Usages upon the Christian Church (Hatch), 235
Inquiry concerning Human Understanding (Hume), 225
Inquiry concerning the Origin of Christianity (Hennell), 34, 41, 234
Internal Evidence (Erskine), 238
Introduction to the Literature of the Old Testament (Driver), 39
Introduction to the Philosophy of Cardinal Newman (Keogh), 87, 249
Insecto-Theologie, 230

Inspiration (Sanday), 233
Isaac, 11
Isaiah, 36, 64

James, St., 35
Jeremiah, 36
J. G. Hamann (Smith), 225
Job, 40
John, St., 47, 64
John Henry Newman, Our Way to Certitude (Zeno), 189, 238
Jonah, 40
Joseph of Arimathea, 41
Joshua, 38
Journal, Newman's, 68, 77, 86, 202, 240
Jowett, Benjamin, 36
Judaizers, 35
Judicial Committee of the Privy Council, 37

Kant, Immanuel, 3, 4, 6, 7, 8, 9, 10, 13, 14, 61, 62, 65, 91, 156, 170, 188, 225, 226, 227, 238, 240
Kaufmann, W., 229
Keble, 77
Keim, 35, 42
Keogh, C. B., 87, 89, 91, 186, 249
Kierkegaard, 11, 12, 13, 50, 195, 226, 230, 236, 263
Kingdom of Christ (Maurice), 227, 231
Kingsley, Charles, 26
Knox, T. M., 228
Kritik der evangelischen Geschichte der Synoptiker (Baur), 232
Kroner, R., 228
Kuenen, 38

Lamarck, 25
La Vie de Jésus (Renan), 42
Lazarus, 42
Leben Jesu (Strauss), 18, 34, 41, 61
Lecky, 51, 52, 57, 236, 237
Lectures and Essays of William Robertson Smith, 233
Lectures on the Doctrine of Justification (Newman), 72, 243
Lectures and Other Theological Papers (Mozley), 231, 236
Lectures on the Philosophy of Religion (Hegel), 17, 228
Lectures on the Prophetical Office of the Church (Newman), 72
Lessing, 49, 50, 236
Lessing's Theological Writings (Chadwick), 236
Letters and Correspondence of John Henry Newman (ed. Mozley), 240
Letters and Diaries of John Henry Newman (ed. Dessain), 239
Letters of the Rev. J. B. Mozley, D.D., 228, 231
Lewis, H. D., 189
Lewis, Sir George, 63
Liberty (Mill), 51, 53
Limits of Religious Thought (Mansel), 247
Liddon, 5
Life and Correspondence of Richard Whately, D.D., 227, 232, 236
Life of Christ in Recent Research (Sanday), 234
Life of Jesus, 18, 34, 41, 61, 234
Life of John Stuart Mill (Packe), 228

INDEX OF BOOKS, NAMES AND PLACES

Life of R. W. Dale (Dale), 237
Lilly, W. S., 91
Light in Winter (Trevor), 238, 240
'Limits of our Thought' (Meynell: article), 83
Limits of Religious Thought (Mansel), 15, 227
Literature and Dogma (Arnold), 233
Locke, 33, 71, 77, 89, 90, 121, 132, 135, 144, 159, 169, 172, 222, 225, 249, 250, 259, 260, 261, 262
Logic (Mill), 28, 121, 141
Loss and Gain (Newman), 79
Lux Mundi (ed. Gore), 40, 50, 231, 234, 236
Lyell, 24
Lyra Innocentium (Keble), 77

Macaulay, 49
Mackay, R. W., 31, 61, 232
Malebranche, 91
Manifesto of the Communist Party (Marx and Engels), 237
Mansel, H. L., 13, 14, 16, 64, 83, 203, 227, 228, 229, 247
Man's Place in Nature (Huxley), 25
Mark, St., 35, 64
Martineau, J., 229
Marx, Karl, 52, 57, 228, 236
Marx and Engels on Religion, 228, 236
Maryvale, 206, 208
Matthew, St., 35
Maurice, 13, 14, 16, 20, 23, 28, 40, 227, 230, 231, 233
Meaning of Certitude (Newman), 204
Messiah, 41, 42, 43
Metaphysics or the Philosophy of Consciousness (Mansel), 15, 227
Meynell, 64, 83, 87, 203, 228, 239, 247, 262
Mill, John Stuart, 13, 16, 18, 19, 20, 22, 27, 28, 51, 53, 65, 90, 211, 227, 229, 231, 240
Milman, 37, 38, 63, 64, 75, 239
Milner, 87
Mivart, St. George, 62, 65
Moberly, 50
Möhler, 45
Montaigne, 91
Month, 239
Moore, Aubrey, 231
Moral and Political Philosophy (Paley), 4, 225
Moses, 24, 36, 38, 40, 63, 64
Movements of Religious Thought in Britain during the Nineteenth Century (Tulloch), 232
Mozley, J. B., 16, 29, 32, 48, 193, 231, 236
Mure, Colonel, 63
Myers, F. W., 229
McLeod Campbell, 20

Napoleon, 49, 50, 51, 151
Natural Religion (Seeley), 234
Natural Theology (Paley), 3, 224, 229
Neander, 63
Neill, S. C., 56, 237
Neue Oder-Zeitung, 236
New English Dictionary, 92, 169
Newman, J. H., 1, 16, 29, 45, 46, 54, 59, 61, 62, 63, 64, 65, 66, 67, 68, 69, 70, 71, 72, 73, 74, 75, 76, 77, 78, 79, 80, 81, 82, 83, 84, 85, 86, 87, 88, 89, 90, 91, 92, 93, 94, 95, 98, 99, 100, 101, 102, 103, 104, 105, 107, 108, 109, 110, 111, 112, 113, 114, 115, 116, 117, 118, 119, 120, 121, 122, 123, 124, 125, 126, 127, 128, 129, 130, 131, 132, 133, 134, 135, 136, 137, 138, 139, 141, 142, 143, 144, 145, 146, 147, 148, 149, 150, 152, 153, 154, 155, 156, 157, 158, 159, 160, 161, 162, 163, 164, 165, 166, 167, 168, 169, 170, 171, 172, 173, 174, 175, 176, 177, 178, 179, 180, 181, 182, 183, 184, 185, 186, 187, 188, 189, 190, 191, 192, 194, 195, 196, 197, 198, 199, 200, 201, 202, 203, 205, 207, 212, 214, 215, 217, 222, 225, 227, 228, 231, 234, 235, 236, 237, 238, 239, 240, 241, 242, 243, 244, 245, 246, 247, 248, 249, 250, 251, 252, 253, 254, 255, 256, 257, 258, 259, 260, 262, 263, 264, 265, 266, 267, 268
Newman, F. W., 18
Newman, Jemima, 64
Newman, The Theologian (Walgrave), 240
Newton, 21, 22, 151
Nicea, 47
Nicholls, D., 235
Nichomachean Ethics (Aristotle), 89
Nicodemus, 41
Niebuhr, 63
Nietzsche, 21
Nineteenth Century, 239
Nineteenth-Century Studies (Willey), 227
Noetics of Oriel, 89, 121
Notes, Theological, Political and Miscellaneous (Coleridge), 7, 227, 230

Objections to Christian Belief (Vidler), 264
Observations Divine and Moral (Robinson), 224
Occam, see William of Occam
Oken, 25
Old Faith and the New, A Confession (Strauss), 234
'On Consulting the Faithful in Matters of Doctrine' (Newman), 54, 237
On the Aspects of Infidelity, 225
'On the Certainty of Faith' (Newman), 81
On the Genesis of Species (St. George Mivart), 62
'On the Interpretation of Scripture' (Jowett), 36
On the Introduction of Rationalistic Principles into Revealed Religion (Newman: Tract), 71
'On the Mosaic Cosmogony' (Goodwin), 24
On the Power Wisdom and Goodness of God as manifested in the Adaptation of the External Nature to the Moral and Intellectual Constitution of Man, 230
On Religion: Speeches to Its Cultured Despisers (Schleiermacher), 10, 226
'Opus Magnum' (Newman: notes), 82
Oratory, the Edgbaston, 61, 67, 77, 105, 106, 203, 205, 209, 228, 238
Oriel College, Oxford, 88, 89, 121
Origen, 88
Origins of Modern Science (Butterfield), 229
Origin of Species (Darwin), 19, 25, 28
Oscott, 87
Oxford, 32, 39, 67, 89, 121
Oxford University Sermons (Newman), 67, 73, 76, 77, 83, 89, 90, 202, 205, 235, 238, 240, 243, 244, 248, 261

Packe, M. St. J., 228, 236
Paley, William, 3, 4, 5, 13, 14, 22, 62, 88, 135, 224, 225, 229
Pascal, 91, 184
Pastoral Epistles, 35

INDEX OF BOOKS, NAMES AND PLACES 279

Pattison, Mark, 235
Paul, St., 35, 36, 40, 47, 48, 233
Peacock, Thomas Love, 24
Pentateuch, 36, 37, 38, 39, 64
Pentateuch and the Book of Joshua Critically Examined (Colenso), 37, 61
Personal Conquest of Truth according to J. H. Newman (Boekraad), 189, 240
Phases of Faith (F. W. Newman), 18
Phenomenology of Mind (Hegel), 17, 228
Philippians, Epistle to, 35
Philosophical Fragments (Kierkegaard), 226, 227, 236
'Philosophical Temper, First Enjoined by the Gospel' (Newman: University Sermon), 69
Philosophy of Mind (Hegel), 17, 228
Philosophy of Religion (Hegel), 235
Philosophy of the Christian Religion (Fairbain), 235
'Physical Science and Theology' (Mozley), 231
Physicio-Theology (Derham), 229
Pieper, Joseph, 60, 237
Pilgrim's Progress, 237
Pinnock, W. H., 230
Place of Christ in Modern Theology (Fairbairn), 234, 235
Plato, 7, 89
Poetics (Aristotle), 89
Pope, the, 66, 238
Portable Nietzsche (ed. W. Kaufmann), 229
Prince Albert, 25
Private Judgment (Newman), 76
Prolegomena to Any Future Metaphysics (Kant), 225, 226
Prolegomena to the History of Israel (Wellhausen), 38
Protestant Thought and Natural Science (Dillenberger), 229-230
Psalms, 39, 64
Pusey, 32, 39, 62, 63

Quarterly Review, 193
Quest of the Historical Jesus (Schweitzer), 234

Rambler, 83, 237
Ramsey, A. M., 228
Ramsey, I. T., 191, 195, 196
Ranke, 49
Rashdall, Hastings, 48, 236
Rationalism in Religion (Newman), 62
Ray, 22
Reality as Social Progress (Hartshorne), 224
Reason in History (Hegel), 235, 236
Reid, 90
Relation between the Holy Scriptures and some parts of Geological Science (Smith), 24, 230
Religion in History and in Modern Life (Fairbairn), 236, 237
Religion of the Heart (Leigh Hunt), 18
Religion of Israel to the Fall of the Jewish State (Kuenen), 38
Religion within the Limits of Reason Alone (Kant), 225, 226
Religion and Modern Culture (Sabatier), 229, 237
Religion and the Modern Mind (Stace), 225
Religion and Philosophy in Germany (Heine), 225
Religious Condition of Christendom, exhibited in a series of papers prepared at the instance of . . .

Evangelical Alliance . . ., 225, 232
Religious Science Congress, 21
Renan, E., 42, 63, 234
Reuss, 233
Revised Version, 40
Rhetorics (Aristotle), 89
Richardson, A., 229
Rickett, Compton, 237
Rise and Influence of the Spirit of Rationalism in Europe (Lecky), 236
Ritschl, 193
Robert Elsmere, 228, 235
Robertson, J. M., 25, 34, 228, 230, 233
Robertson Smith, 38, 39
Robinson, John, 1, 224
Romans, Epistle to, 35
Royal Society, 22

Sabatier, Auguste, 21, 31, 58, 229, 231, 237
St. Chad's Cathedral, Birmingham, 78
Saint-Hilaire, 23
St. Paul and Protestantism (Arnold), 233
Sanday, W., 40
Schelling, 13, 62
Schenkel, 42
Schlegel, 63
Schleiermacher, 10, 11, 13, 15, 28, 62, 195, 226, 231
Schwann, 25
Schweitzer, A., 44, 234
Science and the Christian Tradition (Huxley), 231
Science of Ethics (Stephen), 20
Science and the Modern World (Whitehead), 229
'Scientific and Pseudo-Scientific Realism' (Huxley), 231
Scott, Thomas, 88, 203
Scottish Journal of Theology, 234
Seeley, 42, 43, 63, 234
Shaping Forces of Modern Religious Thought (Alexander), 237
Sheldon, H. C., 228, 229, 230, 231, 232, 234
Siberia, 23
Sickness unto Death (Kierkegaard), 226, 230
Sidgwick, 19
Smith, John Pye, 24, 25, 230
Smith, R. G., 225
Smith, Robertson, 38, 39
Spencer, Herbert, 16, 19, 29, 229
Spinoza, 37
Stace, W. T., 225
Steane, E., 225
Stephen, Leslie, 18, 20
Steward, 90
Strauss, 18, 34, 35, 41, 50, 61, 62, 63
Strauss, Hegel and their Opinions, 61
Stray Essays on Controversial Points (Newman), 91, 239
Summa Theologica (Aquinas), 224
Sundries, book of (Newman), 203
System of Logic (Mill), 229
Systematic Theology (Tillich), 224, 253

Tamworth Reading Room (Newman), 75, 136 141, 143, 166, 244
'Taylor's Translation' of Pascal, 91
Tennant, 177, 193
Tennyson, 23, 26, 27, 30, 230, 258
Theological Essays (Maurice), 230, 233

INDEX OF BOOKS, NAMES AND PLACES

Thesis on Feuerbach (Marx), 228
Thompson, D., 236
Thoughts on Education (Locke), 89
Three Essays on Religion (Mill), 229, 230, 231
Tillich, 183, 193, 224, 253, 265
Toland, 33, 232
Tract 85, 73
Tracts for the Times, 62, 71, 73, 235
Training in Christianity (Kierkegaard), 226, 227
Treatise of Human Nature (Hume), 7, 225
Trench, R. C., 28, 177, 231
Trevor, Meriol, 238, 240
Tübingen, 35, 44
Tübingen School and its Antecedents (Mackay), 61, 232
Two Essays on Scripture Miracles and Ecclesiastical (Newman), 238, 249
Types of Ethical Theory (Martineau), 229

'Ultimate Resolution of certainty of Faith' (Newman), 208
Unbelief in the Nineteenth Century (Sheldon), 228–9
Unbelievers (Cockshut), 228
University Discourse (Newman), 211
University Sermons, see Oxford University Sermons
Usher, Archbishop, 230
'Usurpations of Reason' (Newman), 69
Utilitarianism (Mill), 19, 229

Vatke, 233
Ventnor, 84, 203
Vestiges of the Natural History of Creation (Chambers), 25, 230
Via Media (Newman), 72, 242, 254
Victoria, Queen, 219
Victorian Church (Chadwick), 230, 236
Victorian Essays (Young), 225
Vidler, A. R., 225, 230, 233, 264
Vie de Jésus (Renan), 42

Vincent of Lerins, 46
Voices of the Church in reply to Dr. D. F. Strauss, 61
von Baer, 25

Walgrave, 120, 186, 240, 257, 263
Ward, Mrs Humphrey, 17, 235
Wasser-Theologie, 230
Wayland, Dr. W. S., 4
Webster's Dictionary, 92, 261
Wellhausen, 38
Wellington, Duke of, 115
Wesley, John, 51, 53, 236
Westcott, 40, 233
Whately, E. J., 227
Whately, Richard, 14, 32, 49, 50, 68, 88, 121, 144, 227
What is Christianity? (Harnack), 234
Whewell, 24
White, Hale, 232
Whitehead, A. N., 21, 22, 30, 229, 231
Wilberforce, W. (junior), 61
Willey, 229, 236
William of Occam, 6, 121, 257
Williams, R., 37
Wilson, Henry, 36, 37
Wilson, H. B., 232
Wisdom of God Manifested in the Work of Creation (Ray), 22
Wiseman Review, 240
Wood, H. G., 229, 231, 234
Worship and Theology in England 1850–1900, (Horton Davies), 234, 258
Wrede, 43

Young, G. M., 5, 225

Zechariah, 36
Zeno, 62, 90, 121, 186, 189, 238, 239, 240, 249, 250, 257, 262, 264

www.ingramcontent.com/pod-product-compliance
Lightning Source LLC
Chambersburg PA
CBHW071242230426
43668CB00011B/1543